Marketing for Tourism

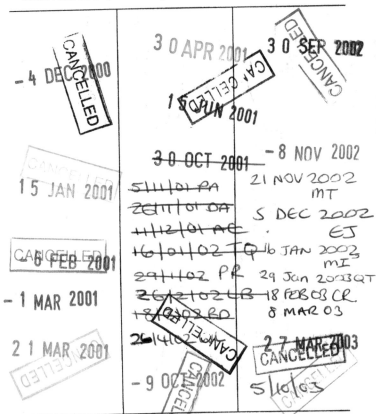

"You booked us a holiday abroad
during the summer. Could you tell us,
please, where we went?"

(Reproduced by kind permission of Punch)

Marketing for Tourism

J C Holloway · C Robinson

THIRD EDITION

 LONGMAN

Pearson Education Limited
Edinburgh Gate, Harlow
Essex CM20 2JE, England
and Associated Companies throughout the world

Second edition published by Pitman Publishing in 1992
Third edition published by Longman Group Limited in 1995
Fourth impression 1999

British Library Cataloguing in Publication Data
A catalogue entry for this title is available from the British Library.

ISBN 0-582-27748-5

Produced by Pearson Education Asia Pte Ltd
Printed in Singapore (COS)

Contents

List of abbreviations

AA	Automobile Association
ABLE	Association of Bath and District Leisure Attractions
ABTA	Association of British Travel Agents
AGB	Audits of Great Britain
AIDA	Attention, Interest, Desire, Action
AITO	Association of Independent Tour Operators
APEX	Advance Purchase Excursion
ATOL	Air Travel Organizer's Licence
ATUC	Air Transport Users' Committee
BA	British Airways
BBC	British Broadcasting Corporation
BCG	Boston Consultancy Group
BMA	British Midland Airways
BRAD	*British Rate and Data*
BTA	British Tourist Authority
CAA	Civil Aviation Authority
CBI	Confederation of British Industry
CIM	Chartered Institute of Marketing
CIMTIG	Chartered Institute of Marketing Travel Industry Group
CIT	Chartered Institute of Transport
CSQ	Customer Service Questionnaire
CTB	Cumbria Tourist Board
DATA	Devon Area Tourist Association
EATB	East Anglia Tourist Board
EFTPOS	electronic funds-transfer at point of sale
EFTS	electronic funds-transfer system
EIU	Economist Intelligence Unit
EMTB	East Midlands Tourist Board
ETB	English Tourist Board
FMCG	Fast Moving Consumer Goods
FTO	Federation of Tour Operators
GIT	group inclusive tour
HCIMA	Hotel Catering and Institutional Management Association
HETB	Heart of England Tourist Board
IATA	International Air Transport Association
IBA	Independent Broadcasting Authority
IIT	independent inclusive tour
ILAM	Institute of Leisure and Amenity Management
IPC	International Publishing Corporation
ISO	International Standards Organisation
ITB	Irish Tourist Board
ITX	inclusive tour-basing fare

JND	just noticeable difference
LTB	London Tourist Board
MEAL	Media Expenditure Analysis Ltd
MIS	Marketing Information System
MORI	Market and Opinion Research Institute
NTB	Northumbria Tourist Board
NWTB	North West Tourist Board
OFT	Office of Fair Trading
OHP	overhead projector
PEX	(discounted airline fare)
PLC	product life cycle
POS	point of sale
PR	public relations
PRO	public relations officer
RAC	Royal Automobile Club
ROI	return on investment
RTW	round the world
SEETB	South East England Tourist Board
SIA	Singapore Airlines
STB	Scottish Tourist Board
STB	Southern Tourist Board
TATR	Travel and Tourism Research
TIC	Tourist Information Centre
TQM	Total Quality Management
TTG	*Travel Trade Gazette*
TVR	television viewing rating
UKTS	United Kingdom Tourism Survey
USP	Unique Selling Proposition
VDU	visual display unit
VFR	visiting friends and relatives
WCTB	West Country Tourist Board
WTB	Wales Tourist Board/Bwrdd Croeso Cymru
WTM	World Travel Market
YHTB	Yorkshire and Humberside Tourist Board

Preface

This third edition is written with the same underlying philosophy as was to be found in the earlier editions, namely, that the principles behind the marketing of tourism are common to all goods and services. The purpose of this text, therefore, remains one of bridging the gap between general principles and their application to travel and tourism products.

A manager who plans to work in this industry must possess a sound understanding of general marketing theory in order to implement marketing satisfactorily, whether that product be an aircraft seat, a holiday resort, a guided tour or a bed and breakfast establishment. This is borne out by the criteria that are listed in advertisements for senior marketing posts in tourism today; experience in tourism is often described as 'useful, but not essential', while evidence is frequently sought of experience in other marketing fields, especially the Fast Moving Consumer Goods (FMCG) sector. This is not only because marketing management depends upon common theory to underpin practice, but also because the FMCG sector has gained years of intensive strategic marketing experience, having introduced the concept far earlier than it was practised in the travel and tourism sector. Many leading entrepreneurs in marketing have cut their teeth in the FMCG sector, before moving on to practise their skills in travel or other service industries.

By and large, small firms within the travel sector – and these continue to make up the bulk of organisations in the industry – have only a hazy idea of what marketing is, and how it can be applied professionally. There is also a general belief within these companies that the investment in skills and other resources in order to carry out effective marketing simply cannot be financed. Yet these companies are increasingly threatened by the growth and influence of large organisations, both in the UK and globally. If they are to survive, their management must become more professional in turn, and nowhere is this more true than in the practice of marketing.

Recognising that an understanding of general marketing principles is necessary to market travel and tourism should not blind us to the fact that equally there are some distinctions in the way travel and tourism (as well as other services) is marketed. Services call for a different approach, with different manipulation of the marketing mix, different considerations in the operation of distribution, a different emphasis in selling and above all in customer services. Tourism is a people industry, in which the product is inseparable from the staff who deliver it, be they waiters, tour guides, travel agents or coach drivers. Each member of the industry has a marketing function to perform in their dealings with the public, and it is therefore vital that they acquire and put into use the practical skills of marketing.

It has been said that selling tourism is selling dreams, but it is all too easy for these dreams to turn into nightmares for the consumers themselves unless there is a clear commitment to the delivery of a quality product to the public. Increasingly, competitive pressures are encouraging those in the industry to forget the other elements of marketing in order to focus exclusively on low price. Price alone has never been the answer to success in travel, and this text will stress the need for a high level of personal service, of product quality and of attention to detail in delivering a tourism service. Increasingly in the 1990s marketing theory is turning to focus on the needs of the 'internal customer' – the employee – who is such a vital link in the chain. Employees who are under-rewarded for their efforts, whether financially or otherwise, who work long hours in high stress conditions, and yet are treated disdainfully by their employers, cannot be expected to deliver the best product. If the best staff are to be encouraged to consider tourism as a career, some means of rewarding satisfactorily these 'front-line marketing troops' must be found.

Marketing for Tourism is designed to lay the groundwork for an understanding of marketing principles, and to reveal how these principles are applied in marketing generally and in the travel and tourism industry in particular. This knowledge will provide the basis for further study of specific aspects of marketing, such as marketing research, international marketing, and advertising, which cannot be covered fully in a basic textbook of this nature. The text will, however, replace those texts, many of them excellent in their field, which have been written to provide an introduction to marketing but suffer either from being goods-oriented or too strongly directed towards the North American reader.

Practical (and factual) illustrations are given throughout of how marketing theory is implemented in the industry, and this edition, as well as being thoroughly updated, introduces a new set of case studies drawn from real-life experiences in the tourism industry. In particular, illustrations are frequently drawn from current real life marketing experience within a major British tour operator, reflecting the expertise of one of the authors. Through these illustrations, the link between marketing theory and practice is further reinforced.

The book is designed to be read by those start-ing out in their careers in the tourism business. It is ideally suited to those studying for General National Vocational Qualifications (GNVQs) in Leisure and Tourism at levels 3 and 4, as well as those on Higher National Diploma (HND) courses, or first degree courses, in which tourism marketing is studied as an option. It will also prove a useful introduction to theory and practice for those taking professional courses such as the Hotel Catering and Institutional Management Association (HCIMA), Chartered Institute of Transport (CIT) and the Institute of Leisure and Amenity Management (ILAM), or others employed in the tourism industry who either hope to move into a marketing post or seek to gain a better understanding of marketing in order to carry out their tasks more effectively.

This third edition sees a new co-author in Chris Robinson, Group Marketing Manager for First Choice Holidays, one of Britain's leading tour operators. Thus continuity in approach is maintained, by linking together an academic with fifteen years' experience of the travel industry, with a senior practitioner who offers wide and current practical experience in marketing management. It remains our hope that through this text, students who are to form the future backbone of the tourism business will have the knowledge and tools to enable them to survive and prosper in the increasingly competitive world in which they plan to make their careers.

Chris Holloway · Chris Robinson

To Immy, in gratitude for her patience and tolerance

Chris Holloway

**To my wife, Dara, without whose support my
contribution would not have been possible**

Chris Robinson

Part 1

1 The marketing perspective

After studying this chapter, you should be able to:

- understand the basic philosophy of marketing
- differentiate between production and marketing orientation
- appreciate the need for marketing in the present travel and tourism business environment
- recognise the constraints under which marketing is conducted
- understand the nature of travel and tourism as a product, and be aware of issues affecting its marketing

'What's this marketing all about, then?'

(a local authority official on his appointment as a tourism marketing officer for the district)

There's probably more talk about marketing today than at any previous time in business. It's the term managers like to use to show that their company is modern, dynamic and forward-thinking. But the fact remains that marketing in the true sense of the word is all too seldom applied in the business world, and still less in the travel and tourism industry. Of course, there are some tourism organisations, both in the public and private sectors, which have wholeheartedly adopted the marketing philosophy, and can be counted among the most effective marketing organisations in Britain; but these remain the exception rather than the rule, and good marketing practice is still rare among the smaller travel companies.

There are a number of reasons for our failure to come to terms with marketing. One is the inherent conservatism of our society, our suspicion of new ideas and reluctance to change old, well-tried ways of doing things. Another is a very real ignorance of what marketing is all about – a result of our tendency to believe that the best way of learning business is to recruit staff straight from school and 'train them up' in the ways of the company. Under this system,

methods of business operation tend to perpetuate themselves, and innovation, where it exists, depends upon the 'gut feel' of the proprietor rather than skilled analysis of the market. Small companies believe that marketing is something that can be undertaken only by large corporations, and is too expensive to be considered within the small firm. The tourism industry itself is a very young one, and only now is it beginning to come to grips with modern business practice. This has also played a part in inhibiting the development of modern marketing techniques.

This book will attempt to show that marketing is not just a 'flavour of the month' jargon term, but a business philosophy that should underline our whole approach to the running of a company. Marketing is not 'something done by the marketing department' alone. Its philosophy should permeate every department. All too often, a company which declares itself to be marketing orientated is in fact product orientated; it is concerned principally with finding ways to utilise surplus capacity rather than tackling the question of what the customer really wants. We see this today in the travel business, in the process known as *consolidation*, whereby package tour charter flights with low load factors are merged or withdrawn, necessitating passengers switching flights, airports or even destinations. The belief, widely held in the travel industry, that low price is the key to success has resulted in inconvenience, discomfort and dissatisfaction among the travelling public. An example of product orientation in travel is the case of a major city bus company which used its buses for sightseeing on Sundays only, because that was the only day on which the company had spare capacity. Unfortunately, passenger demand was for mid-week and Saturday excursions, and the product was a failure.

In other areas of business, Britain's competitors have learned to apply the marketing philosophy very successfully, and have gained a competitive edge over many British goods and services as a result. British businesspeople will need to learn the lesson for themselves.

Let us start by defining the term and taking a look at marketing in the wider context before going on to see its relevance to the travel and tourism industry.

What is marketing?

Perhaps the best way of describing what marketing is is to show what it is not. One of the authors accompanied his daughter while she was shopping for a new bikini. After a fruitless search through countless shops for a top and bottom that would fit her, she tried the branch of a well-known department store. The saleswoman was polite and helpful, but after the umpteenth costume had been tried on unsuccessfully, she cried in exasperation, 'I just don't know what's happening these days; people don't seem to fit our clothes any longer!'

As a postscript to that story, for years in the United States it has been possible to buy the tops and bottoms of bikinis separately, a marketing-orientated solution which is gradually being adopted in Britain. Could the clothing manufacturers have discovered that changing social habits were leading to new body shapes? Exercise, dieting and health foods are all likely to have lasting implications for the average shape and weight of our bodies, which will in turn affect the demand for clothes. Indeed, research at

Manchester University has revealed that women today have thicker waists, lower breasts and more conical figures than they had in the period immediately following World War II – a discovery which is helping the mail order clothes business to market its products more effectively.

Too many people equate marketing with selling, as if the two terms were synonymous. Even a travel trade paper carried an article on travel marketing which defined it as selling – a point quickly picked up in the correspondence which followed in subsequent weeks! Others have defined it as a more sophisticated form of advertising. Actually, both selling and advertising are functions of marketing, which is an all-embracing term to indicate the direction and thrust of a firm's policies and strategies.

Marketing is about anticipating demand, recognising it, stimulating it and finally satisfying it. It is understanding what can be sold, to whom, when, where and in what quantities. There are literally dozens of acceptable definitions of marketing, and this is not the book to discuss the semantics of these definitions. Instead, let us look at the definition offered by the Chartered Institute of Marketing itself:

> Marketing is the management function which organises and directs all those business activities involved in assessing customer needs and converting customer purchasing power into effective demand for a specific product or service, and in moving that product or service to the final consumer or user so as to achieve the profit target or other objective set by the company or other organisation.

The definition has three important implications. First, it is a management function within the company. Second, it underlies, and provides the framework for, all the activities which a business undertakes. Finally, and herein lies the whole philosophy of marketing, it places the emphasis on customers' needs as the starting-point for the business's operations. As Theodore Levitt expressed it, while 'selling focuses on the needs of the seller, marketing focuses on the needs of the buyer'.[1] Marketing is about finding out what the customer wants first, and then producing the product to fit those needs (a marketing-orientated approach) as opposed to producing the product or service and then seeing to whom it can be sold (a product-orientated approach).

Clearly, a marketing-orientated company is one in which the philosophy of marketing pervades the entire organisation. If decisions at board level are production-orientated, or the chief executive is unsympathetic to the marketing philosophy, the marketing manager's task becomes impossible. Equally, marketing cannot function effectively if other departments are inefficient. If the company's costs are high, or inadequate control over product quality results in poor value for money, no amount of 'marketing' will make the company a success. The customer's needs will remain unsatisfied, however well advertised, or hard sold, the product is.

A historical overview

It has taken a long time for British companies to wake up to this need. In the past, Britain didn't need to market its products; Britain's colonies around the world created a ready demand for its manufactured goods. However, with independence, these countries turned to production of their own goods, or bought from Britain's competitors. For too long, Britain traded in the belief that what was British was best; meanwhile, quality deteriorated, British companies failed to match their competitors on delivery dates, and after-sales service weakened. Workers lost confidence in their companies' management, and lost pride in their own performance. In consequence, Britain's share of world markets in almost every commodity became smaller, and Britain grew less wealthy compared with its competitors. At the same time, the introduction of mass production methods meant that Britain needed to sell more goods, in order to take advantage of the benefits of economies of scale by reducing the unit cost of products. Britain's declining markets meant higher costs against those of other countries, making it still harder to sell British goods.

At first, the response of many companies was to sell harder. This failed, so they attempted to undercut their competitors on price, selling inferior products cheaply. This failed to take into account the customers' preference for quality and reliability, and again sales were lost.

While some major industries learned the lesson in the early post-war years, it was only in the late 1960s and 1970s that industry started to apply the marketing concept – some 50 years later than the USA. This process accelerated in the 1980s, with emphasis on design and quality coming to the fore. Firms discovered that it was better to tailor their products to the specific needs of one market, rather than trying to produce products that would meet everyone's needs. They learned to appreciate that people don't buy products, but the benefits which those products offered. This encouraged companies to research specific needs and how to satisfy them. Above all, companies have come to understand that marketing is a dynamic concept; people's needs change over time, requiring companies to recognise and respond to those changes. Successful companies today cannot guarantee that their products will continue to be in demand in the future.

Some issues in travel and tourism marketing

The early post-war years also saw the birth of modern tourism as an industry. Initially, this too was sales-led and product orientated. The spectacular growth of package holidays in the 1960s was generated by the ideas of entrepreneurs who saw opportunities to create holidays utilising spare airline capacity that resulted from the ending of the Berlin Airlift and the introduction of new technology aircraft. Linked with low-cost accommodation in newly emerging Spanish resorts, they were able to offer exciting holidays in the sun for less than 'dreary' holidays in Britain.

Because of the success of the venture, enormous pressures were placed to increase volumes available, and repeatedly hotels failed to be completed on time. Unfamiliar food gave rise to complaints, and aircraft reliability and safety

'. . . holidays making use of spare airline capacity . . .'

gave cause for considerable concern. Then marketing experts began to arrive and to question underlying assumptions.

It was said that in order to sell holidays, one had to overcome three essential fears:

- fear of flying
- fear of foreign food
- fear of foreigners.

The early marketeers in overseas holidays set about providing reassurance and undertook research as a prerequisite for marketing action.

Fear of flying

Such importance is now attached to safety that it seems inconceivable that risks should have been taken with people's lives for commercial gain, yet effectively this was done. Elderly aircraft were being pressed into service to the limits of their capabilities. Due to restrictive pricing policies promoted by state airlines, and backed by bilateral agreements, unsuitable airports were being used (especially the notorious Perpignan in the French Pyrenees). Poor on-board layouts were uncomfortable and resulted in dangers from loose cabin baggage. Even the British government added to individuals' uncertainty by insisting that aircraft used for trooping flights should have seats facing rearward to increase survival probability in the event of a forced or

bad landing. When holiday passengers enquired about the reasons for this bizarre configuration, the answer hardly added to their confidence!

From the original concept of cheap redundant aircraft availability, it soon became apparent that much greater gains could be achieved by purchasing leading edge technology which not only would show actual operational economies through higher utilisation and better load factors, but also would create an aura of customer confidence that would build business levels for those associated with the new standards of holidays.

Fear of foreign food

Foreign foods presented different problems. At a time when British eating habits were much less adventurous than they are today, many of the normal Mediterranean ingredients were reviled as 'greasy' or 'foreign rubbish'. Even the ways of presentation and service were misunderstood, with different traditions, such as serving meat and vegetables separately, and the time taken over mealtimes, much criticised. Hoteliers complained of doing their best under the constraint of tight budgets. They probably complained even louder than the holidaymakers about the awkwardness of customers and the levels of food waste. A little research into methods soon paid off. Catering experts were dispatched, who advised hoteliers how to spend less on ingredients and yet achieve greater satisfaction through changes in cooking methods, presentation and service. As labour became more expensive, many hotels introduced buffets whereby holidaymakers could choose for themselves. Though ingredient costs have risen as a result, the savings in service and in wasted food have balanced the cost and the result is a much better answer for the majority.

Fear of foreigners

Fear of foreigners is really an insoluble problem if taken literally, for it would remove one of the main incentives for travel, which is to meet and understand others better. It arose in part from the unreliability in the provision of accommodation, together with a misunderstanding of local customs and habits. In the 1970s, the large British travel companies decided that the only way of overcoming this barrier was to control totally the overseas accommodation and services. They invested heavily in properties built to their own specification, managed by themselves or their nominees. They introduced expertise that had not previously been available locally and raised standards substantially. Probably the most salutory changes in attitudes were created by the need of tour operators to comply with the Trade Descriptions Act (1968). It meant that the days of careless overbooking were over. Positive moves were made by tour operators to create even greater consumer confidence by offering substantial cash compensation if failure to provide accommodation occurred. The follow-through was that the tour operators' contracts with hoteliers provided that in the event of such failures, the punitive compensation was deductible directly from the hotelier.

On a personal level, the role of the resort representative was changed from merely being an arrival/departure escort and seller of excursions to being a uniformed staff member dedicated to assisting customers to get the most out of their holidays. Now the quality of the product of the major companies is no longer in question, any more than is a sweater from Marks & Spencer or a television set from Dixons.

Marketing as a field of study

While marketing as a field of serious study in the UK goes back to the 1950s, it has now become an essential ingredient of any business course, at all levels up to post-graduate level. While the body of knowledge forming a marketing syllabus has been refined to nationally agreed standards, no one individual who has studied marketing can be expected to be an expert in all facets of the discipline. Marketing tasks are extremely diverse, requiring the application of both management and craft skills. The ability to sell effectively, to put together an effective advertisement, to create an eye-catching and attractive window display,

to conduct research interviews successfully are skills which are as important in their own way as the assiduous research, planning, recording and analysis that we associate with the management function of marketing.

It will be apparent that the strengths of the larger organisation include the ability to employ several marketing staff, who can offer widely differing talents within the sphere of marketing. Certainly, good marketing will always call for an element of entrepreneurial flair, but if our view of marketing is limited to the extrovert, dynamic salesperson who catches the headlines, we are in danger of overlooking the less visible qualities of good marketing: the ability to interpret statistical data and draw rational conclusions, to demonstrate understanding of tourist needs and behaviour patterns. 'Flair' on its own is no longer enough.

Constraints in marketing

Good marketing forms the basis of the so-called 'growth economy', to which the industrialised world is committed. However, it is not without its critics, both on economic and social grounds. Economically, it is criticised for its wasteful use of resources. Huge amounts of money are spent in advertising products which are almost identical to other products, in an attempt to persuade consumers that they are unique, or better in some way than their competitors. Products are designed to date before their normal lifespan, in order to increase sales of more recent models, while consumer goods are designed with parts that will wear out within a given time so that the entire product will require to be replaced. Social critics point to the emphasis that marketers place on material values by playing on consumer emotions in order to build an acquisitive society where wants, rather than needs, are manipulated, with the consumer led to believe that the possession of more and more goods and services is the key to a happy and successful life. As one critic puts it, marketers first persuade you that you have a problem, and then tell you they can help you to solve it!

Defending their role, marketers argue that in creating growth they are helping to create employment and wealth; that Britain's failure to compete against foreign products will lead to its becoming an impoverished country without political power or influence, with the British way of life dominated by its more successful neighbours. This book is not the place for a full discussion of these issues, but some understanding of the arguments and counter-arguments is important, because marketers will need to be aware of the pressures they face in their work. It is also important for those who intend to work in the marketing field that they believe in their work, and in the products they are selling. This is both a moral issue and a practical one; salespeople are not likely to perform to maximum efficiency if they do not believe in the product they are selling. If we are obliged to sell products about which we are cynical, we denigrate both ourselves and our society.

In this respect, we are fortunate that the product under consideration is tourism. Most of those involved in the tourism business can genuinely believe in the product they are selling, as one that is beneficial to their clients, whether holidays are being sold to relieve stress, to aid health or to provide clients with a novel or cultural experience. But those with the responsibility of selling tourism must take care to sell the products which will satisfy their clients' needs. It is not enough for travel agents to sell whatever holidays will generate the most profits. Agents have a moral responsibility towards their clients – and incidentally, by satisfying them, agents will ensure that they will return to book with their company another year. And that is what marketing is all about.

This is not to say that tourism marketers will not face from time to time some serious soul-searching. A destination which is popular will achieve a level of demand which threatens the very attractiveness it offers. This is the paradox of mass tourism – that it can be a victim of its own success. Anyone who has visited a popular seaside resort, such as Clovelly or Polperro, in the height of the summer season will be aware of the problems of congestion and pollution caused by the influx of huge numbers of tourists. Should the industry continue to promote such destinations with impunity? What should the marketing role of a local tourism officer be in such a situation?

In fact, contrary to popular opinion, marketing is not just concerned with selling more. It is also about regulating demand, and this applies particularly where the supply of a product is finite. In this example, the tourism officer's role may be to counter-market the destination in the summer, and to try to switch demand to the shoulder season or off-season; to attempt to select market segments to increase the average spend (by focusing on staying visitors, rather than day trippers, for example); to maintain the quality of the product at present levels of consumption. The management of marketing is about the management of demand, and a marketing manager's role can be to demarket, to stabilise demand levels. Marketing plans by the British Tourist Authority (BTA) include the aims of spreading tourist traffic geographically and seasonally as a means of relieving the pressure of high demand for popular British tourist destinations. Just as a popular theatre show will be packed to capacity throughout its run and unable to expand to satisfy the total level of demand it is experiencing, so a facility such as Heathrow Airport has a finite capacity which calls for demand management. In such a situation, marketing may be restricted to attempts to improve levels of existing service, rather than trying to accommodate all those wishing to use the service.

Since tourism is a product which must be purchased in advance of its consumption, and since it must be described rather than demonstrated to consumers, many opportunities arise for unethical practice in the industry. The product may be oversold, or services promised that are not fulfilled. However, the days when brochures deliberately set out to mislead are now largely gone, killed by a combination of statutory legislation and internal 'policing' in the industry. The Association of British Travel Agents (ABTA) has Codes of Conduct for travel agencies and tour operators and also guidelines for booking conditions, which have substantially reduced the possibility for misleading the public. The European Union Directive on Package Travel (1992) has further tightened regulations requiring that tour operators be more accurate in their brochure descriptions. Constraints are also exercised by the media, always anxious to exploit any evidence of malpractice in the industry, and by organisations such as the Consumers' Association, publishers of *Holiday Which?*. Carriers, too, have their own watchdogs – the Air Transport Users' Committee in Britain, and on a global scale the International Airline Passengers Association. Such organisations have been set up to safeguard the interests of the travelling public.

However, as companies grow, they generally seek for themselves a more professional standard of conduct, and therefore are more sensitive about their public image. A company seeking long-term survival cannot afford to ignore its critics, or have too high a level of complaints from its customers. Newer and smaller companies may be less concerned, but should the industry itself not take effective action to police their activities, the consumer movement will call for more legislation to protect them.

Categories of marketing

If you look back at the definition of marketing given earlier in the chapter, you will see that the aim of an organisation's marketing is to achieve a profit *or other objective*. This distinction is important, since it clarifies the fact that marketing embraces the activities of all kinds of other organisations besides businesses.

Social marketing

Even within the commercial sphere, not all organisations will have profit as their objective. The British Tourist Authority, for example, has no direct profit objective, its goal being to generate tourism to Britain, hence stimulating the economy, employment and the profits of private tourist enterprises. In the same way, other organisations providing non-commercial services, such as educational institutions, have to communicate their 'product' to their 'customers', their students. Ideas, too, will require communicating. The churches, charity organisations, political lobbies, all aim to satisfy certain needs, and the employment of effective communications techniques will help them to do so (has your eye ever been caught by one of those punchy slogans on the noticeboards outside your local church?) Present concern about the pollution of our environment has led to the formation of a strong ecology movement, whose aim is to market an idea to opinion leaders such as Members of Parliament and journalists, as well as to the general public. This concept of 'social marketing' is a relatively recent one, and brings home the point that organisations of all types can apply good marketing practice to their activities.

Consumer and industrial marketing

At this point, it will be helpful to clarify what we mean by the term *product*. In marketing terms, the word encompasses not only tangible goods, but also anything that can be offered to people to satisfy their needs or wants, including services.

Products are sold to two kinds of buyers; those who buy for their own consumption, and those who buy on behalf of others. The term *consumer marketing* is used to describe the practice of marketing to the former category, and *industrial marketing* to the latter. Just as manufacturing industries buy raw materials to convert into finished products for their customers, and retail shops buy stock to sell to their customers, so in the travel world there are many forms of industrial buyers. Many large companies whose staff are engaged in frequent business travel will employ travel managers, whose task it is to arrange all the business travel of the company employees. Business conferences may be organised by professional firms of conference organisers, rather than by firms whose employees actually attend the conference. Hotels, airlines, and other travel companies will be eager to solicit business from these industrial buyers.

Home and export marketing

Finally, we need to draw a distinction between marketing products in the home (or domestic) market, and marketing them abroad to foreign markets. Export marketing, or international marketing, is a specialised field of marketing which will have to take into account different legal systems and business climates, different cultures affecting buyer behaviour, and the problems associated with transporting products abroad. Tourism, again, is substantially concerned with export marketing. British Airways has to sell the concept of flying with a British airline to Americans in competition with American carriers, and the British Tourist Authority must market Britain as a destination to travellers in dozens of countries around the world, in competition with other tourist destinations, while incoming tour operators must learn the needs of visitors from different countries and how to cater for them.

We can now bring all these forms of marketing together in a diagram (see Fig. 1.1).

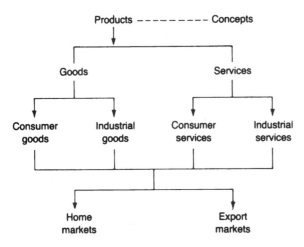

Fig. 1.1 Categories of product marketing

The nature of tourism services

Since we are dealing throughout this book with a service industry, we shall look at the nature of services to understand how their marketing needs, and those of tourism services in particular, differ from those of goods. There are four main factors to be considered:

- intangibility
- heterogeneity
- perishability
- inseparability.

First, services are *intangible*. They cannot be inspected or sampled in advance of their purchase, therefore an element of risk is involved on the part of the purchaser. This is a critically important aspect of the transaction. From one perspective, this makes marketing services much easier; none of the usual problems of physical distribution is encountered, and there is no question of storing the product in warehouses prior to its delivery to the customer. However, intangible products have many drawbacks. The fact that travel agents, for example, do not have to purchase their products before they sell them to their clients reduces their commitment to the sale and their loyalty to particular brands. In place of a distribution system, the travel industry must deal with a *reservations system*, which is simply a method of matching demand with supply. The problems inherent in this form of distribution will be discussed in Chapter 8.

Tourism marketers must attempt to overcome the drawbacks posed by an intangible product, and there are a number of imaginative ways in which this has been achieved in practice. The development of video cassettes, which produce a more faithful (and more favourable) image of the holiday product than can be obtained with a holiday brochure, is one way in which travel can be effectively communicated to consumers. Another idea, introduced briefly during the rapid growth era of the 1960s before oil price rises sent air fares rocketing, was low price 'trial flights' to a destination, whereby unsold charter air seats were made available to the public at a very low fare to enable prospective purchasers of package holidays to 'sample' the destinations and the experience of flying. Sometimes the fare charged (as low as £1) would be refunded against the later purchase of a holiday. In the 1990s, the British company Airtours experimented with low price short flights to help prospective passengers overcome their fear of flying.

The second problem with services is *heterogeneity*. If one buys a tangible product – say, a dining-room table or a television set – mass production methods can go a long way to ensuring that each article produced is homogeneous, that is, standardised, with each unit sharing identical characteristics. With good quality control, 'lemons' occur very infrequently, and the customer can be assured of a product of a certain uniformity and quality. This is not the case with a service. Although the package tour concept has gone a long way to help the standardisation of the travel product, with its combination of flight, transfer and hotel room, there are elements of the product over which the 'manufacturer', that is, the tour operator, can have no control. A holiday taken in a week of continuous rainfall is a very different product from one taken in glorious sunshine. Although operators might offer the consolation of an insurance against bad weather, they cannot guarantee good weather. At the same time, a consumer buying a service such as tourism is buying a range of services provided by individuals, and these too are difficult to control. Hotel waiters who have had a tiff with their partners the previous evening will not render the same friendly service at breakfast that they had offered at dinner the day before. Resort representatives facing redundancy due to a takeover of their company by a rival are unlikely to treat their clients with the same consideration as they would have done in normal circumstances. While good quality control procedures can help to reduce extreme variations in performance, they cannot overcome the human problems inherent in the performance of tourism services.

Third, the tourism product is a highly *perishable* one. If the television set in the showroom is not sold today, it can be sold tomorrow, if necessary, at a reduced price. Or it can be stored and offered at a later date. But an airline seat or hotel room not sold today is lost forever. This fact is of great importance for marketing, particularly when determining pricing. The heavy discounts on rooms sold after 6 pm and the 'standby' fares offered by airlines to fill empty seats reflect this need to off-load products before their sale potential is lost. The problem is compounded by the fact that the travel industry suffers from *time-variable demand*. Often, holiday demand is concentrated in peak summer months such as July and August, and short trips are more likely to be taken at weekends than weekdays. Business travellers wish to fly from Heathrow at a convenient time to them, say between 10 am and noon, whereas airports and airlines prefer to offer a balanced service around the clock to maximise the use of their resources. Once again, pricing strategies can help spread demand by offering substantial reductions during periods of low demand, but this does not totally solve the problem.

Finally, there is the question of *inseparability*. Services are highly personalised, the product being the outcome of the performance of the seller. The simplest way to demonstrate this is again to take the television set as an example. If we see an advertisement for a particular brand of set that we want to buy, at a price which is highly competitive against those of other stores, we are likely to visit the shop. If we find that the salesperson selling the television is unkempt and lacking interest, this alone is unlikely to dissuade us from making the purchase; price and brand reputation have already predetermined our actions. However, transpose the same scenario to a restaurant or hotel, and our reaction will be very different. Whatever the quality of the food, however attractive the décor, service is so much an integral part of the product that it would be unlikely that we should be prepared to purchase from such a poor representative. The travel agent who sells us our holiday, the airline cabin staff who cater to our needs *en route*, the resort representative who greets us on arrival, the hotel's front office receptionist – all are elements in the product we are purchasing, and their social skills in dealing with us are an essential part of the product. It is for this reason that training becomes so vital for the successful marketing of travel and tourism.

The very fact that the product is a composite of several services leads to further problems associated with product development. In a package holiday, customers will normally expect to receive broadly comparable levels of quality in all the components of their travel arrangements, regardless of whether they have bought a high-priced or budget holiday. The tourist booked at a premium-priced hotel who purchases an optional excursion associated with that holiday will justifiably feel cheated if the coach providing the service is dirty or in poor mechanical condition. This 'law of tourism harmony' is an important element in quality assurance in the holiday industry. However, there is now some evidence emerging that patterns of tourist demand are becoming more complex, with better-travelled tourists opting for a mix of variable-quality products to meet their needs – for example, a luxury hotel coupled with budget activities by day. Marketing managers will need to be aware of such trends and become flexible enough to cater for them.

These issues will have helped to demonstrate that, while basic principles of marketing apply to all products, in practice there are special considerations to take into account when marketing tourism. It is the very peculiarity of tourism that makes it such a problematic, and at the same time fascinating, product to create and sell.

Questions, tasks and issues for discussion

1 'In a way, a tourist organisation is not involved in marketing, because marketing *per se* supposes you've got control of the product, and that you can change it'
(Frank Kelly, former director of marketing, BTA)

  To what extent do you agree with this statement?
  Given the position of a public sector tourist board, can it ever be completely marketing orientated?

2 How far do you think the mass market operators of package holidays have successfully overcome the 'three fears' (of flying, foreign food and foreigners) identified in this chapter? Does this remain a problem, and if not, to what extent has good marketing overcome it, rather than other factors?

3 Identify one company in the travel and tourism industry which clearly demonstrates a marketing-orientated philosophy. What are the factors which support this view?

4 What are the 'skills' of marketing? How effectively do you think these skills are actually used in (a) travel agencies, and (b) tour operators?

Exercise

Museums are changing from their traditional role of providing exhibits for inspection at a distance and under glass, to centres of interpretation and experience for their visitors. Visit a local museum and undertake research which will indicate:

● how far the museum appears to be catering from this new approach
● what could further be achieved.

Your research should be based on talks to museum staff – curators, guards, guides, educational assistants – and to members of the general public visiting the attraction. Use semi-structured interviews, aided by tape recorders to record the discussions. Also spend time observing the attraction and its exhibits, noting such features as signs, descriptive boards or literature, interactive opportunities for visitors, etc. Is there an education officer or department responsible for educational visits? How well does the museum meet the different needs for interpretation among its varied visitors – adults, children, foreign tourists, and so on?

Write a brief report indicating what has been achieved, how well this has been implemented, and what remains to be done to improve customer satisfaction.

2 Marketing planning

After studying this chapter, you should be able to:

- explain the planning function and its role within marketing
- understand the elements of a marketing plan and how to construct one
- recognise how uncontrollable factors affect the planning process
- employ SWOT analysis as the foundation for a marketing plan
- describe simple forecasting methods and understand their role in the planning process
- list organisational systems for marketing, and evaluate their suitability for different marketing conditions
- list the elements of the marketing mix, and understand their role in the marketing plan

What is marketing planning?

All tourism organisations, however small and whether consciously or not, engage in marketing activity. The local travel agent, for example, has to make decisions about which services to offer, which brochures to rack and how they will be displayed. The choice of brochures, level of service, type of décor and furnishings, all reflect the market segment the agent has decided to cater for and the ways in which the needs of that market will be met. Advertising the products, drawing attention to special opportunities, perhaps providing free coach travel to the local airport as an incentive for clients to book with that agent, checking past records to see who the regular clients are, and undertaking mailshots with details of holidays that may appeal to them are all examples of marketing activity. There is, however, an important distinction between so-called 'seat of the pants' marketing, where decisions are taken on the spur of the moment, and a carefully thought out and co-ordinated approach to marketing. This latter process is known as the marketing planning process, and it is this process which will be described in this chapter.

Expressed simply, planning is designed to link an organisation's goals and resources to its marketing opportunities, and in doing so to make the best uses of its resources. Clearly then, we have first to know what our goals and resources are, as well as what opportunities exist for us to exploit. If a market is growing quickly, as was the case with foreign holidays from the 1960s to the mid-1980s, opportunities may be comparatively simple to identify, and in these circumstances even relatively inefficient and poorly managed companies may be able to survive and prosper. But the marketing environment is subject to constant change, and if demand stabilises or falls (as happened in the case of package holidays in the early 1990s), the failure to develop a strategic marketing plan which responds to that change may result in the collapse of less efficiently managed organisations. Planning is simply a means of survival in a competitive and quickly changing environment.

Planning for what?

Planning is needed to meet short-term and long-term objectives. At its most basic, short-term planning is required simply in order to identify where the company is now, and where it will be next week, or next month. Managers need to be able to judge their cash flow position, since without knowing how much money will be flowing into a company, it will not be possible to predict whether funds will be adequate to pay the organisation's running costs, such as salaries. The marketing plan determines what needs to be sold in a given period, at a given price, and how this is to be achieved, to meet operating costs.

Beyond this, the company must plan to achieve its longer-term objectives. This could mean finding additional sources of capital for future investment. No banker is likely to look favourably at a request for further funds unless the organisation's aims and strategies are clearly defined. The marketing plan is, of course, only one aspect of a company's overall planning, and as such must be co-ordinated with the financial plans, organisational plans, purchasing plans and other aspects of the organisation's total business activity. Marketing is simply a tool by which an organisation achieves its objectives, by identifying new product and market opportunities, evaluating them and taking action to develop them. In diagrammatic form, a company's Marketing Action Plan will look like that shown in Fig. 2.1.

Setting objectives

Typical objectives likely to be sought by the company will include:

- achieving a certain level of sales growth within a given period of time
- increasing the profitability of the organisation by a given percentage within an agreed time scale
- obtaining a given percentage share of the market within a given period of time (new product), or increasing current market share by x per cent within the period (existing product)
- reducing business risk by diversifying the product range
- obtaining a measured increase in the return on capital employed by the company.

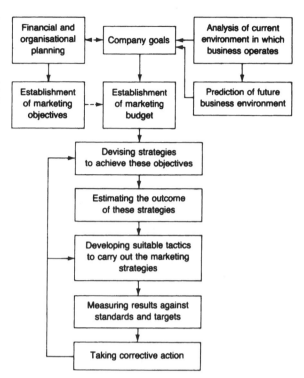

Fig. 2.1 A marketing action plan

The marketing plan will be designed to achieve one or more of these objectives by the use of a selected choice of strategies. There is a danger in trying to achieve too many objectives simultaneously within a marketing plan, since this can result in conflicting strategies. If asked, most managers would declare their aims would be to satisfy all of the objectives listed above; but, as tour operators and other travel firms have learned to their cost, the achievement of increases in market share, or a policy of long-term growth may be at the expense of short-term profits.

A marketing manager is faced with many alternative strategies from which to choose when drawing up a marketing plan. To achieve an increase in the return on capital invested, for example, the tour operator might choose to raise prices, to find ways of reducing costs, to seek higher productivity from present resources, to push for increased sales to present markets served, or to introduce products to new markets.

Which of these is adopted will depend upon the analysis of the current market situation in which the company is operating. A major company such as First Choice Holidays, for example, which has several brands aimed at different market sectors – Sovereign aimed at the luxury market, Freespirit for the more independent traveller without children and First Choice for mainstream family holidays – may set quite distinct objectives, involving different strategic plans, for each of these divisions.

The business environment

In drawing up a marketing plan, a balance must be struck between establishing rigid bureaucratic guidelines and a dependency upon entrepreneurial 'flair'. Any plan has to be flexible, to take into account changing circumstances. If a company sticks too rigidly to its pre-established plans, it stands in danger of missing new opportunities which arise in the course of the plan's implementation. The collapse of a specialist tour operator in mid-season, for instance, will allow another operator to move into a new market or a new geographical area which may have been considered and rejected earlier. At the same time, any company which chooses to ignore its plans will be in danger of heading off in a number of different directions, not only disrupting the organisation's overall planning but also possibly over-stretching its resources.

A business has within its power the ability to change any aspect of its internal operations as it sees fit. However, it operates within an environment over which it has little, if any, control.

This environment comprises the political, legal, economic, geographical and cultural framework in which all businesses operate. It is subject to continual change and the business, if it is to survive, must learn to adapt to these changes. An understanding of the current business environment is an essential prerequisite for planning. We can demonstrate this by taking the example of a typical mass market tour operator. Figure 2.2 illustrates the range of influences on the operator.

Fig. 2.2 The business environment of a tour operator

The operator needs to understand first the nature and scope of the *competition* which it faces from other tour operating companies. How easy is it for new companies to enter the market? Who are the company's main competitors, what share of the market do they possess, and what are their marketing strategies? The dog-eat-dog nature of the tour operating business should not be underestimated. The activity of competitor tour operators is probably *the* dominant factor in planning – spiced by the challenge of second guessing their likely strategy for twelve months ahead. With little consumer loyalty or perception of difference between operators, many holidays are booked after meticulous comparisons between the brochure offerings of the different companies.

In some countries, entry to the market may be controlled by government legislation, a *political* constraint, but in most countries a relatively free market exists, in which, subject to satisfying certain criteria, any company can enter and trade. There will, however, be *legal* considerations to take into account; licences may have to be obtained and restrictions on night flights may inhibit 24-hour operations.

One important factor in tourism, over which companies have no control, is that of *weather*. A poor early summer in Britain will lead to an increase in late demand for holidays abroad (as happened in 1985), while a mild winter followed by a promisingly warm spring may lead British people to plan to take their holidays at home.

A *cultural* factor is changing fashion. While it is true that businesses can sometimes manipulate fashion (the great fashion houses in the clothes trade provide ample evidence of this), there are a great many complex factors at work which will make one country or resort more fashionable than another, and marketing planners have to be sensitive to such changes in consumer demand resulting from changing taste. By and large, the mainstream destinations – Spain, Cyprus, Turkey, Greece, Portugal – remain dominant but enjoy cycles of popularity. Thus in 1992 Cyprus was *the* place to go, 1993 was Turkey's year, and 1994 was the year that Spain bounced back as the star destination country. However, it is not every country or resort that exploits its tourism wisely, or that can sustain it. A glance at a holiday brochure from the early 1980s reveals many 'lost' destinations, for example the Italian Rivieras were then significant destinations, but are now hardly featured.

The other side of the coin of fashion is the consumer's restless search for 'new' experiences and 'unspoilt' destinations. It is not sufficient for operators to offer a balanced programme of holidays across the established resorts. New hotels, new resorts, new countries and new types of holidays must all be part of a continuing programme of product development.

Above all, *economic* influences are at work which will affect demand for the company's products. The business must be aware of the extent to which its suppliers dictate the prices at which accommodation, air seats and other travel facilities are offered. A poor summer in Britain, leading to sudden late demand for foreign holidays, will have the effect of pushing up prices as many operators try to purchase extra arrangements at short notice. Operators negotiating for hotel rooms in Majorca, whatever share they may enjoy in the British market, will find themselves competing with German, Dutch, Swedish and other operators who may be prepared to pay higher prices, or have greater bargaining power, driving up prices for British operators.

Operators must be aware, too, of the *elasticity of demand* for their product; that is, the extent to which a change in price of the holidays leads to a change in demand from consumers. A product such as a package tour, which is not clearly differentiated from products of other tour operators, is highly price sensitive, and price reductions will lead to substantial expansion in the total demand for holidays, as well as attracting holidaymakers away from other operators; just as any price increase not also affecting competitors can lead to a dramatic fall in the company's market share.

Consumer demand for holidays is also determined by the *substitutability* of the package tour, not only against other forms of holidays, but also against other goods and services, such as a new television set or a three-piece suite for the living room. Economists use the term *cross-elasticity of demand* to describe this highly important factor (and one too readily overlooked by many in the travel industry). The annual holiday has now become a habit for millions of Britons, who have shown their willingness to sacrifice purchases of consumer goods in order to continue to take their annual holiday in the sun during periods of recession. However, if prices of these foreign holidays are driven up at a significantly faster rate than other goods and services (due, for example, to changes in exchange rates between, or inflation rates within, the two countries) then consumers may switch their spending patterns. Holidaymakers may decide to stay at home working in the garden, spending the money on shrubs, a greenhouse or garden tools (especially if the summer is good) rather than taking their traditional fortnight in the sun. In 1988, against all economic predictions about prosperity, overseas tourism failed to grow; some pundits have ascribed this to the market's preference to spend on consumer durables. Finally, we must recognise that holiday demand can also be affected by the demand for goods 'in fashion' which compete for leisure money. Video cassette recorders and home computers both represent a considerable outlay for the consumer, who may sacrifice holidays in order to 'join the crowd' in buying the new product on the market.

In addition to the factors we have cited here, a host of other factors can affect the company's business objectives. Demographic changes – a rise or fall in population, a decline in a particular age group, changes in traditional marriage patterns – should be understood, and taken into account when planning for long-term objectives, while the need to take into account shareholders' demands to sustain satisfactory dividends must also figure in the company's short-term marketing plans. Requirements imposed by finance houses and banks, as conditions for loans, will have to be considered. In Britain the national trade body, ABTA, imposes its own standards on its members, while the Office of Fair Trading (OFT) will press for conditions which improve the consumers' interests, such as insisting on brochures showing all-inclusive prices, instead of listing airport taxes and other ancillary costs separately. Environmental lobbyists or Members of Parliament may be pressing for reductions in the number of night flights, or greater utilisation of less popular airports. Even the media exercise influence over the business practices of the travel trade (think of the influence of programmes such as the BBC's *Holiday* or ITV's *Wish You were Here*, for example). In short, the business environment is made up of a huge complex of public and private institutions and individuals, each of which may pose constraints on the way in which the marketing manager functions.

Tour operators, in fact, are in a particularly vulnerable position, since they can be affected both by changes in the environment of their consumers and by changes in the countries in which they operate. They may be operating to a region suddenly beset by political unrest, where the safety of their clients can no longer be assured, or by industrial strife, such as an air traffic controllers' strike in Spain or France. A destination country may change the value of its currency, or impose a higher airport tax on departing passengers, or introduce a swingeing increase in Value Added Tax (VAT), all of which will substantially affect the operators' prices and/or reduce demand to that destination. For this reason, they must be prepared to react quickly to amend their marketing plans.

SWOT analysis

This analysis of the business environment which we have just described is a necessary first step in systematically appraising the present position of the company and identifying its problems, prior to determining objectives for the coming year. Whether the company is preparing a feasibility study for a new product launch, or merely assessing the current market situation in order to prepare a new marketing plan, it must be aware of:

- the economic, political, legal, socio-cultural and technological events which currently affect or could have a bearing on company operations and performance
- the current shape of the markets served by the company, including their size, growth, and trends; product ranges on offer and prices charged in each market; channels through which the products are distributed; and ways in which product knowledge is communicated to the consumers and distributors
- the nature of the competition, including size of each competitor, share of the market they hold, their reputation, marketing methods, strengths and weaknesses
- full details of the company's own market share, sales, profitability, and patterns of trading.

This review is often undertaken using a technique known as SWOT analysis; that is, the identification of *strengths* and *weaknesses* in the business, the *opportunities* presented by the trading environment and any *threats* faced by the company. This information provides the basis for further action.

Let us look at the kinds of issues likely to be considered by travel companies in a typical SWOT.

Strengths

These have to be seen from the perspective of the customer, not the company. For example, with a travel agency, the fact that the internal size of the office will be large enough to accommodate a separate office for the manager is of little concern to the customers. On the other hand, if the company has an established reputation in the region, so that it will be already known in the area for its reliability or service, this will be a distinct advantage in early trading. Convenience of location is extremely important for customers, so a new agency opening in the heart of a new shopping precinct, perhaps adjacent to a popular chain store, will be a clear strength. The attraction of a new shop front and smart modern décor with comfortable seating will be another plus in the company's efforts to win customers from the competition.

A tour operator will be concerned with the image of the brand, as perceived by both travel agents and consumers. A strong image and high levels of awareness within the target market is important to even get on the 'starting grid' of the brochure being considered. Thus a strong and positive brand image is a key strength for an operator. A loyal body of past customers is a considerable asset to be exploited, as repeat business is easier and less costly to win than new sales. Product strengths, particularly those that differentiate the operator from its competition, are important. The operator may also benefit organisationally from unique contracts overseas or other organisational factors that facilitate the delivery of the holiday product and result in higher quality, lower costs, or both.

Weaknesses

One difficulty always facing an agent is that of finding sales staff of the right calibre. If in addition the agency is located in the London area, where employment is high and good staff at affordable salaries difficult to come by, the problem is compounded. At the same time, competitive agencies in the area may have well-established, competent staff, popular with their customers, which will make it difficult to attract business. Perhaps the shop fronts on to a street with a traffic barrier, requiring customers to use an unattractive underpass in order to reach the agency from across the road. This would be a serious weakness in attracting passing trade. So

would inadequate or expensive parking facilities.

The tour operator will be highly conscious of its competitive position: is it disadvantaged in terms of price, scope of destinations, quality of accommodation, product features or service to the travel agents? And is it weak in promotional terms, with the competition advertising its sales messages more effectively?

Opportunities

Opportunities are naturally presented by the chance to exploit any particular strengths of the business. Both agent and tour operator should also be on the lookout for opportunities presented by changes in the market. For the agent this might be a new housing estate being built in the vicinity. A new industrial development may be planned, with potential for business travel; or a new department store may be opening in the near future. This kind of opportunity needs to be not only recognised but also acted upon. Marketing tactics should take advantage of the opportunity, such as directing a mailshot to all residents on the new estate.

The operator might foresee a potential increase in a particular sector of the market, or a competitor might be going out of business, thus opening up the opportunity to capture their share of the market. The market may have reacted positively to particular promotional tactics in the past, presenting the opportunity to repeat or enhance their effect. New destinations, or the enhancement of tourist infrastructure within existing resorts, also present opportunities to the operator.

Threats

Both travel agent and tour operator will be subject to national economic and political events, such as the imposition of a departure tax in the UK, affecting the price of all flights out of UK airports. World politics and terrorist threats can pose major problems for the travel industry, as exhibited by the slump in overseas travel following the Gulf War in 1991. The local economy will affect the travel agent, as it will any regionally based tour operator. The agent will be concerned with such factors as major companies in the area laying off staff or planning to close; the agency manager or one of the sales staff planning to quit in order to open up an agency in competition. Perhaps present traffic patterns are to change as a result of road improvements in the area.

The operator will be alert for threats posed by currency fluctuations and fuel cost increases – both major contributors to fixed costs. Any competitive activity that is affecting sales will also represent a major threat – for example, a price reduction or a significant advertising campaign.

There are always threats in any business; but if they are recognised and tackled early enough, they can be overcome and perhaps even turned into opportunities.

At this point it might be helpful to introduce a case study of a fictitious SWOT analysis undertaken by an up-market city break tour operator which is part of a larger travel organisation. Let us call the operator 'Worldaway Holidays'.

Worldaway Holidays: a SWOT analysis

Strengths

- brand name heritage, providing exclusive cachet and up-market image within the target market
- loyal customer base with high repeat purchase, held on database and thus available for direct contact
- economies of scale linked to parent operation
- uniquely strong coverage of Eastern European capitals
- price guarantee and no-discount policy now well understood and liked by agents and consumers.

Weaknesses

- fewer destinations by comparison with the competition – a weakness perceived by agents to be greater than it actually is
- less attractive flight departure times to several destinations than the competition
- lack of knowledge of reservations staff compared to specialist operators

- lack of flexibility in Viewdata reservation system
- profits unduly impacted by unsold holidays and ineffective 'late sales' tactics
- customer satisfaction questionnaire process not comprehensive – customer names gathered are only 50 per cent of the total customers carried
- existing advertising campaign now 'tired' and response rates are dropping.

Opportunities

- market research shows strong growth in the up-market sector of the holiday business, with social group A/B consumers increasingly taking more than one holiday per year
- direct mail trials have shown that this technique is extremely effective when targeted at customers in order to generate brochure requests and 'push' sales into agents
- overseas staff report good opportunities to increase the programme to Eastern Europe, with good facilities being provided through investment in tourism in cities such as Riga and St Petersburg; there is an opportunity to increase the programme into unspoilt, historic and novel city destinations.

Threats

- relatively 'naive' tourist industry in Eastern Europe, increasing demands upon overseas staff and with a greater risk of a lapse in quality resulting in bad publicity
- specialist operators are offering better, more knowledgeable service to travel agents, and hence are preferred for the more 'undiscovered destinations'
- the major tour operating competitor to Worldaway Holidays is owned by a major airline, from whom 55 per cent of flights are negotiated; a satisfactory contract has still not been agreed
- the same competitor is running a significantly larger promotional campaign than Worldaway budgets would allow.

Worldaway Holidays: resultant marketing plan

Product

To exploit the anticipated increase in the size of the overall market, the programme should be increased to offer a further 10 000 holidays next season. These should be made up as follows:

1 4000 increased capacity to existing destinations. This represents a modest increase in market share of 0.5 per cent, which we hope to achieve through better management of the travel agent channel. The intention is to maximise the profit opportunities available from existing destinations.

2 1000 to 'established' city break destinations which are new to Worldaway, but fill perceived gaps in product portfolio, for example Istanbul. This modest capacity will still mean that we are seen to provide a wider choice of destinations, and it can be highlighted in our promotional activities.

3 5000 to new Eastern European destinations. We are becoming known for Eastern European breaks, and have good contacts through our parent company. This is the logical area for expansion, if sufficient safeguards can be put in place with respect to quality. This will be achieved through a policy of 'quality before rates' – and we should be strongly placed here with little competition and less price sensitivity for these destinations. Quality guidelines will be issued to staff which must be adhered to when contracting beds for next season.

The price advantage that we obtain through economies of scale with our parent company should not be used, as last season, to undercut the competition. The objective is to match the competition for price but use the extra margin we make to add in some 'product pluses' that will differentiate the product. Ideas on this include Worldaway leather luggage tags, taxi transfers from the airport and a free bottle of wine in the room on arrival.

The contracts for all flying should be reviewed. Again, quality standards must be higher – flight departure times should be more attractive. It should also be included in this year's hotel contracts that customer satisfaction questionnaires must be distributed to our customers on departure from the hotel. This will increase the capture of names and addresses for the marketing database.

The knowledge of the reservations staff must be improved to increase our credibility with agents as a specialist operator, and to enable us to sell the new destinations that we have planned with confidence. The reservations staff will be involved with our planned travel agent promotions through a programme of outbound calls to agents. Not only will this be motivating for them, but also it will improve their product knowledge.

Though this will offset to some extent the limitations of our Viewdata reservations system, a budget should be allocated to cover essential systems enhancements ready for on-sale next season.

Price

Prices will be set to match the competition, rather than undercut them.

Our guarantee not to raise surcharges has been well received and should be continued. Equally our policy of no discounting has done much to build our up-market image. Both of these pricing policies can be capitalised upon in promotion.

A feasibility study should be undertaken to investigate the implications of a 'never knowingly undersold' policy of matching the price of an identical holiday if it occurs in a competitor's programme. Hopefully, with the introduction of product pluses such as taxi transfers, the identical holiday will not exist elsewhere anyway. This claim could work well in promotional terms as it builds upon our existing well-received policies.

Promotion

Direct mail campaigns targeted at customers worked well last season and should be expanded. A test group of 'profiled' prospects should also be evaluated next season, and if cost-effective, planned in future years' programmes. The promotion needs a fresh creative treatment to revitalise response figures, but as last year the promotion should generate brochure requests.

Sales messages should include:

- the price promise of no surcharges and possibly 'never knowingly undersold'
- new destinations: a fresher, more varied programme than ever before
- special strengths in Eastern Europe
- emphasise even more the quality heritage of the brand coupled with the value for money from our parent operation.

We shall run a sales promotion to travel agents with the objective of raising awareness of Worldaway as a specialist operator. This should use the device of, for instance, a competition to draw to agents' attention the specific cities we cover. Outbound calls from our reservation teams to key outlets can support the promotion. Prizes of free trips to unusual Eastern European destinations should be backed up by a carefully controlled programme of selective educational visits.

A separate programme of visits for journalists and travel writers should again focus on the new destinations and the growing tourist trade in Eastern Europe.

The value of our customer database is now so great that it is worth incentivising the completion of customer satisfaction questionnaires. A modest donation to a Romanian orphanage project would position us well as an Eastern European specialist.

Further fund-raising activities for this good cause could be undertaken if the incentive proves successful.

Tactical advertisements to generate late sales should be planned in conjunction with a specialist advertising agency. Last year's activity suffered from a lack of skills and resource. In particular, we should benefit from quicker placement of advertisements and better choice of media.

Place

Travel agency distribution remains our key channel. This is to be supported by the activities already mentioned. Nevertheless, the opportunity exists to improve profits through direct sales for late availability. As well as brochure requests, we should trial advertisements quoting our reservations number direct. This will again impact on the training of reservations staff, who will need to be comfortable in dealing with the public as well as travel agents.

A select group of key travel agents will be offered increased commission subject to sales targets. We can further improve our service to these agents through:

- increased calls from sales staff at the expense of less productive outlets
- a joint promotion fund and support for travel agents prepared to mount evening events on holidays in Eastern Europe.

The marketing plan devised above will introduce readers to many of the issues discussed later in this book, dealing as it does with proposals for product policy, pricing decisions and communications with customers and trade buyers. Above all, it introduces the idea that formal marketing planning is essential in any travel organisation, in lieu of *ad-hoc* decision-making. It also leads us to consider issues of strategic planning in travel, which will now be examined.

Strategic planning

Once a company has evaluated its marketing position, it has, broadly speaking, three directions in which it can move, strategically:

- low price leadership
- product differentiation
- market focus.

Low price leadership

If a company is big and powerful enough to undercut its rivals on price, it may choose this strategy as the basis for its consumer appeal. Price reductions are achieved through cost reductions. Large companies can benefit from economies of scale. A company the size of Thomson Holidays, or Tjaereborg with its international markets, can negotiate very low prices with hotels abroad because of the sheer number of beds for which they are contracting. However, large companies also suffer from diseconomies of scale, in that as organisations become larger, so they become more difficult to manage. This can result in problems of impersonality for their consumers and difficulties in communicating effectively among staff within the organisation.

Because large tour operators carry large numbers of clients, this can preclude them from dealing with the many small family-run hotels and guesthouses at the destinations they serve, whereas a small tour operator may be able to negotiate to fill such small hotels at even lower prices than those offered by the major operators.

Product differentiation

As an alternative to price leadership, another company may choose to specialise in certain kinds of products which are not provided by its competitors. It may also opt to focus on quality, justifying a higher price than the large competitors by offering improved value. This will require a heavy emphasis in the marketing plan on quality control to ensure that standards are maintained. One tour operator differentiates its products by emphasising the all-inclusive nature of the package, in which entertainments, excursions and child-minding services are all included in the basic price of the holidays.

In cases where prices are broadly similar, as on certain airline routes where price control is in force, attempts to differentiate products become even more important, since price competition is ruled out. One airline's Boeing 747 is very like any other's, making it necessary to find other means of differentiation than that of the basic product. One airline might stress on-time reliability, another its safety record ('our multi-million-mile pilots . . .') while yet another will seek to create an atmosphere of relaxed informality on board. Singapore Airlines have been widely recognised for the marketing success they have achieved with a campaign aimed at stressing the beauty of their cabin crew and the level of service rendered to their customers. In 1994 Virgin Atlantic Airways introduced Arcadia, a personal in-flight entertainment centre featuring films, cartoons, computer games and a skymap depicting the route with graphical flight information.

'. . . another will seek to create an atmosphere of relaxed informality on board.'

Market focus

In this strategy, the decision is taken to concentrate on one or more specific markets (this market segmentation approach will be discussed in greater depth in Chapter 4). By catering for individual markets in this way, and adapting products to meet the precise needs of those markets, the company reduces the competition it faces and becomes, in effect, a 'big fish in a small pond'. Within these markets, the company can develop a policy of either cost leadership or product differentiation.

In this way, a company can avoid the danger of trying to do all things well but excelling in none. Marketing managers must always ask themselves, 'Why should my customers buy my products rather than those of my competitors?' Unless they can provide a sound answer to that question, the success of their products will remain in doubt.

As the operators in particular have moved more and more to mass market, low price strategies, so smaller operators have turned to specialisation, whether by geographical region, type of activity or market served.

Travel agencies, too, can develop their marketing strategies along similar lines; indeed, many smaller agencies will need to do so in order to survive, as the marketplace becomes increasingly dominated by a handful of large travel chains. The smaller agency may opt to provide old-fashioned, high quality service, or offer specific kinds of product knowledge, such as an in-depth knowledge of cruising and different cruise lines. Alternatively, the agency may choose to deal only with customers from one sector of the market for holidays, or specialise in business house travel.

A popular exercise for marketing managers, now being adopted by travel companies, is to produce a product-positioning map, revealing the customers' image of existing companies competing in certain fields. This can be very helpful both to a company already operating in the market, or one contemplating launching a new product. A survey is conducted among a random sample of holidaymakers, who are asked a series of questions designed to provide an image of the various companies. This image can then be plotted on a matrix. One specialist operator undertook such a study, in which the image of nine competitive operators was mapped along a two-dimensional matrix, as illustrated in Fig. 2.3.

This exercise clearly reveals a gap in the market for mass market, culture-orientated long-haul holidays, which a new programme might be designed to fill. However, a word of warning is necessary in this exercise; it is possible that the product gap exists precisely because there is no demand for the product. Further research is needed to find out if this is the case, or whether it is simply the case that the competition has not yet seen the marketing opportunities.

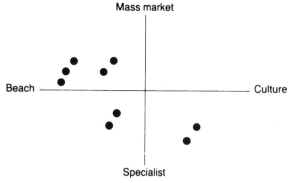

Fig. 2.3 Product-positioning map, showing perceived image of long-haul holidays offered by nine companies

Where a company offers a range of products, each with its own market strengths, it is helpful to analyse this portfolio of products using a tool developed by the Boston Consultancy Group (BCG). The BCG Growth-Share Matrix enables the company to compare the performance of each of its products, allowing the company to identify what planning decisions must be made for each.

A typical BCG Matrix is shown in Fig. 2.4. The eight circles represent the current sizes and market positions of each product marketed by a hypothetical tour operator. The size of each circle is proportional to the amount of revenue that the product range generates, while location in the matrix indicates the growth rate and share of the market compared to its leading competitor.

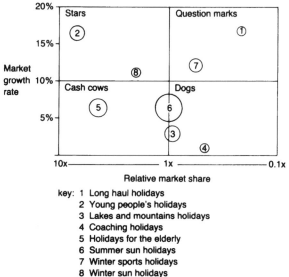

Fig. 2.4 BCG Growth-Share Matrix applied to a major tour operator's package tour programme

The vertical axis shows the rate of growth of the market in which the product is sold, while the horizontal axis represents the market share of the product compared with its major competitor. A market share of 0.1 would indicate that the company has only one-tenth of the market share of its leading rival, while a figure of 10 would reveal it has ten times its rival's share.

The matrix is divided into four cells. If the

company had a product which is both a leader in the market and that market is expanding rapidly, the product is termed a *star*, since it offers the prospect of stable profitability (although not necessarily high profitability, since the company may be forced to defend itself against intense competition for such a lucrative market). *Question marks* offer the promise of success, since they are trading in high growth markets, and here the company's objective will be to seek a greater share of the market for such products. *Cash cows* identify products which have a large market share, but in a declining or low growth market. Their benefit is that they can often prove highly profitable in terms of cash flow to cover the company's operating expenses, since competition will be less fierce, and hence marketing costs less. Finally, *dogs* are weak both in market share and growth rate, and unless the company has some expectation of gaining greater market share or of seeing an expansion in the market growth, it will gain little from pumping additional resources into marketing the product. Planning for each of these products will therefore entail policies of either building up the product to increase market share or sales, fighting to hold the present market share, milking the product for its immediate cash returns, or retreating from the market altogether. If, in the situation explored here, the tour operator sees itself in danger of losing market share to its rivals, it can choose to increase its sales effort, to improve the product in some way, or to find ways of reducing its prices to make it more competitive. These are vital marketing decisions which will form the linchpin of the marketing plan.

Forecasting

As well as measuring where it is at the moment, a company must also determine where it is going, and where it will be at any given point in the future, following the execution of the marketing plan. A forecast is prepared to reflect the anticipated results, with projected sales, profitability and cash flow. In turn, the forecast will influence future marketing plans. If sales are

forecast to fall by 10 per cent in the following year, due for example to a fall in visitors to the UK, it will be the marketing department's task to consider ways in which the shortfall can be made up through new product development, increased promotional activity or whatever other means the department can devise.

Unfortunately, forecasting is a notoriously unreliable science. The sheer number of different factors which influence the flow of international tourism makes it difficult to create an economic model that will permit accurate forecasts to be made. The volatile nature of tourism means that unforeseen events can overtake projected forecasts (particularly those longer than one year into the future).

Marketing plans will usually include short-term forecasts (between three and six months) and medium-term to longer-term forecasts of expected performance. The former can make use of simple statistical principles to project sales, and will be useful in making day-to-day tactical marketing decisions (reduction of prices for late bookings of package holidays is a typical example). Longer forecasts will tend to be more subjective, drawing on a wider selection of forecasting techniques, and will be used as an aid in strategic marketing decisions, such as new product development. The long-term forecast will help to pinpoint changing trends in travel, enabling a company to take advance action if one particular destination appears to be in decline, so that a new product can be developed to fill the gap. Public sector bodies in tourism tend to take forecasting more seriously that the private sector, and forecasts are used to underpin government or local authority development policies in order to aid regional development and employment opportunities. Meanwhile, in the private sector, demand for overseas holidays during the 1980s was seriously overestimated, leading to massive overcapacity (although to some extent this was accounted for by the desire of the largest companies to achieve greater market share). Forecasting for the most part remains a process of 'educated guesswork' among travel companies, few of which employ methods that go beyond simple statistical extrapolation of existing trends.

If forecasting is to be of any value, it must be undertaken systematically, and be made subject to continual revision in the light of changing circumstances. Even allowing for typical margins of error that occur with most forecasts, the process is deemed an improvement over the 'gut feel' method of operation employed by most travel firms. Not all the methods discussed here will be appropriate for small firms, since they can be expensive and time-consuming to introduce; but the simpler ones are easy to incorporate into marketing plans of any sized company.

Demand

Obviously, the basis of any forecast will be the measurement of existing market demand – how many holidays, visits, or whatever the organisation presently sells. This can be relatively easily refined by breaking the figures down by geographical region or market sector. Estimates then must be made of the total market for the product sold, and the proportion of that market the company expects to attract.

Let us take the example of a tour operator who deals exclusively in medium-priced holidays from one particular regional airport. In order to forecast demand, the operator must know or estimate:

- the number of people living in the catchment area of the airport, i.e. within a reasonable travel time compared with other airports that could be used
- the proportion of these likely to take package holidays abroad
- how many of these are likely to take a holiday at the price, and to the destinations, provided for in the company's programme.

There is of course a trade-off to be estimated here, as to the willingness of consumers to pay more for the convenience of a nearby departure point compared with the low-priced package tours available from, say, Gatwick or Luton airports. This figure will represent the served market. The company must finally determine:

- the proportion of those willing to buy the

company's packages compared with those of competitors offering flights to the same destinations from the same airport.

This final figure will represent the sales potential for holidays.

Sales

Forecasting should be taken at three levels:

1 Environmental forecasts, which take into account the uncontrollable factors – economic, political, etc. – which affect travel generally. This will integrate economic growth forecasts, expectations of changes in exchange rates, growth in leisure time and discretionary incomes, the propensity to spend discretionary income on holidays, and comparative studies of inflation rates in different countries. We can refer to such forecasts as macro-studies.
2 Industry forecasts, which take into account levels of competition and profitability in the travel industry, legislation affecting the industry, and other factors within the business but outside the control of the company.
3 Company forecasts, in which the firm projects its own expectations of sales based on controllable and uncontrollable factors operating within the company.

All forecasts will be prepared on the basis of an assumed set of circumstances. However, it is also helpful to include forecasts which examine performance based on the most pessimistic view of future events and the most optimistic view. This will allow for a mid-range of the 'most likely' result, as demonstrated in Fig. 2.5.

Trends in sales

Most short- to medium-term forecasts are based on the use of statistical methods to extrapolate trends from sales occurring in the past. *Time series analysis*, which smoothes out the effects of seasonal or cyclical variation in sales, will be commonly used to project travel sales. Sales may be projected either as a *linear* trend (as in Fig. 2.5)

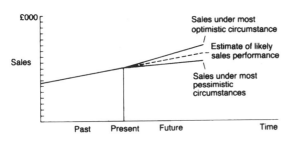

Fig. 2.5 Forecast of future performance based on the marketing plan

or as an *exponential* trend, in which sales are expected to multiply at a constant rate, giving a steady upward curve.

More complicated forecasting methods will take into account a variety of variables to build economic models which are beyond the means of most travel firms, who tend to fall back on *assumptive forecasting*, that is, forecasts developed through a process of making assumptions of what people think will happen. If these assumptions are based on one person's expectations, they are unlikely to provide much degree of accuracy, but if they are refined through a process of integrating many individual views within and outside the company, this will improve their accuracy. Interviews with a cross-section of senior staff within the firm, coupled with trade opinions, the views of sales staff closest to the market, and views of the travel 'pontiffs' can all help to refine forecasts. It should be remembered, though, that sales staff will be inclined to conservatism in their projections if their sales targets are to be tied to forecasts.

Refinements on assumptive forecasting include the *Delphi forecast*, which asks for independent assessments to be made by senior staff, with justifications for their figures. Staff are then shown the forecasts of their colleagues, and asked to refine their own forecasts on the basis of this new knowledge. In this way a more considered view is obtained.

Intention-to-buy surveys, such as those carried out by the English Tourist Board (ETB), are helpful as indicators for short-term trends. Random surveys ask such questions as:

How likely are you to take a holiday abroad this year?

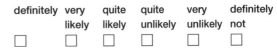

Earlier in the chapter, reference was made to the greater use of forecasting within the public sector. Many of these forecasts can be helpful to private sector companies undertaking feasibility studies for the introduction of new products, too. Let us take a hypothetical example of how a forecast of future tourism flows can assist the planning for new hotels in a region.

Let us say the region currently welcomes some 1.5 million staying visitors a year, and forecasts suggest that this will increase to about 3 million over the next five years. What hotel provision is needed to cater to this influx? The planners will need to know:

- average length of stay of tourists
- the proportion of visitors staying in hotels
- the distribution of visitors over the months of the year
- average hotel occupancy anticipated.

These figures may have to be refined to take into account different rates of increase between business and holiday visitors, different average lengths of stay between these two markets, etc., but for simplicity's sake, let us use the following figures:

average length of stay: 14 nights
60% of visitors stay in the four months of summer
50% of visitors stay in hotels
50% of visitors require double rooms, 50% single rooms
planned high season occupancy rate will be 90%.

The increase in visitors of 1.5 million will require 1.5 million × 14 nights = 21 million bed nights. Assuming that accommodation will be planned to satisfy average demand over the peak period, that is, 15 per cent over each of the four summer months, this would require 3 150 000 bed nights if everyone stayed at hotels (15% × 21 million). But only 50 per cent stay in hotels, therefore we need 1 575 000 bed nights. At an average of 30.5

days in the month, the daily bed night increase required will be

$$\frac{1\ 575\ 000}{30.5} = \text{approx. } 51\ 640$$

If occupancy of these rooms is to be planned at 90 per cent, we shall require 10. per cent more rooms, i.e. 56 804 rooms. Assuming room demand is for 50 per cent doubles, every 100 visitors will require 75 rooms. The region will therefore require another 42 603 rooms within the next five years.

It must be recognised that forecasts are dynamic in nature. If an organisation merely extrapolates its existing sales, rather than planning to achieve a certain level of sales, the result may be a decline in sales growth due to the greater marketing activity of its competitors. Forecasts must be based on what the organisation expects to happen as a result of its marketing plan, as well as what is expected to happen as a result of changes in the environment within which the company operates.

New product development

Based on the overall strategic direction planned by the company and assisted by forecasts of future demand, the marketer can begin to evaluate new product development necessary to meet the overall marketing objectives.

A case study will illustrate the planning process whereby a major tour operator identified the opportunity to introduce a new destination. This operator had already identified a marketing objective: to improve its position in the summer long-haul market.

A tour operator's new destination development

Initially, office-based analysis was carried out on information available from research and forecasts, travel agent feedback and competitor brochures. This analysis identified the following:

- the operator had fallen behind in market share in long haul, compared with competitors' performance

- the operator's current long-haul offering concentrated on Florida, whose market share had shrunk from 55 per cent to 38 per cent
- all-inclusive holidays had grown rapidly in the long-haul marketplace, albeit most destinations of this type were located in the Caribbean; recorded volumes had increased by up to 44 per cent.
- Central/South America was one of the operator's fastest growing destinations and an area where it scored over the competition
- all-inclusive prices in Central/South America were highly competitive when compared with the Caribbean
- opportunities existed for the operator to build upon the experience and buying power of its North American outlet, which already featured resorts in Mexico, many of which were unknown to the UK marketplace
- new free trade agreements between Mexico and the United States promised large future investment in the Mexican tourist infrastructure.

Based upon this initial analysis, the operator decided to carry out further detailed planning to determine the feasibility of introducing such a new resort. This plan was compiled following resort visits to Mexico and further discussion with travel agent contacts, the North American operation, hoteliers and airlines. This resulted in a much more detailed feasibility document recommending the specific resort of Puerto Vallarta. The report contained detailed information on:

- the resort and bed stock available
- quality, service levels and facilities available (star rating, beachfront positions, etc.)
- cost, route, flight times and departure dates that could be negotiated with carriers
- potential for the tour operator's different brands to exploit the resort in different ways (children's facilities for the family brand, 5 star hotel accommodation for the premium brand, etc.)
- promotional opportunities, including joint advertising with the Mexican Tourist Board
- recommended pricing and margin structure
- projected sales volume and profit forecast.

It is interesting to see how the planning process

never ceases. After the successful introduction of Puerto Vallarta, the new product development team went on to assess the viability of a separate 'all inclusive' programme of holidays to be launched in a new brochure for the summer season twelve months ahead.

Setting the marketing budget

The establishment of an overall budget for marketing will be part of the corporate financial planning process, but should represent the outcome of negotiation between the head of the marketing department and other planning executives. These budgets are generally based on estimates of sales revenue and cash flow for the coming year, and introduce a measure of control over cash flow expenditure during the year. The budget determines both the resourcing of the department (including staff) and promotional expenditure.

How this figure is to be calculated is one of the most difficult decisions in corporate planning. Often, budgets are determined, particularly in the case of smaller companies, by no more sophisticated methods than some arbitrary decision on 'what the company can afford'. Alternatively, a rule of thumb is applied, such as the allocation of some percentage of the previous year's revenue, or a percentage of next year's expected revenue. However, in both these cases, what the company is suggesting in effect is that the marketing budget should be the outcome of sales, rather than determining what those sales should be. In other instances, companies attempt to estimate what their main competitors are spending on promotion, and match this sum. It is by no means clear why a competitor should be judged better at determining what should be spent on promotion, but in any case, a rival firm is likely to have very different resources and objectives, which will require different budgetary considerations. A more logical approach to budget setting is an attempt to relate that budget to the objectives that the company intends to achieve. If, for example, the objective is to increase the company's market share by, say, 2 per cent, it is the marketing man-

ager's responsibility to estimate what needs to be spent, and how, in order to achieve this. While it is never easy to forecast revenue based on a given expenditure, this approach is certainly more scientific than the kind of guesswork which more usually takes place in travel companies, and it has the advantage of forcing the marketing manager to consider the relationship between expenditure and sales, through the appraisal of alternative promotional strategies.

One other important consideration is the need to recognise the relationship between profits, as opposed to sales, and the promotional budget. An airline could be expecting to sell 65 per cent of its capacity in the coming year with its present marketing strategies. Assuming its prices are set to enable the airline to break even with a load factor of 60 per cent, this will enable it to make an operating profit on the other 5 per cent sold. However, airlines have very high fixed costs, so that the cost of carrying another 10 or 20 per cent is very small – a few extra meals, a little extra fuel. If an extra market can be attracted, this would represent almost pure profit, and the company would be justified in spending a very considerable proportion of the profit on marketing to attract those other customers, provided it could be reassured that it would not dilute sales to present customers as a result.

Organising for effective marketing

No marketing plan will be effective unless the organisation is equipped to achieve its objectives. In marketing terms, this means that the company as a whole develops a marketing-orientated approach, with staff sharing common aims and the will to achieve those aims.

Marketing is not just 'something which the marketing department does'. Its philosophy should permeate the whole organisation. Many companies pay lip-service to marketing, but remain production orientated, concerned principally with finding ways to utilise surplus capacity rather than tackling the question of what the customer really wants.

At board level in large companies, it is common for marketing to be thought of in terms of sales and promotion activities, rather than the guiding philosophy of the company. Clashes occur between the marketing department and its operations staff, or financial controllers (how often does a company, faced with a decline in sales, take measures to cut back marketing expenditure instead of expanding it?) Chief executives who are sympathetic to the marketing concept can play a major role in co-ordinating a common set of marketing goals for their company.

Within the marketing department itself, staff must be equipped to function effectively. This means effective organisation of staff. Many small travel companies, of course, must function with very few staff, and marketing, such as it is, will be undertaken by the proprietor or managing director, as a part of the general duties of management. While this has the advantage of reducing problems of communications, it does not in itself guarantee more effective marketing. Larger organisations, however, will be likely to employ specialist staff with marketing responsibility, and will have to decide how to organise this staff best for the achievement of their aims.

There are four ways in which a marketing department can be organised:

- functional organisation
- geographical organisation
- product and brand organisation
- market organisation.

We shall look at each of these in turn.

Functional organisation

Perhaps the most traditional way of organising a department is to give staff individual responsibility for one or more of the marketing functions. Marketing entails a great many functions, and in an organisation such as a major tour operator, we may find the marketing organisation chart looking like Fig. 2.6.

This form of organisation has the advantage that each functional manager can concentrate on one specific area of marketing expertise, under

Fig. 2.6 Possible organisation of a tour operator's marketing department

the overall control of a single marketing manager or director who co-ordinates and controls their activities.

Some functionally organised departments are split, with sales and marketing each having independent executives. This arrangement does seem to run counter to the concept of sales as a function of marketing, but it has worked successfully in companies such as Thomson Holidays, and can function well enough if there are good communications, co-operation and goodwill between the respective managers.

When Owners Abroad restructured to become First Choice Holidays, the sales and marketing functions were brought together under the commercial director. The commercial director also controls the research and new product development department and the day-to-day trading function of flights, beds and inventory management. Thus the senior management team provide a focused, all-round commercial view with marketing playing a significant and integrated role.

The marketing department itself separates brand management and brochure production more clearly than many tour operators. This reflects a determination to allow a focus on true brand and marketing issues removed from the actual production of the product. Brand managers are responsible for both summer and winter seasons to ensure that brand values are upheld consistently year round. Marketing also includes the specialist advertising and promotions function, ensuring a close liaison with brand managers, yet a coherent advertising strategy for the whole company (see Fig. 2.7).

Marketing Department Organisation

Fig. 2.7 The organisation of a major overseas holiday company

Geographic organisation

Companies with very large national or international markets may prefer to organise their marketing functions by geographic area. This is particularly useful where the nature of those markets differs greatly, as for example is the case with many travel firms selling to both home (domestic) and overseas (export) markets. A company such as Tjaereborg, which sells its holidays in a number of European countries, will necessarily undertake some, if not all, of its marketing functions separately, with different marketing staff in each country. Indeed, until 1994 the Tjaereborg name and brand were owned and operated in the UK by Owners Abroad, and were thus a completely autonomous operation. It was subsequently subsumed into the new direct sell brand of First Choice Holidays, Eclipse Direct.

Hotel chains take a number of different approaches to the problem, in some cases directing most of their marketing effort from a corporate marketing headquarters in the parent company's head office, with only local sales functions in the hands of marketing staff in each individual hotel, while in other cases chains have decentralised their marketing responsibilities by country or region. The latter arrangement allows a greater measure of response to local market conditions, although naturally it loses some of the benefits of economies of scale and requires larger numbers of staff. According to market conditions, objectives are also likely to vary considerably from one country to another, requiring distinct marketing plans to be developed in each region, although these may be co-ordinated through head office. Regional organisation of this kind can, of course, be further subdivided along functional lines as described earlier.

Product and brand organisation

Where a company produces a variety of different products or brands, it can prove advantageous to provide separate marketing expertise for each. This is apparent in the organisation chart of a major holiday company, in which separate marketing staff are responsible for distinct package holiday programmes. In a large hotel, the banqueting manager is often made responsible for the marketing of catering functions which exclude accommodation services, while the sales manager is responsible for convention and tour sales, and the front office manager for individual transient sales (mail, telephone and personal) and all reservations.

Where companies market their products under quite distinct brand names, the marketing may be organised quite separately for each brand. A company such as the Rank Organisation, which owns such diverse travel businesses as Butlin's, Shearings National, Haven Holidays and Warner Holidays, may find it beneficial to appoint separate marketing staff for each, as long as it is intended to retain distinct identities for the brands. Again, the functional breakdown within the marketing departments is possible.

In practice, product managers often have less autonomy than do marketing managers, but they can control strategies for the marketing of their own product lines, and therefore can react quickly to changes in demand or other circumstances affecting their markets.

Market organisation

Finally, instead of brand or product divisions, it is possible to organise marketing according to the markets served. Hotels, for instance, may separate marketing by business and leisure guests, since the nature of demand is clearly different in each case, and the strategies designed to attract guests will differ in each case, too. This can be further organised according to functional or geographical divisions of responsibility.

It is important to recognise that there are no right or wrong ways to structure marketing departments. Each firm must develop the structure that meets its needs best, and this can often only be assessed in the long term after experimentation. Needs will change over time, too, so that what works best for a company today will

not necessarily suffice as the company grows, or diversifies its product range.

The marketing mix

The concept of the marketing mix is one of the most important in marketing. It determines how the marketing budget is allocated, forms the foundation of the marketing plan's strategy, and provides the marketing manager with the techniques to optimise his budgetary expenditure.

The marketing mix is defined by Kotler[1] as:

> The set of marketing tools that the firm uses to pursue its marketing objectives in the target markets.

These so-called 'tools' are numerous, but can be conveniently grouped together into four categories, popularly known as the four Ps – product, price, place and promotion. Figure 2.8 lists these in more detail.

The variety of ways in which a marketing manager can decide to distribute the budget between these tools is almost infinite. Furthermore, expenditure on some tools can be changed at very short notice (promotion, price) while others (new product development, channels of distribution) are likely to take much longer to alter.

Fig. 2.8 The marketing mix

A tour operator's marketing plan

Once again using our hypothetical tour operator as an example, let us think through a set of possible strategies which the marketing manager may adopt as the basis for the new marketing plan. Within the *product* category, the manager may choose to focus on two new destinations to be added to the summer sun programme, and to change some of the hotels used currently in the programme in order to provide a better overall standard of product and push the programme up-market slightly. For the winter programme, two hotels owned by the company in Fuengirola are to be marketed in holiday packages for elderly people, and all holiday packages henceforth are to include a cocktail welcome party on the first night. Under *pricing*, the operator will offer a 'no surcharge' guarantee for all holidays booked and paid for prior to 30 April, agrees new extended payment terms for holidays in a new credit scheme, and introduces for the first time reductions of 30 per cent for children on all holidays booked for the first week of September onwards. Under the category of *place*, the operator decides to encourage more direct sell, setting a target of 20 per cent direct bookings for next summer's packages, while simultaneously providing extra support for key agents. Agency sales calls are to be reduced, and the company's representatives will no longer call on agents providing fewer than ten bookings in any one year. Finally, under *promotion*, the operator allocates $1.5 million from the budget to be spent on selective television and national press advertising campaigns, and introduces a co-operative advertising scheme with travel agents, whereby it is agreed to pay 50 per cent towards the cost of joint advertising in local papers. Two hundred selected agents are to be taken on educational study trips to the company's recently launched destinations, and twenty travel writers and journalists will be invited on another educational visit to the company's resorts in southern Spain.

These ideas are designed only to indicate the diversity of decisions facing an operator when drawing up a marketing plan for the year. In practice, a much wider range of decisions will have to be made, outlining both the strategy to be adopted and the tactics that will be employed to help achieve the plan's objectives. These issues will be examined at greater length in subsequent chapters.

Controlling the marketing plan

Any plan which a company introduces must be subject to control. In order to do so, the marketing plan must be clear in its objectives, with each objective quantified and measurable. Control will be required over budget expenditure, and the performance of each element in the plan should be continually monitored to ensure the plan is on target. Any deviations from the plan will require action to improve performance, or to consider alternative means of reaching objectives.

Ways in which control is exercised over a firm's marketing activities will be detailed in Chapter 14, and therefore will not need to be further examined in this chapter. However, it should be stressed above all that a marketing plan is dynamic by nature; it is not a set of bureaucratic rules to be followed faithfully for the duration of the plan, but rather a fluid set of guidelines for action that will require constant updating in the light of changing circumstances.

Questions, tasks and issues for discussion

1 List the objectives which a travel agent might incorporate into its marketing plan. Explain how the choice of more than one objective could create a conflict in marketing strategy.

2 Using the diagram in Fig. 2.2, prepare a paper for discussion on the ways in which these factors can influence the marketing operations of a tour operator.

3   Suggest some of the ways a travel agent might 'differentiate' its product, or corporate, identity from those of its competitors.

4   Draft another two-dimensional matrix similar to that in Fig. 2.3, using different variables of your own choice, which a hotel might use to discover marketing gaps.

Exercise

You have been employed as research assistant for a local tourist attraction (you may choose an appropriate attraction near you). Your manager has asked you to carry out a SWOT analysis of the attraction as a prelude to the new marketing plan she is developing. Undertake the research (using both primary and secondary research methods – see Chapter 3), and write a memorandum to your manager containing your SWOT analysis, and any suggestions you feel to be relevant and which will help your manager in her plans for the coming year.

3 Marketing research and its applications in tourism

After studying this chapter, you should be able to:

- understand the need for systematic, scientific research in an organisation
- describe a Marketing Information System and its elements
- plan a simple research programme, construct questionnaires and carry out surveys
- explain and evaluate different methods of gathering research information

What is marketing research?

Marketing research is the planned, systematic collection, collation and analysis of data designed to help the management of an organisation to reach decisions and to monitor the results of those decisions once taken. It embraces all forms of research undertaken to help the marketing of products, including product research, price research, distribution research, publicity research and consumer research. However, research into consumers and their patterns of behaviour is more commonly referred to as *market research* to distinguish it from the more all-embracing term of marketing research.

Research is designed to help an organisation to understand the nature of the marketplace in which it operates, including understanding its suppliers, wholesalers, retailers, competitors and customers.

Research can be *descriptive*, that is, it can help us to find out factual data about what is happening in the marketplace; or it can be *analytical*, attempting to explain the relationship between variables – for example, to find out why these things are happening. Both kinds of information have their place in the process of management decision-making. While in the past, much of the research commissioned by the travel and tourism industry has tended to concentrate on gathering descriptive data – who goes where, when; market shares of the major companies; total sales in each category of travel – since the 1980s there has been a greater interest in, and awareness of, explanatory research which will tell companies why these statistics are as they are.

One important distinction in research methods is that between quantitative and qualitative approaches. *Quantitative research* methods are those in which data are collected and subsequently analysed, normally through surveys employing questionnaires, although experiments may also be carried out to provide answers to certain types of questions. The findings of such research can be verified for accuracy through tests of statistical probability. In general, such research is employed when what is required is a simple count of numbers; for example, of the numbers of people entering a particular attraction, the average spend in the shop or restaurant, or the percentage of people choosing to travel abroad independently rather than on inclusive tour arrangements. Such research is often undertaken to verify or refute a predetermined hypothesis, and the results should be capable of replication in other similar situations.

Qualitative research, on the other hand, is designed to investigate specific cases, often to explore an individual's own behaviour, experiences or feelings about an issue. This is most generally undertaken by observation, or in-depth questioning of the informants, at much greater length than would be possible with a structured questionnaire. Data collection and analysis proceed in parallel and interact, and results cannot be subjected to tests of statistical probability. For this reason, organisations are less inclined to sponsor such research, although the evidence it produces may well be much richer than that which is obtained through a simple quantitative questionnaire. The aim in this approach is to develop hypotheses which may be later subjected to testing through the use of quantitative methods.

Why marketing research?

One potential danger of focusing on the four Ps in marketing is that these omit a key element of the marketing role, on which every other marketing activity depends; the function of research. Unless we know what our customers want, we cannot be certain that the products we produce will appeal to them. If our sales are falling off, we have to know whether this is the result of a general economic malaise affecting all products, a problem specifically affecting the travel and tourism industry, or the result of clients switching their purchases to other travel products. In each case, we should have to devise a different marketing plan to respond to the challenge. Intelligence gathering is therefore a crucial precedent to planning.

Research has a place in the management of any company, however small. The belief, held by many independent travel agents and other small companies, that marketing research is a luxury affordable only by the larger travel corporations, is a dangerous fallacy. True, only the larger companies are likely to be able to buy in the expertise provided by research consultants, to commission, for instance, a survey of trends in travel purchasing. Summaries of such research are, however, often published in a variety of media available at your local library, a specialist library such as that of the English Tourist Board, or even from time to time in the trade press. Keeping up with these reports should be a part of the responsibilities of all travel managers who call themselves professional.

In the larger companies, formal intelligence-gathering techniques become essential, for two reasons. First, by its very nature the larger company has less opportunity for face-to-face contact with its customers; its feedback on changing consumer tastes and preferences has to be planned. Second, large businesses involve greater financial investment, which in turn means greater risk. Think of the investment an airline must make today to re-equip its fleet, with aircraft costing in excess of $100 million each. Consider the investment a hotel chain is making, when purchasing a new property in a large city.

The major tour operators are large spenders and sophisticated practitioners in marketing research. Their thirst for research information, both quantitative and qualitative, is driven by a number of factors:

1 All operators are watching their competitors very carefully indeed. They continually track the opposition's market share, advertising spend, product developments and image in the marketplace. The marketer is looking not just for chinks in the armour of competitors that can be exploited but also for a bench-mark against which to measure own company performance.

2 Consumer attitudes are continually changing and woe betide the marketer who misses out on these trends. For instance, research undertaken by First Choice Holidays into the attitude of holidaymakers towards the environment shows that while major action is not required yet, consumers are significantly more aware than they were in the 1980s. Their concerns were essentially 'selfish' in 1994 – they wanted clean beaches. Come 2004, it is possible that issues such as brochure recycling and the environmental effects of aircraft travel will be important factors when consumers make a tour operator choice.

3 Tour operators need to understand the process

by which their product is selected and bought – and the role and impact of the travel agent intermediary. The retail outlets are changing rapidly in the face of everything from technological advances to the growth of *multiple chains* (often owned or part owned by specific tour operators).

4 The dynamic nature of the market means that tour operators are continually investing in the 'new': new television advertising, new brochure design, new brands, new destinations. These may reflect not only substantial investments in time and money but also a 'make or break' strategic decision for the company. Research is obviously essential to minimise risk.

What information do we need?

All organisations, regardless of size, need to know where they stand in the business environment. In the case of existing products, they need to know how many of each product they are selling; how sales are performing over time, and the forecast for future sales; how their products compare with those of the competitors, and the respective shares of the market held by their own company and their competitors. If a principal or tour operator is involved, they must monitor their distribution strategy, to determine what quantities of their products are being sold by each retailer and which of their retailing outlets are performing best. All companies need to know the effectiveness of their advertising and promotion campaigns. They should also know the profitability and contribution to overheads which each product makes. They must fully understand the customer: who buys what, when, where and why.

Where new products are planned, the company must research the market opportunities, test new product concepts on these markets, find the right appeals to attract attention, test market the product wherever possible, forecast sales and monitor sales performance against forecasts, as described in the following chapter dealing with new product development.

The Marketing Information System

Research should form the basis of an ongoing system for gathering intelligence about the company, its products and its markets. Often, such intelligence is gathered informally and subconsciously by managers in the course of their everyday duties, by observing, listening to discussions, talking to colleagues in the industry and reading trade or other journals and papers. Valuable as this process is, it should be supported by more formal procedures carried out in a systematic and scientific way. Establishing a Marketing Information System (MIS) ensures that the company has a system for the regular planned collection, analysis and presentation of data. Designing an MIS requires a company to undertake two tasks:

- to consider the decisions that its management has to take
- to determine what information is needed to make these decisions.

Obviously, the availability of finance influences the kinds of information that can be obtained. Here, the company must realistically judge what proportion of its profits, or reserves, it should set aside for research, separating the costs of its annual research from any special *ad-hoc* research needs which may arise from time to time (such as a feasibility study to judge the merits of taking over another company).

Since the MIS is designed to ensure that the company has a regular flow of information to monitor its markets and marketing effectiveness, a proportion of the annual budget should be allocated for this purpose, while exceptional research needs, such as those dictated by a decision to expand, will require a topping up of funds, either from reserves or even by way of a loan.

Let's take the case of a small regional chain of travel agents, considering setting up or purchasing a new branch in the region. The location of the branch will be critical for its chances of success, and a feasibility study will have to be undertaken to decide whether expansion in the region is the correct decision, and which of the available sites will stand the best chance of success. While a full-scale survey will be beyond the means of all but the largest chains, some research data can be bought in at moderate cost while substantial fieldwork can be undertaken by a branch manager at the expense only of time and effort.

Figure 3.1 details the setting up of an MIS, and it shows that there are several distinct ways in which information can be obtained in an MIS:

- through the use of *internal records*, that is, the use of recorded data already available within the firm

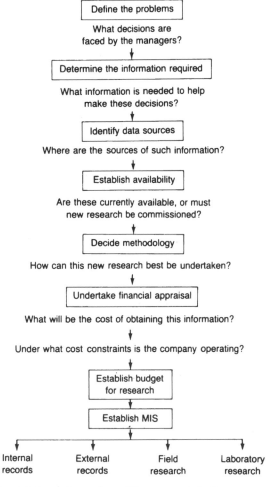

Fig. 3.1 Procedures for setting up a marketing information system

- by identifying and selecting suitable data available in *external records*
- by undertaking or commissioning *primary research*
- by carrying out *surveys*
- by *observation*
- by *experimentation*.

We shall go on to look at each of these methods of research in the sections that follow.

Internal records

The gathering of information from existing records, whether within or from outside the firm, is known as *secondary research*. In some ways it is the easiest method of gathering data, since many of the data are already available to the firm and need only to be collated and analysed. It is also relatively inexpensive to set up internal information systems to collect material as needed.

To take one example, travel agents have a huge range of data on tap. Sales records will advise them which products they are selling and in what quantities. This information, and that provided by their principals, will enable them to break down their sales by company. Some judgement about future sales can be made by comparing forward sales with bookings achieved during the comparable period in the previous year, or with any earlier period of trading, to give a picture of trends in sales over time. Travel agents can compute their average revenue per booking, average commission received for each type of travel product sold, and average sales achieved by each member of the counter staff. Agents can build up a complete profile of their customers: total numbers, breakdown by week of booking or week of departure (giving them the ability to judge whether and to what extent bookings are being made later in the year than formerly), by area of residence and type of holiday preferred. How such data can be used in the marketing of the agency is shown in Table 3.1.

Principals will be continually gathering information of this type both formally and through informal feedback through their personal contacts. For example, sales representatives will

Table 3.1 Travel agency data and their marketing applications

Data	Marketing application
Sales and revenue records	develop promotional campaigns to achieve targets set by selected principals for bonus commissions
	negotiate with principals for joint promotions
	decide which brochures to rack and where
Average commission achieved	decide to drop a product range or give it extra promotion
Bookings/revenue per member of staff	set revenue targets for each member of staff
	determine bonus payments for performance
	ascertain sales training needs
Customer profiles	establish mailing lists for special offers
	devise direct mail campaigns to previous customers, or to catchment areas from which high numbers of bookings are being achieved

continually monitor data on clients and distributors and provide regular reports to their sales managers, which will be integrated into the information system.

With the advent of computers into the travel industry on a wide basis, it has now become a comparatively simple matter to produce data for management decision-making at regular intervals, whether daily, weekly or monthly according to need. The danger of overload must be recognised, however; a manager's time has not expanded to keep pace with the increased flow of information, and therefore data must be selected and presented in a form which is easily assimilated, if they are to be useful.

External records

An enormous amount of data is available to the travel company from existing records. These data can be classified in two distinct ways.

First, we can distinguish between information specifically related to travel and tourism, and information which is more general in nature but nevertheless provides a useful insight into patterns of travel and tourism. For example, statistics produced by the British Government show that the growth of paid holidays since the mid-1970s has been an important factor in the increase in package tours. If the trend towards more holiday entitlement continues over the next 20 years, this fact will be important in estimating the growth of the holiday and leisure business.

The second kind of external data is information which is available freely either as a matter of public record, or available on subscription.

Public record

Appendix 1 at the end of this book provides a list of sources of data. Most of these sources are freely available for consultation in public libraries, or in libraries accessible to the public such as those of colleges and universities which include the study of leisure and tourism in their curricula. Two specialist libraries are:

The British Tourist Authority (BTA) library
Thames Tower
Blacks Road
London W6 9EL

Civil Aviation Authority (CAA) library
Aviation House
South Area
Gatwick Airport, West Sussex RH6 0YR

Many libraries have bibliographies of tourism to consult. Several of these have been published, of which the most comprehensive is probably Jeanne Gay's three-volume *Travel and Tourism Bibliography and Resource Handbook*, published by Travel and Tourism Press, California. However, bibliographies tend to date quickly, and any search of public records must include a study of the most recent data published, which may not yet appear in the listing of any bibliography.

Publications of ABTA, the BTA itself, the BAA, the CAA, the Confederation of Passenger Transport UK and annual reports of major travel enterprises such as airlines, hotel chains and tour operators, all contain valuable statistical information. One unexpected source is the Department of Employment, which publishes the *International Passenger Survey*, which includes information on UK residents travelling abroad and the purpose of their visits defined by destination area. Further material can be discovered in the travel trade press, and academic journals such as *Tourism Management*, *Annals of Tourism Research*, and the EIU's (Economist Intelligence Unit) *International Tourism Quarterly*.

Travel statistics are sometimes brought together in a very useful compendium, such as will be found in the *Keynote Reports* and *Market Assessment Reports*, the *Travel and Tourism Analyst*, and the ETB's *Insights*. The BTA/ETB research library is probably the best place to start one's search, particularly for data dealing with domestic and incoming tourists to Britain.

Information about the advertising spend of major companies in the industry can be found by consulting Research-MEAL, which is also available in many public libraries.

Subscription research

A company with adequate financial resources can choose between commissioning its own specific research, or subscribing to an on-going 'syndicated' survey of consumers which includes information about the pattern of holidays or travel taken.

General surveys of consumer habits of purchasing are conducted by a variety of companies, and use different methods related to scale, speed of reporting and other criteria.

Regular reports by STATS MR provide useful information on the tourism industry and market, based on a national survey. A similar survey is undertaken by the AGB Home Audit. Here a massive 11 000 households are recruited each quarter and the respondents are also requested to complete further questionnaires at three-monthly intervals until the year end. The 24 000 respondents who indicate that they travel abroad are asked to complete a special questionnaire on travel habits.

Perhaps the best known survey is the UK Tourism Survey (UKTS) commissioned by the regional tourist boards. The report (and those of UKTS's predecessor, the British Tourism Survey) is based on in-depth research into the holiday travel of British people undertaken in the past year, comparing this with previous years. In addition to the annual report each March, subscribers now receive copies of monthly survey results which give valuable travel data.

The English Tourist Board, in addition to its joint sponsorship of the UK Tourism Survey, carries out an 'intention to purchase' survey at the beginning of spring, which offers useful data for short-term forecasting of patterns of overseas and domestic holidaytaking among British tourists.

Because of the comprehensive and extensive nature of these surveys, the subscriptions are expensive, and only the largest companies are likely to be able to subscribe regularly. Advertising agents often subscribe to aid their own campaign planning in a variety of fields, and the travel companies using the larger advertising agencies can obtain the benefits of this knowledge through this source.

More specific services are offered by Travel and Tourism Research (TATR), who report regularly upon travel agencies and their attitudes to travel products, as well as their readership of the travel media. Other marketing research bodies provide services such as newspaper cuttings.

One word of warning about the use of published statistics: do not automatically apply general findings to specific situations. Figures which indicate a growth of overseas package holidays may conceal the fact that there is a marked decline to one country at the expense of a growth to another. In the same way, a rise in visitors to the UK will not necessarily mean that there has been an increase of tourism to Northumbria, nor will statistics to the West Country necessarily relate to tourism to Bristol or Bath. There is, in fact, an acute shortage of data dealing with specific locations, making it necessary to use more general data about travel patterns, but unless this can be supported with specific evidence relating to a town or region, findings will be very questionable.

Primary research

If the knowledge required by the organisation is not available through a search of secondary material, it is necessary to undertake primary research, that is, information obtained directly from the market. There are two principal ways by which this is carried out: by asking people questions, and by observing their behaviour systematically.

'. . . by observing their behaviour systematically . . .'

Such research can be undertaken by research organisations on commission, but can be extremely costly. However, for the smaller company, simple quantitative research can be undertaken 'in-house', providing it is scientifically and systematically carried out. It is better to leave more qualitative methods to the experts.

Full-scale national surveys of the market will cost tens of thousands of pounds, well beyond the means of all but the largest travel firms, but some of these data may be already obtainable through organisations such as AGB, and it is as well to shop around to find out what is the lowest cost at which one can acquire the information. At the other end of the scale, a local survey of a travel agent's market is unlikely to be available through secondary research, but could be undertaken by the firm itself. Questionnaires designed to find out, for example, whether existing customers would continue to use the agency if it were to move location, or whether clients would purchase charter flights to Greece if these were available from the local airport, but at a higher cost than from London, are relatively straightforward 'number-crunching' exercises which, if carefully planned and executed, can yield useful information. Researchers do need to be conscious of the fact that what people say they will do and what they actually do are not always the same thing, though!

Let us take a slightly more sophisticated example of primary research which an agent might undertake. A travel agent currently offers free transport to the local airport for all local package tour bookings, as an inducement to book. The agent wants to know how far this incentive is responsible for:

- keeping existing clients from going to competitors,
- attracting clients away from other agencies.

The agent may also want to know whether some other incentive might give greater market satisfaction, without adding to costs, or how much business they stand to lose if they withdraw the present offer. While a questionnaire could be sent out to present customers, this will be no help in reaching competitors' clients, so some form of random survey of people in the *catchment area* will need to be undertaken. This could be done by talking to people in the streets or interviewing them in their homes. Both methods have advantages and drawbacks. Home interviews are more difficult to arrange and more costly in time to conduct, but are likely to result in fewer refusals (if carefully managed) and as more time is taken to consider the questions, responses are likely to be more accurate. Home interviews also allow the interviewer more time to draw out respondents on their opinions and attitudes towards travel generally, leading to more rewarding data; this does call for more skills as an interviewer, however. At the same time, the collation and analysis of information gained in this way is more complex than responses to simple questions in the street survey. Street surveys can be carried out quite quickly, whereas a home survey will take time to organise and conduct, delaying action, which may be crucial.

In short, there are a great many factors which have to be taken into account in deciding which methods to adopt. We shall go on to look at the design of a piece of research, and then consider the different ways in which research can be conducted.

The elements of a research project

The following steps are necessary in planning a research programme.

1 Definition of the problem and the objectives
The organisation must be quite clear about its intentions – clear about what it hopes to achieve as a result of its research. This may seem an obvious point, but a surprising amount of questionnaires carry questions which don't actually throw light on the problem under investigation, but have been incorporated because 'it would be nice to know what the market feels about the issue'. Responses therefore may end up being unused.

Knowledge acquired through this step leads to the formation of the Market Research Brief, as a basis for action.

2 Identification of sources of information
At this point the aim is to find out what, if anything, is known about the problem already. There is little point in paying good money for research which has already been undertaken by someone else, if one can get hold of this. However, a great

deal of research which might be relevant will have been carried out by rival commercial organisations, and would not be accessible. How much will the organisation's existing records help in solving the problem? Where else might the information be found?

3 Develop the research plan
Depending upon the information available in step 2, the main stage of research may now be planned, or it may be thought necessary to conduct some exploratory research first, as a guide in developing a more detailed plan.

For instance, let us assume that a company is interested in developing a low-price multi-centre programme of package tours to the United States, using Greyhound bus for overland travel between the centres. While statistics on the use of Greyhound by British travellers will be available, attitudes towards travel by coach over long distances may be less well understood. As a prelude to knowing what questions to ask in a full-scale survey, it may be helpful first to conduct a panel interview to explore attitudes towards coach travel and to holidays in the USA. The use of this technique will be explained more fully later in the chapter.

4 Research design and methodology
The detailed plan for research can now be prepared. If this is to incorporate a survey, which is the customary means by which facts will be collected, the plan will include:

- selection of respondents – who is to be interviewed, the total size of the sample and how they will be chosen
- the form in which the survey will be conducted (personal interviews, mailed questionnaires, etc.)
- the design of the questionnaire to be used
- the organisation of the fieldwork, including recruitment, training and briefing interviewers
- establishment of the time schedule, and overall budget for the research.

Once these matters have been agreed, it is imperative to 'pilot test' the questionnaire, by trying it out on a handful of respondents selected at random. There will invariably be changes that must be made to the questions, and the pilot will pick these up, as well as giving an idea of the average time taken to carry out one interview. This will help in planning the schedule of interviews.

Once the questionnaire has been refined to a point where the research supervisor is satisfied that the questions and structure are right, the research can be implemented. Survey data are collected and collated. Normally this is done by computer, rather than by hand, making it comparatively easy to *cross-tabulate*, that is, compare responses to any two or more variables in the questionnaire. We could, for example, discover how many women over 18 years of age went overseas for their holiday last year, and spent over £500 per person for their holiday. Here we are examining four variables: female, adult, those who went abroad, and those spending more than £500. This process is known as *analysis*, and calls for skills to select what is relevant, and interpret correctly what the data reveal, so that the correct conclusions can be drawn, and recommendations for action can be taken.

The results of the survey are presented in the form of a report, which will incorporate the following elements:

- the title, date, company name, and name of organisation contracted to undertake the research
- the brief: terms of reference, acknowledgements, and statement of objectives
- a detailed statement of the methodology: methods used, reasons for their selection, and details of how the sample of respondents was drawn, number of interviews conducted, how the fieldwork was undertaken, etc.
- the findings of the survey
- conclusions and recommendations for action
- appendices: these should contain the bulk of the statistical information gathered (full tables of results, etc.) and a copy of any questionnaire used.

We will now look in a little more detail at the ways in which surveys can be conducted.

The survey

Surveys are generally the best means of collecting descriptive information, and will invariably make use of a questionnaire, that is, a series of questions which will be put to respondents designed to help provide answers to the problems the organisation is investigating. The survey can be conducted in many different ways, as we shall see, but regardless of survey method, the procedure must be scientific. This requires that every possible effort is made to avoid or reduce bias in the response. It will usually be impossible to interview all the possible respondents in whom the company is interested, therefore those that are interviewed, the *sample*, must accurately reflect the general views of the total population, or *universe* (the total number of people in the category in which we are interested). Thus, if we are proposing to solicit the views of British tourists to Spain on some issue, we need first to have some idea of the total size of the universe, and must then choose a representative sample of that universe having regard to demographics.

Our first task is then to determine who is to be interviewed. Are we interested in the views only of British holidaymakers, or all British visitors to Spain, including business and VFR (visiting friends and relatives) visitors? Are we interested only in the opinions of those who take package holidays, or also of those on independent holiday arrangements, or staying in second homes? Is it only the views of adults that we seek, and if so do we interview only those over 16, over 18 or over 21? If we intend to include business travellers in the survey, are we interested only in the views of those who use the service, or of those who buy the service (many secretaries make the arrangements for their bosses)? If our interest is in those who travel regularly, how will we define regularity for the purposes of the survey?

Our next problem is the size of the sample we shall select. Large samples provide more accurate results than small ones, but the increase in accuracy becomes less and less significant as the sampling size is increased. As long as scientific methods of selection have been employed to get the views of 56 million people in Britain, we need no more than 2000 respondents to obtain views accurately reflecting the population's views on general matters to within 95 per cent probability; that is, we have only a 5 per cent chance of being wrong in our findings. This is sufficiently accurate for most purposes, where the question is one of a general nature. The additional cost of interviewing enough people to raise the level of accuracy is generally not justified, since we would have to increase the number of respondents four-fold to improve the level of accuracy from 5 per cent chance of being wrong to only 2.5 per cent.

Scientific procedures are crucial, if this level of accuracy is to be retained. A *probability sample* of the universe must be selected. In the case of a simple random sample, this means selecting respondents in a scientifically random way so that each has one chance only, and an equal chance, of being selected. Other acceptable systems of scientific selection include *stratified random sampling*, in which the universe is divided into mutually exclusive groups (such as age ranges), in which the proportion of the total in each group is known, with random samples then drawn from each group in the same ratio as exists in the universe. A third method is known as *cluster sampling*, in which, for example, samples are taken by area of residence, again in the same proportion as the ratio of residents in the universe, and again with each respondent having an equal opportunity to be selected once only.

Major research companies employ sophisticated techniques to ensure that the samples are truly representative. In a national survey they will define how many respondents are to be chosen, and will ensure that the numbers in each category, that is age, sex, socio-economic status, domicile, correspond with the standards they have defined from previous work.

In order to correct any imbalances, a process known as *weighting* is employed, whereby a computer automatically adjusts the results to equate to the standards already set down; thus if the sample was correct in all aspects except the breakdown of respondents by social class, the views of the under-represented sectors may be given additional weight in the final analysis by increasing the relevant answers in proportion to the under-representation detected.

Having said that a 2000 person sample is enough for general questions, it must be emphasised that many questions are much more specific and require different techniques. It is very expensive indeed to establish the views of a minority group.

Example: It has been suggested that we need to establish whether apartment holidays to Spain marketed by major package holiday companies are seen by customers to be satisfactory.

Stage 1: 2000 respondents
Have you booked a holiday in the past year?
   NO 65%   YES 35%

Stage 2: 700 respondents
Was it an independent or a package holiday?
   INDEPENDENT 40%   PACKAGE 60%

Stage 3: 420 respondents
Did you go to Spain?
   NO 70%   YES 30%

Stage 4: 126 respondents
Did you stay in an apartment?
   NO 80%   YES 20%

Result: 25 relevant respondents

Whether 25 people who contribute useful information is adequate will depend upon the nature of the questions to be asked. If the market research firm charges £2 per interviewee, the costing would be as follows:

2000 × £2 = £4000
25 useful respondents
= £160 per usable respondent

It obviously involves going to a great deal of trouble to ensure scientific accuracy, and this is one of the factors in the high costs of such research. Because of this, firms sometimes undertake surveys using non-probability samples, such as stopping every tenth person in the street to ask their opinion. While this may help to throw light on the problem, the results cannot be subject to statistical tests and must always be in some doubt about degrees of accuracy achieved.

It must be remembered that the test of any survey is that the results are both valid and reliable. *Validity* means that the survey proves what it sets out to prove; *reliability* means that if the survey were to be conducted with another sample of respondents, exactly the same results would be achieved (within the limits of probability established).

Let us take the example of a survey of visitors to a seaside resort by means of a *street interview*. An interviewer could be assigned to stand on a particular street corner and question every *n*th person who passed by. This *convenience sample* will have a number of inherent biases. Many visitors to the resort not passing these points will have no opportunity for selection, and the flow of visitors will be greater at certain times of the day and certain days of the week than at others (although this factor can be weighted to obtain more accurate results). It is also possible that other overt or covert biases will emerge. Passersby with more time on their hands will be more likely to stop to answer questions than those who are busy, and there is a strong temptation for interviewers to approach those who look friendly, or are from the same age group, sex or social background. Ethnic minorities might be ignored, and people who cannot speak sufficient English to be interviewed will be rejected. By the use of good interviewer training, by weighting responses, and perhaps by supporting the survey with other forms of research such as hotel occupancy surveys and car park observation (licence plates reveal some very interesting statistics about visitor origins!) bias will be reduced, if never entirely eliminated. This is likely to be the most realistic approach to research for many small companies, such as the travel agent anxious for information about the local market. By instructing interviewers to deliberately choose a cross-section of respondents according to age, sex, group size, etc. (known as *quota sampling*) a wider range of opinions will be obtained, although not necessarily a more accurate one.

While the street interview is the most common form of interview, surveys can be carried out in a number of other ways. *Telephone interviews* are becoming more popular, and as the number of subscribers to telephones in Britain comes closer to 100 per cent, so this form of interview becomes more statistically significant. However, phones are increasingly being used by commercial firms to make *cold calls* (i.e. unsolicited efforts to sell) and there is a growing resistance among consumers to what is seen as an invasion of privacy, which will result in further biases as refusals grow. However, the telephone interview does reduce cost, especially if a national survey is being undertaken – a phone call is a lot cheaper than sending an interviewer to remote corners of the British Isles! Telephone interviews can, of course, also be carried out far more quickly.

Home interviews are best for longer questionnaires, for asking those questions which require some forethought or probing from the interviewer, and for open questions calling for opinions and attitudes. Once again, households must be selected scientifically, so that each has an equal opportunity for selection, and it may be necessary for interviewers to make several calls in order to find the householder at home. This delays the completion of the survey. Possible bias emerges through the closer relationship which is established between an interviewer and respondent in a longer, home interview, with respondents sometimes giving answers which it is thought the interviewer will want to hear, if the respondent finds the interviewer sympathetic.

The cheapest type of survey, dispensing entirely with the interviewer, is the *mailed questionnaire*. This means, however, that response rates are usually lower (although the inclusion of a stamped addressed envelope for the reply will boost responses) and replies are more likely to be attracted from those with an interest in the survey: the research may produce a higher level of people who have taken holidays abroad than those who have not, since they may be more interested in the questions. Respondents also have the opportunity to read the questionnaire through before answering the questions, and what they read later in the paper may prejudice the way they respond to the earlier questions. With this system, there can be no certainty that the person selected for the interview has filled out the questionnaire, or has given much thought to the questions.

Questionnaires may also be distributed to homeward-bound passengers on aircraft or on coaches, given to visitors leaving a tourist attraction with the request that they be mailed back, or left in hotel rooms to be handed in at the front desk on leaving. Each of these approaches has its own advantages and drawbacks. However, where the opportunity is given to have passengers complete a questionnaire on the journey home, the method has significant benefits over others. To start with, one is dealing with a captive audience representing 100 per cent of the universe. Passengers have their experiences fresh in their minds, and they also have time on their hands during the journey, so seldom object to filling in a questionnaire. Response rates will therefore be unusually high, especially if the cabin staff or tour escort collect questionnaires. Staff can also clarify any uncertainties about the completion of the questionnaire. The major tour operators, such as Thomson, Airtours, First Choice (who also own the airline carrying their customers), can make good use of this opportunity to monitor satisfaction, and thus to effect quality control.

When used to its full extent, this technique brings many benefits. Not only can the operators monitor the true level of any difficulties experienced with hotels or resorts, but also they can monitor satisfaction levels in respect of any aspect of the holiday, such as flights used. It is known that when airlines find that their 'ratings' relative to other competitors are slipping, they will take steps to improve service levels in order to impress the tour operator and to secure future business. This process has had a significant effect upon the quality of service given by the major independent charter airlines used for package tours.

Questionnaire design

Good questionnaire design in itself is a well-developed skill, since even the way a question is phrased can bias the response. Questions must be expressed in as neutral a manner as possible,

must be unambiguous and written in a language which is simple enough to be understood by respondents of all levels of intelligence. However, expressing a question neutrally is surprisingly difficult. Take the following two examples:

(a) *Do you think that the Spanish government should allow people to drink alcohol on the beach?*

(b) *Do you think that the Spanish government should forbid people to drink alcohol on the beach?*

Tests have shown that substituting the word 'forbid' for 'allow' suggests a greater level of control which results in respondents being less willing to answer in the affirmative to question (b).

A transport authority questioned respondents' attitudes towards special bus lanes during rush hours by asking:

Are you in favour of giving special priority to buses in the rush hour?

Of those responding, 62 per cent agreed that they were in favour. However, in a later questionnaire, the question was rephrased to read:

Are you in favour of giving special priority to buses in the rush hour, or should cars have just as much priority?

The number of those in favour now dropped to 40 per cent.

The designers of questionnaires must also avoid questions that are:

- vague
- ambiguous
- contain double negatives (making them more difficult to understand)
- set impossible tests of respondents' memory
- lead respondents to reply in a particular way.

There follow some examples of questions that would need to be avoided, or rephrased, to make them acceptable.

1 *On your last trip abroad, how much did you spend on average per day in the bar of your hotel?*
   - this is a memory test, even if the respondent travelled abroad as recently as this year. A fair question to those returning from an overseas trip, or on the last day of their trip,

but even here, at best the interviewer will get only an educated guess.

2 *Do you care enough about the family to ensure that they always carry enough insurance while on holiday?*
   – a loaded question. Who can reply no?

3 *How do the clothes you wear on holiday compare with those that you wear at home?*
   – vague. What is the question getting at? It will tend to encourage equally vague responses such as 'not at all', or 'very well', unless the interviewer has the opportunity to explain the question.

4 *What are your views about arbitrary surcharges for ITX packages?*
   – even if directed to members of the travel trade, the question makes a dangerous assumption about knowledge of technical expressions. Avoid all use of technical expressions, unless it is essential to include them, in which case an explanation of the term should be added (ITX stands for inclusive tour-basing fare). Respondents hate to admit their ignorance!

5 *How did you find the travel agent you booked with?*
   – ambiguous. You may get responses such as 'I looked him up in the yellow pages' coupled with other responses such as 'very friendly and helpful'!

6 *Would you prefer not to travel in a non-smoking flight?*
   – Help! What does it mean? The respondent will have to think too long to work it out.

7 *What do you think of the colour and taste of the ice-cream you have just bought?*
   – you are asking two questions in one. Respondents' views about colour may differ from their opinions about the taste.

As far as possible, for simplicity in collating and classifying information, *closed-end questions* should be used in questionnaires. These are questions in which the respondent is asked to pick from one of several responses possible, or the question is phrased so that the interviewer can check responses from a choice of possible replies. Closed-end questions vary from the

simple dichotomous question calling for a 'yes/no' reply to checklists of responses such as the following:

How many times have you travelled abroad on a holiday of four nights or more in the past year?
   once   1
   twice   2
   three or more times   3
   none   4

Using this form of question, rating scales can be employed to obtain respondents' views about attributes:

What was your opinion of the food served in the hotel?'
   excellent   1
   good   2
   fair   3
   poor   4
   very poor   5

With questions of this nature, it is important that there is an equal balance between 'positive' rankings and 'negative' rankings, otherwise the overall result will indicate a skewing to one side or the other. It is not uncommon to find tour operator questionnaires which ask respondents to choose from the following categories:

   excellent
   good
   fair
   poor

This provides two positive responses, one 'neutral' and one negative. The result will make it appear that the product is slightly better than might be the case in a more objective set of choices. Usually, five choices are provided in scales such as these, but on occasion as many as seven or even nine have been used to provide 'fine tuning' of responses.

Views can also be solicited by the use of a simple scale from 1 to 10 to rate respondents' opinions of a product:

What was your opinion of the service you received while at the hotel?
(Give a mark from 1 to 10, with a maximum of 10 points if you thought it really outstanding, and a minimum of 1 point if you thought it very poor.)

In this way, an average grade for service can be more easily assessed. Similarly, the use of a *Likert Scale* will solicit respondents' extent of agreement to a statement:

French hotels generally offer better food than do British hotels.

1	2	3	4	5
strongly disagree	disagree	neither disagree nor agree	agree	strongly agree

It is a useful tactic to vary the polarity of the scales where several questions of this type are used, so that sometimes 'strongly agree' appears on the left side of the scale, and sometimes 'strongly disagree' appears. This prevents the phenomenon of respondents checking automatically all one column if they generally have a favourable or unfavourable view of the product, causing them to think before responding. The statements should also reflect varying viewpoints, so that people will agree with some, and disagree with others, thus ensuring that thought is given to each reply.

Yet another technique is the *Guilford Constant-Sum Scale* which requires the respondent to apportion 10 marks between two attributes or variables, as in the following question. Since the technique is quite complex, it will require careful explanation to make certain that every respondent understands it.

In the following question, you are asked to divide 10 marks between the two resorts shown, for each of the attributes shown in the left hand column. For example, if you were asked about the quality of the food in each resort, and felt that the food in Corfu was much better than the food in Majorca, you might allocate 8 marks to Corfu and 2 to Majorca for this attribute. If you thought the food to be equally good in both resorts, you would allocate 5 marks to each.

attribute	Corfu	Majorca
sunny and warm	____	____
good beaches	____	____
good resorts for young children	____	____
inexpensive as a holiday destination	____	____

Questionnaires should always be constructed so that initial questions are broad in scope (*Did you have a holiday last year?*) and gradually become more specific as the interview progresses (*In what kind of accommodation did you stay while on holiday? . . . What were your views of the entertainment provided at the hotel?*). Questions of a personal nature, such as age range, occupation, salary, etc., are best left to the end of the questionnaire. Since it is seldom necessary to know respondents' exact ages, this question is best asked within a range, as follows:

15–24	1
25–34	2
35–44	3
45–54	4
55–64	5
65 or over	6
No response	7

In all such scales, make sure that each category is mutually exclusive. It is a common mistake to overlap categories (e.g. age range 25–35, 35–45 etc.).

Whether the questionnaire is to be filled in by the respondent or by the interviewer, clear instructions should be given on how to fill it in, and its completion should be designed to be as simple and rapid as possible. For example, instructions should be issued to circle the number corresponding to the respondents' choice:

Where did you buy your ticket? (circle your answer)	
direct from the airline	1
from a travel agent	2
from a ticket machine	3
from some other source	4
don't know/can't remember	5

This will greatly simplify transposing the answers to the computer for processing.

In some cases, *open-ended questions* will be unavoidable, although the completely unstructured question should be rare in a questionnaire, since it becomes difficult to categorise answers in a form which will enable them to be processed. A question such as *What do you think of British Airways?*, for example, will result in answers in so many different categories that they become unmanageable. The question would be better rephrased to ask separately about respondents' opinions of the airline's service, food, reliability, etc.

The use of semi-structured questions such as the sentence completion question may make answers easier to classify:

When I enter a travel agency, the first thing that I look for is . . .

Figure 3.2 provides an extract from a questionnaire which will indicate how precoding simplifies the processing of information in order to enter this in the computer. With the growth of moderately priced personal computers and survey software such as SNAP, collation and cross-tabulation of survey material has become easier and within reach of the smaller company.

Observation

Whatever the strengths of scientific surveys, they have their limitations. Other techniques such as observation play a useful role in supporting evidence gained through the use of questionnaires. However, if observation is to be taken seriously as a research method, it must be conducted no less scientifically. This requires two things: the use of scientific procedure in conducting an orderly and sustained programme of investigation, and the ability of observers to 'distance' themselves from the event observed in order to record material in a dispassionate and professional manner. This second requirement is difficult for the untrained researcher, since attitudes and behaviour are moulded by our life experiences, and it is hard to step outside them. For this reason, most observation research is used at an exploratory stage in the research programme, and is carried out by professional researchers with psychological training. We should not fail to recognise, however, that much useful material can still be gathered by the non-expert through a process of careful observation, from the travel agent who observe patterns of behaviour of clients who enter the shop and select brochures from the racks, to airline managers who listen to the way check-ins are handled at airports and observe the behaviour of passengers waiting for their flights. The essential thing to remember is that one is doing more than 'gathering impressions'. Patterns of behaviour are being recorded in detail, through the use of field notes or a tape recorder, and over extended periods of time. A very high proportion of what is observed is likely to prove of little use, so that the process is both tedious and wasteful. The technique is none the less particularly valuable when researching competitors' products. The hotelier wishing to know more about competitors and how they handle conference enquiries might call the hotels in question, taking the role of a conference organiser, to see how the enquiry is handled, or may sit in the lobby of a hotel to listen to the comments of guests or observe how front office staff handle incoming guests. One American hotelier (evidently little recognised by his staff) made it a practice to stay as a guest in his hotels to check the levels of service provided. He would ask the lift operator or hotel porter to recommend a good place to eat (usually he was directed to somewhere other than the hotel's own restaurant) and in this way discover how the sales training of staff needed improvement.

On the whole, the technique is best used for generating hypotheses about situations, but it will improve the researchers' knowledge about what sort of questions need to be included in questionnaires.

Experimentation

Experiments usually conjure up an image of a laboratory, and indeed many tests are carried out under laboratory conditions which can be useful in travel and tourism research, such as testing the effectiveness of different advertisements on a cross-section of consumers. Many forms of experimentation can be carried out away from the laboratory, however. An agent who switches brochures around in the racks to see how this affects their selection is conducting a *controlled experiment*. Airlines test different seats on their aircraft to see which proves most comfortable for their passengers, and a tour operator might experiment with the use of different excursions on different departures to see these changes

Interviewer: Follow instructions and read questions exactly as shown

		COLUMN
Interviewer number	☐☐	1,2

Date	☐☐☐☐☐☐	3–8
	Day Month Year	

Day of the week:	Monday	1	
(circle)	Tuesday	2	
	Wednesday	3	
	Thursday	4	
	Friday	5	
	Saturday	6	
	Sunday	7	9
Weather:	Sunny	1	
	Cloudy/Fog	2	
	Changeable	3	
	Rain/snow	4	10

QUESTIONS

A WHERE IS YOUR HOME?

Dorset	1 1	W.Mid/H.ofE.	1 7
(name town or village:)		E.Mid/E.Anglia	1 8
_____		Wales	1 9
Hampshire	1 2	North + NW	2 0
London	1 3	Scotland	2 1
Other WCTB	1 4	N. Ireland	2 2
Other STB	1 5	Other Europe	2 3
SEETB	1 6	Non Europe	2 4 11,12

If respondent gives answer to A giving codes 1 1–1 6, ask questions B1 and B2. If an answer code 1 7–2 4 was given, circle 2 for B1 and B2

B1 HAVE YOU COME FROM THERE TODAY?

	Yes	1	
	No	2	13

B2 ARE YOU RETURNING THERE TODAY?

	Yes	1	
	No	2	14

If respondent answers 'Yes' to both B1 and B2, circle:

and go directly to E	0/0/0/0	15–18

Otherwise ask:

C WHAT IS THE TOTAL LENGTH OF YOUR HOLIDAY OR STAY AWAY FROM HOME?

Days	☐☐☐	15–17

(enter 3 digits, eg 3 days = 003)

D WHAT PLACE ARE YOU STAYING AT?

Weymouth/Osmington/Portland	1	
Lulworth area	2	
Dorchester/Warmwell/Mid + W.Dorset	3	
Wareham/Wool/Bovington area	4	
Swanage/Corfe Castle area	5	
Poole/Wimborne	6	
Bournemouth	7	
Christchurch/New Forest	8	
Other	9	18

E WHAT FORM OF TRANSPORT HAVE YOU USED TO GET HERE TODAY?

Train + bus/taxi	1	
Regular bus/coach	2	
Coach tour/excursion	3	
Minibus	4	
Car: own/firm's/friend's	5	
Car: hired	6	
Motor cycle/bicycle	7	
Other	8	19

F1 IS THIS YOUR FIRST VISIT TO BOVINGTON TANK MUSEUM?

	Yes	1 0	20,21
	No	2	20

If respondent answers 'No' to F1, ask:

F2 HOW MANY TIMES HAVE YOU BEEN BEFORE?

	Once	1	
	Twice	2	
	3–5 times	3	
	Frequently	4	
	Stationed here	5	21

If respondent answered question E with an answer coded 1, 2, 3 or 4:

	circle: 0	22

If respondent answered question E with an answer coded 5, 6, 7 or 8:

	ask:

G WHAT WAS THE JOURNEY HERE LIKE?
(Interviewer: explain this question if necessary)

Been to Bovington before	1	
Easy/well signposted all way	2	
Easy to find the camp, but museum not well signposted	3	
Difficult/poor signposting	4	
Other	5	22

H WHAT SORT OF GROUP ARE YOU WITH TODAY?

Alone	1	
With family	2	
With friends	3	
With family and friends	4	
Organised party	5	23
(state type:) _____		
_____		

If respondent has been to the Tank Museum before, ie answered 'No' to question F1:

circle: 0   24

If respondent is on first visit to the Museum, ie answered 'Yes' to question F1:

ask:

I HOW DID YOU COME TO HEAR ABOUT THE TANK MUSEUM?

Stationed here	1	
Just passing/saw signposts	2	
With organised party itinerary	3	
Military contacts	4	
Tank restoration/specialism	5	
Heard from friends/family	6	
Leaflet in accommodation	7	
Saw or heard other publicity	8	
(specify:) _____		
Can't remember/other	9	24

J HOW MUCH TIME HAVE YOU SPENT HERE TODAY?

less than 30 minutes	1	
30 minutes – less than 1 hour	2	
1 hour – less than 1½ hours	3	
1½ hours – less than 2 hours	4	
2 hours or more	5	25

K HAVE YOU ANY SPECIAL VIEWS ON THE OPENING TIMES?

No special view, times satisfactory	1	
Should stay open at lunch time	2	
Should open earlier in the morning	3	
Earlier morning and lunch time	4	
Should stay open later	5	
Open later and lunch time	6	
Other	7	26

L IF A CHARGE WERE TO BE MADE FOR ENTRY, HOW MUCH WOULD YOU CONSIDER REASONABLE, FOR ADULTS, CHILDREN, AND SENIOR CITIZENS?

(Interviewer: circle one in each column)

	Adults	Children	Senior Citizens	
Free/nominal	1	1	1	
Around 25p	2	2	2	
Around 50p	3	3	3	
Around £1.00	4	4	4	
Around £1.50 +	5	5	5	27–29

(Interviewer: now conclude interview and thank respondent for help and co-operation)

Estimate number of people of different age groups in respondent's group (Enter numbers in appropriate boxes as TWO digits)

	Males	Columns	Females	Columns
under 11 years		30,31		42,43
11–15 years		32,33		44,45
16–24 years		34,35		46,47
25–44 years		36,37		48,49
45–64 years		38,39		50,51
65 + years		40,41		52,53

Number of questionnaire (enter two digits)

54,55

END

Fig. 3.2 Extract from a survey of visitors to Bovington Camp
(Courtesy: University of Bournemouth)

affect customer sales and satisfaction. The technique is useful in helping to establish whether there is a *causal relationship* between two variables, that is, a change in one variable produces a change in another. As well as demonstrating the cause and effect, the objective will be to offer an explanation for it, too.

Qualitative versus quantitative research methods

At the beginning of this chapter, mention was made of the distinction between qualitative and quantitative research. Much of what has been discussed up to this point can be described as quantitative in nature, and involves research which is concerned with gathering statistics to describe what is happening. In this, it is answering questions such as Who?, Where?, When?, and How? Answers to these questions are usually sought through the use of questionnaires. However, there are serious weaknesses with the use of the questionnaire. Their statistical significance is dependent upon their being answered honestly and accurately, but we have no way of knowing whether this is the case. Nor is the survey useful in helping to answer questions dealing with the Why? of travel. Let us say, for example, that we are interested in knowing why people travel by ferry and road or rail rather than by air to the south of France. People may not actually know their real motives, or they may be reluctant to reveal them. Some will not want to admit to fear of flying, or being unable to afford to fly. Even if respondents aim to be totally honest, they may themselves have little understanding of their underlying motivation. Motives can be extremely complex, and result from a great many different factors, while the questionnaire may bring out only the more obvious ones.

Qualitative techniques such as in-depth motivation research come into use for this purpose, and involve less structured interviews in which the purpose is to get the respondent to talk freely about the issue. This may call for interviews lasting two or three hours at a time, and clearly these cannot be carried out on the same scale as a ten-minute street interview. They will need to be conducted by skilled researchers, and this will greatly add to the time and cost of the exercise. They are intensely valuable, though, in probing beneath the surface responses generated in structured surveys.

One such technique widely used in market research is the *panel interview*, in which around six to eight consumers are invited to meet in informal surroundings to discuss a product or topic under research, under the guidance and direction of a skilled interviewer. Through the process of group dynamics, people's deeper feelings about issues are explored, with answers from one participant triggering off comments from other members of the panel. The material is generally tape recorded for future analysis, and as exploratory research can be helpful in guiding the direction of future research needed.

Other forms of qualitative research include *projective tests*, where respondents are asked to project themselves into another person's role. Examples of projective tests include *picture completion* wherein respondents are shown a cartoon or illustration in which one character is making a statement; they are then asked to complete the illustration by stating what they think the second character might be replying. The *Thematic Apperception Test (TAT)* employs a picture depicting a story, and respondents are asked to identify what they believe is going on in the picture. Respondents are able in this way to project what they themselves think as if these responses were a third person's views.

The beauty of research methodology is that there are so many ways in which research can be conducted, and researchers constantly seek new ways in which to secure evidence. One innovatory piece of research carried out by Thomson Holidays will illustrate this. Thomson were interested in finding out what image consumers had of the company, and how this image compared with that of other tour companies. To do this, they used a form of projective technique, in asking respondents to imagine that well-known tour companies had come alive as real people. In this way, Thomson discovered that the company projected an image of the solid, reliable family man, while Enterprise Holidays became personified as the rising young executive and Thomas Cook the pernickety bossy squire.

As an interesting extra insight into the relative positioning of the various tour operators, First Choice Holidays undertook qualitative discussion groups to establish the *emotional values* associated with different operators. They also undertook detailed desk research, analysing the 'tone of voice' and use of language in their advertising. This was interpreted in terms of the psychological technique of *Transactional Analysis*. Put simply, this determines the way the operator is relating to its clients.

Thomson, whose own research identified a solid, reliable family man image, was judged to communicate 'parent to child'. The implications of 'looking after you' and being authoritative and protective are obvious. While such an image is appropriate for the mainstream, rather unadventurous package tour purchaser, it is certainly inappropriate for, say, the more experienced and adventurous traveller. First Choice Holiday's Freespirit brand targets just such holidaymakers. The 'emotional values' associated with the name and brand, and the 'adult to adult' tone of voice, were developed as a result of this research. Such knowledge can be enormously beneficial in planning a company's promotional strategy and knowing what strengths to build on.

Research today is characterised by a growing interest in such new techniques. A museum in the United States, planning to find out which exhibits were the most popular, chose to support surveys by measuring the patterns of wear on the carpets in the museum and the noseprints on the glass cases surrounding the exhibits. Both measures gave a good indication of the levels of popularity of different exhibits.

Although, as has been made clear, many qualitative techniques do not lend themselves to tests of statistical probability, they will often throw light on issues which the more common forms of research technique cannot resolve, and should therefore play a part in the repertoire of any market research department.

Econometric models

A model consists of a set of variables and their interrelationship which reflect real life experience. By identifying how variables move in sympathy with one another, models can be helpful in predicting the future. Their use in travel and tourism research and forecasting is still limited, although they are being developed at a macro level to predict tourism trends by research organisations such as the EIU. This organisation has shown how fluctuating exchange rates and rates of inflation affect flows of international tourism.[1] Research of this kind is essential for public sector planning, and can also be extremely useful in forecasting future sales in the travel business. Models can be constructed on a smaller scale to show the effect of advertising spend on sales, and how this relationship is affected by other factors such as competitors' spend and changes in discretionary income.

Since there are so many variables affecting travel behaviour, the construction of a model to predict changes in the market for tourism is a complex and expensive process, but it is one which is being continually refined and improved.

The effectiveness of research

While some firms in the travel industry, and virtually all organisations in public sector tourism, undertake some form of marketing research, there are still many smaller companies who make no allowance for research in their annual budget, seeing it as inaccurate and an expensive use of resources which can be better channelled into other forms of marketing expenditure. This is shortsighted at best, and at worst can be catastrophic, if managers continue to commit major expenditure to new product development with insufficient background knowledge. Even today, too many small hotels are being bought, and small travel agencies opened, based purely on the 'gut feel' of their proprietors.

Research is never an exact science, but it can reduce the margins of error to which hunches alone are subject. The feasibility study is an essential prerequisite to any new project, whether the launch of a new company, the introduction of a new logo or the development of a new product. Above all, the success of research will be based on three things:

1 Sufficient resources must be allocated to the project to do the job properly, both in terms of time and money. Good research does take time to do, and managers wanting research results 'yesterday', or allocating only a fraction of the necessary funds, will force the methodology to be skimped and the end result to be of questionable value.
2 Managers should be willing to believe the results of the research when they become available, even if they conflict with the management's own preconceived views.

3 The results should be used. All too frequently, research is commissioned in order to avoid taking an immediate decision. Expensively commissioned research is then left to gather dust in a drawer instead of being used to enable managers to make better decisions on the future direction of the company's strategy.

Questions, tasks and issues for discussion

1 Working in small groups, plan an observation exercise which might provide useful qualitative data for a local travel agent.

2 Obtain a questionnaire (preferably one that is used in the travel and tourism industry) and analyse its question construction, suggesting any ways in which you feel it could be improved. What additional questions could be asked that would give the company valuable information not provided by the present questions?

3 Discuss how you would plan a survey to obtain a market profile of visitors to your nearest tourism resort. Using a plan of the resort, identify the points most suitable for conducting street interviews and explain the reasons for your choice.

4 What sources of data exist on the number and profile of visitors to your town or region? What gaps in knowledge about the market exist, and what weaknesses are there in the available data?

Exercise

You are given the task of carrying out a programme of research into your own travel and tourism or leisure course, with the aim of finding ways in which its content or structure could be improved. Produce a report for your course tutor which explains the methods you would plan to use and the reasons for your choosing them.

Include in the report a short comment on the constraints under which the course is operating. Sum up by analysing the extent to which you believe the course is 'marketing orientated', and what areas should become more orientated towards meeting the needs of both students and employers.

4 The tourist market

After studying this chapter, you should be able to:

- understand consumer needs and wants, and the distinction between them
- appreciate the factors affecting consumer motivation and demand
- understand basic principles of psychology and sociology, as they relate to the buying process
- apply behavioural theory to the marketing of travel and tourism services
- understand market segmentation and its uses in the marketing plan

We speak of an individual customer for our products as a 'consumer', but in referring to consumers in aggregate, or groups of consumers, we use the term 'market'. A *market* can be described as *a defined group of consumers for a particular product or range of products*. Exactly how that market is defined is of crucial importance for our understanding of consumer behaviour, since it will shape the marketing response we make to our consumers' wants and needs.

Tourists are consumers who purchase a number of diverse travel and tourism services. If those in the industry have a clearer understanding of why their products are in demand, they will not only be able to tailor their products more closely to the needs of their clients, but also be better able to select the advertising and sales messages used to inform and persuade those clients to buy the products.

Curiously, most research expenditure in the travel industry has tended to focus on what tourists buy, when they buy it, where they buy it and how they buy it; vital enough information, to be sure, but these bare facts tell us little about *why* the client purchases the product. Why, for instance, do certain tourists choose to holiday in Florida rather than Greece? What variables are at work here apart from cost? Why do they choose to travel with British Airways rather than, say, Virgin Airways? Why do they buy an indepen-

dent inclusive tour rather than a group tour? Why have they taken the trouble to go direct to the airline to book, rather than through a local travel agency? These questions are not only interesting academically for an understanding of tourist behaviour; their answers can be enormously helpful in the preparation of marketing plans.

Understanding needs and wants

As elsewhere in this book, our aim will be to understand basic principles, while relating these to the context of tourism. We shall start by looking at consumer needs and wants, and learning to understand how these arise.

As consumers, we often talk about our 'needing' a new television set, a new dress, or a holiday. Do we in fact really *need* these things, or are we merely expressing a desire for more goods and services? We live in a society orientated to increasing material consumption. We measure our success as a nation against other nations in terms of Gross National Product (GNP), a measure of material wealth; we are therefore encouraged to discover new wants, or 'needs', as soon as existing ones are satisfied. One result of this is that it becomes increasingly difficult to distinguish between wants and needs. Many people will search through a packed wardrobe of clothes and agonise that they haven't 'a thing to wear' for their forthcoming holidays. To what extent are the new clothes they intend to buy to take abroad actually fulfilling a need?

To answer that question, we have to determine what is meant by a need. People have certain physiological needs that are basic to survival; the need to eat, to drink, to sleep and to keep warm, and to reproduce, are all essential for the survival of the human race. However, for our psychological well-being, we also have other needs which require satisfaction; the need to give and receive affection, the need for self-esteem, for recognition of our abilities by others, for status and respect. There is also a fundamental human drive for competence, a desire to control the environment, and to gain understanding for its own sake. Abraham Maslow has conveniently categorised these needs into a hierarchy (Fig. 4.1), theorising that more basic needs have to be satisfied before our interest will focus on higher level needs. Until we are fed and sheltered satisfactorily (and 'satisfactorily' means according to the needs of our cultural group) we are unlikely to give much thought to self-esteem or 'mastering our environment'.

The way we perceive our needs is built up of a complex interrelationship of beliefs and attitudes which arise out of our knowledge and opinions. Let us take the purchase of a car, for instance. At its basic level, a car provides us with transportation, and our choice is based partly on economic considerations. It may be more convenient to use

a car than public transport, and we look for a car that is cheap to run, reliable in operation, with easy access to maintenance and servicing, roomy enough for ourselves and our luggage. But we may also seek to satisfy certain psychological needs in the purchase of our car. The design of a particular model may appeal to us, either for aesthetic reasons or because its fast, sporty shape will be envied by others, gaining us status. Different colours appeal for similar reasons, and we may choose a bigger car to demonstrate our wealth to others. Our choice of car, as with our choice of so many other goods and services we buy, reflects the way we see ourselves – our perception of the kind of people we are.

It is not the role of this book to moralise about individual lifestyles. Our aim is only to bring the reader's attention to the impulses that shape consumer motivation. It is sufficient at this point to emphasise that there is a very complex set of motives influencing most of the products we buy, and this is true of holidays as much as other products.

The variables affecting human needs

All of us have the same basic physiological needs. But how is it that in various countries and regions, different needs arise, leading to different patterns of demand? Why are many Americans satisfied with 'convenience' food, but insist it be served quickly and accompanied by a glass of iced water, while many French people will consider the meal the most important event of the day, to be lingered over and enjoyed? Why is the demand for personal computers and video recorders in Britain among the highest in the world? Why is the sale of toothpaste so relatively small in France compared with other western nations?

Variables affecting the demand for goods and services may be conveniently divided into two categories: *demographic variables*, which are broadly population statistics, and *psychographic variables*, which are concerned with our patterns of lifestyle and personality.

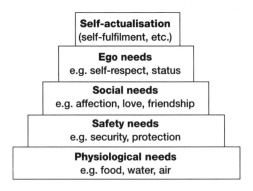

Fig. 4.1 Maslow's hierarchy of needs

Demographic variables

Population statistics include the numbers of people living in a country or region, and the component make-up of that population – the proportion in different age ranges, the marital status, proportion of those with children, number unemployed, and so on. Marketers will be interested to know not only the present statistics of the population, but also the changing trends taking place in the population.

If the number of young people is declining, for instance, while the number of those of retiring age is increasing, this will have important implications for tour operators who are specialising in holidays for the elderly and those concerned with young people's holidays. If a company produces shirts, it would obviously be helpful to know the proportion of males in the population taking a size 15" collar, and whether demand for larger collar and shirt sizes is increasing – due perhaps to the population eating better, or doing more sedentary jobs without exercise.

'. . . to know whether demand for larger collar sizes is increasing . . .'

If, in addition, we know something about the disposable income of these groupings (i.e. the amount of money these families are left with to buy goods and services after their regular commitments to mortgages, insurance, taxes and other essential household expenses have been paid), this will further aim our marketing planning. In Britain, for example, two groups with substantial discretionary income are young single people and 'empty nesters' – those aged about 40+ whose children have grown up and left home, and who may have two earners in the family at the peak of their earning potential. It is also a characteristic of Britain's changing population that, due to lower birth rates, the numbers of young people are declining, while the numbers of those in middle age are increasing. We are likely to see much more attention focus on marketing new goods and services to middle-aged people instead of young people from the mid-1990s onwards.

Psychographic variables

Simply counting heads in this way unfortunately tells us little about the motivation of individuals within these groups. How many will prefer coloured shirts to white ones? How important to young people is it to buy clothes made with natural fibres (cotton, linen, wool) rather than with synthetic materials? To answer questions such as these, we need to know much more about the cultural climate of a country and the psychological needs of its population.

Countries and regions develop their own unique cultures and values, which are learned rather than instinctive. Thus the British tend to seek a greater measure of privacy in their lives than do Americans, leading to a greater demand for products such as garden fencing. The British Tourist Authority, as part of its marketing research undertaken abroad, regularly monitors differing consumer needs of tourists from those destinations which provide substantial tourist demand to Britain. They have found, for example, that many Germans love beauty and art, appreciate their environment, and are obsessed with physical well-being; their tourists demand accommodation with private facilities, accommodation that is clean and simple, and offers fresh food with large helpings in the restaurant. They enjoy family-run accommodation and a 'local atmosphere'. Knowledge such as this will be much more helpful in determining the basis for a hotel's marketing plan designed to attract German tourists.

Regional differences within countries are also often pronounced. The demand for so-called health foods in Britain is far greater in the south than the north, while products such as mushy peas, popular in the north of England, are hard to sell in southern England. Although North Americans share a common culture that is quite distinctive from the British, there are huge differences in culture and lifestyle between those residing in the north and south of the United States, and between those in the east and the Mid-West; US marketers have long been aware of the need to treat domestic markets as consisting of up to nine distinctive *market regions* when drawing up marketing plans.

Within national and regional groups, we can further distinguish a number of sub-cultural groupings. *Ethnic groups* are those with differing racial or religious characteristics. The high levels of immigration from Britain's former colonies has led to concentrated populations of West Indians, Pakistanis, Chinese, Indians and other ethnic groups in Britain's major cities, which in turn has given rise to demand for specialist food, clothing and other products (including long-haul air travel to the maternal countries). In Germany, specialist travel agencies have sprung up to cater for the huge foreign travel demand created by the *Gastarbeiter* – foreign workers from countries such as Turkey and former Yugoslavia – who return home periodically for their holidays. Since German reunification, the flood of Eastern Europeans entering the country has given rise to further opportunities for specialist travel. In the USA, New York counts among its population a high proportion of Jews, who have marked preferences for travel – weekend breaks in the Catskill mountains, and holidays in Miami Beach, for example. In turn, this has led to hotel proprietors learning to cater for the particular needs of these markets, by providing Kosher food and traditional Jewish dishes, such as 'lox and bagels'.

Social class continues to play an important role in all societies, whether capitalist or communist, although its importance is so often thought to be declining. Class is usually defined in terms of occupation of the head of household, although this variable alone can be misleading. The system of social grading most commonly employed among marketers divides occupations into six categories, known as socio-economic groupings:

Socio-economic groupings

A Higher managerial, administrative or professional
B Middle managerial, administrative or professional
C1 Supervisory or clerical, junior managerial
C2 Skilled manual workers
D Semi-skilled and unskilled manual workers
E Pensioners, unemployed, casual or lowest grade workers.

In this categorisation, ABC1 are broadly defined as middle class, while C2 and D categories are working class. E groups, as a catch-all, are less easily defined in terms of social class, but represent those at the lowest level of subsistence in society.

Between these groups, norms, values and patterns of consumer behaviour are distinctive, to an extent not explained by purchasing power alone. In fact, it would not necessarily be the case that those in the ABC1 categories have more discretionary income than do C2D categories. Many skilled manual workers today have more discretionary income to spend than those in traditional 'white collar' jobs, especially when taking into consideration the added burden of expenditure among middle-class consumers on items such as private schooling for their children. Of equal importance for those providing leisure services is the relative amounts of leisure time available for short breaks or holidays. Many managers and professionals are obliged to take work home and can give less time to relaxation than can the 'nine-to-five' manual worker, who today may enjoy as manyas four to five weeks holiday each year.

Sociological groups

We have shown that consumers can be divided into a number of cultural and sub-cultural groupings, according to nationality, racial origin, or other form of common background. There are two further groups to be discussed here, of which marketers must be aware.

Peer groups

The first of these is the peer group. This is defined as the group with which an individual is most closely associated in his or her life. Such groups include fellow students, workmates, friends and relations or close neighbours, and there is a strong tendency for individuals to conform to the norms and values of their peer groups. The latter therefore exercise considerable influence on the buying decisions of individuals within their group. We have only to remember the pressures on us to conform in matters of dress or hairstyle in school to realise how great this pressure can sometimes be! The expression 'keeping up with the Jones's' reflects the desire to emulate the purchasing patterns of our neighbours.

Reference groups

In addition to the groups with which we as individuals are most closely associated, there are other groups with which we would choose to associate ourselves, either because we admire them or simply because we would like to emulate their lifestyle. These reference groups, as they are known, exercise strong influences on aggregate patterns of consumer demand. Some members of the Royal Family, for instance, become trend setters in introducing fashions in hairstyles or clothing, as do film, television and pop stars. The so-called 'jet set' which surround prominent personalities are widely admired by impressionable people, who copy their way of life and purchase goods and services which are, or are thought to be, purchased by these 'innovators'. When products receive the personal endorsement of members of the reference group (film stars advertising soap or perfume, for example), this can lead to huge increases in sales. Many marketers for this reason are keen to see links established between their products and prominent people in society.

This desire to emulate those in an esteemed position in society gives rise to the phenomenon of the *trickle down effect*, whereby products originally purchased by elite members of a society are adopted by those further down the hierarchy. Many products once thought of as 'up-market' gradually trickle down the social scale, while those at the top of the social scale are continually seeking new products and services to distinguish themselves from the mass consumers. Articles such as filofaxes, cafetières or Austrian blinds spring to mind as examples of the trickle down effect, which holds true equally for tourism. Consider, for example, the way in which resorts such as St Tropez have over the years been transformed from exclusive holiday centres for rich and famous people to popular resorts for mass market tourism.

Earlier, we made clear that social class is not simply a factor of occupation or income. It is, rather, a compendium of norms and values to the extent that a marketer's real concern is less with social class than with lifestyle; the ways in which social groups choose to live. Those following an unconventional lifestyle may be drawn from different social classes, but select the products and services they buy on the basis of their peer or reference groups. For example people following an 'alternative lifestyle' may demand wholefoods, natural fabrics for clothes (handwoven rather than machine made), fashions in ethnic styles and designs, minimal use of cosmetics and simple 'folk' furniture. It is interesting to note that in spite of the growing influence of this group in buying behaviour, little is known of their habits in holidays and travel. However, many specialist operators have introduced new types of package tour arrangements to cater for the needs of this fast-growing sector of the market. One example is Cycling for Softies, a small specialist company which provides independent cycling holidays in France coupled with comfortable accommodation in traditional hotels.

The psychology of the consumer

Up to now we have dealt with patterns of consumer behaviour in aggregate. For a thorough understanding of consumers, we must also know how they act and react as individuals.

Various models have been suggested by researchers of human behaviour, who are in general agreement that the number of, and interrelationship between, variables affecting product choice is extremely complex. In this chapter we can do no more than provide an introduction to consumer choice and outline some of the factors as a prelude to understanding how marketing can aid product choice.

Many models have been developed, of various levels of sophistication, to show how consumers react to stimuli. Howard and Sheth,[2] for example, have argued that consumers can be classified as being in one of three stages of behaviour: an initial extensive problem-solving stage, where they have little knowledge about products or brands, and are seeking information from a wide range of sources; a stage of more limited problem-solving, where decisions have narrowed and information seeking has become more directed; and routinised behaviour, where buying has become based largely on habit and previous satisfaction with the product.

Buyers choose products which they perceive as having the best potential to satisfy their needs. Buyers choosing a dietary product as an aid to slimming will be motivated by a product that offers some combination of low calories, nutrition, taste and value for money. Buyers learn about such products partly through experience with the same or similar products in the past, and partly by seeking information. Information is sometimes sought actively (as when the buyer has an immediate need), or passively (where the buyer may be responsive to information and stores it away for future use). Sources of information may be the commercial world, or the buyer's social environment. The commercial world produces messages about products which act as stimuli – for example, advertisements which describe a product's quality, price, availability, service, and its distinctive qualities against its competitors. Social sources of information include word of mouth recommendation from friends or family, or objective articles about the product in newspapers or periodicals. A number of variables which we have discussed earlier mediate the effect of these stimuli. Our social class, personality, culture and group influences, as well as economic influences such as our financial means, pressure of time and the importance of the purchase, all interact with our internal state to affect our decision-making. Internally, individual decisions are based on the way we perceive and learn about new products. Research has shown that our perception of products is highly selective. We tend to 'screen out' information which is too simple or too familiar (hence boring), or too complex to take in, while we are more receptive to information to which we are predisposed. If, for example, we are thinking about a holiday, we become more aware of holiday advertisements. However, our perception of information is also biased: we tend to distort information to suit our own frame of reference. Many people who have never visited Britain quite genuinely believe that the country is veiled in permanent rain and fog. Such preconceptions form a formidable problem for the BTA, but they can be modified by strong stimuli, such as the personal experience and recommendation of a member of the family or a friend.

Learning theory

One of the simplest models of the theory of how we learn is shown in Fig. 4.2. The model suggests that our individual needs give rise to a drive which we take action to satisfy. If our action does indeed result in satisfying the need, we tend to repeat the experience, leading to the development of habit formation and customer loyalty to particular brands. In the same way, we tend to generalise from past experience of a product, so that the satisfaction we receive, for example, by

Fig. 4.2 A model of learning theory

taking a cruise will lead us to take another cruise, or another type of holiday with the same company. However, Howard and Sheth have shown that constant repeat purchase of the same product leads to monotony and a search for a new product or brand, with the consumer once again returning to intensive problem-solving activity. An awareness of this phenomenon is useful to marketers attempting to switch loyal users of rival products to their own company's products.

The interaction of *stimulus* and *exogenous variables* results in buyers responding in a number of ways. First, their attention to new products may be achieved. Second, they become aware of the product, either broadly, or to an extent that they will recall and recognise it again in the future, or acquire a deeper knowledge of the product's benefits. Third, consumers may form the intention to purchase the product at some future time. Finally, they will engage in overt purchasing behaviour, that is, they will purchase a particular quantity of the product at a particular time, through particular distributive outlets and at a particular price.

This hierarchical pattern of response is known as AIDA – Attention, Interest, Desire, Action – representing four stages of response by consumers to a product. The marketing strategy is aimed at achieving one or more of these consumer responses. This will be discussed in greater depth in Chapter 9.

Applying consumer theory to tourism marketing

We have necessarily taken a number of pages to explain the fundamentals of consumer theory. But theory has value only when it is applied, so we now turn to examining ways in which our understanding of consumer behaviour can help the practice of marketing, and of marketing tourism specifically.

Although individual behaviour has been shown to be complex, it is possible to identify patterns of generalised group behaviour among consumers sharing common characteristics.

Marketers have long recognised that few organisations are powerful enough to aim their products at the consumer in general. The cost of such a strategy is huge, and, particularly if the company is engaged in selling to international markets, such a 'shotgun' approach, which fails to accurately target the markets for which products are aimed, does not make effective use of resources.

In very few cases are the products of one organisation attractive to all consumers in the marketplace. It therefore makes good sense to target the products to specific types of consumers, for which the product offers specific benefits, thereby making it more distinctive from its competitors: adopting, as marketers refer to it, a 'rifle' approach. This approach is known as *market segmentation*, the basis of which is that the company first determines the market or markets it will serve, and then develops its products to serve the needs of those markets. This *concentrated marketing* strategy reflects a marketing-orientated approach to business that is fundamental in planning.

A market segment can be defined as

> A subgroup of the total consumer market whose members share common characteristics relevant to the purchase or use of a product.

The value of market segmentation is that the subgroup is also reachable through advertising messages aimed exclusively at them.

Let us now look at some of the ways in which markets can be segmented in the travel and tourism industry.

Segmentation in travel and tourism marketing

Markets can be segmented in many different ways. If we go back to our earlier description of the variables affecting the demand for goods and services, we can start by segmenting our customers according to these criteria.

We could, for instance, decide to cater for groups of holidaymakers according to their age, their social class, or their regional distribution.

Let us assume that we have decided to become specialists in developing package holidays for customers living in a particular region of Britain. We might feature, as benefits for this group, the convenience of local airport departures, free transport to the airport and/or free parking at the airport. While we would be carrying smaller numbers of clients than the large mass market operators, and would not therefore gain the same economies of scale, many consumers will be satisfied to pay slightly higher prices for the convenience of a local departure and the additional benefits offered. We could stress that we are a local company supporting the economy of the region, and be active in local community events, so that local residents tend to think of our company first when planning their holidays.

Other tour companies have specialised by age. The success of companies such as Club 18–30, which focuses on the provision of youth holidays, and Saga Holidays, which specialises in holidays for older clients, reflects the success of concentrated marketing strategies. Incoming tour operators have specialised in handling groups of tourists from specific countries, such as Japan, the USA or Israel. They make it their business to know, and cater for, the needs of nationals from these countries. In the USA, some tour operators have aimed to capture the black ethnic market (by, for example, establishing tours to West Africa for black Americans curious about their roots).

Just as with demographic segmentation, so can we segment by psychographic variables. Some companies have developed specialist villa holidays catering for young professional people, while other organisations have packaged tours for those with specific lifestyles. Research by the Irish Tourist Board (ITB) has found that holidays in Ireland tend to meet the needs of those seeking to know and understand themselves better – a 'self-actualisation' need in Maslow's terms. This knowledge can be used by those promoting holidays to Ireland, by their emphasising Ireland as a destination for self-reflection and tranquility. Stanley Plog[3] in the United States has found that tourists can be categorised broadly as either psychocentrics or allocentrics. The former are self-inhibited, nervous and lack the desire for adventure, preferring well-packaged routine holidays in popular tourist destinations, mainly of the 'sun, sand, sea' variety, while the latter are more outgoing, have varied interests and are keen to explore new places and find new things to do. Such tourists are more likely to travel independently.

This model in itself is no doubt too simplistic. Most of us have some mix of these characteristics, and it is a noticeable fact that many mass tourists to popular destinations, who would fall into the psychocentric category, gain confidence after a number of trips abroad, and become more adventurous. They may hire a car, for instance, and drive to areas less frequented by tourists, during their routine package holiday. Nevertheless, the model is helpful in thinking about the facilities we should provide to meet these differing needs.

Yet another way of segmenting our markets is according to the benefits the product offers. In many cases, different benefits appeal to different markets, and this can be seen in the case of a hotel which attracts both business people and holidaymakers. Sometimes both markets are attracted at the same time (as with hotels in major cities, although weekend visitors are more likely to be leisure clients), while in other cases different markets are attracted at different times of the year. Seaside hotels may find that they are attracting a more up-market clientele, and from an older age bracket, during the shoulder season than in the peak summer season.

Some hotels, particularly in country towns, will have to cater for different guests, based on whether their visitors are 'transient' (stopping only overnight while touring) or 'terminal' (using the hotel as a base for touring). Hotels in US cities (and certain other countries) have recognised the need among day trippers and shoppers for a base in the city to rest, leave their purchases or take a bath, and hoteliers have hired rooms by the hour for this market, thus finding a new way to use the product.

Major hotel chains have identified a steady rise in the number of business women to whom they are catering, and have responded by providing facilities to meet their needs, including more feminine décor, cosmetic mirrors, hairdryers and other benefits. In some cases floors in large hotels have been experimentally restricted for the use of women only, to enhance the security of female travellers. The development of motels in the USA was a direct marketing response to an identified need. Transient tourists required easy check-in and check-out facilities, minimal service or public rooms but convenient parking and low prices. The motel meets all these needs.

Major tour operators might be thought at first to be largely undifferentiated in their market segmentation. In fact, their products have in some cases become highly differentiated, even if less specialised than with small companies. To take advantage of the many different needs of their national market, they offer a huge range of different resorts, the convenience of local airports, holidays of different lengths, a wide range of hotels and prices, and catering arrangements varying from self-service to half board and full board.

Volume segmentation

There is one other form of market segmentation to which we must make reference, that of volume segmentation. This distinguishes between light and heavy users of the product (or loyal, repeat purchasers compared with occasional or infrequent purchasers). Hotel companies offer discounted rates, and other benefits, to regular purchasers such as companies booking employees regularly, or airlines who have contracts for crew accommodation. In some countries, loyal users of certain airlines may benefit from 'frequent flyer' programmes: once members exceed a certain annual mileage of travel with the airline, they are rewarded with a free trip for themselves, or their partners. While this strategy has proved highly successful in building brand loyalty, it has also suffered from an unforeseen drawback: all recipients tend to cash in their vouchers at the same time, and the resultant decline in cash tickets creates cash flow problems for the airlines!

Other lessons from Maslow

It will by now be appreciated that an understanding of consumer needs is critical for successful marketing. It might be helpful at this point to summarise consumers' travel and tourism needs and relate these to the Maslow hierarchy discussed earlier.

Motivation for travel and tourism can be categorised as follows:

- holiday travel
- business travel
- health travel
- visiting friends and relatives (VFR)
- religious travel
- travel for economic benefit (e.g. shopping)
- travel for educational purposes (study tours, etc.)
- sports and activities travel (participation or observation).

In fact, we can summarise all of these activities under five basic needs: *physical, cultural, interpersonal, status and prestige,* and *commercial.* Although there will be some overlap of motives between these categories, it will be useful to see how these needs are met by tourism facilities or destinations, and how they relate to levels of need in Maslow's hierarchy.

The demand for business travel is quite different from that for leisure travel, since it is by nature less 'discretionary', that is, less a matter of personal choice. Business people travel because of the demands of their business. As a result, such travel is less price sensitive, since the company rather than the individual will be footing the bills. Business people tend to make frequent short-duration trips, which are generally taken mid-week rather than at weekends, and travel is not subject to seasonal fluctuations. Travel decisions often have to be taken at short notice, so that they need regular scheduled flights available and a fast and convenient reservations service.

At a basic physiological level, travel can sometimes be essential for health as in the case of treatment overseas for complex surgery, or the need to travel to warm, dry climates to recover from illnesses such as asthma and tuberculosis. These are then survival-related needs. Many people in stressful occupations also need a break from the mental or physical strain of their work to avoid a breakdown in health, and this 'cathartic' travel is no less necessary for survival. Even business travel, usually only thought of in terms of economic need, may be required for the survival of the organisation in the face of overseas competition – but we must also recognise that quite a lot of business travel is in fact taken for prestige purposes – the requirement for first-class travel and top-price hotels, for instance – while conference travel may be ascribed to competence needs.

Many people fail to travel, due to real or imagined fears – the fear of flying, or fear of being attacked. In these cases, the failure to travel is again related to basic safety needs of survival. In these cases, the marketer's responsibility is to overcome such fear, for example, by the national tourist office mounting a campaign to reassure visitors of the safety of their country, or bringing pressure on the government to provide protection for tourists, while airlines have to take steps to educate their clients about air safety. British Airways, for example, have run a series of flights designed for those with a psychological fear of flying.

Our social needs for loving and belonging are often met through package holiday programmes, since many tourists find group tours an excellent way to make new friends or seek romance. Cruises fulfil this function well, as well as providing a recognised outlet for those recently bereaved, who need a change of environment to escape their distress. A desire to appear attractive to others may be achieved by gaining a suntan, despite the health risks. Visiting little known and distant tourist destinations may give tourists prestige in the eyes of their friends who are less travelled. Cultural travel provides opportunities for self-actualisation, the process of achieving or fulfilling one's potential.

These examples will be sufficient to show that travel satisfies many physical, social and psychological needs. They will also have shown us that travel motivation can be both general and specific. We experience the general drive to get away from our present environment, to escape from routine and seek new and different experiences, while at the same time we demonstrate individual motivations to see specific destinations and undertake specific activities while on holiday.

Some of the ways in which tourist needs for physical and cultural experiences are met are shown in Table 4.1. It is important to appreciate, however, that tourists seek to satisfy not one single need but a number of quite distinct needs simultaneously. The most successful products are those which respond best to this 'bundle of needs' within a given market segment. As Pearce says,[4]

> It is not the specific qualities of a destination and its attractions which motivate, but the broad suitability of the destination to fulfil particular psychological needs.

It is perhaps significant that, in a Gallup poll taken in 1983, it was found that if one looks at the countries in Europe to which British tourists aspire to travel, and if differences in cost are ignored, Switzerland, France and Germany are listed as the three favourite destinations, with Spain lying only fourth. Clearly, the bundle of benefits provided by these countries is greater than that provided by Britain's premier package holiday destination.

Having now discussed consumer needs for travel, we can now examine one other important aspect of consumer behaviour, that of decision-making.

Decision-making for the travel purchase

Studies of the decision-making process are becoming more common in tourism research. How decisions are taken, as well as when they are taken, are important factors in helping to understand the consumer purchase.

We earlier discussed the process by which consumers are influenced in product decisions, in models such as AIDA. The process is further

Table 4.1 Tourist needs and the marketing response

Need	Response
Physical	
Rest and relaxation	Beach holidays
	Lakes and mountains
Action and adventure	Trekking
	Ponytrekking, skiing
	Canoeing, sailing
	Safari parks
Health	Gentle walking trails
	Spas
	Health farms
Cultural	
Educational	Lecture cruises
	Study tours
Historical/Archeological	Tours of war sites
	Birthplace museums
	Nile cruises
	Ironbridge Gorge
Political	Tours of Kremlin
	Tours of Berlin
	Tours of UN
	Houses of Parliament
Scientific/Technical	NASA space centre
	Big Pit mining museum
	Car assembly plant
	Hollywood film studio
Arts	Music festivals
	Theatre visits
	Folk dance shows
	Craft or painting holidays
Religion	Mecca
	Lourdes
	'Retreats'
	Oberammergau
Commercial	Shops/restaurants
	Conference facilities
	Freeports
	Craft centres
	Wine/beer fairs

complicated by the degree of risk inherent in the purchase. Obviously, deciding whether to buy a new bar of chocolate involves minimal risk, whereas deciding where to take the annual holiday involves substantial expenditure and a high degree of uncertainty. The consumer often lacks sufficient experience on which to base a decision. Experience is a key element in the learning process, and gaining objective information about new destinations is not easy. For this reason, word of mouth recommendation plays a very significant role in encouraging decisions.

Risk can be reduced in several ways. First, *familiarity* gives confidence and results in the regular repeat purchase of a product; hence the tendency among more conservative holidaymakers to return to their traditional seaside resort year after year, or to buy another holiday from the same tour operator (brand loyalty).

Second, risk can also be reduced by *lowering our expectation* of the product. However, consumers tend to idealise their major purchases, so this is rarely practical in the case of travel purchases. Nevertheless, there is great danger of overselling a travel experience, because of the frame of mind in which holiday purchasers are making their decision.

A third way of reducing risk is to *maximise knowledge*, seeking as much information about the product and selecting the 'best' choice from a wide selection of alternatives. An individual's personality plays a role here, as certain types of people tend to optimise their choice, while others, especially those with authoritarian personalities, consider fewer alternatives and are more easily satisfied. Advance booking is a characteristic of the search for security, reflecting not only the desire to make the booking of one's choice, but also the need to gather and consider information about the product well in advance. The tendency to book later in the UK is not only the result of expectation of bargains, but also reflects the increased sophistication of the British travelling public, who have become more familiar with overseas destinations.

The booking process is protracted, and there are a number of different influences at work here. The interplay between tour operator and travel agent is an interesting case in point.

The tour operator works hard to be included in the initial selection of brochures through brand image and advertising. The clearer and more helpful the brochure, the more likely the operator is to survive the 'homework' stage. It follows that a little known operator whose brochure is poorly produced and 'me too' in style will stand little chance of winning the booking. Hence the chosen strategy of many small operators to specialise and excel in certain types of holidays. Hence also the price and advertising wars between large operators whose products offer very little real difference.

The travel agent is seen as the means to resolve the perceived lack of difference between operators, the easy and safe route to resolve the perceived complexities of price calculation and availability, and ideally as an information resource adding personal knowledge and expertise to back up the information in the brochure. It therefore follows that a travel agent who hasn't read the brochure and can add no information on a potential destination is not meeting consumer expectation and also stands little chance of winning the booking.

In consuming a product, risk is reduced by searching for familiarity. However, tourism by its nature involves some novelty. Hence the common tourist problem of how to balance the need for adventure and new experiences with the need for familiarity and reassurance.

Studies of North American tourists show that this problem is resolved in a number of different ways. First-time US visitors abroad may venture into the border towns of Mexico, where they are close to the 'perceived safety' of their home country and culture. US visitors to Europe frequently make the UK their first stop, as the two countries share a common language and culture. Perceived security may also be increased by travelling to the foreign country in one's own national airline, and by staying in hotel chains operated or owned by a travel company from the home country.

In the case of British tourists, Jersey has successfully promoted the island as a 'bit of France that is British', while Gibraltar is marketed as 'so British, so Mediterranean', effectively combining the appeal of security and familiarity with that of a warm climate in a foreign destination.

The package tour is the marketer's response to the need for familiarity. Tourists travel to mass tourism destinations where they will be in company with others from their own culture, where many locals will be conversant with their language, and where it may be possible to buy familiar food and drinks, but there is scope to sample new foods and different ways of life. The guided tour, particularly when led by a guide from the home country, gives psychological security, while the guide not only acts as 'culture-broker' but also caters to the tourists' social needs by acting as a catalyst in getting members of the group to know one another.

Family group decision-making

Where decisions have to be made together, rather than individually, it is important to understand who participates in the decision, and the degree of influence each member of the group exercises. In family travel, how far is the choice of where to go, and when to go, made by one member of the household, or is it a joint decision by all members of the household? Evidence suggests that women play a much more important role than was formerly thought in the process of deciding the family holidays. An IPC magazine survey undertaken in 1984 found that nearly twice as many women as men played the major role in influencing the holiday choice, while women were also found to be mainly responsible for the planning and organising of holidays. What has to be borne in mind when marketing travel is that, where joint decisions must be made, the parties involved may have different needs and objectives; consequently different messages may have to be directed to women and men. The typical travel brochure, with its pretty bikini-clad models on the cover, appears to be aimed at men, but may also appeal to a fantasy in some women which encourages them to believe that just possibly the holiday will make them become more like the model.

Market segmentation as a guide to marketing planning

It might be helpful to close our discussion of consumer behaviour by reviewing a segmentation exercise undertaken by one of the major tour operators. It has already been noted that the travel market is complex and can be segmented in various ways from destination to age of traveller. A very interesting exercise in segmentation started with the individual and identified different *archetypes* or *mood states* into which consumers could be grouped. These archetypes were by no means 'once and for all' categories. Individuals might well progress between them, with experience. They might also approach, for instance, a second holiday in a rather more cost-conscious mood within the same year.

The research went on to identify what the different groups were looking for from their tour operator – and the differences are very marked indeed, as shown in Table 4.2. This research clearly identifies to the operator opportunities for product differentiation to match the different types of consumers, and gives a strong indication of the advertising messages likely to be most effective in promoting the different products.

In-depth qualitative research of this kind can be invaluable in aiding a company to put together and deliver the kinds of holidays which different market segments are seeking, and then attract them with appropriate promotional themes.

Table 4.2 Tour operator segmentation exercise

Archetype characteristics	Expectations of tour operator by customer
1 Once in a lifetime tripper One-off special trip, e.g. honeymoon, retirement, 25th anniversary. ● high emotional investment ● very high expectations ● expects something memorable ● would like 'perfection'	Tour operator should recognise importance and 'specialness'. Expectation to be pampered and provided with extras. Desire to be treated like a king/queen, not to be one of many.
2 Mainstream package taker Often families with diverse needs within group that includes children. Not confident in own self-sufficiency abroad. ● enjoy sociability of package holidays ● seeking UK on the Mediterranean	Tour operator must take care of everything and provide a buffer against the foreign location. Rep should be helpful but not intrusive, and the focus for a diverse range of facilities and excursions. Familiarity, especially food, is important.
3 Resort repeater Loyal to resort or even hotel, possibly also to operator. Often enjoys being 'old hand' and own expertise. ● repeats a 'perfect' match for own needs ● seeks the security of familiarity ● knows exactly what to expect	Expectation of operator is lower. Wants certain level of comfort and a sense of security. Expects recognition of own knowledge and looks for some degree of sociability from a package. Basically looking for hassle-free organisation at the best price.

Archetype characteristics	*Expectations of tour operator by customer*
4 Up-market package taker Prizes individuality and doesn't want to mix with hoi polloi. Frequently DINKYs or empty nesters (i.e. couples pre- or post-children). ● may take only long-haul packages ● often destination-driven ● 'one-upmanship' a factor	Tour operators should provide something a little out of the ordinary, high quality and a 'tailored' product. There needs to be a sense of individuality and recognition of experience/confidence of the consumer. The fewer other Brits the better.
5 Aspiring individualist Takes fewer packages than up-market package taker above. Often more experienced traveller. Not interested in mass sociability. ● may seek package as not confident of location ● likes sense of 'trail-blazing' ● Often picks less popular destinations	Tour operator is expected to provide efficient expertise and organisation, but no interference. Wants rarity from a package that's 'not a package'.
6 Deal seeker Out for a good deal. Limited desires, e.g. sun, sea, sand, cheap booze, can be satisfied by a number of locations.	Looking for a deal from the operator. Wants 'cheap and cheerful', not 'cheap and nasty'. No costs should be hidden. Still wants effective organisation and help if it is needed.
7 Up-market deal seeker Looking for bargain, but among 'different', up-market holidays. ● often long haul or up-market ● unable or unprepared to pay more ● often experienced in short haul and 'graduating' ● confident via experience	Expects operator to provide a deal, yet still wants high level of looking after and cosseting. Wants guidance and expertise and a holiday that is different but not too different or unknown.
8 Confident individualist Anti-package and sees self as independent traveller. Very price conscious and seeks to achieve one-upmanship over operator. ● wants to be in control ● may do own independent research	Wants operator for cheap price, no interference, avenue for specific enquiries and help in a real emergency.

Questions, tasks and issues for discussion

1 Examine and analyse:

   (a) the factors which led to your own choice of a recent holiday, and
   (b) your ambition to visit any destination in the world.

   What are the motivations behind these choices, and how were they influenced?

2 It is known that travel agents have comparatively little effect in influencing their clients' choice of holiday. Why do you think this is? Can anything be done to alter this situation?

3 Design a holiday which will appeal to an alternative lifestyle market segment, and suggest ways in which the product might be promoted to the market.

4 What evidence is there that the 'trickle down effect' operates in travel? Is the process desirable from a marketing point of view, and if not, can it be arrested?

  In the role of a tourist officer for a resort which is going down-market, suggest how a reversal of this trend might be made possible in the marketing plan.

5 Describe some of the ways by which tourists achieve a satisfactory compromise between their desire for novelty and adventure, and their need for security and familiarity.

Exercise

You have recently taken up a position in the research and development unit in the marketing department of a large tour operator. Research carried out by the unit has shown a significant market gap for holidays for the broadly defined 'middle-aged' – the 35–55 year-old group.

You are required to carry out further research on this market, to identify the types of holidays that this age band demands, following which you are to devise a programme of holidays aimed at this particular age group. You may further segment the market in any way you think fit.

Working in small groups, construct a questionnaire and carry out a survey of people in this age group. Use the results to plan an itinerary which will identify:

● the destination (country, resort)
● the type of accommodation to be used
● the package arrangements (Independent or group? Escorted? What meal arrangements? What activities to be included? Any special considerations?).

Produce a mock-up of a brochure for the programme. Detailed copy and costings are not required.

Your team will be required to make a presentation to an audience of independent travel agents who specialise in unusual holidays, outlining the programme and the reasons why it has been selected.

5 Tourism product policy

After studying this chapter, you should be able to:

- define product policy and understand its importance in the marketing plan
- explain how products are differentiated
- understand the role and importance of branding in the marketing mix
- describe the product life cycle, and the actions necessary to launch a new product and revitalise a flagging one
- understand the concepts of product benefits and added value

What is product policy?

Getting the product right is the single most important activity of marketing. If the product isn't what the market wants, no amount of price adjustment, dependable delivery or brilliant promotion will encourage consumers to buy it – or at least, not more than once, and very few companies produce products which are 'once-in-a-lifetime' buys. On the other hand, if the product produced does satisfy the consumer, the purchase is likely to be repeated, and the purchaser may go on to buy other products offered by the same company, and to recommend that company's products to other consumers: three very strong reasons why a company must make sure the product is right for the market at which it is aimed.

As we indicated in Chapter 1, a *product* is defined as anything that is offered to a market to satisfy a want or need. The term therefore includes tangible goods, services, people, places, organisations or ideas.

The tourism product is really quite a complex one, since it can comprise a place (the holiday destination), a service (a tour operator's package, incorporating the use of an airline seat, hotel room and sometimes other facilities) and on occasion certain tangible products such as free flight bags, or a free bottle of duty-free spirits to encourage booking.

When consumers buy products, they are buying features, of a perceived standard of quality and style which reflects the product's design. The product's image and value may be further enhanced through the use of a brand name, which acts as a cue, helping the consumer to identify a product as of a particular standard. Further enhancement may result from the product's packaging, which both protects the product and increases its attractiveness. The brand may also be indicative of reliable delivery and after sales service. Such characteristics are features of any product. Let us now, by way of example, look at the features of a package holiday.

Let us say Mr and Mrs Jones are looking for a two-week beach holiday abroad. They have two young children aged 8 and 5 accompanying them. They aren't too concerned where they go, as long as it's fairly hot, and the price fits their budget. But in fact they are looking for a complex bundle of features to fit their needs, some of which may not even be spelled out when they book the holiday, since they will presume they are included anyway (but if absent, this would constitute grounds for reasonable complaint). Table 5.1 provides a summary of what the Jones family may be expecting. The list is not necessarily exhaustive, and could be expanded into greater detail, but it is sufficient to demonstrate the complexity of the product being purchased,

Table 5.1 The composition of a package holiday product

Product segment	Features
1 Destination	not too distant in flying time, clean, sandy beaches, reasonable certainty of sunshine, lively entertainment at night, good shops, reasonable prices, interesting excursions, friendly locals, safe to walk about, English widely spoken
2 Airport	convenient local airport, car parking, not too congested, duty frees available
3 Airline	flights at convenient time, reliable, good safety record, thoughtful, polite service. type of aircraft
4 Coach transfers	clean, modern coaches, reliable, competent and friendly driver and courier
5 Hotel	location: accessible to beach, shops, etc. Staff: trustworthy, English speaking, competent, friendly; facilities: well-maintained, attractive décor, quiet at night, adequate public rooms, swimming pool, child care service. Bar with good range of drinks at moderate prices. Adequate size bedroom with balcony, sea view; comfortable beds, phone, colour TV, adequate cupboard space, wood (not wire) hangers, shower, toilet, shaver point, good lighting for make-up. Restaurant/meals: good food, well cooked, served hot, adequate portions, good variety and choice, pleasant atmosphere, comfortable seating, flexible meal hours, fast, polite and friendly service
6 Resort representatives	knowledgeable, competent, friendly, reliable, accessible
7 Tour operator	price reflects good value for money, secure, reliable, offers guarantees, extras
8 Travel agent	convenient, competent, reliable, friendly, pleasant 'shopping atmosphere', extra services provided (e.g. free transfers to airport, free insurance)
9 Miscellaneous	companionable fellow travellers with common interests, 'expectation', widening of general knowledge and interests, pleasant memories of experience

and the range of needs it is designed to satisfy. Almost inevitably, there will be some conflict between these needs, such as between cost and quality, or between the different needs of each member of the family (what Mrs Jones finds attractive hotel décor may not appeal to her husband, while the children's idea of entertainment will differ from their parents). Consumer decisions invariably require some compromise.

In fact, the needs listed in Table 5.1 are not *core needs* at all, but rather *second-level* needs. Core needs are those which give rise to the demand for a holiday in the first place, as discussed in the chapter on consumer behaviour. Mr Jones may be expressing his need to get away from the work environment, while Mrs Jones seeks a break from the responsibility of caring for her children 24 hours a day, from cooking and from housework, and may be looking to make new friends and widen her social contacts. Underlying needs of fitness, status, adventure and romance may all be implicit in the demand for this particular holiday.

Differentiating the product

It is important to recognise at this point that what consumers are demanding are not products, or even features of products, but the benefits these products offer. What is sought is the satisfaction of needs; or, as Theodore Levitt amusingly put it, 'purchasing agents don't buy quarter inch drills; they buy quarter inch holes'. Our needs are very diverse, and the greater number of needs that can be satisfied through the purchase of one product, the more attractive that product becomes to the consumer.

It is this essential role of marketing, to produce

added benefits, which enables the marketer to distinguish one product from another. The marketer must ask: 'If the product which I am supplying offers no appreciable benefits beyond those offered by my competitor, why shouldn't my customers buy my competitors' products?'

The need to invest distinctive benefits in a product gives rise to the concept of the *Unique Selling Proposition* (USP). This is the feature or features in a product which offer unique benefits not found in those of its competitors. There are a number of holiday companies specialising in the organisation of package tours aimed at the young (18–30) travel market. While the product offered is similar in many respects, companies focusing on this market segment seek ways to differentiate their product from others. Thus for example, 2wenties emphasises that their hotels are used exclusively by their customers, while Club 18–30 places stress on the added adventure and, some might say, almost blatant sexual promise of their holidays.

Companies will distinguish products in a wide variety of ways. Some may provide added features at an inclusive price, others may choose to emphasise the reliability of the product on offer. Quality is an important attribute of many products, and not only premium-priced products. Japanese car manufacturers have established an excellent international reputation for their products by the application of careful quality control in their manufacturing process, ensuring better finish and reliability than most of their rivals throughout the price range. In the travel industry, certain airlines have chosen to identify their product with reliability ('multi-million-mile pilots', 'on-time arrivals'), and Thomson Holidays have chosen to stress their careful process of checking foreign resorts and hotels to reduce complaints and improve customer satisfaction.

At the opposite extreme, companies have also tried to distinguish their product by making it cheaper than their rivals, with their marketing emphasis on the reduction of production costs and/or low promotional expenditure. This will reduce unit profits, but the resultant increase in volume demand created by the attraction of low price can be sufficient inducement to adopt such a policy to establish a leading market share. The 'pile it high, sell it cheap' philosophy that was at one time the principle of Tesco Supermarkets has been taken up by a great many British companies, sometimes at the expense of quality control. The travel industry, too, has fallen victim to the belief that low price is the key to success; and over time, the belief becomes a self-fulfilling prophecy, since if companies promote low price, their customers will come to believe the message and demand low price. However, they are not necessarily willing to forgo the other attributes they seek, such as reliability and quality, with the result that overall satisfaction falls.

Tour operators will concede that they receive a higher ratio of complaints on, and their customers often have higher expectations of, their cheapest holidays! It must be remembered that price is only one aspect of a product, and countries such as Germany, Sweden and Switzerland, which have relatively high labour costs, have nevertheless successfully marketed products on the basis of value for money and high quality. Their success in export sales, at the expense of cheaper British products, is all too apparent, while British products that have gained an international reputation – Jaguar and Rolls Royce cars, Pringle knitwear, Royal Doulton china, Tiptree jams – have done so on the basis of reliability and quality.

It is significant that in the late 1980s Tesco itself changed its marketing approach, no longer relying on the old 'pile it high, sell it cheap' concept.

Good design, or 'style', can also form the basis of product differentiation. This is perhaps more readily appreciated in physical products, and the success of companies such as Gucci clothing and accessories, Bang and Olufsen hi-fi, Braun consumer durables or Olivetti office equipment spring readily to mind as examples of companies where style is closely associated with both distinctiveness and quality. Good design provides three important aids to the consumer: it represents the perceived value of the product, it enables the company to create a 'personality' for its products, and by judicious periodical alterations in styling, it creates demand through replacement with more fashionable new styles.

Style also has a role to play in travel, too, both in terms of the physical features of the travel product and the image which certain companies have generated. The design and décor of hotels, ships and aircraft provide opportunities for companies to personalise their products, as well as periodically to update them, while some hotels and carriers have actually played on the nostalgia of travellers, with the Orient Express perhaps being the outstanding example of 'style' in travel design.

Style can be a two-edged sword, however. Hotels are as subject as other products to the vagaries of fashion, and must allow within their marketing plans for frequent refurbishing and new themes to attract their customers.

The creation of a particular image or personality for a company or its products is a particularly astute form of marketing, especially in those companies in which physical design can play no part. In this case, the marketer aims to create an 'aura' for the product, distinguishing it from its competitors in sometimes indefinable ways. Companies such as Jules Verne Travel are offering a product which is perceived as distinct from competitors, even though they may be selling the same destination and accommodation. In the airline industry before deregulation, when differentiation under International Air Transport Association (IATA) regulations was virtually excluded, none the less certain airlines were able to develop distinct 'personalities'. Eagle Airlines created an entirely new market between New York and Bermuda, for example, by developing an image of a friendly, easy-going airline quite distinctive from other airlines serving the route. A similar style was evident in Freddie Laker's brief foray into 'Skytrain' and is apparent in Richard Branson's Virgin Airways – helped, no doubt, by the ebullient personalities of their respective chairmen, but not dependent upon that alone. Certain hotels are renowned for their atmosphere – the Algonquin and Plaza in New York, Brown's and Claridges in London – giving them a unique quality that cannot be captured by their competitors. A history or tradition is obviously helpful in creating this atmosphere.

Marketing managers must never forget that their customers are buying experiences, and the atmosphere of a hotel, cruise ship or destination is a major contribution to overall tourist satisfaction.

Branding

Giving a product a brand name is not only a useful way of differentiating it from others but also a means of adding perceived value. This has implications for the price that can be charged for the product and the profit margins attainable on each unit sold.

A brand may be defined as a 'name, sign, symbol or design, or combination of these, intended to identify the products of an organisation and

Fig. 5.1 Some examples of logos in use in the travel and tourism industry

distinguish them from those of competitors'. This name , symbol or combination is referred to as a 'logotype' or *logo*. The brand may be registered as a trademark, legally protecting the company's right to use it exclusively in the home country and overseas. Registering the brand also makes it an offence for competitors to copy the design too closely; conversely, to be acceptable for registration, a brand must be sufficiently distinctive from others already registered.

Branding a product is one of the oldest forms of marketing technique, but has become a potent tool of marketing in the twentieth century. Virtually anything can be branded, from matches (Swan Vestas) to petrol (Shell Oil) and turkeys (Bernard Matthews has been a notable success story). Service industries have also become aware of the benefits of branding, and brand names are beginning to become household names in tourism. One has only to think of aircraft livery, the funnel colours of shipping companies, such familiar logos as those sported by Holiday Inn, American Express or Thomas Cook, to realise the extent to which branding has become important to the industry. Figure 5.1 offers some common examples of branding in travel.

The benefits of branding

Ascribing a brand name or symbol to a product offers a marketer a number of advantages. First, it helps to identify a particular product and distinguish it from competitors, as we have described. Second, it becomes associated with the particular benefits offered by the product, acting as a 'cue' to purchasers in their decision-making. In particular, it indicates to purchasers what level of quality they can expect, since a range of products marketed under the same brand name will carry similar expectations of quality standard (and for this reason it is essential that companies branding their products exercise very strong control over the quality of their production). Third, where the product is intangible, such as is the case with tourism products, since it cannot be seen or sampled in advance, the purchase of a branded product helps the consumer to avoid risk.

Consumers who are satisfied with the brand purchase are likely to repeat the purchase and, over time, to become regular purchasers of the brand. Repeat purchase becomes instinctive and habitual over time, at which point we can describe the customer as being 'brand loyal'. Some travel companies are already dependent upon brand loyalty. Cruise companies such as P & O, for example, claim as many as 60 per cent of their customers are regular repeat purchasers; it is also becoming a feature of the mass market tour operators, although the present emphasis on price tends to undermine efforts to build brand loyalty.

Branding becomes a key tool in market segmentation strategy. Associating a brand with a particular segment of the market can help to expand a company's market share at a time when the total market for a product is saturated. As one example of this in the field of tangible products, consider the range of different washing powders (arguably one of the most homogeneous products available) offered by Procter & Gamble or Unilever in their attempt to widen their respective companies' market shares.

Major tour operators such as Thomson Holidays and First Choice Holidays have developed new brand names for their products as part of their market segmentation strategy. Thomson's use of the 'Skytours' brand, for instance, distances that programme aimed at the cheaper end of the market from the broader, more up-market programme sold under the Thomson banner. Similarly, First Choice retained the Sovereign brand (which began life owned by British Airways) because of its strong brand image and association with top-end quality holidays.

Finally, use of a brand name enables companies to employ a technique known as *brand stretching* – the introduction of new products into an existing range under the same brand name. In the Fast Moving Consumer Goods (FMCG) market, this is a critical factor in the launch of new products by companies such as Heinz or Campbells. Well-established travel brands such as Thomson or Cosmos could be stretched to include new ranges of holidays such as cruises or seat-only flight programmes, enabling them to gain immediate credibility in the market, as well as willingness on the part of travel agents to deal with the new products. 'Big name' brands become increasingly important as the competition intensifies to get brochures displayed on travel agency racks.

A final advantage of brand stretching, for instance with Cosmos Travjet, is the fact that promotional spend works in favour of all the brands – regardless of the specific brand being promoted – through increased recognition of the core name Cosmos.

Branding decisions

If a company decides to introduce a brand, it can do so in a number of ways. It can introduce a 'blanket', or family brand name, as is the case with Heinz; or, as with Procter & Gamble, it can introduce different brand names for each product it manufactures. There are examples of each of these approaches in travel. Accor Hotels trade under a range of company names (Sofitel, Novotel, Mercure, Ibis and Formule 1), while Forte may choose to project a family image with some properties, and differentiate with other products (Forte Crest Hotels, Forte Posthouse Hotels, Forte Heritage Inns, Forte Grand Hotels and The Exclusive Portfolio). International branding has been established with the takeover of the Meridien chain from Accor Hotels in 1994. Scheduled airlines may run charter offshoots under different brand names (Lufthansa: Condor, Iberia: Aviaco).

A new brand name may be chosen if an existing brand is too closely associated with a particular type of product, making it difficult to stretch and encompass new concepts. Companies such as Yugotours, Olympic, Austrotours or Paris Travel, whose original choice of name reflected the policy of specialisation in specific travel destinations, would find it difficult to introduce new destinations under the same brand name (although some have tried to do so – and indeed, Yugotours, prior to its collapse, tried to generate a new name and new destinations when travel to Yugoslavia was decimated),

whereas a company with a more ⌐ name, such as Global or Cosmos, w restricted.

In first developing a brand, the objectᴠ the brand need to be carefully thought out. brand is not just a means of drawing attention to the product: it should stand for something. It must act as a cue to the product characteristics, including the product's quality. Is it to be low, medium or premium quality? Is it to offer the economic appeal of 'value for money', or the more emotional appeal of high price for a status product? Think of the diverse messages associated with clothing labels such as Harrods, C & A and St Michael to realise the immense power of brands to communicate effective messages about product characteristics.

Branding provides the opportunity for a company to enhance its corporate image, because how consumers feel about a brand reflects their feeling about the company. Companies such as Shell use their brand names as a means of enhancing the corporate image, and this is reflected in travel companies such as Swissair, Cunard and Hilton Hotels.

Brand sponsorship

When a firm decides to introduce a new brand, it has several options open to it. First, it may choose to develop and use a brand exclusively for itself. Second, it can manufacture the brand of another organisation under licence. This applies equally to a service product. Thomas Cook, for example, buys in holidays of Jules Verne, among others, to market under its own name.

Third, it can franchise a brand. In this situation, the company owning the brand allows others to sell the product, with certain preconditions attached, such as the obligation to purchase raw materials exclusively from the supplying company, or the obligation to pay a proportion of the earnings to the franchiser (royalty payments). Franchising offers the benefits of rapid expansion for a brand, and the security, on the part of consumers, of consistent and recognised standards of quality. To be effective, though, the brand must be well established in the market efore it is launched as a franchised product. Fast food firms in particular have expanded rapidly with the use of franchises, so that companies such as Kentucky Fried Chicken and McDonalds Hamburgers have become household names world-wide. In the travel industry, Holiday Inns and Hilton International are just two hotel chains which have benefited from the use of franchising, and other sectors of the travel industry are just beginning to experiment with the technique. Franchising as a distributive technique is discussed in Chapter 8.

What makes a good brand name?

A number of guidelines have been drawn up by marketing theorists for the development of a good brand name. Since a critical function of the brand name is to obtain immediate recognition for both the product and its attributes, the name or symbol has to communicate these attributes with appropriate imagery. Names must be easy to pronounce and remember, as well as helping to convey the product's benefits. Symbols should be distinctive, their design and colour supporting the product concept.

Although corporate names, often associated with the founder (Thomson, Hilton) remain popular brand names, words conveying the nature of the product or with pleasant associations (Sunair, Serenissima) help to reinforce the benefits in the purchaser's mind. 'Catchy' brand names (Britrail) retain the parent organisation's name but reduce it to a more easily memorised logo.

It is important, particularly in such an international field as travel, that brand names are registerable in all the countries in which the company can expect to operate, and that these names are both easy to pronounce and to remember by those speaking foreign languages. Words may need to be screened to ensure they don't project a different association in other languages: the French may be hard put if they were to try to market their popular soft drink 'Pschitt' in Britain There are companies which will help international brand name choice by screening new product names in advance and singling out any judged unsuitable for any reason – a wise precaution.

The simplicity of a word or illustration will enhance recall and recognition. This is important in the travel industry, where the brand may have to be displayed on a fast-moving object such as an aircraft or coach.

Finally, one must remember that there are always examples of companies that have managed to break all the rules and nevertheless succeeded. Who would have imagined that Kawasaki or Mitsubishi could become household words in Britain? Or that Tjaereborg could be successful in selling package holidays to the British? These companies succeeded in establishing a reputation through the quality of their products alone; but this is not to deny that their marketing task might have been easier had they been marketing their products under names such as Honda or Touropa.

A brand will enhance the corporate identity of an organisation so that product and company become inseparable in the minds of the consumers. But to gain maximum impact, it must be used in all areas of the company's marketing; on stationery, brochures, representatives' uniforms, shopfront, literature racks and in promotional aids such as flight bags, carrier bags or other 'give-away' material. This represents the 'total marketing' approach so essential in modern marketing.

Repositioning a brand

Periodically, it may prove necessary for a firm to reposition its brand; that is to say, to modify the brand in some way so as to widen its appeal or direct its appeal to another market segment. This becomes necessary when, for example, the original market associated with the brand experiences a decline or when fashions change. This usually, although not invariably, also requires a modification in the product itself. Since the early 1980s, the marketing strategy of several Japanese car companies is a good example of periodic repositioning. Originally marketed as a cheap but reliable alternative to the domestic product in Britain, the companies have moved 'up-market' by repositioning and refining the image of the cars sold, leading in some instances to products which are designed to appeal to a sophisticated market willing to spend for added refinement. In doing so, the companies have developed a high status image for their range, adding product benefits and increasing profit margins. This is an exercise which must be undertaken with considerable care, however; images, once established, may be hard to adjust. Tesco has not found it easy to rid itself of its original product concept and move up-market.

A good example of brand repositioning in tourism is that of the resort of Torbay in Devon, embracing the Torquay and Paignton coastal area. Research suggested that the image of this region was confusing to the public, and, coupled with a downward trend in holidaytaking at English seaside resorts generally, it was apparent that a new image would have to be found for the area if customers were to be attracted. The brand and its image were changed, to recreate an earlier theme of the 'English Riviera', reminding holidaymakers that the area enjoyed a comparatively good climate. Even with a small budget for promotion, the area was able to increase its visitor numbers and reposition the product in the public's eye to make it a more attractive proposition.

What's in a name? The power of branding

We have already discussed the fact that there are many different segments of the travel market with very different requirements. While this can be very helpful for the smaller 'niche' operator to create a very precise image and positioning for a specialist product, it makes it difficult for the mass market holiday operator to create a brand image that isn't 'bland'.

Research bears out how strongly the name in particular, but also the logo and design styles of different brands, can affect the perception of the holidays represented by those brands.

The under-40s in particular are very design conscious and are influenced by good design as implying a good operator. Birds and sunsets have to be used with care as they are seen as rather unimaginative and tired. Colour too can condition expectation, for example a lot of blue in the brochure cover design immediately positions the holidays as 'Lakes and Mountains' holidays.

While there is such a variety of different requirements among holidaymakers, research shows a remarkable degree of agreement among consumers about what they don't like. Basically, all consumers were found to dislike:

1 Regimentation or any perceived suppression of individuality: whether it was mothers reacting against the standard issue T-shirts for the children's club, or single holidaymakers dreading attempts by reps to organise congas.
2 Crowds: mothers feared they would lose children; young singles needed peace on the beach to catch up on sleep and get over the hangover before the next night of revelry; older people saw crowded beaches as down-market, and believed they could afford a bit of peace and quiet.
3 Children: all groups united in a loathing of too many children. Singles were unwilling to be woken early by other people's children, and feared families complaining about the noise that they themselves made at night. Empty nesters whose own children had left home felt they were 'free at last' to enjoy a holiday without children. Even mothers recoiled from the idea of too many children and wanted just a few potential friends for their own children (with whom the latter could then go off and play, relieving mothers of the need to entertain).

These fears have a strong impact on the reaction of consumers to different brands, and affect the likelihood of selecting a particular operator's brochure for consideration.

Thus Thomson 'Small and Friendly' is very positive, in that it allays fears of crowds and large regimented resorts. First Choice 'Freespirit' again has strong connotations of individuality. Names such as 'Transun', 'The Sun Club' and 'Fanfare' all evoked images of crowds and regimentation.

As well as countering negative aspects, consumers are looking for a certain cachet and implication of quality in the name. Thus any name that sounds 'silly', or would be embarrassing to mention to 'the Jones's', puts an operator at a disadvantage. So, for instance, while a holiday booked with First Choice 'Sovereign' is considered up-market and brings the consumer positive social status, the identical holiday branded 'Sunflower' was viewed much less positively.

This is even true of names that describe the nature of the holiday very accurately. Singles holidays have built up such a poor reputation that it is slightly embarrassing to admit to having gone on one, even among avid consumers of such holidays. It follows that even a hint of such an image is a large turn-off to non-singles. Thus names like 'Spree' invoke negative reactions among all consumers.

Bland and unimaginative names for the tour operator or brand conjure up the image of a rather unimaginative and 'ordinary' holiday. Asked what kind of company is the fictitious 'Sun Star', consumers read a tremendous amount into the name. Sun Star, they said, must be:

- a Mediterranean operator
- cheap and cheerful
- basic sun and sand holidays
- operating from a shabby 1960s office block in Oxford Street, London
- rather dodgy and disreputable.

Asked what kind of company is 'First Choice Holidays' (before Owners Abroad had adopted the name, and therefore at this point an equally fictitious name), consumers were united in declaring that it must be:

- operating to a wide choice of destinations
- providing quality but not dauntingly up-market
- not just sun and sand, but promising more
- operating from a plate-glass high-rise office
- a very professional company with uniforms and BMW cars outside.

The product mix

Few companies produce a single product. Companies are therefore faced with making marketing decisions on the mix of products which they proposed to offer to their customers. The product mix comprises the range of different product lines the company produces (the *product width*), together with the number of variants offered within each product line (the *product depth*). A white goods manufacturer such as Hoover, for example, will have to decide on the range of products it will manufacture (washing machines, dryers, dishwashers, vacuum cleaners, toasters, irons, etc.) as well as what options will be made available in each product – different motors, designs, capacity, colours, and so on. Such decisions have implications for the whole marketing mix. Different products may be targeted at different market segments, for example, requiring different advertising and promotional strategies. Some products may be marketed in an intensely competitive environment, with consequent implications for pricing, and profit margins. Some, because of technical complexity or other factors, will need exceptional sales back-up, while others may be suitable for self-selection, affecting distribution strategies.

In the manufacturing process, a critical factor is to what extent existing resources such as machinery and skilled labour can be used in making diverse products. If a machine has spare capacity and can be used in the manufacture of a new product line, this may make all the difference as to whether it will prove profitable for the company to make the new line. For each product line, the manager must be knowledgeable about the market; who is buying the product and why, how competitive it is against those of rival organisations, what market share the product enjoys, the level of sales achieved, and the contribution it makes to overall revenue and profits. Such knowledge will enable further decisions to be made about new products: should existing products be strengthened or extended, should some options be withdrawn, should new product lines be introduced and should such products be consistent with the existing product range, or would it be better for the company to diversify into entirely new lines?

Just as with any other business, a travel or tourism business must also decide its product width and depth. A large mass market operator has to make a number of critical marketing decisions.

Although at first glance one might be inclined to think that a tour operating programme is a single product line, in fact the nature of package holidays makes them quite distinctive, appealing to different market segments and satisfying different needs. For this reason, a company may organise its products into separate divisions, under separate product managers, producing separate brochures, and even operating these holidays under different brand names. Thomson, in addition to operating its winter and summer sun programmes, offers long-haul holidays, lakes and mountains holidays, programmes for elderly people ('Young at Heart'), as well as holiday programmes under separate brand names ('Skytours' and 'Horizon'), and even some brands operated as quite distinct divisions from the mainstream company, with a separate distribution system (Portland Holidays). Within each of these programmes, decisions must be made on product depth: what holiday length to offer (3, 7, 10, or 14 days)? From which airports to operate? To which destinations and airports? How will the price of each product be determined in order to achieve the overall target profitability for the company?

Sometimes, as we have seen with branding, lines can be 'stretched', to encompass new market segments. Such decisions might be taken if the current market is experiencing slow growth, or the company finds itself increasingly under attack from the competition. A company at the bottom end of the market may find profits squeezed, and attempt to reposition its products further up the market to allow a greater margin of profit; or a company which has focused on the upper end of the market may choose to widen its appeal by reaching a larger market, capitalising on its reputation for quality in the top-market field. Such policies carry the inherent danger that the public image of the company and its markets may become confused, causing it to lose its niche and original marketing strengths. Some shipping companies, for example, in their attempt to widen their appeal to reach new mass markets for cruising, downgraded the product, thereby losing the confidence of their loyal, original customers. It is interesting to note that this lesson was learned and the experience acted upon. P & O, in taking over Princess Cruises, retained both the distinctive names and separate marketing activities for the two companies, who drew their clientele from discrete markets, while Cunard, in purchasing the former Norwegian ships *Vistafjord* and *Sagafjord*, retained distinctive marketing policies for the two ships although absorbing them into the Cunard shipping division.

The product life cycle

Although the exact duration of a product's life cycle cannot be forecast, all products exhibit characteristic life cycles, which can be illustrated graphically, as in Fig. 5.2.

The 'S' curve of this graph indicates that typically a product will experience slow initial sales after launch, while it is still comparatively unknown, with accelerating sales as it becomes better known and its reputation established. Steady growth is then achieved until almost all the consumers likely to buy the product have done so, at which point sales even out. The product also faces increasing competition as its sales expand, so that at saturation point it may be fighting harder to retain its existing share of a stagnant market. If newer products are seen as better than the existing one, sales will decline. At this point the company must take some action, either to restore the fortunes of the product or to kill it off.

This theoretical model holds true for all products, including tourism. A destination will gradually become known to tourists, who are initially attracted in small numbers. As it becomes more popular, and exploited by other carriers and tour operators, sales will rise rapidly; perhaps a different market is attracted. The uniqueness of

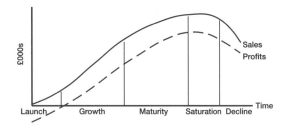

Fig. 5.2 The product life cycle

the resort is lost, and it becomes another mass market destination, appealing to a more down-market holidaymaker. The expansion of hotels and other facilities at the resort may lead to a surplus of supply over demand, while the despoliation of the resort may make it less attractive to the holiday market, who will move on elsewhere. Eventually, the resort may decline to a point where tourism is no longer significant and other industries may be encouraged into the region, or the local authority decides to take action to improve the appeal of the destination again.

Of course, each product has its unique life cycle. In some cases, this pattern of growth–maturity–decline may be quite rapid (skateboards, Rubik's cube, novelty items) while in others, the product can sell at saturation level for a very long period (Oxo). It is also important to recognise that brands are subject to similar life cycle stages, although generally of a shorter duration. Clearly, the marketing manager must be aware of what stage in the life cycle the brand, as well as the product, has reached. As competition increases, brand life cycles tend to shorten, requiring the introduction of new marketing strategies designed either to increase sales or to kill off one brand to make way for a new one.

Forecasting product life cycles, and when a product is about to move into a new stage, is clearly no easy matter, although the danger signals heralding a decline are clear enough – declining sales or market share, especially in relation to one particular brand or product in the product line. There is evidence to show that when life cycle forecasting is attempted, it can prove surprisingly accurate. More generally, however, an understanding of the relationship between a product and its life cycle enables marketing managers to plan their campaigns more effectively and to be in a better position to judge product sales and profit potential.

As can be seen from Fig. 5.2, as profits rise and fall at different stages of the life cycle, the extent to which a particular product will contribute to overall profit objectives of the firm can be anticipated, based on its position in the life cycle. At the launch stage, the marketing costs associated with a new product will be substantial, as the company tries to bring the new product to the attention of its market. Only as sales accelerate will these costs be recovered and the company start making a profit. Highest profitability is generally achieved at the maturity stage, with profits falling back thereafter as sales decline, although by careful manipulation it may be possible to maintain high profit levels at advanced stages, by reducing advertising expenditure and allowing the product to 'live on its reputation'. This is known as 'milking a cash cow', and as long as loyal purchasers continue to purchase the product, it may be worth the company's while to continue to produce it.

The value in understanding the nature of the product life cycle is in its relationship with marketing strategy. It will alert the company to the need for positive action at the *threshold point*, where some change to strategy will be essential if the product is to continue. But beyond this, the marketing mix will be different for every stage of the life cycle.

First of all, the type of consumer who purchases the product may be different when a new product is introduced, compared with those purchasing the product at a later stage in the cycle. This fact enables a company to use a market segmentation approach based on 'lifestyle'. Early buyers of a new product are frequently experimenters, willing to take chances for the novelty or status of being in possession of a little known product. This market segment will generally have more disposable income, and will be more 'value-conscious' than 'price-sensitive'. The product image will be based on its uniqueness, and its appeal to status or curiosity. Advertising and promotion will be aimed at communicating this message to a specific market, using the most suitable channels and giving potential consumers maximum information about the product's benefits. Price at this point may be relatively high. The system of distribution may be fairly selective, since it may be difficult for the company to support, or gain acceptability from, a wide selection of distributive outlets.

Once the product is well established, and has achieved a wide market through a process of emulation, competitors will have introduced their own version of the product into the market. Faced with a growing choice of products, the consumer may become confused and uncertain about which to select. The marketer's role then becomes one of persuading and constantly reminding consumers about the product's benefits, ensuring convenience of purchase by maximising distributive outlets, manipulating price to keep the product competitive and reinforcing the brand image associated with the product.

Finally, as sales peak and falter, the company has to look at the merits for revitalising the product, or allowing it to decline slowly, or killing it off and planning a replacement.

Revitalising a product

There are many different ways in which a company can rejuvenate its product, and the method it will choose will depend on the reason or reasons for the product's initial decline. If this occurred through the introduction of a new competitive product with additional benefits, the company might choose to add similar benefits to its own product, to add new but different benefits, or to reduce the present price and emphasise its value for money perhaps trying to reach a new, more price-sensitive market in doing so. If on the other hand in the company's view the competitive product is not superior to its own, the decision may be taken merely to increase advertising spend, or introduce sales promotion to regain market share. Marketing is about selecting strategies which are either designed to counteract threats, or to take advantage of opportunities in the marketplace. If you remember the 'four Ps' of marketing, you will realise that the action a firm can take is limited to one of four areas: it can alter the *product*, the *price*, the *promotional* campaign, or the *place* (where and how the product can be bought). Let us take an example.

Maddington Hall: revitalising a product

Maddington Hall is an English stately home open to the public between Easter and the end of October each year. It is not a major visitor attraction, but has the appeal of a smaller home which has been in the hands of the present family for over three hundred years. It has historical connections with the English Civil War, and prior to that was the home of a leading member of Queen Elizabeth I's court. There are also links with the USA through the settling of some members of the family at the beginning of the eighteenth century in New Jersey.

The house attracts over 20 000 visitors a year, but in recent years the pattern has shown a steady decline:

Entrants to Maddington Hall, 1983–94

1983	27 300 (peak year)
1984	27 120
1985	26 580
1986	20 084
1987	21 312
1988	22 033
1989	22 441
1990	18 256
1991	18 002
1992	18 334
1993	18 457
1994	18 448

The decline in 1986, and the sharp downturn in 1990 and 1991 were attributed to the fall-off in American visitors in those years. The combination of recession, the Gulf War and poor spring weather in Britain held domestic visits down in 1991. Moreover, there was no compensating increase in visitors from EU countries, especially Germany, in spite of a steady increase in European visitors to Britain, nor did the house benefit from the general increase in domestic summer visitors to visitor attractions following a good summer. More worrying, however, has been the relatively static market that the attraction had experienced in the previous three years; the house is clearly not recovering in spite of a slow but persistent recovery in the economy as a whole. This failure to pick up in the mid-1990s is of particular concern.

Management faces the following choices. It can spend more money on advertising; but income from the house is barely enough to pay for upkeep and running costs, and the budget for promotion is very low. Because of the diversity of the market, it would be unrealistic to be able to advertise directly to overseas visitors, and much of the budget is spent on publishing a leaflet which is left in hotels and other places frequented by visitors. Attempts to interest coach operators and tour operators to include the house in packages have been unsuccessful, as the hall is not seen by the trade as sufficiently famous or interesting in itself to attract a market.

It could lower the entry price, but it is believed that this would result in a fall in revenue, as the increase in numbers attracted would be insufficient to make up for lost revenue. It could even increase the price, if it is believed that the added revenue will more than offset the fall in visitors.

It could also consider ways in which the product could be made more attractive to a wider market. For example, it could seek additional revenue by becoming more commercial – adding tea-rooms, souvenir shops or other revenue-producing facilities, or staging events such as the re-creation of Civil War battles or jousting tournaments to attract larger crowds on specific days of the year. If willing, the owner could arrange to preside over candle-lit dinners for exclusive groups of visitors who would be willing to pay handsomely for the privilege of meeting him and his family (particularly if titled). Some of these activities would need considerable capital expenditure, requiring a bank loan or other means of raising funds. Management would have to consider carefully whether this expense would result in a big enough jump in attendance to ensure profitability.

Finally, ways could be considered of improving the distribution, for example, by identifying specialist tour operators abroad who could be interested in marketing the attraction, or by joining a consortium of other attractions in the region, or a group of stately homes who would produce a joint leaflet reaching a wider audience.

Whatever decision is made, it needs to be carefully thought through and researched. Each choice would need to be considered on its own merits, just as in the case of the launch of a new product.

Launching a new product

Launching a new product, be it aircraft, ferry route, hotel or tour package, is the riskiest undertaking in marketing. The statistical failure rate of new products is daunting, but the likelihood of product failure can be reduced (though never totally removed) by following a process of careful screening. But we should be quite clear about what is meant by a 'new product'. Improvements to an existing product can render that product so new as to make it seen by prospective purchasers as a genuinely new product. Similarly, if an existing product is launched to a new market unfamiliar with it, that product is also, to all intents and purposes, a new product. This can best be illustrated by Fig. 5.3.

		Market	
		existing	new
Product	new	introduce new product to present market	launch of new product to new market
	existing	modification to existing product for present market	reposition present product to attract new market

Fig. 5.3 New products

Clearly, the least risk is taken by the company which chooses to modify an existing product to make it more attractive to the present market – by adding additional benefits, for instance. If the product is losing its appeal to the present market, it may be feasible to *reposition* the product, that is, to direct its appeal to a different market segment – or to sell the product overseas instead of to domestic consumers. This may also call for changing the concept of the product to make it more appealing to a new type of consumer. Another alternative is to develop a genuinely new product (or new brand) to be sold to one's present consumers. The appeal of this is that if the company has an established reputation, the likelihood is that present satisfied customers will be prepared to give the new product a trial also. Finally, the company can choose to introduce a genuinely new product to a new market segment – a double risk, but one where research may show significant profit potential in the long run, hence a gamble worth taking.

It is difficult to determine exactly when a

product can be termed genuinely 'new'. Most products we buy are advances on and modifications of existing products, but every now and again a concept is so original and different from any other product on the market that it can be defined as totally new. The ball-point pen, although a modification of existing writing instruments, used technology so totally distinct from anything employed before that it must be accepted as unique, as must the photocopier or the folding bicycle. In travel and tourism, Concorde offered a totally new concept in air travel, while the motel was distinctive enough from the traditional hotel to be termed a new product. Billy Butlin, looking in the 1930s for a way of keeping seaside visitors entertained in all weathers, introduced the concept of the holiday camp, which was unlike any existing form of holiday at the time.

Market gaps

The aim with any new product is to find the 'market gap' – a product opportunity with a ready market which has not yet been tapped. Again, this is derived from taking a market-orientated approach to new product development, in which the first step is to see what new products, or modifications of existing products, are wanted by consumers. The high cost of labour in Scandinavian hotels was resulting in prohibitively high prices for hotel food; the solution was to introduce self-service breakfasts which, although a break from the traditional service expected in hotels, proved to be very popular with hotel guests because it both reduced prices and offered a comprehensive choice of quantity and menu selection. The *Sea Goddess* cruise ships incorporated an intriguing drop-down stern which converted the ship, when anchored, into a floating base from which passengers could swim or windsurf – a marketing breakthrough to reach a new type of clientele for cruising. Luxury coaches have been converted to appeal to business executives, by altering the layout of seats and making it possible to hold meetings round a table while travelling. All these concepts are based on modifying existing products,

but in doing so, making them sufficiently distinctive to offer substantial advantages over existing products and filling wants, whether expressed or unexpressed, of consumers. But the launch of each of these products should be more than a hit-or-miss gamble based on some executive's hunch. It should be the end product of a process of new product development which is carefully structured at each stage of its development.

Why do products fail?

Before looking at the process of new product development, we need to ask ourselves why so many products fail. It is not enough to say that this is simply the outcome of too much competition. Products have succeeded in exceptionally competitive markets, while others have failed despite having no serious competition. Again, explanation for the failure must lie within one of the four Ps.

If the product is not really new – if it is only an attempt to emulate existing products on the market, offering no appreciable advantages over what is currently available – it stands a poor chance of success. It may be that the competition in the marketplace is already too great to give the new product much scope for success; but oversupply in itself does not threaten a new product. When Holiday Inns announced plans to build a new hotel in Liverpool in the 1970s, hoteliers poured scorn on the idea; the city was already over-supplied with hotel rooms, and present hotels were achieving poor occupancy levels. But the hotel chain had correctly identified its market. The existing business clients of hotels in the city were dissatisfied with the facilities available, but their business required them to be in the city. When they were offered a more modern hotel, with the facilities they preferred, there was a rapid switch to the new hotel and away from the more traditional hotels, some of which were soon forced to close.

This is a simple illustration of the fact that there is more than one kind of demand. In fact, four distinct kinds of demands can be listed:

1 *Existing demand* the demand which results from inadequate supply of the products the consumers want.
2 *Displacement demand* the demand resulting from the dissatisfaction experienced by current consumers.
3 *Created demand* the demand which marketers can develop, which results from wants that are latent and unrecognised by consumers, but can be awakened and promoted by effective marketing.
4 *Future demand* the demand that will arise naturally in the future as a result of demographic or other changes in the population.

Projections on the future sales potential of the new product should take into account all four of these demands.

The product must also be sold at the right price. What is a 'right price' for a product must clearly depend on many different factors, which are discussed at length in Chapter 6. Suffice to say at this point that the price must be right in relation to other, competitive products, providing an adequate level of profit for the company while remaining within the range which the market can bear.

While no amount of promotion will sell a poor product, the promotion must be adequate to accomplish its task. Unless consumers are made aware of the product, no matter how good it is it will not be bought. That means that the choice of medium must be appropriate for the market segment at which the product is aimed; Forte's classical concert weekends may be better advertised in *The Gramophone* than the *Golfer's Weekly*.

Lastly, it is no good creating demand for a product, if the consumer cannot buy the product easily. This means having the support of travel agents who are prepared to rack your brochure and sell the product, or else some equally effective form of distribution on which one can rely for sales. It also means effective briefing of agents. Many travel sales have been lost through inadequate briefing of retailers on new products and their benefits.

Screening the new product

The process of screening new products is illustrated in Fig. 5.4. Let us look at each of these steps in turn.

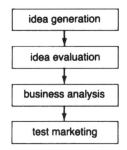

Fig. 5.4 Screening the new product

Ideas can be generated from many sources, both within and outside the company. Most typically, an idea for a new product is generated by a company executive, and may then be discussed between a group of executives responsible for new product development. However, other employees further down the ladder can also make significant contributions to new product development if encouraged, and this needs to go further than the usual suggestion box. The sales force in particular are in touch with dealers or customers, and can feed back to management many useful ideas for product improvements, based on either what competitors are offering or what customers and dealers are saying is needed. Regular reviews should be undertaken in retail outlets to ensure that the company's products are remaining competitive with others on the market. In larger companies, departmental heads can encourage individual staff to suggest improvements to products, or new product ideas, based on their separate spheres of knowledge.

Each of these ideas should be carefully evaluated, so that those whose advantages seem less clear-cut are screened out from the alternatives put forward. This is most easily attained by drawing up a checklist of the strengths and weaknesses of each idea. The market at which the product is to be aimed must be identified, a listing of the benefits of the product over existing products made, and suggestions made on the price that could be charged for the product.

Once the most promising new ideas have been refined, they need to be tested for business viability. An estimate must be made of sales potential, based on the market expected to buy the product, the profit potential, and the cash flow, so that management has a clear picture of how long it will take before the new product starts to realise a profit. Research will be undertaken at this stage to test public reaction to the concept. If this is positive, the programme can move on to the final stage, at which the product is made in limited quantities for test marketing.

In the case of tangible goods, test marketing has usually meant selling the product in one region of the UK to see if the potential sales are realised. If the projections on sales are met, then a full-scale launch is undertaken.

In the case of travel, test marketing is less easily undertaken. Aircraft cannot be produced for test marketing, and hotels cannot be built with the ability to be withdrawn if they are unsuccessful. Nevertheless, there are ways of reducing risk by testing product concepts, and some innovatory ideas have been used to overcome this problem in travel. Hotels, for example, have been able to test proposed new room décor by having a few rooms redecorated in existing properties and having guests pass comments on the appeal of the décor. There is also scope for introducing new package tours on a limited scale to test the market, before committing the full resources of a company to mass marketing a new destination. However, in general it has to be recognised that launching a travel product entails much greater risk than is the case for other products, and for this reason alone it is essential that much greater care is taken to follow the earlier screening processes outlined above.

Owners Abroad: repositioning a company

In early 1994, Owners Abroad undertook a complete review of its products and branding. At that stage the company was selling holidays under fourteen discrete brand names. This branding structure was regarded as having several distinct disadvantages:

1 The brands were overlapping and it is difficult to differentiate fourteen products strongly.
2 Competitors – Thomson and Airtours – were spending more and more on above-the-line advertising behind 'monolithic' brands. By having a single flagship, the promotional spend is concentrated much more on to this single brand identity, achieving far greater market presence or 'share of voice' against the same spend spread across fourteen different brands.
3 Without a flagship brand, the opportunities for brand stretching were limited.
4 With so many brands, brochure production overheads were high (over fifty separate brochures were produced annually) and travel agents were struggling to rack so many different Owners Abroad products prominently.
5 Consumer trends were indicating a drift towards quality, and Owners Abroad's own customer satisfaction questionnaires were indicating that the market was shifting into three distinct groups – the pre-family and couples (without children), the families, and the quality up-market.
6 While the family-orientated mass market represented the familiar volume/value product, the other two groups exhibited the trend towards social group AB type travellers and multiple holidaytaking in one year. As such, they represented growth areas for the future.

Careful validation of these three groupings against published figures led Owners Abroad to believe that the market potential in each of these sectors was large. Much research was then undertaken to understand the three sectors and to arrive at the correct naming and branding structure for the whole company.

Essentially, the chosen strategy was to adopt three brands only, each brand representing distinct holiday types that reflected the needs of the different target groups. The names and logos of the three brands would reflect the right image and emotional values of the product they represented.

This represents a very flexible segmentation. It is not simply a price or life stage segmentation. It provides a conveyor belt which allows the consumer to move steadily from pre-family to family to up-market holidays. It also allows the same consumer simply to select the holiday that best meets their needs at the time through attractive and relevant positioning. Thus the same couple might have a summer holiday with the children chosen from the mass market family brand, and a second, winter, holiday without the children chosen from the pre-family/couples product.

Lastly, the name of the tour operator itself would be changed to the same name as the mass market brand. This was following the strategy of Thomson and Airtours, and allowed a repositioning of the company as a mainstream competitor against the other two volume players in tour operating.

The restructured Owners Abroad was thus completely metamorphosed. From fourteen unrelated brands, it changed into First Choice Holidays, with a rationalised brand and naming structure designed to attack aggressively the competition and to meet the changing nature of the package tour market in years to come (see Fig. 5.5).

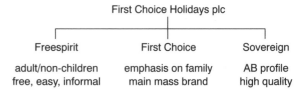

Fig. 5.5 First Choice Holidays plc branding structure

Questions, tasks and issues for discussion

1 In 1986, Weymouth Tourist Office publicised the blowing up of its obsolete bandstand as a special event for visitors. What other innovatory ways of creating tourist products can you think of?

2 What examples can you provide of travel or tourism companies that have developed products with distinct 'personalities'? How important has this been for the success of the company?

3 The value of a slogan to promote a town for tourism is revealed by the success of such examples as Bradford's 'a surprising place', South Tyneside's 'Catherine Cookson Country', and 'Glasgow's Miles Better'. Suggest a slogan for a town in your own locality which attracts tourists, or has the potential to do so.

4 Collect what are, in your view, good logos of four travel companies, and write brief notes for a presentation at which you will explain why you consider each effective, and what its image aims to project. What role does colour play in this?

Exercise

Following the work undertaken in Chapter 4, in which you planned a programme of package holidays for the 35–55 year-old age group, you have now been asked by your manager, Rosemary Clarke, to make comments on the best manner of 'test marketing' these holidays before they are fully launched on the marketplace.

Write a memorandum to your manager, suggesting how the holidays might be screened and tested before introducing them to the market.

6 Pricing the product

After studying this chapter, you should be able to:

- understand the factors affecting demand for products at different prices
- explain basic economic principles of price demand
- understand how pricing can be used as a tool to achieve marketing objectives
- explain how costs affect price, and the significance of marginal costing in travel and tourism marketing
- recognise that price is only one factor influencing the demand for travel
- list key pricing policies
- know how to use strategic and tactical pricing as elements in the marketing plan

What determines the price of a product? Price is as much a tool of marketing as promotion, and plays a critical role in the marketing mix. The price of a product should be seen not only as the outcome of market forces. A marketing manager will be aware that price says something to the consumer about the nature of the product, and by manipulating price in combination with product quality and the promotional messages, sales can be orientated to a new market, or market share can be increased at the expense of competitors.

In order to understand how to use price as a tool, we need to have a clear picture of how customers interpret product prices. Here, the concept of the *fair price* is paramount. Buyers judge whether a product is fairly priced by asking themselves whether it represents value for money. Unfortunately, however, all consumers do not share the same view about what represents value for money, because, even assuming that we have the same disposable income, we establish different priorities for what we purchase, and attach different values to the benefits products offer.

Many people are bemused by the willingness of avid collectors to pay huge sums of money for a work of art. Others will go heavily into debt in order to pay for a car or a house they covet, while still others treasure the ambition to experience a world cruise, and may well 'blow' an inheritance on such a luxury.

In the late 1980s, a room little bigger than a broom cupboard in Knightsbridge, London, was sold for £35 000; its appeal was its proximity to Harrods as a *pied-à-terre*. Two collectors, trying to outbid one another for a unique 'collectible', can drive auction prices to incredible heights, simply because it is one of a kind, or is the only one remaining in private hands. Following the decision of the USA to reclassify the work of the potter Hans Coper as sculpture rather than craft, prices of his work rose from around £6000 to around £40 000 at subsequent auctions – yet the quality of the work remained unchanged! Clearly, the meaning of value is complex as indicated by examples such as this.

The economics of price

Price and demand

From these examples of non-tourism products, what will have become clear is that price has little to do with cost, and far more to do with what customers are prepared to pay for a product.

In a market where the product is unique, or without satisfactory substitute, or where the product is manufactured by a company which enjoys a monopoly or near monopoly, price will be set high. A luxury item, the purchase of which offers the owner prestige, will also command a high price. A flight on Concorde, or a round-the-world (RTW) cruise, are two examples; and significantly, the top-price suites and deluxe cabins are often the first to be sold on RTW cruises, due to both their prestige and uniqueness.

However, it is more customary for travel products to be sold in highly competitive environments, where price is constrained by the substitutability of the product by other, similar products. To understand the interplay between price and demand, we need to know something about how the individual responds to products at different prices, as well as how aggregate demand (the sum of all individual demand) is determined.

Individual demand

Individual consumers make judgements about products based, as we have seen, partly on price. Price acts as a guide to quality, and where consumers have the means to make comparisons with other products, price must be perceived as neither too expensive nor too cheap. If the price lies outside an acceptable range, customers will either reject the product outright, or will seek much more information before committing themselves to a purchase. This can be demonstrated in Fig. 6.1.

If the price of our holiday lies within the sectors AB or CD, customers will require much

more information about the product to be convinced that it offers value for money.

If customers are unable to examine the product in advance of purchase, as is the case with many tourism services, judgements about value for money are equally difficult to make. For example, overseas package campsite holidays, combining long-distance express coach transport with tent, mobile home or chalet accommodation, attract many buyers due to their low prices. Where the customers are first-time travellers abroad, have no prior knowledge of site, resort or nature of the programme, and have no clear way of establishing an acceptable price range, they may find their expectations are not met. Full information must be given in advance to customers, either through the medium of the brochure, or through the advice offered by the travel agent. Since many of these products are sold direct to the public, the information conveyed by the brochure alone may be inadequate to gain an accurate and objective picture of the product.

Aggregate demand

The aggregate demand for a product is the demand resulting from the total of each individual consumer's demand patterns, and these will constantly change according to the price and market circumstances, such as availability, convenience of purchase, and competition level. The extent to which a change in price alone will affect a change in total demand is known as the price elasticity of demand, and is illustrated in diagrams A and B in Fig. 6.2.

In diagram A, Q_1 represents the number of products (e.g. package holidays offered by a particular company to a specific destination) sold at the price of P_1. Now let us assume that the company finds itself able to reduce the price of these holidays to P_2, as a result of better negotiations with airlines and hotels. More holidaymakers now want to buy these packages, so the number of holidays sold rises to Q_2. If the revenue achieved by these extra sales exceeds the revenue lost by the reduction in price, we say that demand is relatively elastic. By the same

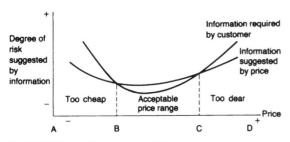

Fig. 6.1 Information conveyed by price

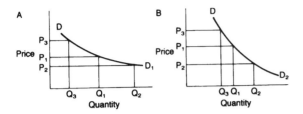

Fig. 6.2 Price elasticity of demand

token, an equivalent increase in price, from P_1 to P^3, will cause sales to drop off substantially to Q_3.

A different picture is presented by diagram B. Here, Q_1 represents the number of units sold at a price of P_1, where price is not the major consideration in the purchase; say, club class seats in airlines operating on a major business route such as Frankfurt to London. In this case, if the price falls to P_2, sales will still increase only to Q_2, since business travellers for the most part have to travel to a particular destination, and are unlikely to be influenced to travel there more frequently, or to switch from other routes. If the gap between economy and club class fares narrows, it may cause a few holiday travellers to switch to the higher class, but such changes will be few and the increase in revenue achieved by the extra seats sold may be less than the revenue lost by reducing the seat prices. Equally, should the airlines on the route increase the fares to P_3, business travellers will be unlikely to cancel their journeys. Only a very substantial increase may cause the company to look at other means of travel such as rail, or to reduce the number of trips their staff makes, or cut back the staff sent to this destination. The quantity of seats sold drops therefore only to Q_3. We can say that demand is relatively inelastic for this product, and this will be reflected in the fairly steep demand curve shown in D_1D_2. However, demand patterns will be very different if the route is deregulated, and each airline has the freedom to set its own price. In such a competitive market, the business traveller may well switch to an alternative carrier, unless the airline charging the higher price can convince its customers that the extra expense is worth paying for – for example, by offering more convenient flight times, schedule reliability or superior in-flight service. Price decisions are always subject to the extent to which customers can find an acceptable substitute for the product. Low prices to Maastricht in the Netherlands, or to Luxembourg, could tempt some travellers to fly there instead, and continue their journey by road or rail into Germany.

In setting prices, the company will want to know what levels of demand it is likely to experience at different prices. For a new product this is hard to gauge. The two most common methods of assessing demand are:

- asking potential customers what they would be willing to pay for the service
- test marketing the product at different prices in different regions.

The difficulty with the first method is that what people say they will do does not always translate into actual behaviour when the product is launched, while with the second method, it is difficult to control all the factors apart from price which will influence consumer decisions in different areas. With a major item of expenditure such as tourism, it is possible that consumers from other areas may take advantage of the low prices in other regions. German tourists, for example, have discovered that they can make substantial savings on their package tours abroad by booking them and joining them in Britain.

Pricing to meet objectives

As with other elements in the marketing mix, pricing should be treated as a tool to achieve one's marketing objectives. If the target market has been clearly identified, and a decision taken about where the product is to be positioned, pricing bands will become easier to determine.

Looking back to our introduction to strategic marketing, you will recall that companies can adopt one of three broad marketing objectives. They can attempt to lead the field by keeping prices down; or they can adopt a strategy of *niche marketing* by differentiating their product from the market leaders or by selecting a particular market segment to which they will aim their appeal. A company with a substantial hold on a market may seek to maximise its profits by finding ways to reduce cost while maintaining or moderately increasing prices; or it may seek to increase still further its share of the market by cutting prices in line with its reduced costs. Companies with a more tenuous hold in the market will then either be forced to price low in order to survive, or to attempt still further to differentiate their product – for example, by using price as an indicator of quality.

As we have seen, below or above a certain price range there will be no demand for the product. But within the range, there will be some scope for flexibility to adjust prices, within three *concept bands*.

1 Premium pricing

Here the decision is taken to set prices above market price, either to reflect the image of quality or the unique status of the product. The product may be new, or it may have features not shared by its competitors, or the company itself may enjoy such a strong reputation that the 'brand image' alone is sufficient to merit a premium price.

2 Value for money pricing

Here the intention is to charge medium prices for the product, and emphasise that it represents excellent value for money at this price. Marks & Spencer have traded very successfully using this policy, which enables a company to achieve good levels of profit on the basis of an established reputation.

3 'Cheap value' pricing

The objective here is to undercut the competition, and price is used as a trigger to purchase immediately. Unit profits are low, but satisfactory overall profits are achieved through high turnover. Low prices will often be introduced by a company seeking to gain rapid expansion in the market, or a toehold in a new market.

It must be stressed that any of these policies may be seen as 'fair pricing' policies, notwithstanding the criticism sometimes directed at companies achieving higher than average profits. Market orientation seeks to ensure that the customer is satisfied with the product at the price paid. A fair price can be defined as one which the customer is happy to pay while the company achieves a satisfactory level of profit. Thus a premium pricing policy is acceptable providing that the customer receives the benefits appropriate to the price. Only where companies are able to force up prices against the consumers' will, such as in the case of monopolies, can it be said that fair pricing is inoperative.

Internal influences on pricing

In the long run, all commercial organisations will continue to produce a product only if it can realise a profit; but profit can be defined in a number of ways.

Gross profit is the price of the product less the direct costs of its production. For a travel agent, the figure represents the difference between the price paid for travel services and the price charged to the consumer, that is, the commission received on the holidays and travel services sold. These commissions will usually range between 7 per cent and 10 per cent depending upon the travel services supplied. In some sectors, e.g. airlines and tour operators, *override commission* of an extra 1 to 5 per cent or even more may be paid for volume-based performance. Use of this override commission to pass on discounts to the consumer is now a major weapon in the armoury of travel agents. The cost of a package tour to a tour operator is the price that the operator must pay to airlines, hotels and other organisations offering the services which are included in the package – the *raw materials* cost. To these costs must be added the *overheads* which the company must meet – the costs involved in running the company, including administrative costs (office rent and rates, light and heat, telephones, etc.), salaries, and marketing costs such as advertising, distribution, reservations and brochure production, plus any other miscellaneous expenses incurred in running the business. These costs are deducted from the gross profits to ascertain the net profits.

Accounting practice dictates that total costs are divided between *variable costs* (VC), that is, costs that vary with the amount of products made, and *fixed costs* (FC), which are relatively difficult to change in the short term and will accrue regardless of the amount of products made. The cost of renting an office and cleaning it cannot be changed in the short term regardless of how many, or how few, of its products the company succeeds in selling.

The marketing manager will need to know at what point in sales is *break-even point* achieved, that is, where total costs exactly equal the total revenue received from sales; it will then be possible to establish how this break-even point will be affected by charging different prices for the product. This will reveal how many more holidays (or other products) must be sold at a lower price in order to recover costs.

Let us take an example of a theme park or tourist attraction which is considering three different pricing possibilities as its basic entry price: £2.50, £3.00 and £3.50. In Fig. 6.3, the lines VC and FC represent respectively the variable costs and the fixed costs associated with running the project. In a venture such as this, fixed costs represent a very high proportion of total costs, since the major expenditure is in the capital outlay to construct the attraction and to staff it. Variable costs will be a small element, and will include some staff costs (seasonal part-time labour), catering, and energy costs (power for amusement rides, etc.), plus some additional maintenance

costs associated with the added wear and tear resulting from larger crowds. Diagrammatically, the break-even chart tells the marketing staff how many customers they must attract at each level of price in order to cover their costs.

TR_1, TR_2 and TR_3 represent the total revenue received at entry charges of £3.50, £3.00 and £2.50 respectively. Presenting the diagram in this form tells us not only where the break-even points occur, but also what contribution the revenue will make to the fixed costs at each pricing level, should sales fail to break even. If sales fall below the break-even point, and as long as the variable costs are covered, the income received will still make a useful contribution to the ongoing costs of the project, which will have to be paid regardless of the number of visitors.

Recognising the importance of contribution has been a significant development in pricing policy in the travel industry. Public railways for example, have high fixed costs in maintaining their track and signalling equipment, as well as in capital expenditure on rolling stock. Apart from peak routes and periods such as the rush hour, much of this rolling stock would lie idle, unless low-priced off-peak excursion fares were introduced. These fares will easily cover the small element of variable cost involved in operating the equipment (extra power, maintenance) and make a significant contribution to the high capital costs of running a railway. Another example is provided by the educational institutions who make available student accommodation out-of-term for holiday use. Students are away from universities and colleges for up to twenty weeks in the year. Many of these weeks coincide with peak holiday periods. This, coupled with the fact that many educational institutions are situated in geographically attractive regions of the country, means that the colleges have found it worthwhile to sell their accommodation at 'marginal costs' little above variable cost, to avoid closing down during the holidays. They have gone on to promote their public rooms for meetings and conferences, thus increasing the demand for such accommodation during the holiday periods.

Costs establish the floor price below which a

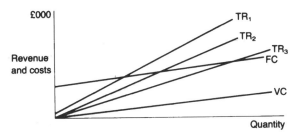

Fig. 6.3 Break-even chart

company would be unprepared to consider sell-ing its products. But simply ascertaining costs and adding a 'mark-up' of some arbitrary per-centage to determine the selling price does not represent a marketing approach to pricing, since it ignores the dynamics of the marketplace – what competitors are charging, the elasticity of demand for the product and what the market will bear. It also fails to take into account that price actually influences cost through its effect on the volume of sales. Low prices stimulate demand leading to high turnover, which pro-vides increased negotiating power with suppliers, enabling tour operators, for instance, to drive costs down by promising very large pur-chases. If the proposed selling price appears too high against competitors' prices, an appraisal of the costs is needed. Can costs be shaved? Might it be possible, for example, to adopt a new distri-bution system such as direct sell, to reduce costs and make the product competitive in price?

One further complication in costing is the allo-cation of fixed costs to a product. Some acceptable means has to be found to apportion the fixed costs of a company to each product and range of products in a manner which can be judged fair. An airline might divide its costs by the routes served, in proportion to the passenger ton kilometres flown, or based on the anticipated revenue for a given route. No single system of cost allocation is perfect, however, and it is not uncommon for a lower level of fixed costs to be assigned to new products launched, in order to give them a better chance to achieve quick prof-itability in the market.

Pricing and the product mix

It is important that the price set for a product is right not only in itself, but also in relation to the other products marketed by the company. If the product appears cheap by comparison with oth-ers in the range, consumers may switch their purchasing patterns and sales overall will fall; or equally, the market may view the cheaper prod-uct with suspicion, unless a satisfactory explanation is given for the price differentials. As

'. . . the market may view the cheaper product with suspicion . . .'

most travel products are increasingly viewed as homogeneous, a low-priced holiday in, say, Greece will divert holidaymakers from Spain, unless Spanish holiday benefits are promoted very heavily.

However, with many travel products it is com-mon to find that each product in the range faces entirely different market conditions. An airline may experience significant competition both in price and service on one route, while enjoying market leadership on another. Airlines are gener-ally reluctant to allow authorised routes to lapse, allowing competitors to step in (and market patterns can change very swiftly, as British Caledonian were to find with their routes to the Middle East and South America), and instead may be willing to cross-subsidise a loss-making route with profits made on more successful routes, provided that a satisfactory overall level of profitability can be achieved in the year.

Let us take a hypothetical example of cross-subsidies, using the services of Britainair, a British carrier with three routes. Let us assume that the marketing plan for the airline calls for targeted profits of not less than 7 per cent overall. This could be achieved by balancing the profit levels on all routes as follows:

Route A is a recently awarded route which faces

intense competition from other airlines who are well established in the market, and who are themselves cutting prices in efforts to increase their market shares. Britainair is anxious to get a toe-hold in the market and gain a 10 per cent share of what is thought to be a potentially lucrative route.

Route B is one on which the airline is already well established; it is shared with two other carriers, with roughly equal market shares. While market share is stable, and profits satisfactory, the route is not growing and load factors, while adequate, could be healthier. All three airlines are anxious to discourage any new entrants to this market.

Route C is one on which Britainair is the market leader. There is strong flag loyalty from the major market segment, and the company enjoys an excellent reputation in the market.

The marketing plan for the coming year suggests the price structure shown in the table below.

Such cross-subsidies would be considered appropriate only in the comparatively short term, to achieve strictly short-term objectives. In the long term each product will normally be expected to become profitable in its own right (although in the case of certain airline routes which serve the needs of the community, the public sector may provide grants to keep otherwise unprofitable routes in operation). However, it is not uncommon for companies which are horizontally or vertically integrated to accept lower

than normal profits when 'selling' or transferring their products to other divisions within the company. This practice, known as 'transfer pricing' or 'shadow pricing', could be employed, for example, where a tour operator owns its own airline, and the aircraft are 'leased' to the tour operator at an artificially low price to enable the operator to compete at a time when cut-throat competition is restricting profits generally. It should be added that the leading tour operators owning their own airlines deny that this practice occurs within their own sphere of operations. However, it is generally accepted that profits on sales of duty-free goods on board cross-Channel ferry services are substantial enough to enable the ferry operators to sell tickets for their services at much lower prices than would otherwise be possible. In effect, the ferry companies are attracting passengers with low prices in order to recoup profits overall through the sale of on-board goods and services – a situation which will be radically affected if, as planned, the European Union withdraws duty-free rights among member countries after 1998.

Price's role in the tourism marketing mix

Pricing, as we have already emphasised, is only one tool in the marketing mix, and pricing decisions must be determined in relationship with all the other elements of the mix. The impression is gathering strength within the travel industry that price is the sole criterion of importance to the

Sales		Average unit price per seat (£)	Total revenue per route (£)	Target profit % at average prices	Target profit (£)
Route A:	50 000	90	4 500 000	3	135 000
Route B:	250 000	110	27 500 000	5	1 375 000
Route C:	200 000	100	20 000 000	11	2 200 000
Total revenue, all routes:			52 000 000		
Total target profit overall:					3 710 000
Total target profit (weighted average)				7.13	

consumer, or that other elements are relatively insignificant. While it is true that brand images (with a handful of notable exceptions) have not played a big role in tourism marketing up until the present, this is not to say that symbolic values in travel products are any less important than in other industries, and 'futures' forecasters such as the Henley Centre are suggesting that as discretionary income rises, the symbolic and emotional values attached to brand names will increase.[1]

All too often, however, travel companies have chosen to ignore the creation of added value in their marketing plans, and have concentrated exclusively on the promotion of price. The major tour operators in particular have used low price as a means of increasing their market shares, at the expense of profit levels. There can be little doubt that this policy was highly successful during the 1980s, although this may have had as much to do with the publicity that resulted from the price wars between operators, causing consumers to become conscious of price rather than value. Over-optimistic sales projections led to heavy discounts to 'dump' unsold seats through late bookings, encouraging consumers both to shop around for the best bargains and to book later. It is likely that increasing disposable income and other favourable factors such as exchange rates would have led to substantial increases in the number of package tours sold during the 1980s, even had discounting not been introduced.

The 1990s, however, apparently presented a very different scenario, with lower volumes but higher prices the stated goal of most companies. This did not prove to be the case for the first half of the decade: profit margins for many travel companies – particularly tour operators – remained comparatively poor. At the same time, the aggressive competition for market share has pushed the overall market size higher, often on the back of price competitiveness.

Other influences on price

Earlier, we explored some of the factors affecting price decisions over which the company will have very little control. Chief of these are:

1 The economic health of the country (or region). It is notable that at the time of the depression in the 1970s, unemployment was less of a problem in London and the South East of England than in the North and Midlands, and consequently travel bookings from the former areas were less affected. However, at the beginning of the 1990s the slump in the South East proved to be severe, while the situation in the North remained relatively unchanged.
2 The elasticity of demand for travel and tourism products.
3 Levels of competition faced by individual companies and substitutability between competing products.
4 The nature of the target market, which will determine what kind of holiday or other travel products they will buy and at what price.

There will also be ethical considerations to be taken into account. A company concerned about its public image will wish to reassure its public that it is not making excess profits, even assuming it is in a position to do so without challenge from the Monopolies and Mergers Commission. It would also be short-sighted of companies to attempt to introduce substantial price increases at a time when the political climate favours price restraint, even were the market able to bear such increases.

Legal constraints

Under certain conditions there may even be legal constraints affecting price decisions. Periodically in Britain prices have been politically controlled under price and wage 'freezes' to hold down inflation, while legislation exists to affect pricing tactics in a number of ways. In the hotel industry, for instance, the Tourism (Sleeping Accommodation Price Display) Order (1977) requires hotels with four or more letting rooms to display room prices at reception, and the Price Marking (Food and Drink on Premises) Order (1979) enforces similar requirements for the display of food and drink prices where they can be seen by customers before entering. The Price

Marking (Bargain Offers) Order (1979) requires any money-off offers to be genuine reductions on original prices.

Codes of practice

Additionally, there are a number of organisations, quasi-governmental and industrial, which exercise some influence on pricing policies and strategies, which marketing managers must bear in mind. Many of these exercise control through Codes of Practice which companies are either obliged, or strongly advised, to follow, if they are to be accepted as professionals. The Independent Broadcasting Authority (IBA) has its own code relating to advertising, to which reference is made in Chapter 9. The Chartered Institute of Marketing, the professional body representing marketing staff in all sectors of industry – which, incidentally, has its own travel and tourism sector, the Chartered Institute of Marketing Travel Industry Group (CIMTIG) – has its own Code of Conduct, and ABTA itself enforces Codes of Conduct for both tour operator and travel agent members. The Tour Operators' Code, for example, includes a section devoted to standards on brochures which, under Section 13, requires the brochure to carry 'the total price, or the means of arriving at the total price, together with a precise statement of the services included therein'. It goes on to demand of tour operators that where a variety of prices is offered, the operator must make clear in the brochure what the basic price is and what it covers (1994 Edition of the Members' Handbook). Clear directions on surcharges and how these can be imposed must be given, and in the event such surcharges are imposed, a detailed explanation of the reasons for the surcharge must be provided to customers. Airport and seaport taxes must be integrated into the price of all European holidays.

The Office of Fair Trading (OFT) now prohibits the imposition of resale price maintenance on travel agents, who are at liberty to discount their own commission to reduce the price if they wish to do so. Agents are permitted to charge fees for services they render, but such fees must be determined individually, not 'in collusion' by ABTA, under OFT rules. Bodies such as the Air Transport Users' Committee, who are the watchdogs concerned with the protection of passengers, closely monitor air fares and will react strongly where they find evidence of price anomalies (this could mean concern with low prices, too, if these are seen as evidence of 'predatory pricing' – prices set below cost, designed to drive a competitor out of business). The National Consumers' Council, Consumers' Association and, indeed, the media themselves, all play a role in publicising prices thought to be out of line with the achievement of normal business profits.

Developing a price policy

Policies are plans for the future direction of the business. A company's price policy therefore appears in the marketing plan as an indication of the company's objectives in setting prices.

In some cases, price policy may be no more than a reaction to market forces or the result of a failure to plan, but good marketing implies a more positive approach to considerations of price, and the development of an active plan to influence the market through price. These policies will now be examined.

Profit maximisation

This is a commonly stated objective which combines charging what the market will bear with attempts to reduce costs. One difficulty associated with the policy is to know exactly what any market will bear, and the problems inherent in constant price adjustment cause many companies to settle for a policy of 'satisfactory' rather than maximum profits. There is also the danger in maximising profits that the firm will attract unwelcome competition; by keeping profits moderate, and prices low, this may deter opportunist firms from entering the market.

There is another argument against the reduction of costs to their minimum. A hotel, for example, could adopt a strategy of employing casual labour in season and closing down out of season, as a means of maximising profits. This may still be true even after assessing the marginal contribution of staying open throughout the year, which we have discussed earlier. However, there is a social cost in hiring and firing indiscriminately in areas of already high unemployment. Such jobs will attract the less committed casual workers, and a hotel which relies as much on providing good service may find it hard to attract the qualified staff necessary for the achievement of this. Customers who are disappointed do not rebook, and the long-term effects may be to actually reduce profits.

Target return on investment (ROI)

A common practice is to measure the amount of profits achieved each year as a proportion of the total capital invested in the company. This can be helpful, since comparisons can then be made with the profit potential if the capital were invested in other forms of business. Many small tourism businesses do not achieve the same level of profit which might be possible through other investments (indeed, higher returns could generally be achieved simply by investing capital in building society accounts!) and it has to be assumed that profit is not the only motive in setting up a tourism business. Many small business people are content to achieve low returns on their invested capital for the privilege of working for themselves, or running their own businesses. This has always been the case with proprietors of small hotels and guesthouses, which are frequently family-run concerns, while proprietors of travel agencies and others in the travel industry enjoy the opportunities for cheap travel offered by their jobs. Larger companies tend to measure success purely in economic terms.

It should be recognised that in the case of some sectors of the travel business, capital appreciation on assets is as important as operating profit. Hotels in London, for instance, have seen the scarcity of building land in the city centre lead to huge rises in the value of their property during the 1980s, far exceeding any operating profit they were achieving.

Finally, ROI is not a good measure of travel agency success, since the actual cost of setting up an agency is quite small, involving as it does no investment in stock. The cost of purchase of a well-established travel agency will include a large element of 'goodwill', based on the assumption that present customers of the agency will continue to trade there after the change in ownership.

Pricing for market share

Many companies will set their prices at a level designed to ensure that they will achieve a certain share of the market. This, disparagingly known in the industry as 'playing the numbers game', generally calls for price restraint, especially in the early stages of the product life cycle (PLC), where the aim is market *penetration* (as opposed to market *expansion* in later stages of the PLC). However, if it is the intention to deliberately curb profits in the early stages of the PLC in order to achieve a given market share, there must be the underlying objective of achieving a good profit level in the longer term, since there would be little point in becoming locked into a long-term price war without some evidence of ultimate benefit to the company.

Falling profitability on the tour operating business has resulted from the combined objectives of major companies to restrain prices to build market share. This has had the effect of driving some medium-sized and small companies out of business, but the substantial growth achieved by the market leaders has led to potentially large turnover and profits. The major operator, as at May 1994, held about 27 per cent of the summer package tour market, while the leading three companies (Thomson, Owners Abroad – later First Choice – and Airtours) accounted for about 55 per cent of the total market. However, this is a fall of some 15 per cent over the previous two years, as other, usually large, operators fought back to survive.

For this policy to succeed, the product itself must be elastic in demand, and costs per unit must fall as 'production' increases (as they do in the case of tour operations, where lower prices can be negotiated if more customers are guaranteed to the suppliers). Additionally, the product should anticipate a long life cycle (expansion of leisure time and discretionary income suggests that holidays and travel will enjoy a long-term growth curve). Any company embarking on such

n a very rice war ie reader ompany share of lowed if ne more et, since ers (rel- also be ncerned t where ht come es and of some on, the n inves- y policy turated ompany ay from ill offer harkets, growth. rsonnel atic or recruit- ffers to mpeti- ope to xisting etween rnover, share.

e than market share, but using turnover as a yardstick for success may disguise the fact that a company's actual share of the market is falling.

If, for example, demand for overseas flights increases dramatically, an airline could experience a 3 per cent growth in its traffic although its total market share might have fallen by 10 per cent or more, suggesting that its management has not maximised its opportunities. Concern with turnover can also overlook a decline in profitability.

Turnover may be increased in one of four ways:

- by getting more people to buy the product
- by getting present purchasers to buy it more frequently
- by finding new uses for the product
- by increasing the price of the product.

A large country hotel may attract more visitors by improving its facilities without an increase in price, and promoting this improvement in the main regions where its current market is generated. It might encourage its summer guests to return for a three-day winter break, with special package prices available to guests who book while on their summer holidays. It could also choose to market its facilities to conference users, with new meeting rooms and improved catering, at a commensurately higher price. It could make more cost-effective use of its public space by subcontracting retail shopping space in its lobbies, with a percentage of the revenue accruing to the hotel turnover. Hotels have further innovated by offering off-season occupancy on a timeshare basis. All these are strategies which will help the hotel achieve its price policy, which is to price to increase the operating turnover of the hotel.

Price restraint

Sometimes companies will take the decision to maintain or lower prices simply in order to retain existing markets. This could be a response to falling sales generally, or even a goodwill gesture at a time when the government is actively seeking price restraint to control inflation. This will normally be a short-term policy designed to meet current market conditions.

Meeting competitors' prices

On the face of it, this is an attractive policy for consumers, since it reassures them that they will not find the product more cheaply by shopping around. Although the outstanding example of this is to be found outside the travel industry, in the John Lewis Partnership's guarantee 'we are never knowingly undersold', the policy has been used by Thomas Cook in their 'price promise' which offered to refund the difference in price on package tours which could be bought more cheaply elsewhere.

If a policy such as this is adopted by more than one leading competitor, a price war can develop, with smaller companies adopting 'survival pricing' to remain in business. Without sufficient reserves, they will be driven out of business as in the case of severe market share pricing policies. If this results in a handful of major companies forming an oligopoly to dominate the market, this will be against the consumer's long-term interests, since new companies will find it difficult to get established in the market, and the larger companies may force up prices and profits. This in turn can lead to the formation of new market gaps for cheaper holidays.

Short-term profit maximisation

Often known as 'skimming the cream', this policy calls for the setting of high prices at the launch stage, with a progressive lowering of price as the product becomes better established, and progresses through the life cycle. Reducing prices to boost sales is an alternative to innovating the product to rejuvenate it when sales falter, as discussed in Chapter 5. This is illustrated in Fig. 6.4.

The policy takes advantage of the fact that most products are in high demand in the early stage of the life cycle when they are novel or unique, or when supplies are limited. A new museum with exhibits that will attract many tourists such as the Jorvik Centre in York, or a theme park with exciting new rides, will both be limited in their ability to expand sales when popularity peaks. Longer opening hours may be one possibility, but if the event is very popular, long queues will form. Demand can be managed by setting very high prices initially to cream off those prepared to meet them, gradually reducing the price to meet different market segments' price elasticities.

If there is no problem with supply, the object will be to obtain the highest level of sales possible in the post-launch period at the highest price. This will call for a large promotional spend at the launch stage to make the market aware of the new product as quickly as possible and influence them to buy it.

The particular value of this policy is that it provides a high inflow of funds to the company when the marketing costs are highest. As high prices in travel will increase the revenue earned by travel agents, this will also encourage the distributors' support. If the product also anticipates a very short life cycle, as is the case with event tourism such as the Olympic Games, where costs of organising and marketing the programme must be recovered quickly, this is a sensible policy to pursue. Care must be taken, however, not to antagonise regular markets for short-term benefits. All too often hotel prices have been increased very substantially during events such as World Fairs, and if accommodation thereby becomes unavailable or overpriced to the regular markets, there may be a consumer reaction: loyal customers may simply go elsewhere.

Premium pricing

In premium pricing, the intention is to price high in the long term, using price as an indication of quality, or symbolic value, as with the case of high status holidays. Here one is dealing with a highly inelastic market demand, but the product must deliver what it promises. Its scarcity value

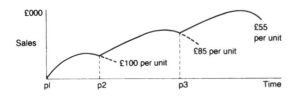

Fig. 6.4 Skimming the cream

may be a major part of its appeal, therefore such products in travel are more likely to be developed by small specialist firms. The package tour sold largely to the North American market, comprising a visit to a British stately home, with dinner hosted by its titled owners, is one example of such a product which has both scarcity and prestige value.

While all the above policies involve active decisions to influence markets through price, some companies will adopt passive price policies, of which three can be identified:

- following price leadership
- price agreements
- cost-plus pricing.

Following price leadership

Sometimes referred to as *going rate pricing*, this policy is adopted by those who feel that their products are insufficiently distinguishable from those of their leading competitors. Prices are set based on what the competitors charge.

A drawback to the policy is that prices cannot be established or marketed until the competitors' decision on price has been publicised. Small seaside hotels and guesthouses traditionally wait to see what shape prices are taking before determining their own for the coming season, while many tour operators in Britain wait for the launch of the major companies' brochures to see the prices charged before going to print with their own brochures. This policy will obviously inhibit forward sales.

Price agreements

The concept of a *cartel*, a group of companies coming together in order to set uniform prices, is now rare, and indeed in Britain – virtually without exception – it is illegal. The OFT has made it clear that fixed price agreements cannot be imposed on travel agents for package tours, nor is ABTA permitted to agree uniform fees for the services provided by agents. Distributors are therefore required to determine their own pricing

policy, which allows them to discount inclusive holidays by some proportion of their commission if they so choose.

Tourism, however, is an international product, and may be subject to other regulations. Until the 1970s, price regulation in the air transport industry represented one of the very few examples of an officially sanctioned cartel, with prices agreed through the International Air Transport Association (IATA). The growth of deregulation of air transport, first in North America and later in Europe, has significantly reduced the effectiveness of the air price cartel, although on many Third World routes price regulation is still in force. In other areas of tourism within the UK, the OFT will investigate any suspected cases of price collusion.

Cost-plus pricing

This is the simplest mechanism of all for pricing decisions. The company establishes its costs for a particular product, allocates some share of overhead costs to production plus a percentage markup for profits, and this then becomes the selling price. Clearly, this takes little account of market forces, and while costs do have to be covered in the long run, policies have to respond more to changing market conditions and 'what the market will bear', as we discussed earlier in this chapter.

However, the concept of *marginal costing*, which attempts to identify the cost of one more unit of a product, is an important one in cost-plus pricing, since it offers the marketing manager a flexible tool for pricing. We earlier examined the concept of 'contribution' to fixed costs, in which the variable cost of one more unit is ascertained. In the case of, say, an airline ticket to the USA, the additional cost of carrying one more passenger is extremely small: an added meal, a minute addition to fuel and equally minuscule costs for ticket issuance, etc. Therefore, once break-even is achieved it becomes very attractive to price the 'marginal seat' (any remaining seats over the number that have to be sold to break even) at a price which will attract market demand from those unwilling to pay regular fares. Scheduled carriers introduce such fares as 'stand-by' to fill these last remaining seats, and charter services originally introduced 'seat only' sales to achieve the same purpose.

It makes good sense for all companies to pre-determine their pricing policies, but in fact of those that do, most tend to be the larger corporations, where the marketing concept is treated more seriously. One study on pricing policy in the hotel industry found that smaller units (hotels with up to 24 beds) for the most part either had no policy or one in which they simply followed price leadership. Hotels up to 200 beds in size tended to use cost-plus pricing, with some emphasis on the achievement of target profits, while only in the largest hotels was price used as an active marketing tool, with an emphasis on return on investment.[2] The idea that pricing policy is linked through marketing plans to the achievement of organisational objectives is still to receive widespread application in the travel and tourism industry.

Price policies have many important implications for other areas of the marketing mix. The price determined for a product will influence the decision on whether 'push' or 'pull' strategies are more appropriate to use, with promotional tactics developed to support one or the other approach. A decision to price for rapid penetration in a new market will call for the widest possible distribution of the product, while the decision to 'skim the cream' would suggest a more select distribution system to be appropriate.

We shall now turn to the ways in which pricing policies are implemented as part of the overall marketing campaign.

First Choice Holidays: tour operator pricing

The pricing of a tour operator's programme is clearly crucial in such a price-sensitive market; the scale of the task is awesome. First Choice, for instance, produced some 2300 brochure pages for the 1995 summer season. Most pages featured a price panel with perhaps 100 separate prices – making a total of almost a quarter of a million individual prices. Small wonder that computer systems play such a fundamental role in aiding the marketer to evaluate different pricing options and their implications, and to calculate the unit prices.

With such a huge and complex pricing operation to perform, the basis underlying pricing policy is, of necessity, a straightforward cost-plus pricing approach. By comparing margins achieved across the programme for different levels of margins, and different levels of sales, overall profitability can be evaluated and financial targets fixed.

Naturally, this approach alone would be too simplistic and it was overlaid with a considerable number of individual policy decisions at brand, brochure, country, resort and hotel level. These are aimed at achieving specific marketing objectives and reflect the product manager's skilled understanding of their product and the market. Here are just some examples of these detailed policy considerations.

First, each major operator cannot wait for the competition to launch their brochure and then follow suit – the delay in reaching the market would be unacceptable. Further editions of the brochures (see p. 101) provide an opportunity to respond to the competition's prices. In addition, a detailed analysis of shared accommodation and historical sales levels can be taken into account in an attempt to judge the likely competitive pricing position. Competitive strategy is also vital.

Second, the pricing policy also reflects specific objectives, such as 'regain market leadership in Kos', 'achieve an overall 2 per cent price advantage', 'maximise profit on 14 night villa accommodation to capitalise on exceptionally competitive rates negotiated', or 'maximise profit on unique resorts and reduce margins on units shared with the competition'.

Third, the brochure price is determined but so too is the proposed policy on early booking discounts, child discounts, late sales reductions, travel agent commission incentives and the like. This is because the overall profitability target of the programme must be set against the actual sales price likely to be achieved.

Strategic and tactical pricing

Strategies are concerned with the overall plans for the implementation of policy, while tactics relate to the day-to-day techniques in pricing which can be rapidly altered to suit changing conditions in the marketplace. Thus a strategy of discriminatory pricing, involving the setting of different prices to different market groups (e.g. business travellers and holiday travellers) may be introduced, but the actual prices to be charged (APEX, PEX, GIT, ITX fares, etc.) and the ways in which these fares will be adjusted will imply tactical decisions.

One of the strategic decisions which must be taken will be whether to price differentially to different geographic areas. Should the price set be common to all customers, or should it vary to reflect different market demand in the various regions of a country, or between different countries? It may be more costly to sell one's incoming package tour arrangements in the USA, for instance, than in France, or it may be necessary in one country to boost commission levels to agents to secure their support. Long-haul holidays sold in Britain are cheaper on the whole than identical holidays sold in Germany, partly because of higher marketing costs in mainland Europe, partly because the market will bear higher prices, but too great a differential will result in travellers diverting to the UK to pick up their package holidays. Alternatively, should the price be the same to all markets, but adjusted to take into account varying conditions - night flights versus day flights, low season versus high season?

When Billy Butlin launched his first holiday camps, his pricing strategy was *all-in pricing*; a single price gave his customers access to every entertainment facility in the camp. This meant that there was always plenty to do even in inclement weather, and the strategy proved highly successful. Club Méditerranée was later to build on this model for their successful chain of holiday resorts around the world. The decision to charge a low basic entrance fee and recoup profits through *add-ons* is a critical one for the tour operators, who choose different approaches. A package tour to China, while having a high basic cost, is often fully comprehensive, to include excursions, all meals, even drinks, while a similar tour to the USA may be limited to flight, room and transfers. Each decision must be made on its own merits and reflect market conditions in the host and generating countries. The two destination countries in this example have totally different tourism industry structures, the former being highly centralised and therefore far simpler to organise on a fully comprehensive basis, while costs are extremely low and therefore the package will be seen to be offering good value.

Strategies must be designed to respond to the marketing initiatives of competitors, too. As market leaders, Thomson Holidays became concerned that not only were their competitors waiting for them to launch their brochure before determining prices, but also some were adjusting prices to undercut Thomsons after the Thomson brochure appeared on the market. They responded by relaunching the brochure with lower prices, and this has now become a well-established routine to the point where relaunches are built into the print run, and a 'second edition' with adjusted prices can be introduced if the market shows signs of flagging at originally published prices, or if the leader is too far out on price. While this significantly adds to print costs, it gives the company much greater flexibility for fine tuning on price. This trend to multi-editions is accelerating. For its summer 1995 programme, Thomson followed its initial launch in August with a second edition in late September, just seven weeks later.

How should a company respond when challenged on price? The immediate decision to slash prices is not necessarily the best one, and only has the effect of reducing profits for everyone. It may be justifiable where there is evidence of extreme price sensitivity, or where it is thought to be difficult to recapture market share once lost. However, if the company has a strong brand image, believes in the quality of its products and has the financial strength to survive a price attack, it may well ride out the threat, or it can counter-attack by improving product quality, or by heavy promotion. With a sufficiently distinctive product, it may even be possible for the company to increase the price, and hence the psychological 'distance' between its own products and those of the competition. In short, there are a variety of solutions, of which price reduction is only one, and the company under attack needs to consider each option carefully.

Beaulieu, the heritage attraction in Hampshire in the south of England, provides an interesting example of the use of tactical pricing to solve a problem. Its strategy was to charge a high entry price giving access to a wide range of attractions which had involved substantial capital investment. The fear was that the entry cost would be perceived as providing poor value by those unfamiliar with what the attraction had to offer, or the length of time they could expect to spend at the site. The solution was to make little advance information available about the actual cost of entry, and to site the parking area at some distance from the entry kiosk. Customers, having parked and walked as far as the kiosk, would be reluctant to forgo a visit at that point because of cost alone, and grudgingly paid up, only to find themselves with much more to see and do than they had anticipated. A survey of visitors leaving the site found that they were well satisfied with the visit and voted it good value for money.

A contrasting approach is taken by other attractions, where *off-set pricing* (sometimes known as *bait pricing*) will set a very low entry charge, possibly even a 'loss leader' at below cost, in order to attract visitors, who then find themselves facing extra charges for every event (a common tactic for fairground amusement sites such as the Tivoli, Copenhagen). One interesting example of bait pricing is shown by the hotels in Las Vegas, USA, where prices are extremely reasonable for rooms and food because profits are reaped through gambling on the premises. Fruit machines are to be found in every lobby, public rooms, even around the swimming pools. DFDS Danish Seaways has also used bait pricing to attract off-season visitors to round voyages on their UK–Denmark service, on the basis that the service will operate anyway (for freight needs) and the additional on-board spend during the 24-hour crossing will enable satisfactory overall profits to be achieved, or will at least provide a substantial contribution to operating costs during the winter.

Discounting tactics

Discounting became a highly controversial topic in the travel industry during the 1980s and early 1990s. In a market situation where 'money-off' incentives became widespread, where hotel receptionists were given unlimited freedom to adjust prices for late arrivals, where it became common for travel agents to split commissions with their business house clients in order to retain a sale, and where tour operating reservations staff conducted 'auctions' with agents on the telephone for seats on late booking holidays, the idea of a set price for travel services was a fast disappearing concept. This might be seen as an almost inevitable result of deregulation in the industry and the tactical pricing which, for instance, had led to an airline fare structure in which more than a hundred fares could be applied on a single route between two points.

Travel discounts are obviously here to stay. The question is whether they can be controlled, and how far the practice is contributing to the development, or decay, of the industry. Evidence suggests we have moved too far to making the discount the major selling tool, and have chosen to ignore the other tools of marketing.

Marketing theory recognises at least six forms of discounting, although not all these are to be found in the travel and tourism industry.

1 *Discounts for cash payment, or early settlement of invoice* Common in business where credit is normally given.
2 *Price reductions for quantity purchases* (bulk discounts) Common in negotiations between tour operators and their suppliers, and proposed for businesses purchasing large numbers of air seats.
3 *Trade discounts* Discounts offered to people in the travel industry for their personal travel.
4 *Trade-in allowances* Only applicable where tangible products are surrendered as part exchange on the sale of a new product.

5 *Seasonal discounts* It is customary to charge lower prices for tourism products purchased 'out of season'.
6 *Distressed stock* (and similar discount tactics) Includes examples such as Advance and Late Saver discounts. The former, by encouraging early bookings, offers two benefits to the company; more precise information on its forward booking situation and (assuming full payment is also made early) the use of prepayment for investment. Late Savers are the equivalent in other businesses of sales, that is the clearance of distressed, or unsaleable, stock. This is doubly important in the case of travel, since unsold stock cannot be stored and sold later.

The popularity of Late Savers among travel consumers has played an important part in the market's tendency to book travel later each year, in the hope of securing a bargain. However, apart from advance booking of tickets on airlines, early booking discounts have been rare in the travel industry. In the mid-1990s, however, operators also attempted to introduce discounting for early bookings, in an effort to reverse the consumer trend towards late bookings. In 1994, the First Choice Holidays direct sell brand, Eclipse, ran a very successful 10 per cent early booking promotion, successfully boosting sales. In the same year, the industry launched a campaign of 'deep discounting' (offering up to 15 per cent, and in some cases as much as 20 per cent, off for 1995 bookings made a year in advance). This confirms the trend towards the retail price of a package tour reflecting the pricing policy of *both* tour operator *and* travel agent. The fact that these may not be in total harmony was illustrated by the fact that two of the three big multiple travel agents were offering 15 per cent off Airtours and First Choice Holidays, but only 5 per cent off Thomson Holidays packages. This was because of Thomson's uncompetitive policy on agent incentives for larger volumes of sales.

While this campaign aided the larger multiples and operators to increase their market share, it can have done little to improve profitability in already thin margins.

Perhaps the most common discount for early booking is to be found in conference bookings, since the decision to hold or abandon the conference must be made well in advance of the event.

There is an important distinction between 'discounting', which is a regular pricing tactic, and 'money-off' offers which accompany special promotions. The use of the latter tactic will be discussed further in Chapter 11.

Clearly, any discounting schemes should be introduced only where there is evidence of price elasticity, i.e. that lower prices will sell the product. In order for discounting tactics to be successful, the discount must be large enough to be seen as a bargain. Here, the concept of the *just noticeable difference* (JND) needs to be understood. This is the amount by which a product must be reduced in price in order for it to attract the bargain-hunter. Some firms make it a practice successively to reduce prices until stock is clear, and this too is a practice which is being introduced experimentally by some tour operators pricing their Late Savers.

Yet another price tactic is the use of the 'psychological discount'. The firm in this case introduces an artificially high price, with the expectation that this will seldom, if ever, be used. Instead, all markets will be offered attractive 'bargains' against the hypothetical price. In the field of consumer durables, references to 'manufacturer's suggested price' provides a base for retailers to fix their own price. While the practice is less widespread in travel and tourism, it is found in areas such as some hotel printed 'rack rates' from which a wide range of discounted prices are offered. Hotels, and cruise ships, have been able to offer apparent bargains by selling accommodation at the basic price and upgrading clients to superior accommodation without additional charge, while airlines have scope to upgrade clients from economy to higher category seats, subject to availability. This provides apparent bargains, but without any cost to the principals.

The total number of price tactics which can be employed is beyond calculation, and limited only by the initiative of the company introducing them. The pricing tool remains a powerful technique for market manipulation and a means to respond quickly to changing market conditions.

Questions, tasks and issues for discussion

1 Under what conditions is 'meeting the competitor's price' an unsuitable policy for a travel company?

2 What are the arguments in favour of reducing prices for advance bookings instead of later bookings? Why have not more travel companies chosen this policy?

3 What should be the pricing policy for a tourist hotel in the Scottish Highlands? Explain the relationship between price and market opportunities for the hotel.

4 What lessons can be learned from the collapse of the International Leisure Group (ILG), and their major summer sun brand Intasun, in 1991? (Secondary research will be necessary to find out why this occurred)

    Has the industry yet learned the lessons from ILG's collapse?

5 Prepare a report which argues the case against an 'open skies' policy on European air routes.

Exercise

Conduct a random sample street survey to test the sensitivity to price for travel on cross-Channel routes between England and France, and discuss the importance of the relative price differentiation between Eurotunnel's prices, ferry prices and air prices on these routes.

On the basis of your findings, write a report which criticises current pricing on these routes.

7 Marketing communications

After studying this chapter, you should be able to:

- understand the role of communication in marketing
- list the elements of the promotional mix and assess their qualities for communicating
- evaluate alternative strategies for budgeting
- understand what is required to create successful promotional messages
- recognise the importance of personal presentation skills in the travel and tourism industry
- recognise the importance of design in the retail shop

Once a product has been created and a price determined for it, the marketing focus switches to promotion. However good a product, it will seldom sell itself. Knowledge about the product has to be communicated to the potential customers, either through word of mouth, advertising or some form of display. Furthermore, the company has to decide not only the best means of bringing the product to the attention of the market, but also the best means of physically delivering the product to its customers. In the case of travel and tourism, even though we are not dealing with a tangible product, we still have to find a means of delivering knowledge of our products to customers, and certain tangible items associated with travel – brochures, itineraries, tickets and vouchers, insurance policies, for example. This process of delivery is known as distribution, and it involves both the selection of suitable channels for distribution and the physical movement of items associated with the marketing of the product. We will be looking in more detail at the function of distribution in the following chapter, while in this chapter we will be considering issues concerning the communication, or promotion, function.

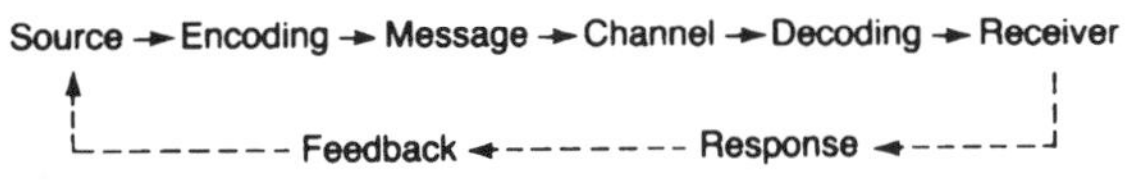

The communications process

Figure 7.1 explains the process by which an organisation communicates with its target market. The process of communications starts with a *source* of information – the person, organisation or company with a message to deliver. The source must determine what message to deliver to its target, the receiver. An airline, for instance, may have many different messages which it wants to deliver to different target markets it serves. To the businessperson, the purpose of the message may be to communicate details of convenient mid-morning flights to European capitals, or information about the airline's outstanding on-time record, while the leisure market will be more interested to hear about free airport parking facilities or new low prices to the main holiday resorts served by the airline. The kind of message we want to deliver will determine the form in which the message will appear, that is how we will *encode* the message to achieve the greatest likelihood of its being received by our target market. If we have a lot of facts to

Source → Encoding → Message → Channel → Decoding → Receiver

Feedback ← Response ←

Fig. 7.1 The communications process

communicate to our customers, such as a list of cheap fares and their dates of availability, we shall probably need to have the message printed, so that our customers can study it at length, absorb it and even tear it out and keep it for future reference. Encoding means determining not only the best way of getting our message across, but also the most effective way given the typical constraints under which the company operates. With unlimited money, it is relatively easy to ensure that every potential customer is made aware of our product; but in the real world, funds are always limited, and we have to ensure a profit at the end of the day. Encoding means putting the *message* into a form in which it will be clearly understood and absorbed by the target market. We could choose, for instance, to place an advertisement in English in a European magazine, designed to attract people to visit Britain and take a tour, but this would hardly be an effective way of getting business. Not only would many non-English-speaking Europeans fail to understand our message, but also we could anticipate some antagonism from those who do speak the language, on the grounds that we are not making a very serious effort to sell our product if we don't put it into our customers' language. If on the other hand we are advertising for a new member of staff who speaks fluent Japanese, to deal with incoming tour clients, it would be highly appropriate to prepare an advertisement in Japanese, for an English newspaper, to ensure that we won't receive applications that waste our time. We have to design our message for maximum impact.

The next step is to decide which *channel* we shall use to deliver our message. If we have already decided that it must be a printed message, this partly determines the medium we shall use. We could advertise in magazines or papers read by our target audience, or we could place advertisements in the travel trade press, directed to travel agents, to make them aware of our product's attributes, so that they in turn will recommend our product to their clients. We could also send a newsletter through the mail to agents with the same message, or provide our sales staff with a circular to give to agents during their calls. This latter technique would also give us the added advantage of being able to reinforce our message with a personal selling presentation.

Having in this way settled on our strategy for putting our message across, we sit back and wait for the bookings to start rolling in. Unfortunately, though, all our best efforts can be frustrated if the *receiver* doesn't *decode* our message. *Interference* in the communications process can affect the decoding of messages in a number of ways. A big news story breaking in the morning paper on the day of our advertisement could mean that many of our customers fail to notice our message.

Our mailshot to travel agents may be ignored because the agent that day has unusual pressure of work and doesn't find time to read 'non-priority' mail. A train derailment could mean that newspapers for one region of the country fail to get through, and nobody in that region gets to see our advertisement. Some of our potential clients may simply not be in the right mood for receiving messages when they see our advertisement, while others may have had a poor recent experience of our service, and are unwilling to read anything positive about the service. Some people, about to read the message in the newspaper over morning breakfast, may be interrupted by a phone call. There are many ways in which interference can prevent our message getting through, and these are frequently beyond our control. Even if the message is received and believed, many potential customers will have forgotten it within a few minutes; clients are bombarded with messages every day of their lives, and only a small percentage are likely to be retained. All we can hope to do is to minimise the loss of our messages by careful initial design of the communications process.

Hence the famous quotation, 'Half of my advertising is wasted; the problem is, I don't know which half', attributed to Lord Leverhulme. We must realise, of course, that the communications process is not a 'one-off' advertisement or promotion. The need to communicate is always with us; a never-ending process of drip feeding our message to the market. It is the cumulative effect over time of perhaps many different types of communication –

advertisement, mail, personal contact – that builds the consumer's image of a company and its products.

Determining the promotions mix

The marketing manager has four distinct ways of communicating the promotional message to the public:

1 By *advertising* the product through a selected medium such as television or the press.
2 By using staff to engage in *personal selling*, either behind the counter, over the phone, or calling on clients as sales representatives.
3 By engaging in *sales promotion* activities, such as window display or exhibitions.
4 By generating *publicity* about the product through public relations activities, such as inviting travel writers to experience the product, in the hope that they will review it favourably in their papers.

It should also be recognised that much communication about products actually takes place by *word of mouth recommendation*. The benefits of a satisfied customer suggesting your product to another potential customer cannot be over-emphasised. This 'hidden sales force' costs a company nothing, yet it is the most highly effective of all communications modes, since the

'. . . much communication about products actually takes place by word of mouth recommendation . . .'

channel has credibility in the eyes of the potential customer, and will be judged as objective in the assessment.

The converse is also true, of course; an account of a bad experience relayed by word of mouth has a very strong negative influence on purchase. And human nature being what it is, research shows us that consumers tell ten times as many people about a bad experience as they do about a good one!

Recognition of the importance of influencing those who can in turn influence others to buy new products has led to the concept of the *two-step flow of communication*, in which messages are directed by the company to the opinion leaders in society, rather than to the general public. Opinion leaders include representatives of the mass media as well as those most likely to initially purchase new products. A travel company with a limited promotional budget might be best advised to concentrate its expenditure on influencing travel writers, by providing study visits to view their products at first hand, since a favourable report on television or in the press will have a huge impact on sales. In 1991, Pluckley in Kent, the scene of the highly successful television series *The Darling Buds of May*, developed a wholly unexpected tourist market, while Brittany, where some of the scenes were shot, received a boost in visitors from Britain. Similar success was enjoyed by Stamford in Lincolnshire in 1994, following the filming of the classic novel *Middlemarch*; by mid-1994, Scotland was eagerly anticipating a huge growth in inbound tourism based on the filming during this time of the blockbuster *Rob Roy*. One film such as this can generate enormous curiosity on the part of viewers, which is translated into a significant rise in visits.

Factors influencing the choice of the mix

What determines the mix of these four promotional tools in the marketing plan? In some cases, companies will choose to employ only one of these elements in the mix, while other companies will use a combination of all four. There are no right or wrong answers about such choices, although guidelines based on the following criteria can be helpful.

1 *The nature of the product*   Clearly, it will be difficult to sell a complex or technical product without personal sales advice. Many in the holiday trade would argue that, although resorts are often thought of as homogeneous and interchangeable, a customer actually needs quite a sophisticated level of knowledge to make a decision about what resort or hotel to choose. A brochure can spell out in cold print what kind of beach the resort offers, or the facilities the hotel provides, but more subjective issues are difficult to put across in print. Questions such as the ambience of the resort, the quality of the food served in the hotel, what kind of fellow holidaymakers the client will encounter in the resort can properly be answered only in a direct face-to-face sales situation, where the salesperson can help to match the customer's needs to the products on offer to ensure customer satisfaction.

2 *The target at which the communication is aimed*   A decision will be made on the mix of communications directed to the consumer and to the trade. Communications aimed at the trade employ what is known as a 'push' strategy, that is, the aim of the company is to encourage dealers to stock the product, and to push it to their customers. This will often involve direct selling, supported by trade advertising, or sales promotion techniques such as the payment of bonuses for achieved targets.

A 'pull' strategy, on the other hand, is designed to generate consumer demand for the product, pulling customers into the shops and forcing retailers to stock the product through the sheer level of demand. Here, the emphasis will be on extensive national advertising, with perhaps some sales promotion support. No intelligent retail travel agent can afford to ignore the products of major tour operators such as Thomson, Airtours or First Choice Holidays to concentrate on selling smaller companies, because of the sheer popularity of the biggest companies, which would mean turning business away.

3 *The stage in the life cycle in which the product is to be found*   The communications task for a new product is to make customers aware of its existence. This means informative messages, usually carried by mass media advertising, with some sales support, to let as many people know what it is you have to sell, and the product's benefits. Later, as competition for the new product increases, the task will switch to that of persuading the public that your product is the best of those available, calling for greater emphasis on sales promotion. As the product becomes well established and sales have peaked, the task will be to remind clients of the product's existence, and encourage them to think of their brand first when shopping. This is achieved by a mix of 'reminder' advertising (perhaps little more than constant repetition of the brand name) and point of sale display material. These tactics will be discussed more fully in subsequent chapters.

4 *The situation in which the company finds itself in the marketplace*   In a highly competitive environment, a company will be under pressure to employ many of the same promotion techniques as its major competitors, to ensure that its products are seen by the same consumers. This may require regional adjustment of the communications mix, depending upon the relative strengths and weaknesses of the company in different areas. This is particularly the case where a company is also selling its products abroad, where both the message conveyed and the channels used to reach the market may be quite different to those in the home country.

5 *The company's budget for its promotional strategy*   This is the most important factor that the company must determine. This budget can, of course, include a contingency to allow for *ad hoc* activity that exploits unforeseen opportunities as they arise, as well as ensuring sufficient funds for a planned programme of activity.

The communications budget

How much should a company spend to promote its products? Theoretically, the answer is simple. It should continue to spend money on promotion until the point is reached where the additional cost of producing and promoting the product becomes greater than the sales revenue it produces; that is, you keep spending as long as marginal revenue exceeds marginal cost, in economic terms. In practice, this point is not easily ascertained, and the marketing manager will fall back on one of several traditional approaches to budget setting.

It is still not uncommon in the travel industry to find expenditure on promotion being determined on an *ad-hoc* basis, without any attempt to budget for this in advance. The criterion is, 'What can we afford at present?' and an advertisement is inserted into a local paper as the need arises. While this has the advantage that the company is being seen to respond to changing market conditions, the procedure lacks foresight and planning. It may be that at the point where expenditure is needed to take advantage of an opportunity (a tour operator, for instance, offers a retailer a 50/50 deal to jointly advertise its services), no funds are available. It makes more sense to budget at the beginning of the financial year for anticipated promotional expenditure.

At its least sophisticated, this simply means deciding what it is believed the company can afford to spend in the coming year. This could be based on some percentage of the previous year's sales, or the expected sales in the coming year. The exact percentage to be allocated again tends to be arbitrary. Some managers have fixed ideas about the appropriate proportion of sales to be allocated to promotion; in the travel industry, figures ranging between 1 per cent and 6 per cent are commonly quoted, although many travel agents make no advance commitment for promotional spend whatsoever. If the trend in sales is linear, that is, progressing each year at roughly the same rate of increase, some justification might be found for the principle, although it would need some 'fine tuning' to take into account such changing circumstances as inflation

rates; obviously any major change in marketing such as the launch of a new product would call for a total reappraisal of the system.

Without specifically matching promotional funds to objectives, there is also a danger that marketing managers will be tempted to overspend in the early months of the financial year, to avoid any possibility of cutbacks occurring later in the year. When travel businesses face a decline in sales, they tend to look at how costs can be readily pruned, and the communications budget is an easy target by which to effect savings.

In a highly volatile industry such as travel and tourism, it is anyway problematical to forecast accurately anticipated sales for future years. But a more serious criticism of this method of budgeting is that it suggests that sales should dictate promotion, rather than being the outcome of promotion. One could even argue that if sales are expected to go up by so much next year, why should one invest money for promotion anyway? Availability of funds is only one criterion for determining the budget, and if it becomes the sole criterion there is a danger that promotional opportunities will be missed.

Other firms set budgets on the strength of what their leading competitors are planning to spend. This is seen as safe, in that it will at least reduce promotional competition if all companies spend the same amount. However, there is no reason to suppose that other companies have better means of judging what is an appropriate budget for promotion, and their circumstances are likely to be different anyway. While the expenditure of major companies can be ascertained (the *Advertising Statistical Review* carries such information), the information may not be available at the time the company's budget is prepared, and in any case most travel companies are small, and are working with comparatively small budgets, details of which are unlikely to be easily available.

It is far better to argue that the promotional budget should be decided on the basis of the sales objectives for the coming year. This technique is known as *objective-task budgeting*. The company predetermines what it would cost in promotional spend, for example, to increase the level of awareness of its products to 60 per cent of the total market, or to increase sales by 10 per cent, and sets aside a budget sufficient to achieve these aims.

There should be a clear relationship between the size of the budget and the overall size and share of the market at which the product is aimed. Market size and share determine profit expectations, and the promotion plan should be geared to achieving a satisfactory level of sales in that market. This can be most effectively quantified when planning an advertising campaign; Chapter 9 will illustrate how budgets are related to objectives.

The message objectives

If communications are to be effective, it is critical that they follow clear objectives, and are designed to maximise the achievement of these objectives. This means that we must start by having a very clear idea both about the market's knowledge of the company and its products, and its attitudes towards these. The sorts of questions the company must ask itself are:

- 'What proportion of our market is aware of who we are, the products we produce and the benefits they offer?'
- 'What image of the company do our customers have? Is it specific, that is, does our market share a common view? Is it diffused, that is, do people have different or confused views about what the company is trying to be and to say?'
- 'What image or beliefs about the company or its products do we need to change?'
- 'What have our present goals been aiming to achieve?'

Readers who take a short-term view about communications, believing that they have only to do with promoting current opportunities to the market, may feel that this emphasis on image creation is academic, or at best appropriate only to the largest companies. This is not true at all. The image that a company is projecting greatly aids the process by which the consumer differen-tiates one company and its products from another. While a travel agent should certainly include as part of the promotional activities a list of Late Savers in the shop window, and perhaps advertise such opportunities in the local press, there are also many far-sighted agents who are concerned about their long-term image. This may mean taking a regular column in the local paper with photographs of their staff, drawing the public's attention to the fact that the staff regularly visit resorts abroad to improve their product knowledge. This is part of the process of polishing the image, by building public opinion to see that agent as 'caring', 'expert' and 'personal' in its approach, for example if the first names of individual staff members accompany the photos in the advertisements, new and potential clients will become familiar with the name, location and image of the company, and will tend to think of that agent first when booking a holiday. For personal security reasons it is advisable not to publish surnames with people's photographs.

Consumers should be reached at three different levels by the communications process.

1 At a *cognitive* level, consumers must be made aware of the product and understand what it can do for them.
2 At an *affective* level, consumers must be made to respond emotionally to the message, to believe it and to be in sympathy with it.
3 At a *behavioural* level, the message must make consumers act on what they have learned; in short, consumers must be motivated to buy the product.

These points will remind us of what we learned about the purchasing, or adoption, process in Chapter 4. One model of this is illustrated below:

awareness→interest→evaluation→trial→adoption

Here, awareness represents the cognitive element; interest and evaluation represents the affective; trial and adoption represents the behavioural. The company's aim is not only to get consumers to try the product for the first time, but also to convince them that this particular product serves their needs best so that they will buy again either the same product or another product from the same company; in short, to turn the consumer into a loyal user of the company's products.

At any given point in time, individual consumers in the company's total market will have reached different stages in this process of adoption. Some will already purchase the product regularly, others will have tried it for the first time and are still evaluating it, still others will have only just become aware of it, while a number of potential purchasers will have yet to become familiar with it. Each of these buying stages represents a different challenge for the communications team.

The full range of possible objectives in communicating have been well categorised by Russell Colley, in his DAGMAR (Defining Advertising Goals for Measuring Advertising Results) model.[1] The value of Colley's approach is that it forces the communications team to define their objectives in terms which can be measured, so that the effectiveness of the communication can be judged. A communication campaign has to be planned to specify what each individual message is designed to achieve, to which stage of the buying process it is directed, and how much is to be spent in achieving it. This will be made clearer in Chapter 9.

In all, Colley identifies some fifty objectives, but for our purposes it is sufficient to list these under three groups of objectives:

- those intended to *inform* clients about the product;
- those designed to *persuade* customers to buy
- those whose purpose is to *remind* customers of the product or the company.

As we revealed earlier, these different objectives are closely linked to the stage in the life cycle of the product, but there are other criteria, too, which will influence the form of the message.

A package holiday may represent anything from a highly homogeneous programme of sun, sea and sand aimed largely at a mass market, to an escorted cultural tour which may be unique in the market and is aimed at a small but discerning

clientele who have money and are prepared to spend it on esoteric travel. In the former case, the holiday is being sold in a highly competitive environment where price has become a critical factor; there is little or no brand loyalty, and little to distinguish the product of one company from another. Assuming that this product is already well established, the task becomes largely one of persuading clients to buy this product rather than those of competitors. In the latter case, we are dealing with a sophisticated market making the choice between a far smaller number of distinctive holidays. Paying perhaps £2000 or more per head, the clients will want a great deal of detail about what they will be getting for their money. Brochure photographs of exotic locations can draw their interest, but alone are unlikely to do the selling job. They must be supported by comprehensive details about the historical and cultural sites to be visited, the background to the accompanying guide-lecturer's expertise, the size and composition of the group they will be joining for the tour. While some of this information can be conveyed by a good brochure, it is likely to be achieved far more effectively with word of mouth selling, and a knowledgeable travel agent is indispensable in counselling clients about such holidays.

The advertisement for Wigan Pier in Fig. 7.2 is an example of a message targeted at group organisers. As such it aims to make best use of a small budget by addressing an opinion-leading subset of the total potential market.

Likewise, the trade advertisement launching First Choice Holidays was specifically aimed at travel agents, who of course are the front-line source of sales for the tour operator. In 1994, Owners Abroad changed its name to First Choice Holidays, and rebranded all its products. It was imperative to ensure that the travel agents were immediately fully aware of this change, and also that they regarded it very positively. The advertisement ran in *Travel Trade Gazette* and *Travel Weekly*, taking eight consecutive full colour pages. As befits the rebranding of one of the largest tour operators, this eight-page coverage represented the largest advertising space ever booked in these magazines. It was only a part of

Fig. 7.2 An advertisement aimed at group organisers, emphasising product benefits and price concessions
(Courtesy: Heckford Advertising/Metropolitan Borough of Wigan)

a multi-media communications programme to the trade that also included direct mail, sales promotion and personal sales visits to every productive travel agency in the country.

Designing the message

Message design has to take four factors into account:

- the source of the message
- the message appeal
- the channel to be used
- the target audience.

The source of the message will be a major factor in establishing its credibility, and it goes without saying that credibility is vital if the communication is to be effective.

A message gains credibility in a number of

ways. First, it will be believed if the source is seen as dependable. A recommendation by a close friend or relative, whose judgement we value, will be a strong stimulus to buy, and this is reinforced by person-to-person communication, where the receiver has the opportunity to question the source and elicit more details about the product. If the product information is coming from a stranger, other means must be found to judge its trustworthiness.

If, for example, the person delivering the message is seen as an expert on the subject in question, this will greatly add to credibility. Travel writers who commend a holiday on the BBC *Holiday* programme will be immensely credible both because of their perceived expertise and objectivity and because the message is delivered by the BBC itself. (The *Holiday* programme appears to represent an interesting bending of the rules governing advertising on the BBC!)

Second, trustworthiness can be achieved by using someone closely associated with the product. The use of John Nettles of *Bergerac* fame to promote Jersey as a destination for holidays was a neat, if unsurprising, strategy of the Jersey Tourism Committee, adding credibility to the message since the actor was assumed to 'know' the island intimately. Moreover, the memory of this link in the public's eyes, and hence, the effectiveness of the advertisement, has long outlived the termination of the TV series itself (see Fig. 7.3). A permanent link between a destination and a well-known personality can be of enormous benefit in the promotion of that destination.

There is a risk with such personality based advertising, however: if the personality suffers adverse public relations exposure, the credibility of the advertising suffers too. One example is the withdrawal of the Michael Jackson campaign by Pepsi in 1994.

A third way to offer credibility to a message is to ensure that it is likeable. A message delivered by someone who is natural, straightforward, or able to inject an element of humour into the delivery, will help to aid its credibility. In a non-tourism context, Victor Kiam's wonderful series of advertisements for Remington achieved their objectives because the source proved to be genuine – not an actor playing a role, but a real company president whose business acumen was unquestioned – as well as natural and humorous. The combination of these qualities proved outstandingly successful in creating a memorable series of television ads. One caveat, however: research has shown that there is a danger in making messages too humorous, since the humour can interfere with the learning process. It is the product that the advertiser wants remembered, not the personality!

Messages can be devised to appeal in two ways to an audience. First, the appeal can be rational, using an economic argument to sway the consumer: an airline may feature its low prices on key routes, or its punctuality record. Second, the appeal may be emotional, such as those ads of Singapore Airlines (SIA) which feature its attractive female cabin staff. Of course, these appeals are not necessarily mutually exclusive. If SIA's objective is to encourage travellers to believe that its stewardesses provide a level of service not found in other airlines, the appeal combines logic and emotion. There are, however, dangers in using such sexist advertising in western countries. We can use emotional benefits such as safety, by playing on fear (although care must be taken not to become counter-productive here; there is a danger that by suggesting one's competitors are unsafe, one may instil a fear of flying in general!). A more subtle approach is reflected in British Airways' message, which plays on the theme 'the world's favourite airline'.

In the late 1980s, Thomas Cook produced a controversial series of television ads in which its aim was to encourage consumers to choose Cooks rather than other travel agents because – it was hinted – only Cooks offered complete financial stability. This 'fear appeal' of losing holidays had strong market impact, although the decision to produce what was tantamount to 'knocking copy' produced many complaints from other agents to ABTA, who ruled that Cooks were casting unjustified doubts and damaging the business *per se*. There is a danger in such campaigns that the impression left with consumers may be the total instability of the retail travel business which could have the effect of increas-

Fig. 7.3 An example of 'personality' advertising directed at the trade
(Courtesy: Jersey Tourism)

ing direct bookings or last-minute bookings.

In considering whether to use rational or emotional arguments in communications, it is worth bearing in mind that rational messages are more likely to appeal to the better-educated consumer than are emotional messages.

The First Choice advertisements for Sovereign combine both rational and emotional messages. The copy concentrates on exclusivity, quality and 'getting away from the crowd', while hinting at the kudos associated with booking a Sovereign holiday. The beautiful photography and classic design work together to support the story and generate desire. The overall intention of the advertisement is to differentiate the Sovereign product from its competition through clear product identity.

Promotional messages are sometimes criticised

on the grounds that their arguments are too one-sided. In fairness to the communicator, the aim of commercial messages is to present a company's products in the best possible light. However, in some instances they will achieve more by presenting a more balanced view of the products. This is particularly true when one is dealing with better-educated consumers or where the consumer is potentially hostile to the concept. In the travel world, the hyperbole of the copywriter and past inaccuracies in brochure texts have led to some suspicion about travel brochures in general, although the ABTA Code of Conduct and an increase in control through statutory law have led to marked improvements. However, some travel companies have taken to producing 'objective guides' to resorts and hotels which present a two-sided picture of refreshing honesty, and this has greatly helped to increase the trust in, and loyalty towards, those agents by their clients.

Successful communications

We can summarise this introduction to the communications process by saying that good communications require that a company:

- determines its objectives clearly, and defines these in terms that are measurable
- assigns sufficient funds to the campaign to ensure that the mission can be accomplished
- limits the objectives set, so that the receivers clearly understand the message and remember it
- wherever possible, directs the message to a specific market whose traits and characteristics are known and understood
- designs a message which is short, attention-getting, credible and which reinforces the desired image of the company and its products
- tests all communications before launching the campaign, to ensure that they will be effective.

Huge sums of money are spent by the larger travel companies on promotion. Major campaigns such as those offered by leading airlines, shipping companies, hotel chains or tour operators can cost over £1 million – too much to gamble. The companies must make every effort to ensure that the campaign achieves the sales level, or other target, determined. In the following five chapters, we shall go on to look in detail at each of the communications tools available to marketing organisations, and see how these can be most effectively used.

Personal selling

Travel and tourism is a people business; that is to say, the people who attend to the needs of tourists form an essential ingredient in the product itself. Whether referring to sales staff who are responsible for dealing with customers behind the counter, resort representatives who cater to their needs when they arrive at their destination, or any of the hundreds of staff with whom the customer will come in contact – hotel waiters, barstaff, porters, hotel cleaners, coach drivers or airline cabin crew, all play a major role in ensuring that the total product satisfies the client.

It may be self-evident, but it has to be stressed, particularly to young people, that service does not mean servility. People must learn to take a greater pride in their skills at serving the needs of others. Above all, this means being outgoing or friendly in dealings with tourists at all times: the phrase 'the customer is always right' applies especially to the business of tourism, and irrespective of the long hours and hard work which travel staff are called upon to perform, the customers will always expect them to be friendly and cheerful on or off duty. In short, *the travel product is indivisible from the staff who deliver it*. If we are buying a television set from a sales assistant who is poorly dressed, unkempt or unfriendly, we may be disappointed, but the reputation of the brand name may still ensure that we go ahead and buy it, if the price is right. With travel, no reduction in price will compensate for an impolite tour guide, a surly coach driver or a slovenly dressed waiter.

Those who intend to work in the travel industry in a role which will in any way bring them into contact with tourists must be willing to present a well-turned-out appearance, to be patient and helpful, and above all to smile and appear friendly. The way we express ourselves on paper when communicating with clients is also an important element in the travel transaction. Good written communications call for tact, especially when dealing with complaints, attention to detail and the use of correct English; poor grammar and spelling reflect badly on the company employing you, and the effect is compounded when you rise in position with the company (our inadequate grammar doesn't mysteriously improve when we are promoted!).

Sales technique goes much further in the travel business than merely effecting a transaction. Interpersonal communications are part of the 'after sales service' which is provided in all travel products as part of the tourism experience, and when these communications are good they can compensate for many shortcomings which are inevitable in a tourism product, such as poor weather or air traffic delays. As such, they are therefore a vital element in the company's marketing strategies, and adequate training must be built in to the marketing plan to ensure that these communications, too, are effective.

The use of social and personal skills

Two types of skills are required to be employed when dealing with clients (and with other colleagues); personal skills and interpersonal, or social, skills. Both involve verbal and non-verbal communications, the more important forms of which we shall deal with here.

Personal skills

In the initial encounter with clients, first impressions are crucial. The way that travel clerks, hotel receptionists or resort representatives appear and present themselves will set the scene for a successful company–client relationship. For this reason many companies impose strict rules on matters of appearance and grooming. Yet people live in an age of freedom that would have been inconceivable even in the 1960s, and do not readily accept restrictions on their right to dress as they please, adopt the hairstyles of their choice,

and use their preferred cosmetics. For many people, the world of employment provides the first challenge to these rights, and tourism employees must learn to adjust to the constraints that the conditions of employment will impose.

At a basic level, this will mean conforming to a style of dress and grooming that the employer requires. Airlines, for example, will insist that cabin staff adopt a conservative and manageable hairstyle. Women who have formerly felt that the 'natural' look suits them will be told to use make-up, including perhaps a bright shade of lipstick. They conform, or they don't stay in the job.

Needless to say, travel staff coming into close contact with customers must be fastidious about personal hygiene. Regular washing and bathing is essential, together with oral and dental care, avoidance of food which may offend clients such as garlic or onions, and the use of anti-perspirants being strongly recommended, especially for those engaged in physical work (such as stowing hand baggage in overhead compartments).

Deportment is important, too; we communicate non-verbally as well as verbally, and the way we walk, sit or stand reflects an attitude of mind towards the job. Staff will be expected to look alert and interested in their clients, to avoid slouching when they walk, to sit upright rather than slumped in a chair. Clothes must always be clean and neatly pressed, as well as suitable for their purpose. The objective of most companies is to present a 'uniform' appearance, to convey a corporate image of the company, and increasingly this means actually wearing a uniform. Hotel, airline and car rental staff, couriers, resort representatives and even travel agents are being asked to adopt uniforms. Representatives serving in warm climates are having to give up the casual leisure wear that has been customary in order to present a more formal image, with skirt, blouse and neckscarf, or slacks, shirt and tie. Of course, in such conditions, it is doubly important that uniforms are washed and pressed regularly. Jewellery is generally frowned upon, and must be kept to a minimum.

These are all indirect and non-verbal communication skills which tell the client something about the company and its employees. Next we shall turn our attention to direct communications skills, both verbal and non-verbal, which involve interaction with clients.

Social skills

Reference was made earlier to the importance attached to friendliness in dealing with clients. Employees must approach customers in a friendly and confident manner. This means a welcoming smile, eye contact, attentiveness and a willingness to listen. When shaking hands, a firm handshake will convey a sense of confidence and responsibility – vital for the client seeking reassurance or help, or opening negotiations to buy a product. The use of the client's name enhances the image of interest and attention (hotel porters are trained to read the labels of incoming guests' baggage, so they can use the client's name as early as possible in the host–guest relationship). The tone of voice is important, too; voices should be well modulated and soothing, especially when dealing with an irate customer. Fortunately, earlier prejudices against regional accents have largely disappeared, but a strident or whining voice grates, and it requires only a little effort to change this.

When handling complaints, the voice should convey concern. Many clients look for a sounding board to work off their anger, when they have a legitimate complaint, and agreement rather than argument will help to modify their anger. A wronged customer is seeking two things, an apology and a reassurance that action will be taken to investigate the complaint. It costs a company nothing to deliver both.

Attentiveness to the client's needs can be demonstrated by volunteering an interest in the client. A resort representative, for instance, can enquire in passing whether clients are enjoying themselves, or a counter clerk can ask a customer browsing through the brochures 'Is there any particular kind of holiday you have in mind?' to generate a sales sequence.

In general, people working in service industries in Britain have far to go, to perform at the level of service which many of our foreign competitors offer. This is perhaps the greatest weakness of the British travel product, and it is a salutary experience to observe a professional waiter in, say, Italy or Spain, and compare the quality of service they offer with the general level to be found in Britain. There are many excellent and well-trained staff in the UK, however, and the increasing emphasis on training is steadily improving the picture, at least in the larger companies. In the USA, which is not always thought of as a service-orientated country, the level of control exercised over staff in tourism often astonishes the British observer. Training programmes for Disneyworld, for example, dictate the exact form and level of performance of all employees coming into contact with clients, even down to an obligatory smile and saying 'Have a nice day' on parting. Whether it is possible, or even desirable, to emulate this example in Britain is debatable, but our concern for our clients must improve in all sectors of the industry. Above all, our attitude of mind towards service must change, to a pride in one's job and a respect for the client. The use of derisive terms for customers such as 'punters' is symptomatic of a poor attitude to service which is indefensible if the industry is to become professional in its approach.

The sales sequence

We have talked about the vital ingredients – deportment, appearance and facial expression – which are needed to give clients initial confidence when dealing with representatives of a company. In this final section on communications, we shall look at the sales sequence itself.

While the most common setting for selling is the retail agency, and the examples below will be particularly appropriate to that setting, the principles of selling skills apply equally in all situations where client and sales staff come face to face, as in the case of resort representatives selling trips or cruise staff selling shore excursions.

The sales sequence requires a salesperson to proceed in five steps, by

- establishing rapport with clients
- investigating client needs
- presenting the product to clients
- handling objections
- closing the sale: getting the clients to commit themselves.

Establishing rapport

The sales sequence has two aims: to sell the company's products, and to match these products to client needs so as to ensure that the client receives satisfaction. In order to meet the latter objective, the initial task for any salesperson is to engage the client in conversation, to gain the client's trust and learn about the client's needs. This process, known as establishing rapport, will reveal how open the client is to ideas, and how willing to be sold. Some customers are suspicious of any attempts to sell them products, preferring a self-selection process. They may see sales staff as ignorant about the products, or 'pushy', but even such clients as these can be put in the right frame of mind to buy from a particular shop if they receive friendly and helpful service.

In order to strike up a conversation with a client, one must avoid the phrase 'Can I help you?', common as it is. The phrase simply invites the reply, 'Thank you, no, I'm just looking'. A more useful opening to generate discussion would be, 'Do you have a particular kind of holiday in mind?', or to a customer who has just picked up a brochure, 'That company has a particularly good choice of holidays this year. Were you thinking of a particular destination?'

The good salesperson must be something of a psychologist, judging from clients' facial expressions their frame of mind and their reactions to questioning. Customers in a hurry, who appear to know exactly what they want, will not thank you for holding them up to engage in a conversation, but a fast, efficient service accompanied by a friendly smile will encourage them to return. Above all, the salesperson should act as naturally as possible. Being yourself will best reassure clients that you are genuine in your desire to help and advise.

Investigating needs

Having gained the client's trust, the next step is to investigate their needs. Once again it is necessary to ask open questions which elicit full answers, rather than closed questions which call for yes/no replies. The sorts of questions the sales staff will need to know include:

- Who is travelling, and how many will be in the group?
- When do they wish to travel, and for how long?
- How do they want to travel?
- Where do they want to go to?
- How much do they expect to pay?

Clients will not necessarily know the answers to all these questions themselves, so one needs to start out asking those that they can reply to easily, and gradually draw out their answers to questions they may not have thought about yet. Some of these answers will be vague to start with ('We had thought about somewhere hot, not too pricey, sometime in the summer') and can be gradually detailed as the conversation proceeds.

Needs must never be assumed. Clients might say that they don't want to go on a package holiday. There could be many different reasons for this, ranging from a bad experience on earlier packages to a desire for complete flexibility or a wish to escape from the holiday masses. The exact reason for the preference should be known so that the salesperson knows what products to offer – there are, for instance, very flexible (independent inclusive tour) (ITT) packages where the client would not be one of a crowd. It may be that friends have put the client off the idea of a package because of their experiences. In any case, at each stage of the investigation, it is as well to make sure that the needs identified are agreed between the client and the salesperson:

'Let me see, you wanted somewhere quiet and remote, just to lie back and relax, is that right?'

'You did say that you didn't want a large hotel, is that right?'

Presenting the product

Once the salesperson is satisfied that there is enough information about the client's needs, then the next step is that of presentation. This means presenting the right product to meet the client's needs, and presenting it in a way which will convince the client that that is the right product. Here, the key to success is to mention not only the features of the holiday or other product being sold, but also the benefits to the client:

'I would suggest that you stay in Igls rather than Innsbruck itself. It's quieter at that time of the year, less congested, and offers some very attractive woodland walks, just what you were saying you wanted. There's a small hotel, the Ritter, which is owner-managed and has an unusually friendly and personal atmosphere, ideal for someone like yourself staying alone.'

Obviously, product knowledge is crucial to the success of this stage, but personal experience of the resort itself isn't always necessary; sound knowledge of the brochure material will generally suffice.

Even if the product you are offering is exactly what the client requires, it is always well to offer one or two alternatives. Clients like to feel they are being offered a choice. Pick out the benefits of each, but stress that the first choice really seems to meet the client's needs best. Too many alternatives, on the other hand, will lead to confusion, and may delay a sale.

Handling objections

One important aspect of the sales sequence which generally arises here is the need to handle objections from the client. Objections may be genuine, based on price, or they may be due to the client being offered insufficient choice. On the other hand, they may be made because the client has an additional need that has not yet been met, and this may require the salesperson returning to the investigation stage to draw out this need. It may also be because the client is not yet ready to buy, and may need more time to consider.

If the product is more expensive than was originally envisaged, the client will need reassurance of the extra benefits included and that the product is offering real value for money. This is best achieved by showing clients a product at the price they were willing to pay, and comparing the two, pointing out the additional benefits of paying a little more.

Whatever the reason for the objections, it must be identified and countered by matching all the client's needs to a product as closely as is possible to achieve.

Closing the sale

The final stage in the sequence is to close the sale. This means getting clients to take action and commit themselves. There can be several outcomes to a sales sequence. Clients may buy the product, either by paying in full or leaving a deposit; they may take an option on it; they may agree to the salesperson calling them later, or agree to call back later; or they may leave the shop without any commitment of any kind. Although ideally the aim of all sales conversations is to close with a sale, this is clearly not possible, and the important thing from the salesperson's point of view is to ensure that the best possible outcome is obtained. Clients may want to go home to talk over the product with their partner, but if they leave satisfied that they have received good service, there is a high likelihood that they will return to make the booking. Of course, if they are merely uncertain, the sale may be clinched by going over the benefits once more, and reminding them that it is better to take an option (which does not commit them) to avoid disappointment if the particular holiday they have in mind has been sold by the time they return.

A good salesperson is continually looking for the buying signals emitted by clients: statements such as 'Yes, that sounds good' clearly indicate a desire to buy. Where the signals are not clear, a comment from the salesperson such as 'Would you like me to try and book that for you?' may prompt the client into action. However, clients should never be pushed into a decision; not only will they not buy, but also they may determine never to return again.

Finally, remember that the selling job doesn't end when the clients have paid. Hopefully, they will become regular customers. Reassurance of your desire to help them at any time with their travel arrangements, and a closing comment such as, 'I know you will be happy with that particular hotel. Do come and tell me about it when you get back' will reinforce the sale and reassure customers that they have made the best possible choice, not only of the product but also of the retailer through which they purchased it.

Sales training for overseas representatives

An important part of the role of a tour operator's overseas representative is to sell excursions, car hire and merchandise to the clients in resort. This makes a significant contribution to profits for little extra cost (see Chapter 6). It is fair to say that many clients wish to take advantage of excursions and consider them an important part of their holiday experience. They therefore appreciate a representative who can put over the benefits of different trips in a professional manner. The local economy and job prospects are also boosted by the extra business generated for taxi and coach firms, restaurants, tourist attractions and shops.

Tour operators are increasingly investing in training for their overseas staff, and sales training represents an important part of this. All First Choice Holidays representatives, for example, attend a two-day course where they learn sales skills and practise them in role plays. Of course, the basic principles of selling and the sales sequence already discussed remain the same whether you are selling the main holiday package or an excursion. Therefore First Choice Holidays representatives are trained to follow the following pattern:

1 *Establishing rapport* The 'Welcome Get-together' is an important vehicle for representatives to establish rapport with their clients. The tour operator provides help and support to ensure that representatives know how to introduce and structure such an event for their clients. The company provides help in terms of 'welcome packs' and support material. However, representatives must also learn how to gather and present the specific,

local information unique to their own resort.
2 *Investigating needs* Exactly as with matching a holiday type to an individual, representatives must often spend time on a one-to-one basis with their clients asking open questions in order to find out what they like doing and the sort of trip which matches their needs.
3 *Presenting the product benefits* The art of matching product benefits to needs is emphasised, as this is the heart of selling. There is a difference between a mere itinerary and the specific appeal of certain excursions to individual clients. Thus the representative must learn to tune into the wants of each different client:

> 'The coach is air-conditioned so your kids will enjoy the trip without getting too hot.'

> 'The boat is open decked, so you need not worry that you will miss out on an opportunity to work on your tan!'

> 'The cabaret night is a really sociable and fun evening, so it's a great opportunity for people travelling alone to meet other guests.'

4 *Handling objections and closing the sale* While the principles remain the same, in practice the representative probably has a shorter time span in which to achieve the sale, as the days rush by on a seven night holiday. Their ability to close the sale and make a firm booking is therefore imperative.

Travel agency design

It is appropriate to close this chapter with a look at travel agency design, since the effective presentation and design of an agency is critical to its acceptance as a location for the purchase of travel by consumers.

It has often been said that travel agents are fortunate. All they need is a shop, some posters and a telephone, and they can set up in business. Of course, it is not as easy as that, and today's competitive climate makes it certain that design of travel agencies will become ever more important to their success.

While it used to be considered that a travel agent need not take premises in the centre of town because customers would seek it out when they required advice, this too is no longer the case. Most high streets have their own travel agency and the number of customers they attract is directly related to the position they occupy within the town. Good visibility of the shop, such as being on a prominent road junction, may well be a bonus, but the greatest test of any shop site is the number of pedestrians who pass the door. A counting machine and a stopwatch employed at various times during the week will give the best indication of the relative merits of the position when considering new sites. Availability of car-parking facilities is also worth exploring and considering, especially in the small town location.

Any retail concern will normally obtain the best site it can afford for a new business, and will then do its best to maximise the use of that site. Similar considerations can be applied to existing agency locations.

Most research into why customers choose one travel agency in preference to another leads one to the conclusion that the most important factors are that it is in a convenient location and that it is noticed. Thus the outside appearance is of critical importance. In increasingly professional-looking high streets, other traders have led the way with crisp, colourful fascias stating their identities, and merchandise to entice the shopper in. A theme is almost always apparent, and the displays are changed frequently to create interest. Travel agents would do well to learn these lessons, especially to forgo their 'bargain bazaar' approach, characterised by numerous stickers with conflicting messages.

In terms of layout, all trades now favour open windows which allow a view of what is beyond the window display. They also favour a fairly flat shop front which maximises the space available within.

From the outside, and within, two factors dominate first impressions – colour and light.

Colour

Colour plays a key part in establishing an identity. Different colours are credited with individual values:

- red conveys warmth and vitality
- white is clean, cold and clinical
- green is considered natural, caring and wholesome
- blue is seen as crisp and efficient
- yellow is happy and joyful (though sometimes it can be garish)
- burgundy looks sophisticated
- brown and orange are comfortable, relaxing colours.

Above all, to choose a colour will establish a background for all that you want to display. Never forget that it will look very different when stocked with brochures and posters.

Good examples of colour usage are red for Thomas Cook, royal blue for the Going Places fascia, and burgundy for American Express.

Three leading tour operators have a policy of publishing a wide variety of brochures (Airtours and First Choice Holidays between them publish some 60 brochures for summer alone), and few agents can afford not to stock most of these on their racks; indeed this represents a deliberate ploy on the part of these operators to monopolise the available racking space of the agencies. Increasingly, the agents themselves (particularly the large multiples) are following a policy of restricting the display of brochures to those companies which are well established with the retailer, while independents generally try to compete by offering a wider selection of smaller operators' products. The choice of what to display and sell is referred to as *racking policy*.

Several of the major agency multiples are owned in turn by tour operators. This so-called *vertical integration* means that the parent company has considerable influence over the racking and sales policy of the travel agency, with preference obviously being given to the brochures of the parent operator.

All travel agents will be quick to agree that these brochures are the most important sales tool. They cost a great deal of money to produce, and supplies are often restricted; yet very often little control is exercised over them. Whatever racking policy is in force, the positioning of brochure displays is critical. If they are freely available in the open area of the shop, then certain basic rules will apply. The most effective positions for display will be those close to the door, or opposite the entrance, at around shoulder to eye height. Should the brochures displayed there be the ones you want to use to attract attention, or the ones that will sell readily anyway? Once policy has been decided, it should be positively translated into the display facilities (and the related storage capability) in shop design.

Lighting

Lights can make or break any scheme. Fluorescent lighting is economical and highly efficient for overall background levels, but is extremely poor for creating impact. Concentrations of light in small areas of relative darkness will highlight any goods much more effectively. The intensity will depend upon the method chosen, with tungsten bulbs, spotlight bulbs and quartz halogen low-voltage units improving in effectiveness by degree. Modern lighting deserves expert advice, once the objectives of the shop design have been decided upon.

Lighting also leads into practicalities, for the overall light levels within a shop will affect the environment for both the customer and the workers. High overall light levels are seldom attractive, and they will also interfere with ease of vision on computer screens. However, the level of light in which staff undertake clerical duties, especially poring over closely packed timetable information, must be good.

Within the travel agency, the first impression should be friendly and welcoming, and designed to put customers at ease. It must be clean (and therefore designed to be easy to clean), up-to-date in design and practical to operate. Figures 7.4, 7.5 and 7.6 provide illustrations of travel agency layout design, lighting and racking considerations.

Practicalities

To convert enquiries into bookings will need not only a desk, but also access to telephones, com-

puter visual display units (VDUs), and reference material. These facilities must be to hand and tidily arranged. Consideration must be given to storage and security of money; it must be decided whether each clerk will have a personal till or whether a central cash desk is to be operated.

Display, demonstration and excitement

Travel is about images of places far away and highly desirable. It is about people enjoying themselves and taking a break from their drab daily routines. Travel agencies should exude some of this excitement of possibilities, but it is very easy for the travel agency to become boring and ineffective. Thus the use of display panels with emotive photographs, dramatic (not 'so what?') posters, video walls and video demonstration players for travel information and even the use of modern computer booking systems, all help to add to the atmosphere of growing excitement.

As with most moods, however, never assume that things happen by accident. The relationship of space and distance is important. Staff positioned too far away from brochure racks will tend to appear uncaring. The way in which layouts are thought out will help to provide a tidy appearance, e.g. one must not leave convenient space where new brochure supplies can be dumped by delivery carriers in full view of customers. The shop will need to be comfortably warm in winter and cool in summer. The layout has to be equally effective for customer comfort and staff convenience – no mean task. What is certain is that to do the job well is both important and expensive.

Desks or counters?

One debate that has continued for many years is whether desks or counters are the best methods for carrying out transactions with the customer. There are divided views, and these can be summed up as follows:

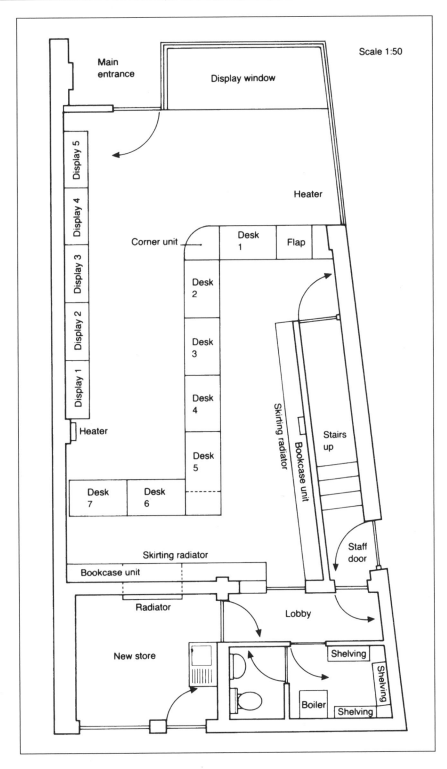

Fig. 7.4 Shop plan for Go-Right Travel

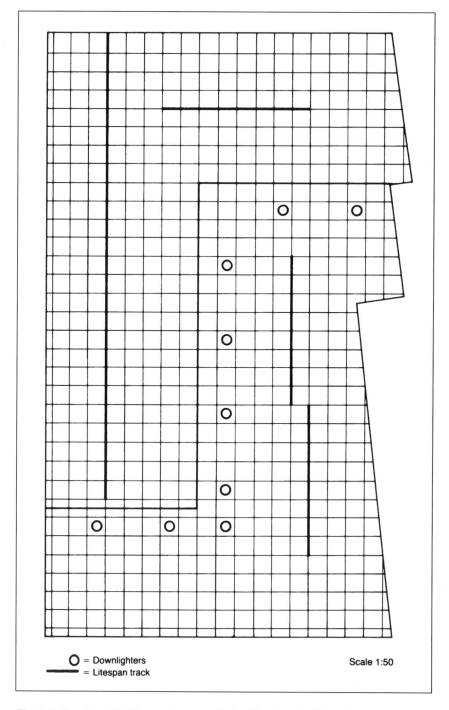

O = Downlighters
▬ = Litespan track

Scale 1:50

Fig. 7.5 Overhead lighting and suspended ceiling for Go-Right Travel shop

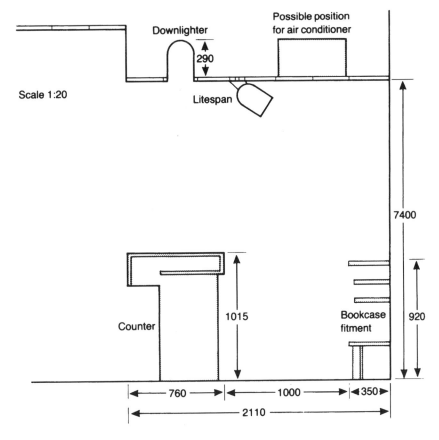

Fig. 7.6 Elevation of interior, showing counter, bookshelves and lighting for Go-Right Travel shop

Counters

- do not encourage customers to 'settle in' and stay for longer than necessary
- enable staff (on high stools) to work at the correct height to deal with customers standing up and prevent them feeling dominated by the customer standing above them in a 'superior' position
- provide a security barrier and enable cash to be kept at each position
- provide adequate space below the desk top for either a split level desk with computer screens, etc., tidily built out of view, or for other storage and reference facilities.

Desks

- are more friendly, encouraging customers to sit and chat

- can be set out informally near brochure racks
- are much less expensive in shopfitting terms as they are able to be deployed without being fixed or specially fitted.

Which policy is chosen is not important, as long as it is implemented well.

The emphasis on corporate design in all areas of business will ensure that the travel agency of the future, if it is to survive as a distribution system, must employ the newest techniques in retailing and above all must provide the welcoming, attractive and comfortable trading outlet which customers are coming to expect in all shops (see Figs 7.7 and 7.8).

Fig. 7.7 Modern desks for personal selling in a multiple agent's office
(Courtesy: Thomas Cook Group)

Fig. 7.8 Bright, modern and efficient layout for a multiple agent's office
(Courtesy: Thomas Cook Group)

Questions, tasks and issues for discussion

1 How effective is the communications process in your classroom? From which
   forms of teaching and through which learning processes do you:

   (a) remember information best?
   (b) acquire skills best?

   What 'interference' occurs to prevent your receiving messages?

2 Discuss the merits of personal selling through travel agents compared with
   advertising direct to the public, in the promotion of package holidays.

3 Identify one TV programme or film which has influenced you to see or want to
   see a destination. What exactly was the appeal that motivated you? How best
   could the resort or area in question be promoted to you to reinforce this
   motivation?

4 Collect two advertisements which offer contrasting messages, and explain why
   the appeals are different.

5 Assume the role of a small, independent travel agent, and design a message for
   an advertisement aimed at counteracting messages from the major multiples
   which appeal to 'security' and 'price sensitivity'.

Exercise

You have been asked to undertake an appraisal of the effectiveness of
communications in a local travel agency. Select any agency of your choice (if you
have a student-run agency within your college, you may care to choose this) and,
based on the issues discussed in this chapter, observe the effectiveness with which
the agency communicates with its market.

Write a report to the manager of the agency which critically assesses each of the
criteria you have identified. Include in your report an appraisal of the importance
which price plays in the marketing of travel products in the agency, as identified in
the products displayed in the windows or within the agency. What other
promotional appeals are being used to support sales by the agency?

8 The distribution system

After studying this chapter, you should be able to:

- identify the factors affecting the choice of different distribution systems
- appreciate the role of the travel agent as retailer of travel services
- distinguish between methods of co-operative distribution and evaluate the respective merits of each
- recognise the importance of the sales representative's role in marketing, and understand how this is successfully managed
- understand the function of inventory control in travel and tourism reservation systems

It is convenient to think of distribution as part of the overall communications process, since it involves the selection and operation of channels by which a company communicates its products to its markets. Technically, in marketing theory there are two aspects to distribution. One deals with the distributive channels, the other with the physical delivery of products to those channels, and ultimately to the consumer. The latter process entails the keeping of inventories of goods to balance supply and demand, the warehousing and storage of goods, and the transportation of goods to dealers and customers. However, these latter functions relate largely to the marketing of tangible products, while in the case of travel and tourism, customers are brought to the product rather than the product being delivered to the customer.

We are therefore concerned here with somewhat different aspects of the distribution process. Nevertheless, there are common issues in distributing goods and services. Particularly, tourism requires the establishment of a *reservations system*, both to handle the sales process and in order to act as an inventory control system to balance supply and demand. This reservations system can usefully be thought of as a 'travel distribution system', which is closely linked to the way in which channels are managed, and will be dealt with in this chapter as part of the examination of the role and function of distribution channels.

The prime purpose of distribution channels, however, is to sell a company's products, and for this reason we shall also look at the functions of sales skills and sales management as part of this chapter.

Channel choice

Before we consider how channels are chosen, let us first make ourselves aware of the options open to a company, when planning its distribution strategy.

A principal, such as an airline, cruise company or hotel, can if it so wishes choose to deal entirely direct with its customers, entirely through intermediaries, or some combination of direct sell and sales through intermediaries. The term *intermediary* is used to describe any dealer who acts as a link in the chain of distribution between the company and its customers. Most companies choose to deal through one or more intermediaries. The reason for this is simple: it is cheaper for a company to do so than to set up its own network of retail shops or sell its products directly in any other way. By paying a commission or other agreed form of financial remuneration to their intermediaries, companies buy the use of a distributive network. The system also acts as a convenience to consumers, as they can choose from a range of different products under one roof, instead of having to visit each producer's shop in turn to select their product.

Should an airline decide to sell its flights direct to the public, it must provide a network of shops for the purpose; at least one in every important trading centre in the UK and abroad. Alternatively, it could find other means of selling tickets, such as through automatic vending machines, through telephone bookings or by mail order, but all these offer disadvantages to the customer, and moreover each separate airline will have to set up its own distribution system, duplicating the retailing effort (although some airlines on non-competitive routes would undoubtedly act as representatives for the distribution of other airlines' tickets). The resulting airline shops will have only a limited number of products to sell: flights, and package holidays using that particular airline's services. Customers would be forced to move from shop to shop to compare flights and prices, or to buy other products such as car hire associated with their trips.

Multiply this picture by the huge number of different travel principals, and you will begin to understand the enormity of the direct sell problem, and the sheer impracticality of cutting out the intermediary entirely. A few key travel products could well be distributed in this way, if the market is very large, highly concentrated geographically and the product is purchased frequently; or alternatively if the company is very small, but the product is highly specialised, and one which potential customers are prepared to search out. Certain short break and activity holidays are sold in this way.

Many US airlines do have their own retail outlets in major commercial centres in their own country, while in Britain the level of demand for air tickets can just support a limited number of British Airways (BA) shops in major cities. Most travellers, however, will find it more convenient to book their BA flights through their local travel agent, which handles 70–80 per cent of the total volume of air tickets. BA must also be careful, therefore, not to antagonise their travel agents by expanding their direct sell efforts too forcefully, which would threaten agency support. With low brand loyalty among the flying public, it could be relatively easy for many agents to persuade their clients to switch to other airlines.

Figure 8.1(a) explains the process by which goods and services reach customers through a *chain of distribution*, starting at the producer and ending at the point where the customer accepts 'delivery' of the product. The diagram has been simplified to indicated a typical number of links found in the chain, but in the case of some products, additional intermediaries can extend this chain considerably. Using the analogy of the airline once again, an airline is a producer of a transport product, and is therefore at the start of the 'travel chain of distribution', although the reader should be aware that the product chain actually stretches back through the aircraft manufacturer to the supplier of raw materials for the aircraft.

An airline sells its seats in a variety of ways. Individual seats can be sold direct to a customer, or they can be sold through a retail travel agent. The airline will also sell seats in bulk through tour operators or 'air brokers'. Tour operators in turn use these seats to create package tours (some argue that in so doing, they are creating new products, and should therefore more correctly be termed 'producers' of products rather than wholesalers), which are then sold either direct or through agents. Some types of air brokers enter the chain at a level between the airline and the tour operator, purchasing large blocks of seats at bulk prices and selling these in turn to operators, while other brokers act as 'consolidators' for airline charter flights, helping tour operators with low load factors to integrate their flights with other operators who are similarly placed. Some of these consolidation seats will find their way on to the market, being sold individually through travel agents to the public at 'late booking saver fares'. Tour operators may themselves off-load unsold seats at 'saver fares' to the public through travel agents or direct. The distribution system for air seats thus becomes

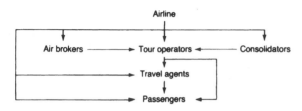

Fig. 8.1(a) The chain of distribution

Fig. 8.1(b) Distribution channels for airline seats

quite complex, with seats being sold through a variety of different dealers. This can be seen in Fig. 8.1(b).

An airline operating both scheduled and charter flights will typically use all of these distribution methods to maximise its load factors, but must continually re-evaluate the service provided by each of these links in the chain, to ensure that the current system offers the most effective means of reaching customers at the lowest possible cost commensurate with the quality of service required.

Selecting the channel

New companies to the travel and tourism business must determine their strategy for distribution, just as existing companies must re-evaluate it from time to time. There are three key factors which a principal must bear in mind when making this choice:

● cost
● control
● level of service

Cost

Much has been made of the belief that so-called 'direct sell' tour operators can sell their product more cheaply to the public by cutting out the intermediaries. In fact, the issue is not clear-cut. Certainly, some holidays sold direct are cheaper than identical holidays sold through more traditional channels, but this is not always so, nor is it necessarily the case that the same level of profit is being achieved on the holiday. The critical factor in reducing price is the reduction of cost, and while this may be a factor of lower distribution costs, it may equally be the result of more successful negotiations with airlines and hotels, or greater 'muscle' because of the greater number of beds or seats being contracted.

Companies selling their products through retailers have one great advantage over the direct sell operators. Most of their costs are variable costs, that is, distribution costs arise only when a sale is made. A direct sell operator, however, will have the fixed costs of operating the shop whether the public come in to buy the product or not. This means that either the direct sales operator must enjoy a high level of turnover to support the cost of the shop, or the product must be unique and so certain to find a ready market that the promotional costs are comparatively low. In this respect, those mass market operators who have chosen to sell direct such as Portland Holidays (a division of the Thomson Travel empire) provide us with an interesting case study. The homogeneous nature of mass market package holidays requires the direct sell operator to invest heavily in promotion at the launch stage, both to bring the product to the public's attention and to persuade them to adopt a novel system of buying it. In addition to a programme of national television advertising, there are heavy direct mail expenses in sending brochures to prospective customers, and the company must provide an exceptional telephone service to ensure that members of the public can get through to the company once their interest is aroused. Any failures here will drive the customer back to the more familiar travel agent.

Great care therefore must be taken to ensure

that the information and booking system is capable of supporting the level of demand which it creates. However, once the direct sell company achieves a satisfactory market share, enabling it to reduce marketing costs relative to other costs, its avoidance of intermediaries' commissions will enable it to compete on price with other operators of similar size.

The problems faced by Portland and other direct sell companies in getting an established share of the travel market is typical of other problems facing companies seeking new ways of reaching the market. British customers are conservative in their buying habits, and it has been difficult to overcome the strengths of traditional channels. The convenience of the location is a critical factor in the success of the travel agent, just as it is a critical factor in the distribution success of any fast moving consumer good. But with the low brand loyalty towards travel products, the convenience and accessibility of the retail outlet becomes second only to price in importance for the product's success. This is one aspect of the level of service which a company provides for its clients.

The desire for control over product distribution systems has led several tour operators to develop or buy their own retail outlets. Thus Thomson has ownership of Lunn Poly, the largest retail multiple in the UK; Airtours purchased two major multiples, Hogg Robinson and Pickfords, and merged them into the retail chain Going Places, the second largest multiple agency. Both of these are examples of vertically integrated companies, whereby the travel organisation wholly owns the tour operator, retailer and the airline which carries its customers. To this may be added resort accommodation (Airtours, for instance, also owns cruise ships).

Such vertical integration in respect of retailers carries the powerful advantage of protecting the sales channels of the other parts of the organisation. As competition has intensified, this had lead to strong *directional selling* by such retailers: under firm corporate direction, the multiples concerned are becoming progressively more successful at channelling sales into their own tour operations. It is estimated that in 1995 Thomson accounted for more than 50 per cent of the tour operator sales in Lunn Poly.

While this trend has become a very important part of commercial reality in the 1990s, it is not without its problems. An alternative strategy, adopted by First Choice Holidays, is to avoid ownership of retailers, in order to form strong commercial relationships across a broader range of retailers. The tour operator is thus not also seen as a retailer competitor, and avoids the tit-for-tat directional selling exemplified by Airtours' poor representation in Lunn Poly and Thomson's lack of sales in Going Places.

Control

The principal must also consider the degree of control which it can exercise over its distributive outlets, when planning the distribution system. The use of intermediaries necessarily results in some loss of autonomy, although if the principal owns its own retail shops it can exercise a much higher level of control.

There is the loss of personal contact with clients, if the sales function is in the hands of an independent distributive outlet. It becomes more difficult for the company to understand its market, or identify changing market needs, and it is very dependent on receiving regular feedback from dealers or agents who, without a personal vested interest in one company's products, may not keep their ear so close to the ground. A greater problem still for effective marketing is that the travel agent, dealing with many hundreds of products, will be less committed to any one product than would the staff of one's own company. Bonus commissions can be used to provide some incentive, but other companies are offering similar financial rewards to increase sales, and travel agents will have their own priorities in pushing products. In a field where there is so little brand loyalty, this lack of control over distribution is of great concern to principals, especially in the case of companies such as airlines which have massive capital investment in equipment, but very little control over its sale. It is for this reason that some airlines will determine to have their own retail sales shops, even at the expense of higher distribution costs.

Level of service

Having one's own distributive outlets offers a further advantage. It becomes far easier to co-ordinate the company's level of service and marketing activities generally. An airline launching a new route can be certain that the route is featured in the retail shop windows, that brochures are in stock and prominently displayed, that special point of sale material is on show, and that the sales staff know the product and bring it to their customers' attention.

Product knowledge among retail agents is a controversial issue among principals. Any company that can convince agents that their staff have intimate and first-hand knowledge of the destinations they feature in their brochures will have a considerable sales advantage over other operators, as the agent will feel more confident in calling that operator's staff to discuss their clients' needs. Similarly, a company retailing its own products, such as Portland Holidays, can far more effectively mount a promotional campaign to support their sale, and ensure good co-ordination between all aspects of the promotion. The promotional support that any travel agent can give to one product among all those they represent is necessarily limited. Their staff's product knowledge, too, having to be wide enough to know something about all the hundreds of holidays they sell, must equally be more shallow in dealing with any individual company's products.

Intensive versus selective distribution

A medium to large-sized company has a far easier choice of alternatives open to it when planning its distribution strategy than does a small company. If the larger company sells products appealing to the mass market, and that market is geographically widely distributed throughout the country, it could be anticipated

that the company would normally seek to maximise the number of possible outlets through which its products can be purchased. Such a strategy is termed *intensive distribution*.

Earlier, it was pointed out that sales achieved by way of commission paid to travel agents involve a proportionately small fixed cost element of the total transaction costs. However, this should not disguise the fact that establishing a network of dealers does involve a substantial ongoing cost to a company. There are some 7000 branches of ABTA travel agents in Britain. Each must receive at least a minimal level of servicing if they are expected to be productive for the company. In addition to supplying brochures, this will mean regular mailings to keep agents informed of new products or changes to existing products; the offer of merchandising assistance and materials such as window displays; providing agents' educationals or other forms of training in product knowledge. Additionally, strong supporting agents will expect a regular call from the company's sales representatives.

All these support services will have to be committed over and above any commissions paid to the agents for sales achieved. Such support is clearly beyond the means of the smaller company. A tour operator expecting to carry, say, 5000–6000 passengers in a year could not begin to contemplate a strategy of intensive distribution, since on average less than one booking from each agency will be received. Instead, the operator will opt either to sell products direct or go for some form of *selective distribution* network. If for instance the market is strongly London-based, a certain number of agents located there may be chosen to represent the company; if the market is more evenly distributed throughout Britain, a strategy of *exclusive distribution* could be employed, by the appointment of a 'sole agency' in each major conurbation.

Hotel representative agencies are also appointed by hotels to represent and market their services, particularly to overseas markets where the hotel may find it difficult to reach the client direct or through travel agents. These hotel representatives receive 'overriding' commissions from the hotels they represent which are sufficient to allow them to accept bookings from travel agents to whom they allow the normal agency commission. Sometimes the contract between hotel and representative will include a clause that the latter will not represent any of the hotel's leading competitors.

The agency relationship and its distribution implications

This is a convenient point at which to explore in more detail the relationship between agents and principals, especially tour operators, and to consider how this relationship affects the distribution issue.

Since the mid-1960s, following the collapse of Fiesta Tours in 1964, ABTA provided a voluntary protection scheme for its members known as 'stabiliser'. A fund was established to which both tour operators and travel agents contributed. Both classes of members also agreed to be vetted annually to demonstrate their financial viability and committed themselves to a binding agreement whereby ABTA agents would sell only the package holidays of tour operators who were ABTA members, while in turn the tour operators agreed to sell their products only through ABTA retail members.

Although this restrictive practice was judged in the public interest in the UK, it conflicted with European Union (EU) legislation on trading, and in consequence was abandoned in 1994. This has resulted in a much freer trading environment, with ABTA tour operators selling through new, non-ABTA retailers, and agents in turn being free to sell the products of any supplier they choose (financial security of the companies may be still guaranteed through bonding arrangements). In practice, however, choice is narrowing, for a number of reasons.

There are nearly 7000 tour operator members of ABTA, and most are comparatively small-scale operators who find it difficult to distribute their products through the retail agents. Even if they found that all ABTA agents were willing to stock their brochures, just to provide each with a file copy would involve them in distributing 7000

copies, many of which would be wasted. To send a bale of, say, 50 copies per branch immediately establishes a print run of 350 000 copies. The distribution costs will also be substantial, as they are unlikely to cost less than £1 per bale, and could cost considerably more, dependent upon weight or size.

If every smaller operator followed this policy, then the travel agent would be deluged with brochures. The display area is unlikely to take more than some 100–150 spaces (facings) – even the biggest seldom exceed 300 – while the agent might have as many as 1000 brochures to promote. No agent could conceivably become expert in all the information in this number of brochures, and the value of the advice offered would necessarily be less than adequate. It is certain that the agent is unlikely to have adequate display space to maximise the effect of all the brochures in stock. It follows that those featured will almost certainly fit industry norms, such as the ability to fit the racks. An unusual shape or size will affect its chance of being promoted. A 'clever' heading in a position other than at the top of the page will probably mean that in an overlapped display it simply isn't seen.

Availability and suitability of distributors

A willingness on the part of the operator to distribute brochures to any agent demanding them is one side of the coin. The other side is the willingness of agents to accept the brochures.

Agents are highly selective about the range of products they are willing to sell and the companies they will represent. With the limited rack space available, by the time 'preferred operators' have been racked – major companies' brochures (which are virtually guaranteed to sell anyway) and those paying bonus commissions and receiving the approbation of management – there will be very limited space for new products coming on the market, or for products from small companies, however attractive. Even should the travel agent be keen to adopt the new product, there must be a good match between the agent's catchment area and market and the company's intended market. To some extent, the image of a company is reflected in the image held by its distributor.

The suitability of retailers is also determined by the level of service they will provide for their customers. Convenience of a local outlet to the market is only one attribute of service: the times at which the outlet is open to the public are no less important. Some agents have experimented with late night openings one evening a week, and increasingly, others are opening on Sundays, since trading laws were relaxed. This has led to considerable antagonism from agents and their staff. However, the introduction of more flexible working hours, giving customers the ability to book holidays outside the normal hours of opening, has been popular, and may help to combat the threat of direct home computer bookings which should be feasible by the turn of the century. In areas such as city centres where a lot of travel bookings are made during office workers' lunchtimes, agents are learning to become more flexible by providing part-time staff during the peak lunch periods to cater for the extra demand. Such work is attractive for former employees who have left their companies to raise children, for example.

Technology in distribution is making a major impact, as increasingly tour operators are expecting agents to deal with reservations direct through their on-line computer systems. If agents are unprepared to invest in computer technology, they lose out in the ability to offer clients fast access to information. What is more, the facility to telephone tour operators for bookings is being withdrawn by the larger agents, making it impossible for non-computerised agents to represent these services. Equally, non-computerised tour operators are finding it difficult to compete against high technology reservations systems, with agents increasingly preferring to deal through the on-line reservations systems of the better-equipped principals.

As long as agents continue to provide the level of service which their customers want – good product knowledge, objective advice and convenient location and opening hours – and as long as

these services can be provided at a cost competitive with other distribution systems, the travel agent will continue to flourish.

The travel agent as distributive system

The travel agent's role in the distributive system is to provide a convenient location for the travelling public to seek out information about travel, to make reservations and to buy their tickets; and to do this at a cost which is comparable with other forms of distribution. The proximity of location to the market has always been the principal factor in the success of a travel agent. A street-level shop in or close to the high street is essential, even at the expense of the higher costs which the shop must bear. However, since a travel agent's stock is composed entirely of brochures, less space is required than in most other forms of retail outlet, and costs can be held down by sacrificing square footage. This does mean that the travel agent must measure success in terms of turnover per square footage, and consequently modern shops are designed for a fast throughput of clients, even though the product might in some cases (e.g. cruising and long-haul holidays) be thought to need the care and attention of a professional counselling service.

A characteristic of agency operations since the late 1980s has been the low margins of profitability which most have achieved, as an outcome of the intense competition between tour operating companies, which has made package holidays relatively cheap against other goods and services. This has been exacerbated by the introduction of late booking discounts, greatly reducing the average turnover per booking. Without a commensurate increase in levels of commission to atone for this decline, agents have had to push for higher turnover per branch, and per staff employed, in order to survive. At the same time, the total number of travel agents, at around 7000 ABTA members, has remained remarkably stable throughout the recession of the early 1990s. Historically, when increases in commission levels have been negotiated, this has usually resulted in expansion of the number of retail outlets, rather than in increased profitability of existing units, making principals reluctant to raise commission paid to agents as a means of achieving higher levels of service for customers.

Perhaps the most significant development of the 1980s and 1990s has been the so-called 'march of the multiples', the phenomenal growth of the largest retail chains which has led in Britain to the three largest chains (Lunn Poly, Going Places and Thomas Cook) controlling a quarter of all agencies and nearly half of total retail turnover. This trend is set to continue with all three committed to further expansion. For the first time, power is moving from the principals to the distributive sector in the travel industry, with chains being able to negotiate increases in commission for the higher levels of sales they achieve. At the same time, their greater capital resources have enabled them to invest heavily in computer systems for their reservations, accounting and management information needs, widening the advantages they enjoy over their smaller competitors. Their higher market profile, resulting from national television advertising coverage and a willingness to offer booking incentives, threatens the survival of small agencies. Additionally, many independent agents must pay cash for transactions, while most multiples have credit agreements with all their major suppliers, easing their cash flow position.

These developments have forced the smaller agents to rethink their role in order to survive. Since the small agent cannot compete on price, it must adopt alternative strategies to compete. Four possible solutions include:

- more aggressive sales techniques
- developing 'exclusive distribution' contracts, to represent the smaller, specialist tour operators whom the larger chains are reluctant to support
- providing a superior professional service with informed recommendations rather than merely retailing whatever the consumer asks for
- emphasising the value of the independence of the advice given – the agency has no vested

tour operator interests to bias its recommendations.

In the past, travel agencies have been seen largely as 'order takers' – a convenient point for the purchase of travel arrangements – but competition has now forced a reappraisal of the role, and agents are placing greater emphasis on the ability of their staff to sell, to establish rapport with their clients, and to offer a superior level of product knowledge, so that clients actively seek them out to receive advice, particularly for independent, tailor-made travel arrangements that provide greater earning potential than the standard package holidays.

Independent Holiday Shop: new techniques in travel retailing

One agent has sought to change the methods by which retailers do business. The Independent Holiday Shop, based in Winchester, southern England, was formed in 1993 by two partners who had formerly run a small company chartering classic yachts in Turkey and Greece. The difficulty they found in reaching their potential market was one that they recognised they shared with other specialist holiday companies. Their non-ABTA agency was established with the objective of representing exclusively up to 120 of the smaller, independent specialist operators, and focusing particularly on the tailor-made holiday built around an independent package arrangement.

The company was launched with a novel approach to the contract with their principals: these were charged a fixed fee per calendar month or year for racking their brochure. Premiums were charged for eye-level racking, and for window display of brochures. Commission rates were then negotiated, but at rates lower than the traditional 10 per cent received by agents. This meant that the retailer could cover start-up costs in advance through the charge to principals.

In practice, the agent has found that in the longer run profitability has been improved by eventually reverting to a normal commission structure without a racking fee, but the initial changes proved a highly successful way of launching the agency. Agency commission is payable in retrospect by the principals, with clients paying the principal direct. While this results in a poorer cash flow for the agent, it obviates the legal necessity to be bonded.

The company is now seeking to develop a franchise for up to 45 branches, based on a licence fee and a monthly charge to its franchisees (rather than the more traditional payment of royalties on sales).

Co-operative distribution systems

Consortia

One means by which agents, and principals, can market themselves more effectively is through becoming part of a co-operative marketing venture. The consortium is a characteristic development in joint travel and tourism marketing, allowing organisations to unite for marketing purposes while retaining their financial independence. Consortia are prominent in the marketing of tourist attractions, hotels, and retail travel agents.

The consortium provides a means by which individual companies with common but not competing interests can join together for some mutual benefits. Perhaps the most common benefit is the publication of a joint brochure. A group of tourist attractions, such as ABLE (Association of Bath and District Leisure Attractions) or DATA (Devon Area Tourist Association) can in this way afford to produce thousands of brochures for extensive distribution to hotels, restaurants, tourist information centres, libraries and other sources where holidaymakers in the area are likely to enquire for information (see Fig. 8.2).

With each member's facilities listed at proportionate cost, an attraction can gain far wider circulation and publicity than would be the case if each company were to produce and distribute its own brochure. Groups of stately homes, heritage sites and small hotels have similarly banded together to publicise their products nationally and internationally.

While the production of a joint brochure is the most common benefit to be found in consortia,

Fig. 8.2 Co-operative promotion: Bath's ABLE consortium of tourist attractions brings together 36 local attractions in a joint brochure

there are many other benefits to be achieved in a marketing consortium. In the case of travel agency consortia, a major benefit is the negotiation of higher rates of commission for group members. A number of agents coming together within a region can equal the sales power of a major multiple in the same region, and can therefore gain substantial bonus commissions for targeted sales. One such consortium, Woodside Management Systems (with headquarters in the USA) has built up an international network of business travel agents to negotiate lower prices for hotel accommodation and other travel products for its members.

A consortium can also reduce its members' operating costs by offering opportunities for bulk purchase of supplies such as stationery, computers, and services such as window dressing, while hoteliers gain from the economies of scale inherent in the bulk purchase of food, drinks and other hotel supplies purchased through a central buying organisation.

Hotel consortia in particular have developed common themes as part of the consortia marketing policy; for example, hotels have formed group marketing consortia with themes of historic interest, common price categories or similar standards, such as 3 star, while area marketing consortia such as Torquay Leisure Hotels have been formed to promote the sale of hotel rooms in the same geographical region of the country. Marketing consortia provide the added benefit for hotels of enabling each to act as an agent of the other hotels in the chain, providing an international distribution network. In this way the smaller hotels are capable of competing with the larger chains, although the superior reservations procedures of the latter, usually with advanced computer reservations systems, still give the large organisations a lead.

One other advantage of the consortium is that it provides the means to recruit management expertise on a scale unthinkable for the small company alone. Travel agents and small hotels can for the first time employ centralised accounting, legal assistance, staff training, as well as marketing expertise for the members. Other small tourism units are just beginning to recognise the scope which consortia offer, and sectors such as farm holiday operators are forming groups to integrate their marketing.

While the benefits of consortia are self-evident, readers should be aware that the operation of consortia is not without its problems. One is the result of the autonomy of each individual company within the consortia. Determining the financial contribution of each member to the consortium's common fund is one such issue; should this be in proportion to the turnover that each achieves? Should the amount of space in the brochure be equal for all members, or variable according to the number of products each company offers, or the relative size of each member? Hotel consortia, for instance, generally determine their contribution according to the number of beds in each unit. Then a method of

determining which pages will be allocated in the brochure must be agreed. Members prefer to have their products listed in the opening pages, since the consumer is more likely to notice the first pages than those towards the back of a brochure. Should members therefore pay proportionately more for the early pages in a brochure than those occurring later? Equally important, how is the consortium to be managed? Generally speaking, in the early years of a new consortium, members take it in turns to appoint someone from their management to administer the consortium's affairs, although as time progresses, and the success of the consortium becomes more assured, a small secretariat is usually formed.

Franchises

A second means by which an organisation can expand its system of distribution rapidly is by franchising. This is an arrangement under which a business (whether principal or distributor), known as the franchisor, grants an organisation (the franchisee) the right to use the company's name and market its products in exchange for a financial consideration – usually some form of 'royalty', or percentage of turnover. In most cases the rights are exclusive within a district, so that the franchisee becomes the sole distributor of the product in the area. The franchisee will also usually pay an initial sum to the franchisor to cover various 'set-up' costs, which can include help with site planning, practical advice in setting up the business, and staff training. The franchisee will also agree to conform with the terms of the contract, such as purchasing raw materials or products exclusively from the franchisor, and maintain clearly defined standards of quality.

While there are a number of different ways in which a franchisor may operate, the most common benefits which the franchisee gains are the rights to sell an established brand name product, and the centralised marketing support provided by the franchisor. In turn, the franchisor gains by the rapid expansion of sites operating under one name, and a fast-accumulating central fund with which a national or international advertising campaign can be launched. This campaign creates brand awareness and a ready demand for the product, which leads to further demand for franchises by those eager to start up in business by themselves at reduced risk. Since franchisees are their own bosses, they can also be relied upon to work harder to ensure the success of the organisation.

The franchise concept is not a new one; indeed, its origins go back over 200 years to the breweries' 'tied house', under which an inn or pub is licensed to sell ales and beers of the brewer only, still a common practice in Britain in the 1990s. However, the modern franchise was introduced on a major scale in the USA in the early 1970s, and has become particularly prevalent in the expansion of the fast food business (Kentucky Fried Chicken, McDonalds, Pizza Hut, Spud-U-Like).

The travel and tourism industry has been in the forefront in franchising developments in Britain, as well as elsewhere. Apart from catering institutions, hotels, camping grounds, car hire and travel agencies have all launched successful franchise operations. Hotel chains such as Holiday Inns achieved enormous growth in the 1960s and 1970s with their operating franchises around the world; in the 1980s car hire franchising led to the expansion of companies such as Budget Rent-a-Car, as well as Hertz and Avis. Although attempts to franchise travel agencies in Britain go back to the 1960s, these and other initial attempts to franchise the travel business failed. A number of reasons can be put forward to explain this failure. In the first place, a successful franchise must have a name with strong drawing power, as well as offering a unique product. The franchising of a travel agency offered no product nor price advantages, nor did the possession of a franchise in itself guarantee an IATA appointment or other principals' approval.

Exaggerated claims were often made about potential profits that could be expected, while the training or other back-up marketing facilities did not materialise. In a business such as travel where the product is highly specialised, lack of adequate training for staff is fatal. Even promises of exclusivity were sometimes broken. All too often, in order to get franchisee support, the franchisors were tempted to appoint anyone with the money to pay, regardless of their business acumen, with the result that standards were inconsistent and quality suffered. An additional legal hurdle to the franchising of retail travel was the fact that at that time, commissions could not be split between an agency and another organisation, and the payment of royalties was in itself a form of split commission. Not until the freedom to discount and to split commission in the 1980s did the door become fully open to travel agency franchising, with the now defunct Exchange Travel group the first to introduce it. One attraction of that franchise was the accounting backup provided by their head office, which relieved branch managers of many administrative tasks and allowed them to concentrate on marketing. However, by that point the narrow profits being achieved by agents and the additional turnover needed to pay the 1 per cent management service fee made the venture questionable. The competitive environment in which retailers now operate, and the opportunity for franchisees to increase their margins by negotiating higher levels of commission, subsequently have made franchising more popular, and a number of new attempts were being made in the mid-1990s to establish retail travel franchises, notably by the Canadian company Uniglobe, with its focus on business travel.

Building links with the retail agent

Although the two examples given above indicate ways in which agents themselves can unite to form more effective sales units, the 'manufacturers' of travel products will be chiefly concerned with finding ways in which they can provide the most effective support to their retail agents to maximise their own sales.

In order to see how this can be achieved, first let us examine the relationship between the travel agent and the principals. The agent's main role, as we have seen earlier, is to provide a convenient outlet for travellers to enquire about, and book, their travel arrangements. In exchange for this service, the agent receives commission, varying between 7 and 10 per cent of the travel revenue, from the principal. It is now increasingly common for principals to pay higher rates of commission to agents meeting set sales targets, as a means of increasing their commitment to selling, since agents purchase no advance stock and show little brand loyalty to principals. Multiple retailers such as Lunn Poly have become so powerful that they may demand a minimum of 15 per cent commission from small operators before they will sell the product. It is therefore pertinent to ask what other factors, apart from higher financial remuneration, will encourage an agent to support one principal rather than another.

The answer to this is more complex than is at first apparent. Certainly, agents will take account of opportunities to increase profits through increased commissions, but if this were the only criterion, every principal would be forced into a commission war with their competitors. Furthermore, a decision taken by the management of an agency to rack a company's brochures is only the first step for the principal, who must also ensure that the staff of that agency actively push the company's products.

Market share is clearly a factor here. All agents who succeed in gaining appointments will sell the products of the six or so leading tour operators, since not to do so would be tantamount to commercial suicide. Even here, though, one company's products may be more actively sold than another's, notwithstanding comparable levels of commission, as we have seen in the form of directional selling. The determinants in this 'trade-off' can be listed as follows:

1 *The image of the company and its perceived stability* There must be no danger or rumours that the company is headed for collapse.
2 *The match between the company's products and the client's needs* Most agents see that it is in their own interests to satisfy their customers.
3 *The reliability of the company in such issues as overbooking, consolidations, delivery of tickets, and communications* Thus, if agents find it

frequently difficult to get through to the reservations department of one particular company on the telephone, they may switch to another company who proves easier to reach. The significance of computer reservations systems at easing this communications process will be discussed later in this chapter.

4 *Agency staff product knowledge* There is no substitute for personal experience gained by sales staff, in encouraging them to sell hotels or destinations, and enabling them to be more convincing in doing so.
5 *Co-operative programmes* Many companies will actively support travel agents in their sales efforts by paying 50 per cent of the costs of special promotional events run by agents, or as contributions to specific advertising programmes. These joint promotions enhance the image of both organisations in the other's eyes. To the agents, it shows a willingness to support their efforts to sell, while it reveals to a principal that agents are more than merely order takers, and are actively selling the company's products.
6 *The personal relations generated between a principal's sales representative and the agency counter staff* This factor must never be underestimated. For many agents, the sales rep *is* the company he or she represents, and the rep's personality is a significant factor influencing agency support, both in terms of recollection and recommendation. For a small specialist company, the role becomes even more significant, since the principal's aim will be to get the agent to think first of their company when handling enquiries.
7 *The relative ease with which transactions can be completed* Time is money to an agent. If procedures are too complicated, and especially where the total value of the sale is small, the amount of work in which the agent becomes involved will cost more than the relative commission earned. A study undertaken by Upminster Travel examined the relative profitability of the various travel services sold by the company. It was concluded that the sale of rail, cross-Channel ferries and domestic air tickets were subsidised by the profits

achieved by selling package tours, shipping and long-haul air bookings. Many agents subsequently have chosen not to deal with coach and rail bookings because of the relatively small commissions paid. Some services, such as hotels, require agents to claim their commission after clients have used the facilities. Not only is this an onerous procedure, but also it slows the agent's cash flow. Agents are also reluctant to deal with hotels which are without booking offices or representative agencies in the agents' home country, since telexes or telephone bookings abroad boost booking costs.

8 *The sale of domestic holidays* Many agents have been reluctant to deal with UK domestic package holidays, either believing that commissions are inadequate or that booking procedures are too complex. However, the increase in short-break holidays in Britain, coupled with the aggressive marketing of packages by companies such as Rainbow Holidays and the tourist boards' efforts to integrate commission-paying holidays into single comprehensive brochures have all gone a long way to making the products more acceptable to agents.

9 *The availability of credit terms* Most principals allow a measure of credit to their better supporting agents. The small, less well-established independent agents are therefore doubly disadvantaged, in that they not only find it difficult to negotiate higher commissions but also are required to pay cash for transactions. Managing cash flow is a critical issue for agents, and its successful management can increase profits substantially, while the absence of credit is a major operating drawback.

10 *The acceptance of credit cards* Many agents have resisted accepting credit cards for the purchase of travel, since the agency costs of 1–2 per cent make further inroads in already slim profit margins. The wide-scale phasing-in of EFTPOS (electronic fund transfer at point of sale) allows clients' bank accounts to be debited immediately and funds transferred to the principals' accounts. Cards such as Switch and Barclay's Connect, with which agents are coming to terms, have the effect of further reducing the cash flow of non-credit intermediaries.

Two other factors should perhaps be mentioned here. First, patriotism is hard to measure, but does play a role in some agency recommendations, where air travel or cruising is concerned. A British travel agent may well recommend a British product, where other things are equal. The recovery of British Airways' fortunes during the 1980s was undoubtedly aided by the goodwill of the British public and agents. Second, on a regional scale, a similar attitude towards local companies can be detected among agencies which is not merely a result of commercial interest. A local tour operator will often be on closer personal terms with travel agents in the area and will derive goodwill from being part of the local community.

Based on an assessment of these points, and the organisation's relative strengths and weaknesses in each area, principals can develop a distribution strategy within the overall marketing plan to improve their standing with agents in one or more of these directions.

It will also be helpful for principals to be aware of the agent's policies regarding the racking of brochures. Each agent or chain of agents determines its individual policies as to what products it will sell and what brochures it will display. Many will also have clear guidelines about how the brochures of the various companies represented will be displayed. Thomas Cook's approach is not untypical, in their designating four categories of tour operator product:

- *winners' list*: roughly the top 20 operators in size
- *recommended operators*: roughly the next 35 in size
- *authorised operators*: those which the company is also prepared to sell
- *non-authorised operators*.

Those companies on any agent's winners' list will automatically receive full agency support; recommended operators receive more limited support; policy for authorised operators may be to sell but not display brochures, so only a file copy of the company's brochure may be kept in the office.

Clearly, such a policy is demand-led. Some agents may reserve space for local operators, for companies in which they have a specialist interest (for instance, car ferry companies' brochures will be prominently featured by travel agencies run by motoring organisations such as the AA and RAC), and any companies for which special commission deals have been negotiated, or jointly sponsored promotions have been arranged.

This selection and categorisation also operates in reverse, with principals grading their distributors according to the level of sales they achieve. As in all businesses, the 'Pareto Principle' applies, in that a small proportion of agents tend to produce the bulk of the business for any company's total sales. Typical ratios would result in 20 per cent of retail distributors making 80 per cent of the bookings.

It is this feature of distribution which determines a company's policy regarding agency support. Companies could, justifiably, decide to support only those agents providing them with a reasonable level of bookings. This will reduce distribution costs, but it will inhibit the maximisation of sales, especially in its tendency to discourage new, or marginal, agents from selling the company's products. With the current emphasis on expanding market share, tour operators in particular are keen to receive all the bookings they can get, with the result that agents are categorised into bands based on turnover achieved. This will determine how much support the principal gives the agent.

One operator, a specialist medium-sized company, has used the following grading system for its agents. While the number of bookings will vary according to the total number of passengers carried by the company, the principle is common to most operators and other travel companies:

category	definition
P	preferred multiple, with substantial number of bookings achieved each year
AA	agency with at least twelve bookings
A	agency with minimum of six bookings
B	agency with two bookings each year
C	agency making at least one booking
D	agency failing to make any bookings
Z	agency without bookings but demonstrating some potential

'Preferred multiples' will generally be supported with bonus commissions for targets achieved, based on some percentage increase over their performance in the previous year. They are also likely to receive offers of 50/50 promotional help, a regular cycle of calls by sales representatives, full merchandising service such as window display material, a regular mailing of information in the company's newsletter, invitations to brochure launches in the region and offers to attend educationals to experience the company's package tours. Those in lower categories will have reduced levels of support, to a point where those in the lowest category may be given only an office copy of the company's brochure and minimal support in other directions. This still enables the agent to 'prove itself' and be offered increased support when bookings are received.

The principal must also exercise control over the number of brochures distributed to agents. A watch must be maintained on the ratio of bookings to brochures. This ratio can vary widely, with some agents achieving bookings for every three brochures they give out, and others perhaps making only one booking in twenty brochures. A high ratio of brochures to bookings is indicative either of poor sales techniques, with little attempt being made to do more than distribute brochures in response to enquiries, or lack of control over brochure orders given to principals: junior agency staff may be given the task of reordering brochures without any clear idea of actual numbers needed, resulting in a high wastage rate at the end of the year.

John MacNeill, then managing director of Thomson Holidays, once pinpointed seven characteristics by which a principal could identify the efficient travel agent. These are listed below as a useful checklist for those considering making agency appointments:

- the agent will have a Viewdata reservations system in use
- staff will have enough product knowledge to satisfy their more demanding clients
- the agency shows evidence of efficiency in reducing its costs
- the agent operates a well-planned policy of selective brochure racking
- its management has the ability to recognise booking patterns and trends over time
- the agency actively sells, using its initiative to tap the local market
- helpful feedback is provided to its principals regarding the local marketplace

The role of the sales representative

A principal's sales representatives play a crucial role in the relationship between the company and its agents, since the 'local rep' will be the main, and sometimes the only, point of contact between the two. In spite of this, there is a tendency among principals to reduce this function in the organisation or seek other means of communicating with their agents. This is due to the comparatively high cost of keeping sales reps on the road. It can cost upwards of £30 000 per year to maintain a sales rep, including travel expenses. However, there is arguably no more effective way of building links with retailers, and it is perhaps significant that while principals have been searching for alternative methods of servicing their distributive outlets, travel agents themselves have begun to employ their own external sales reps to call on businesses and other organisations to increase sales, often using part-time staff paid on commission to generate such business.

However, most principals continue to employ a field sales force, whose task is to develop existing business and generate new business, by making regular calls on retail agencies and by calling direct on businesses (in the case of transport and accommodation principals) or organisations likely to offer the prospect of group travel bookings. By this means, travel agents are

'. . . the representative's most valuable service . . . is to act as a troubleshooter.'

kept regularly informed about product development in the company, and are offered merchandising help and advice on any promotions they might wish to make featuring the company's products. However, undoubtedly the representative's most valuable service, in the eyes of many agents, is to act as a 'troubleshooter' to solve problems. Knowing them personally, agency managers will call them first if they have a problem, or if they need, for example, to clear a fully booked flight for valued customers. The rep's own personality, and his or her ability to help in these circumstances, will play an important part in the development of the agent's image of the company.

Although, with the advent of computerised reservations systems, most companies will have up-to-date information about sales achieved by agents in each product category, the sales rep is still the best person to advise the company on agency potential, to determine what level of support each agent should receive, and to recommend specific counter staff for agents' educationals.

Reps have a responsibility to get to know personally each agency manager and member of the counter sales staff on whom they call. They must be thoroughly familiar not only with their own company and its products, but also with those of their leading competitors and their relative prices. They should have clear objectives to achieve on each visit, to ensure that it is cost-effective.

Attitudes towards the visit of sales reps differ considerably between agents. While most prefer to see a company representative at some point during the year, they may resent 'cold calls' made without prior appointment, and some object to giving up their time to dealing with the many different representatives who call on them. In the early 1990s two of the retailer chains enforced a complete ban on sales representatives calling at their shops. This was seen as a move to ensure that head office directional selling control was not undermined at a local level by external representatives. The reps therefore have to ascertain the views of each travel agency manager towards their visit, using considerable tact, picking convenient times for visiting and determining whether an agent is interested primarily in learning about the company's products, exchanging social and trade gossip, or keeping the visit as brief as possible and merely noting that the principal is expressing an interest in them.

In the past, reps were frequently used to deliver the principal's brochures, but this is now more cheaply undertaken by professional carriers, usually employed by the printers. In reaction to bans on sales calls made by the multiples, several of the larger tour operators have disbanded their teams of sales representatives altogether. In their place they employ teams of *merchandisers*, who are sales personnel employed by an external agency and used by operators on an *ad-hoc* basis only. They may be used to sell in the new season's brochures or to execute a trade promotion. Freespirit – a brand launched for summer 1995 – used such merchandising forces in order to:

- explain the concept of the new brand
- ensure the brochures were being racked correctly
- motivate retailer staff to sell the brand through a sales promotion.

The success of such activity depends upon a tight and specific focus, together with detailed briefing from the tour operator. Merchandisers in no way replace the role of the sales representative: they have little knowledge about the company and its products outside their specific brief, but their use is becoming widespread.

Two other means are also increasingly used to communicate with agents. These are:

- the telephone sales force
- the external sales team.

Telephone contact has become an increasingly common means by which principals keep in touch with their agents. Many of the functions common to sales reps can be conveniently undertaken by making a telephone call periodically from head office. At the very least this has the effect of considerably reducing sales calls, and therefore costs. However, some airlines and other organisations have switched entirely to the use of the telephone to maintain agency contact, with some consequent loss of personal contact between agency and principal. This is symptomatic of the pressure on companies to reduce their marketing costs as competition increases. Some principals make use of quieter booking periods to utilise their reservations teams to make telephone contact calls to retailers.

Employment of an external sales team to service companies is also finding favour as another means of cost reduction. Under this scheme, a contract is drawn up with an external agency which provides a team of knowledgeable sales staff to call on the company's agents and generally represent the company's interests. Members of the sales force are frequently people with prior experience of repping with travel companies, and are therefore well acquainted with the industry, so only minimum training is needed to update them on the company's own products. Costs are reduced because these teams may also represent a number of other travel products (generally non-competitive in nature) at the same time, when they call on agents. The cost of each individual agency call is therefore divided between several principals. While undoubtedly reducing distribution costs, it can be argued that the system fails to establish either a unique image for the company or a genuine relationship between principal and agent, since these intermediaries are not direct employees of the company. Moreover, the level of control which can be exercised over the sales force is reduced. Nevertheless, for the smaller principal with a limited budget for sales representation, this can provide a solution to the need to service the retail agent.

The management of the sales representatives

Whether company policy is to employ its own sales force or to buy in the use of an outside team, the sales manager's role starts with the need to set objectives for the team. This will include establishing the tasks they are to undertake, and setting any targets which they are to achieve. However, many of their tasks will not be directly revenue-generating. As we have seen, sales staff have a servicing function, building good relations with the travel agents and with businesses, grading agency potential, gathering feedback from agents about market trends, providing merchandising assistance, and generally acting as a source of reference for agents. Reps will play a key role in the annual brochure launch presentations (see Chapter 11), helping to organise regional functions and participating in them. However, where an outside sales force is employed, the objectives are likely to be less ambitious. Based on objectives given to the sales force, its size can be determined. This requires four steps:

1 Totalling the number of customer contacts to be made, whether agencies or other sources of potential business, and dividing these into categories according to the level of service each is to receive.
2 Deciding how often each category is to be visited, and what other forms of support the sales staff are to provide.
3 Totalling the number of sales calls required and assessing time allowances for other activities.
4 Establishing the number of sales staff to be employed in order for these duties to be performed, and dividing their responsibilities into geographic regions.

In the case of a large company, this could mean employing a sales team of perhaps 20–30 people. Obviously, a much smaller company cannot afford to offer the same direct representation, and must reduce the call frequency or employ an outside sales team. A further drawback to employment in a smaller company is that there is less opportunity to establish a career structure for sales reps. Larger companies will enable reps to be promoted to district, regional or area sales managers, perhaps going on to controller of sales or sales director, whereas in a small company the sales rep may report directly to the general manager, and may indeed have less autonomy in determining the budget spend than is the case with a larger organisation.

However, smaller companies do offset some of these disadvantages by providing more flexible employment for their sales reps. Often, in the case of tour operators, staff will work as overseas resort representatives during the summer season, and will be brought home during the winter either to call on agents as sales reps or to complement the reservations staff during the busy booking season which follows the Christmas holidays. This has led to full-time employment for many former seasonal staff, which has improved staff quality and ensured that sales staff have excellent product knowledge through direct personal experience.

Other tasks of the sales manager are to determine scales of remuneration and conditions of work for the sales team, and plan their training. These functions are likely to be undertaken in conjunction with other members of staff in a large company, such as the personnel or human resources manager and the training officer. However, the sales manager alone has direct responsibility to motivate staff, direct them and monitor their performances. We shall examine these latter functions briefly here.

It is wise to give sales reps as much autonomy as possible and minimise direct supervision. Greater individual control over their job leads to greater job satisfaction for the reps, who will give better performance as a result. Sales reps will require a period of induction training, to give them a background on the company and its products, sales methods and record keeping and other procedures specific to the company; they will also require updating from time to time as procedures or products change. Although more commonly found in the larger organisations, training manuals given to new staff can play a helpful role, providing they are kept up to date, so a loose-leaf manual is probably best fitted for this purpose. Record keeping is one means by which the sales rep will communicate with the sales manager, but this should be complemented by a regular pattern of meetings to exchange feedback. Reps are frequently separated from the events in their head offices for long periods while on the road, and can become divorced from events taking place at the head office unless a regular programme of meetings is organised for them. Increasing usage of mobile communications, such as car phones, within the sales forces allows the representative to keep in hourly contact with head office if necessary. For the most part, however, contact is maintained through the use of report forms which are completed by the sales rep each week.

The report form provides the basis for the schedule of visits planned by the rep each week. A typical report form will come in three-sheet self-carbon format, in which sheet 1 outlines the weekly plan, indicating to the sales manager the planned schedule of calls for the coming week. This is sent in advance to the sales manager, who will then know where to find the reps should any of them be needed urgently. Sheet 2, the weekly check sheet, includes the information from sheet 1 together with comments by the sales rep on the outcome of each visit. Explanations are given for any changes to the programme that had to be made during the week. This is mailed at the end of the week's cycle of calls to the sales manager. The rep retains the third copy, with all this information, for his or her own records.

In this way the sales manager is kept fully informed of events in the field, and in the same way, any sales leads received at head office need to be passed quickly to the sales rep in the area for prompt action, within an agreed time scale.

Details of any new agency appointments must be passed quickly to the reps, since a new agent is highly motivated to generate business for principals and will benefit from early encouragement. Leads followed up by the rep are reported back on the weekly report forms, with an assessment of the potential for business. New agents or potential sources of business will be given the rep's name and contact address.

Most travel companies' reservations systems are now computerised, giving the sales manager access to a vast amount of statistical data regarding sales by area, agency and period. This will give sales managers details of revenue within the responsibility of each rep, enabling comparisons to be made between targeted and actual sales performance, and indicating trends over time. These figures must be regularly disseminated to the reps in the field, so that they have access to full information on their own performance and that of their agents. At the same time, reps must receive up-to-date information on other promotions under way or planned by the company, and the organisation's overall marketing plans, so that promotion efforts can be effectively co-ordinated. Opportunities should be created for the sales force to provide structured feedback to the marketing function; many excellent marketing initiatives have had their roots in pertinent observations of the market made by the sales team. Conversely, lack of communication with the sales force can be the downfall of otherwise sound marketing ideas. Discussions should take place between the sales manager and the reps themselves when agency sales targets are determined each year, particularly if these are to be linked with bonus commissions. Finally, the travel expenses incurred by reps must be monitored by the manager. While these are generally predetermined as part of the overall sales budget, they need to be reviewed from time to time, not only because costs change but also because a company should not inhibit the potential for increased business by too tightly controlling a rep's expenses. A sales rep over budget on expenses should not be criticised if these expenses have resulted in a comparable increase in sales as a result of the rep's efforts.

Inventory control

In the long term, the marketing manager's task is to manage demand, that is, to achieve a balance between supply and demand. This is not easy in the travel business, where demand differs seasonally; it is difficult to predict, being affected by political as well as economic circumstances; and where resources are finite, so that, for example, a popular destination or tourist site cannot accommodate all who are interested in visiting it, or access may have to be limited due to ecological damage caused by excessive demand.

In the short term, the marketing manager may employ any of three techniques to control demand without changing supply:

- prices can be raised or lowered to influence demand
- waitlists can be built up
- forward booking systems can be introduced.

Forward booking leads to the formation of a *reservations system*, which is a key element in the travel distribution system.

Reservations systems

Reservations systems are used in most forms of transport and accommodation, and in booking theatre tickets and package tours. These services cannot easily increase their supply in the short term. There are also limited reservations systems in operation for some other services used by tourists, such as up-market restaurants, campsites during peak season, and popular museum exhibitions (especially for group visits). Arguably, reservations systems could also be more widely used to control demand at other tourist facilities such as beaches (which become unattractive if unlimited access is permitted) and ski slopes (where long queues can form during periods of high demand).

Reservations systems also enable organisations whose resources are not finite to forecast future demand more accurately and arrange to expand supply. Thus, inclusive tour companies can negotiate for more airplane seats and hotel rooms during the peak season at those destinations which, while not full, have shown indications of being more popular that was first forecast. Advance reservations have also made possible pricing structures such as the Advance Purchase Excursion (APEX) fares on airlines, which enable the airline operators to predict more accurately their future patterns of demand and load factors. Above all, reservations permit principals to maximise their load factors (or occupancy rates) by repricing or by repackaging, or in some cases by switching customers from products experiencing excess demand to those where demand is light.

The criteria for a reservations system, whether it be manually operated or computer operated, are that it is capable of displaying availability, can register bookings as they are made, and can effect cancellations and redisplay the cancelled booking for resale. The cost must be kept low as a proportion of total service charges, whether to travel agents or to the general public (if access is direct). Access should be easy and user friendly, that is, simple to understand and to operate.

Reservations systems can be organised in one of three ways:

1 *A manual system, in which entries are made into diaries or other record books*   A common practice among tour operators is to hang huge charts of hotels and airline seats on the walls of the reservations department, with staff entering bookings with erasable marking pens. Bookings are then expunged as cancellations are received. Other operators have used a system of colour-coded discs hung on pegs, or cards stored in slots, on the charts, which can be removed if cancellations occur. With this form of reservations system, travel agents telephone their bookings through to a reservations clerk, who registers options, or makes bookings, over the phone, by removing discs or cards, subject to deposits received by mail.

2 *Reservations are held in the principal's computer system*   Agents telephone the reservations clerk, who consults the computer and offers bookings over the phone, again normally subject to receipt of deposits by mail within a period of seven days.

3 *The principal operates an entirely automated computer reservations system*   Agents access the computer live ('on-line') by means of a visual display unit (VDU) in their offices, and can take options, or make a booking, without the intercession of any member of the principal's staff.

Both manual and computerised reservations systems may provide for *overbooking*, whereby more units (plane seats, hotel beds or whatever) can be sold than can be supplied. Although widely condemned (and under certain circumstances illegal), principals argue that overbooking is a necessary distributive technique to allow for the 'no-shows' which are common practice in travel, especially where business travel is concerned. Business people have been in the habit of making several return flight reservations if they are uncertain about when their business dealings will be completed. The alternative would be for companies such as airlines to settle for lower overall load factors, with a commensurate increase in prices to the consumer. Attempts to introduce the payment of deposits or cancellation fees have proved inoperable in the past, and the overbooking system has become a fact of life to which the travelling public have become accustomed, within the bounds of 'acceptable risk'. However, where overbooking becomes too extensive, as has occasionally happened in the case of hotel bookings on package tours, other control mechanisms come into force, such as the intercession of government agencies or threats of action from bodies such as the Federation of Tour Operators (FTO), consisting of leading members of the inclusive tour business in Britain. Tour operators themselves can no longer legally claim exemption from responsibility for overbooking by others, and therefore have to resolve overbooking problems for their clients as they arise.

The cost of using different reservations systems is a major consideration for travel agents, who seek to reduce their overheads. Most reservations for the products of small companies are still made by telephone, with reservations clerks who become well known to travel agency staff. However, for this system to be effective, the agent must be able to obtain a connection quickly with the principal. If an agent finds difficulty in getting through to the reservations department, or if calls are 'queued' at busy times, leading to high telephone bills, there will be a marked reluctance to use the services of that company unless no suitable alternatives exist. Principals can reduce agents' overheads through the use of telephone calls in which the agent is not billed for the cost of the call (e.g. 'Freefone' 0800 calls in Britain) or by using a system in which telephone charges are billed at only the local call cost for long distance calls.

Computerised reservations systems

The major development in the 1980s and 1990s has been the rapid switch to computerised reservations systems providing on-line reservations facilities to agents. The installation of such systems had been so costly that only principals carrying many thousands of customers each year could consider their installation, but continuing falls in the price of computer software and hardware have now made it possible for much smaller principals to consider automated reservations systems. Thomson Holidays' introduction in the 1980s of their 'TOPS' system, a low-cost, user friendly and extremely reliable reservations system, enabled that company to increase sales substantially and establish a huge lead over the rest of the inclusive tour business. Their later decision to abandon telephone sales entirely for their summer holiday programme points the way to future developments and the need for all agents to be linked by VDU to principals' computer systems in order to survive.

In the airline world, the rapid development of computer reservations systems has provided a new tool for the marketing manager. Originally seen merely as a method of controlling huge inventory speedily and efficiently, it soon became apparent that the way in which information was made available could radically improve sales potential.

In the USA there were a number of systems, each of which grew out of an internal inventory control system for the airline itself. Originally the agent, or the client, was required to telephone a reservations clerk who would operate the VDU and respond with the answers required. The speed of the system in responding to the enquiry, and the amount of information given, soon became a critical factor, with the travel agent often calling the airline with the most efficient booking system, rather than one with the flight most likely to suit the client.

Airlines then realised that not only would there be huge staff cost savings if agents were given their own VDU and access to the system, but also they would become more committed to that airline, particularly if it assisted agents in other ways, such as ticketing, invoicing and financial controls.

From the agent's point of view, however, there was the nightmare prospect of having several VDUs in the office, each dedicated only to the provision of information and processing for one concern.

Two approaches developed. In the USA, the *single access system* meant that all information, irrespective of the carrier to be used, became available from the computer system of the chosen airline. Anti-trust legislation has now made it necessary for the airline to supply information without bias, and it must list flights between a pair of airports in strict timetable order, rather than listing its own flights first. Two airlines have been at the forefront of development (United Airlines with the Apollo system, and American Airlines with the Sabre system): both offer competitive and extremely comprehensive systems that can deal with many additional travel components, as well as the air ticket transaction, such as hotels, car hire, resort information, weather and entertainment details. They are also capable of printing tickets, itineraries and invoices, and coping with accountancy functions.

The alternative approach, which was favoured in the UK, was to establish a *multi-access system*, known as Travicom. Financed principally by British Airways, this set out to operate a totally unbiased system on behalf of all the major carriers. The enquiries generated by a travel agency's VDU were directed to a central computer which acted as a switchcentre and a translation device.

The message was then connected to any of some thirty airlines throughout the world and an immediate reply sought. The systems major drawback was that the reservation, once made, was stored in that distant computer core, rather than at one central point. This made paper back-up essential at the agency and delayed the introduction of the paperless office.

In 1987 both Sabre and Apollo became available in Europe for the first time. British Airways saw the need to operate on a larger scale, and reached agreement with other major carriers, initially within Europe, to commission a totally new system which could operate on a global scale. This system, Galileo, has merged with the US Apollo system, to reinforce the global strength of this organisation. Travicom users and technology have been absorbed into the new system progressively.

Lufthansa and Air France have also set up a different but parallel system, codenamed Amadeus, with similar objectives, which has its headquarters in Munich and has already gained the support of many European agents. Battle is now joined to see which of these global reservations systems will become the market leader.

Reservations technology is advancing at such a pace that a discussion of the merits of current systems has little place in a textbook such as this. Suffice it to say that these developments will have profound effects on future distribution strategies, not least in terms of extending direct marketing opportunities. Airline tickets can be purchased in some countries from machines at airports, and this system is easily extended to the use of EFTPOS to pay for the ticket. Such expansion in direct selling, which threatens to cut out the retail agent, must be a further cause for concern among agents.

Future directions

Apart from computer technology, other new factors are beginning to shape the future of distributive systems. The practice of *networking* between travel companies is leading to expansion in potential new distribution systems.

Tourist Information Centres (TICs), for example, are increasingly acting as commercial booking agents for travel and tourism products, especially for the sale of bedroom accommodation. In Britain, *Etna* is a computerised information and booking system in use in TICs for the booking of hotel beds.

The trend to *integration* in the travel industry, which will allow tourism principals to exercise greater control over the distribution systems through their ownership of retail agencies, is another direction which must concern the independent agent.

Reciprocal referrals between hotels, links between hotels and airlines, and between hotels and car hire companies, all provide alternative routes for the sale of travel products which can be further exploited.

Finally, the concept of *net bulk purchasing*, by which travel agents actually purchase in advance travel products and are responsible for selling them, offers a new means of retailing, and a threat to the smaller agent who will be less able to fund this type of investment or stand the risk that it implies. While this concept has not developed to any great extent yet in the travel industry, there is no doubt that principals will give it more serious consideration in the future, in their efforts to find new means of distributing their products.

Questions, tasks and issues for discussion

1 Examine the feasibility of British Airways' extending direct sell travel shops and reducing their reliance on travel agents as distribution outlets. Would this be a wise decision (a) immediately, and (b) within the next five to ten years?

2 Computer technology is a fast-moving subject. Prepare a paper which updates the latest developments in computers as they affect the distribution of travel products. What conclusions would you draw about the place of technology in travel distribution by the year 2000?

3 How effective are travel agency consortia? Could they become more powerful in retail travel over the next few years?

4 One possible future strategy for the Thomson Travel Organisation is to restrict sales of its tour operation (Thomson Holidays) to its retailing chain (Lunn Poly) only. Comment on the strengths and weaknesses of this option.

Exercise

You have been commissioned by a firm of consultants to solicit the views of travel agents in your area on the role of sales representatives. You have been asked specifically to find out what agents require of both airline and tour operator representatives, and how satisfied they are with the services provided by these representatives.

Plan a research programme which will involve interviews with selected agents in the area, and collect data. Based on the results of your investigations, draw up a short manual for the use of **either** an airline representative **or** a tour operator's representative, which will provide new employees in this role with some guidelines in their dealings with agency managers and counter staff.

9 Tourism advertising

After studying this chapter, you should be able to:

- understand the purpose of advertising
- know how to create effective advertisements
- appreciate the role of the advertising agent
- understand the factors behind choice of media
- recognise the need to plan for promotional budgets

In the context of this book there are three main areas of advertising, namely advertising by the principal to the consumer, advertising by the agent to the consumer, and advertising by the principal to the agent.

Advertising in tourism is similar to advertising for any other medium. It essentially follows the AIDA principle of:

- attract *Attention*
- create *Interest*
- foster *Desire*
- inspire *Action*

It can, and often does, follow this pattern stage by stage. A good example in another field was the series of privatisation launches carried out for British utilities (gas, water and electricity), in which television advertising played an important role. *Attention* was attracted by advertisements which were less notable for their promise than for their bizarre, attention-getting qualities. *Interest* was created by an invitation to receive information that had been specially prepared to convert curiosity into readiness to consider a proposition that would follow. *Desire* was fostered by a combination of public relations activity surrounding the prospects for the launch and the likelihood of profit. *Action* was inspired by sending application forms, or publishing them in the newspapers, and was further encouraged by advertisements reminding the consumer of the closing date of the offer.

Fig. 9.1 Example of tactical late sales price promotion. (Note the strong emphasis on low 'lead price' together with the credit card reservations hotline number.)

(Courtesy: First Choice Holidays)

The indirect sales channel has, in the past, led tour operators in particular to focus more on the first two criteria, attention and interest, possibly using desire as a motivant. Major strategic brand awareness campaigns at periods of peak booking are examples of this. However, the continual drive to make the most of tight budgets has increased pressure for advertisements to feature some kind of 'call to action' which can be measured. In addition, tour operators will underpin their strategic advertising with a year-round programme of tactical activity.

The call to action to the consumer is often to request a brochure, and the operator dispatches a brochure direct to the consumer. As the ultimate booking will still usually be made through a travel agent, the retail trade has come to regard this with less suspicion. They increasingly realise the benefits of an operator driving clients into their shops and of co-operative advertising.

Tactical 'late sales' advertisements and special price deals, whether placed by operator or travel agent, have strong calls to book the holiday then and there (see Figs 9.1 and 9.2). Telephone hotlines, credit card facilities and seven-day 24-hour service are a major feature of such advertisements.

Fig. 9.2 A series of branded advertisements that highlight aspects of product differentiation. The call to action is to request a brochure
(Courtesy: First Choice Holidays)

Expenditure

Inevitably the real problem is the amount of money available in an industry where margins are traditionally low, and where public relations activity is more common because of the ease with which interest can be created by journalists, resulting from the offer of free facilities to them.

Above and below the line

Two of the most used phrases about the advertising expenditure is *above the line* and its corollary *below the line*. Above the line advertising is normally considered to be advertising placed in television and the national press whose objective is primarily that of brand awareness. Advertising and direct mail which has a coupon or other response device, and whose objective is primarily

to generate enquiries and/or direct sales, is normally referred to as below the line.

Advertising agencies

Paying the piper

Just as the public are encouraged to use the services of a travel agent and are promised that it will cost no more than booking direct (with a few notable exceptions), advertisers are likely to use an advertising agent to create, design, prepare and place the campaign. One benefit is that an advertising agency will have access to statistical information from major market research programmes that are not readily or economically available to the advertiser.

Traditionally, the basis of employment has been the premise that whereas the customer would pay in full for each £100 of space in the press or on television, the advertising agent will pay only £85. The advertising agent will, however, become the principal in the transaction and be expected to pay the media owner even if the eventual client defaults or becomes unable to pay. This margin actually establishes a 17.65 per cent mark-up on the spend by the advertising agent. It has become common practice for this margin also to be added to any other work that an agency commissions on behalf of a client, such as related point of sale displays, promotional videos, etc. This can be very arbitrary, however, and there is nothing magical about the figure of 17.65 per cent. Where the actual production costs are low, and/or the media spend is small, the agency may not be adequately remunerated for their management time involved by a 17.65 per cent mark-up. Equally, a promotion involving a very large production cost, such as a very large print run, might result in an artificially high agency commission. Increasingly, agencies are paid on the basis of a mixture of fee and commission.

The principle applies just as much to small as to large advertisers, and even local travel agents may find that in return for placing a regular series of advertisements in the local newspaper via an advertising agent, they will be able to have the layout and designs created professionally, instead of being set up in boring type in an uninspired fashion (compare the layouts illustrated in Figs 9.3 and 9.4). Though fortunately becoming less common, the type of layout shown in Fig. 9.3 is referred to disparagingly as a 'tombstone' advertisement.

The client–agency relationship

The worst possible foundation for a client–agency relationship is the client's belief that the agency is being paid for through media commission, and therefore that the client has no responsibilities and is entitled to virtually unlimited service for free.

Fig. 9.3 Advertisement A: example of unimaginative 'tombstone' style layout

Fig. 9.4 Advertisement B: example of imaginative layout

In reality, truly productive business relationships are complex two-way processes. Agencies need the income provided by any particular client's work, and this makes it difficult for them to dictate the course of the relationship alone. Who can blame an agency for not proffering unpalatable advice to a difficult client who does not want to hear it? And yet it is the client who loses out ultimately, and who has everything to gain from the most effective relationship possible.

It is important for clients to establish at the outset exactly what they want to get out of using an agency. The motivation to use an agency will normally be one of the following, or some combination of them:

1 The agency has the resources available to produce the promotional campaign and the client does not have such resources in-house. It is often much more efficient to call in the services of the agency as and when required, as opposed to employing full-time staff. This is especially so if the requirement for promotion peaks and troughs, or is not large enough to represent a full-time job.
2 The agency has special skills that the client does not possess, e.g. creative and design talents.
3 The agency has specialist knowledge and experience, e.g. media knowledge, an understanding of international advertising, or business and marketing expertise drawn from within the client's own market sector.
4 The agency has, by definition, a more objective view than the client, who is too close to the product. In addition, the agency has a breadth of vision drawn from working with different clients across many different industries.

When choosing an agency it is important to have a clear view of the nature of the service that will be required. The strengths and resources of a prospective agency can vary tremendously in the skills and experience of their personnel, and hence in the service that they can offer.

A client who needs to mount a major strategic press campaign on an international basis within short time scales would ask such questions as:

'Does this agency physically have enough people to manage a campaign of this size quickly?'

'Does the agency have in-depth experience of media buying overseas?'

'Does this agency have experience in my market sector?'

'What proportion of this agency's work is press as opposed to other media?'

Equally, a small tactical advertiser with a low budget would ask such questions as:

'Am I paying for high calibre agency staff with business expertise that I don't need and can't afford?'

'Is this agency's creative team used to producing good campaigns but on low budgets?'

'Would my account be very small relative to the agency's other accounts, with a resulting low priority?'

Once a relationship is entered into, the onus is on both parties to create the correct environment for effective working. There are several vital ingredients.

1 *Mutual and honest information exchange* The client will need to devote time to ensuring the agency understands the business, its products and its markets. The more strategic the campaign, the greater the agency understanding has to be. A long-term relationship is often beneficial to capitalise upon the time and effort both agency and client devote to arrive at a detailed mutual understanding. Also, an agency needs to discuss honestly with the client the progress of a campaign and any problems they may be encountering.
2 *Clear lines of communication* There is a tremendous amount of detail surrounding even a small campaign. A good agency will submit work at set points in the production process for client approval. These milestones must be agreed in advance, and all parties must be clear about who within the client organisation is authorised to approve each stage. Thus the managing director may approve the initial creative idea, while the marketing manager may sign off the final prices that appear within an advertisement.

3 *Mutual respect* A good personal relationship and 'chemistry' between client and agency staff undoubtedly helps, as it does in any service business. Mutual respect is vital. A client who employs an agency, but does not value its advice, may be missing out on the objective view. Equally, an agency that cannot assimilate input and opinion from the client into its creative approach is failing to benefit from the greater in-depth product and market knowledge of the client. An open mind is essential. While most clients complain of an agency's creative work 'going stale' over time, most agencies complain of clients being 'boringly resistant to new ideas'.

4 *Specific and reasonable objectives need to be assigned to every promotion* Whether the advertising is 'good' advertising can be assessed only against tangible measures of effectiveness.

5 *The service required determines the choice of agency* At a day-to-day level, the client should not assume that all agencies are the same (they are not), and should define exactly what is expected from the agency, such as attendance at weekly progress meetings, detailed post-campaign response analysis, all changes in the media schedule to be notified in writing. This not only makes it clear to the agency what is expected, but also allows it to resource and cost the campaign accordingly.

6 *Budget and time scales available* These should be clear at the outset, and realistic in terms of the objectives.

7 *Basis of the agency renumeration* This should be fair and clear at the outset. A client who values a long-term relationship will want the agency to make an honest profit. Larger clients will know that they play a significant role in the business survival of their agency. One of the most contentious areas of costing is which party bears the cost of amendments to advertising ideas and copy, and if possible a policy should be agreed in advance.

Advertising effectiveness

Advertising in itself is a product and like any other product its effectiveness must be decided by a number of factors. Some of the most significant will be:

- the idea chosen and the medium in which it is to be promoted
- the number of people to whom it is promoted and the frequency of repetition
- competition from others at the time of the campaign
- the timing of the campaign in relation to the buying pattern.

All too often, those responsible for advertising budgets dry up in terms of creativity. Sometimes, in order to maintain annual appropriations, they will place advertisements in a half-hearted way, lacking in original thought. If this is blamed upon lack of budget it is an excuse for waste, for a boring advertisement is sure to fail the first two criteria – attention and interest.

Sadly, this is sometimes seen in the advertising of national tourist offices, who, faced with inadequate budgets, try to satisfy too many interests and impress few. A series of slide photographs on television, with an end caption of 'Surprising Germany', surprised no one. Italy obtained its first appropriation in many years and instead of catching attention by promoting some unique aspect of the country, produced 'Italy has Everything' advertisements – hardly believable or attention-getting.

In contrast, the Swedish Tourist Office were winners of the CIMTIG/TTG (Chartered Institute of Marketing Travel Industry Group/ *Travel Trade Gazette*) awards in this category for a memorable advertisement on television in which a moose puppet told of Sweden's virtues in a sing-song voice that combined clear English and a Swedish accent.

The CIMTIG/TTG awards scheme has for many years promoted better understanding of what makes for good advertising in the industry. Television, radio, newspapers, magazines and other media are included and awards are made to those responsible for the best creative work each year. Experts then comment about their good and bad points at the presentation ceremony.

Media choice

However good an advertisement may be intellectually, it would be wasted in a dark room; and the medium or media through which it is to be communicated will be a fundamental factor in its success. Local travel agents' budgets may run to the use of local newspapers, local radio and possibly to local or regional publications, but only the larger agencies can consider television as a medium, even within the immediate vicinity. In determining which to use, the agent will weigh up not only price but also the relative advantages and disadvantages of each medium.

Publications:
- how many copies are produced and distributed?
- of these, how many are distributed in the catchment area?
- is there evidence of their being read by more than one person?
- are they wanted or unwanted, i.e. paid for or 'freesheets'?
- how frequently are they published and how long is their effective life?
- is the publication considered highbrow or lowbrow?
- is colour or spot colour available?
- what is the reproduction method and quality like?
- can the position of the advertisement be controlled?

Television or radio:
- how many listeners or viewers can one expect on average?
- is it possible to choose the days and times and relate them to a relevant programme?
- what proportion of the listeners or viewers live within the catchment area?
- are customers likely to be attracted from a wider areas than would otherwise use your services?

Publications

For the advertiser on a larger scale there are many more opportunities and thus a wider choice of questions to be answered. The question of demographic segmentation will become much more important. The cost of reaching each thousand readers in itself may be less important than the likelihood of those readers being target clients; for example when advertising cruises it is not sufficient to assume that they are an expensive commodity and that sales are more likely to emanate through the columns of *The Times*. It could well be that *The Times*' readers would be more likely to purchase highbrow trips up the Nile to see the Timepes of Abu Simbel than readers of the *Sun*.

Conversely, for a Mediterranean cruise there may well be more *Sun* readers per pound spent on advertisements who are able and willing to afford the trip than there are *Times* readers.

The International Publishing Corporation (IPC) has done considerable research into patterns of holiday purchase. It contends that women have more effect than men upon holiday choice, thus it promotes the value of advertising in its weekly and monthly women's magazines as a high priority for sellers of holidays. It also analyses readership profiles for each magazine in the group so that advertisers can choose the one that best fits the profile of targeted consumers.

Television and radio

That television is effective as a medium is obvious. Equally understood is the fact that it is extremely expensive and can be quickly forgotten. Because of the costs involved in screening, major advertisers employ the best creative talents to devise, produce and test their schemes. All of this further increases the budget necessary if your advertisement is to rate alongside the excellence of others. Furthermore, having produced a superb advertisement, it would be foolish not to use it frequently, preferably at peak times for your target audience.

As a medium, television is outside the range of all but the largest travel and tourism businesses.

By contrast, commercial radio is often much more local in its coverage, and requires much less investment in production costs. Imagination is the key to its effectiveness, as listeners are not limited to what they see on the screen. It is a particularly effective medium for tactical messages, as production is rapid. Whereas television is generally limited to large businesses, radio can be used by even small travel agencies, and for regional promotions.

When budgets are large, the complexity of choice is much greater, but fortunately a great deal of information and advice based upon research is available. A wise advertiser will use the expertise available in defining media requirements.

Frequency

Whatever the medium, and however good an advertisement may be, its effectiveness increases upon repetition, even if this sometimes seems to be *ad nauseam*. To spend a large amount of money on the creation of an excellent campaign and not to repeat it is often a waste. A really good campaign will be worth repeating year after year, subject only to amendment and updating.

Competition

As Chapter 2 made clear, there are three marketing strategies that lead to commercial success, namely:

- *low-cost leadership* selling cheaper than your competitors
- *differentiation* creating a high added value, a desire for your product in preference to that of your competitors
- *focus* specialisation to a substantial degree that makes your product unique and difficult to copy.

Competition from others makes it essential that your advertising campaign is robust and it is unlikely to be so unless it achieves one of these criteria.

A *price platform* is fragile, and *low-cost leadership* is always vulnerable. To simply claim 'we're cheapest' is difficult to maintain when a price war results in each firm deliberately undercutting its main competitors. Eventually prices will drop to a level that is impossible to sustain, and it is the nerve, or wealth, of each competitor which will determine who survives, rather than the merits of the product, or the management quality of the company. There is an inherent belief by the public that cheapness in itself leads to poor quality, and thus a disbelief in claims for quality allied to low price.

Differentiation is the path chosen by most brand leaders in any industry. The fact that cellulose tape became known as 'Sellotape', and that vacuum cleaners are referred to as 'Hoovers' is a great credit to the originators. Kellogg's Corn Flakes, Nescafé, Heinz Baked Beans and other top-selling products never promote price, but the reputation that they have built up for product reliability. They exploit this with advertising that builds upon their standing. They become natural *first choice brands* against which all competitors are judged. This inherent quality is referred to as *added value*, and it can be increased by advertising. It is, however, a quality that does not come readily or quickly and which can easily be lost if production standards fall and consumer expectations are not realised.

This technique can be used by a local travel agent who concentrates on the experience of staff and their ability to advise more competently than competitors. On a larger scale, a memorable campaign by Thomson Holidays built their reputation for reliability by depicting their quality controllers as serious businessmen (typified by city suits and bowler hats). In both cases the advertisements are about the quality of service provided rather than about the product itself.

Focus is about specialisation. It might be concentration on a new product, or upon virtues that are unique to a company. It is much more difficult to copy quickly a campaign that is based upon a true marketing advantage that has been planned, such as 'all our villas have private swimming pools', or 'we have trained baby patrollers at each of the hotels marked', or 'every cabin has private shower and toilet'. Assessment of unfulfilled customer needs is an integral part of a marketing plan, and enables selling advantages to be established which are unique to the company concerned.

Timing of the campaign

If you had an unlimited budget, you might wish to advertise throughout the year. Inevitably, however, judgement has to be exercised about when the most effective time will be. Tour operators traditionally published brochures well before Christmas for the next summer season and hoped that the expectancy among past customers plus a little help from public relations would carry them through to Christmas. Little money would be spent prior to Christmas as it would be unlikely to divert thought from Christmas goods anyway. Immediately after Christmas, advertising on television and in the weekend papers would deluge the potential customer.

Unfortunately for the industry, booking patterns have changed, and whereas it was traditional for the majority to book their holidays in January or February, many people now wait to do so until a short time before departure. We are now seeing launch advertising by tour operators in the August/September period, coupled with

'**Tour operators traditionally published brochures well before Christmas . . .**'

discount promotions by travel agents, in an attempt to reverse this trend. However, it flies in the face of a marketing principle – that of giving the customers what they want, rather than what you want to sell them. It follows that persuading customers to commit themselves early needs a substantially larger advertising budget and some extremely persuasive reasons – such as savage discounting, a feature of the early sell advertising campaign of the leading travel agency chains in 1994.

Conversely, unsold holidays and transport facilities are a prime example of 'perishable goods' for they have no value whatsoever after departure. Anything paid for them must be better than nothing and the way in which late booking opportunities are promoted can greatly affect the fortunes of any company. If they become too attractive, however, then they will impact upon the willingness of others to pay the full price and commit themselves early. A very substantial part of the travel industry's advertising budget is now spent on this 'tactical advertising', normally offering remaining holidays at knockdown prices.

Who advertises?

Another feature detected has been the tendency for advertising to be placed by substantial national travel agency chains in place of the tour operators. This undoubtedly reflects their changed bargaining power, as it relates to additional commission paid to them for achieving high sales. It is a normal feature of the retailer–supplier relationship that the efficient large-scale seller of goods in the high street will be able to influence what is provided and to demand terms far beyond those available to the independent (the control which Marks & Spencer exercises over its suppliers is a good illustration of this), and this is becoming as true in the travel industry as elsewhere. Increasingly, it can be expected that brand loyalty will become more the province of the retailer than the supplier, and that advertising will play a significant role in this transfer of power.

Fig. 9.5 Advertisement C: emphasising price benefit

Fig. 9.6 Advertisement D: emphasising price benefit

Cost justification

One thing that is certain is that no business actually wants to advertise, to give a proportion of sales revenue to a media owner. Thus it will need to be convinced of the benefits to the business before taking space. If this is so, then the corollary also applies, that the effects should be measured afterwards.

On a small scale this is difficult unless the product advertised is a specific one, for which sales would have otherwise been unlikely or more limited. Two examples of this in a travel agency context are shown in Figs 9.5 and 9.6. Both advertisements demonstrate the importance of price in making offers, but neither is actually based on price alone.

The 'Early Bird Ski Savers' advertisement was placed in July, very early, and at a time when only enthusiasts normally book. In order to obtain their first preferences they pay the highest prices. This travel agency had not transacted many ski sales previously. By making a clear discounted offer they managed to attract not only many skiers who had previously booked direct, but also a worthwhile number of group bookings for whom early booking was essential to obtain rooms together. The result was a measurable increase of 400 per cent over the bookings received for the whole of the previous year, up to the closing date. Such bookings, which would have been relatively simple to transact with first choices still generally available, gave a greater cash flow benefit and helped in achieving volume bonuses.

After building up expertise in negotiating air fares to Australasia for clients of the agency, it was decided to advertise outside their natural catchment area. The air fares used as 'lead-in' prices were attractive and resulted from negotiations with second-line carriers, but in addition a special '£50 free insurance' offer was made in respect of full tariff fares. Either way sales were predicted, and proved to be, substantial in net profit terms. By keeping a record of enquiries received from addresses outside the catchment area, it was possible to relate the actual cost of advertisements and net benefit each week.

A common practice is for travel agents to obtain 50/50 support from tour operators and other principals, whereby they benefit from professionally produced advertisement layouts describing the particular company's wares, and into which they slot their own identity. This is said to extend by association the benefits of the national advertiser's campaign to the agency. Sometimes it looks as if agents get a raw deal, as their proportion of the space is rarely more than 20 per cent. The benefits are invariably difficult to measure.

For a large-scale advertiser, particularly if carrying out a brand identity campaign rather than one related to a specific product, the success can be judged in two ways. First, the results will show in the statistical analysis of bookings or enquiries received. Second, it can be tested by 'before' and 'after' market research of brand awareness, particularly as regards products or brochures that a potential customer would 'definitely consider' before making a purchase.

Hoseasons: cost justification in practice

A remarkable example of cost justification is demonstrated by Hoseasons, a leading tour operator whose business is based upon pre-eminence in the letting of waterway craft on the Norfolk Broads and other stretches of water. Their range of products increased immensely during the 1980s, and they now market a wide range of self-catering accommodation as well as boats, both within the British Isles and in mainland Europe. Hoseasons estimate that around two-thirds of their customers each year are either previous users of their services or contact them as a result of recommendations. In order to encourage this sector they follow them up with direct mail. This leaves around one-third of their million-plus customers whose bookings are derived as a result of advertising or public relations (PR) activities.

Traditionally, advertisements for boats and self-catering in the UK have been in small spaces in a variety of newspapers and magazines, especially at weekends, in the *Radio Times* and *TV Times*, and in publications of the English Tourist Board. With a multiplicity of media it is very difficult to guess at individual effectiveness, and this could lead to the advertising budget getting totally out of control. It is thus critical to their success that they can compare effectiveness of their advertisement spend, and this covers around 1000 insertions each year, ranging from small circulation specialist magazines to national publications and television advertising.

Hoseasons do it by asking all enquirers to define which advertisement caused them to make contact. This information is logged, as are similar data requested on each booking form received. It is then possible to see not only what brings the most enquiries, but also which advertisements result in the best conversions.

Thanks to a sophisticated computer system they are able to compare such aspects as:

- the publication chosen
- the style of the advertisement
- the date of publication
- the space cost
- the replies received
    - by phone
    - by post
    - through other sources.

Hoseasons are able to establish a cost per reply analysis which is extremely accurate and gives guidance in future policy making. It also enables them to test the success, not only of general advertising themes, but the more specific product-led or tactical messages too.

Door-to-door distribution

If direct mail is the logical quality route for communication to selected customers and/or potential customers (see Chapter 12), door-to-door distribution is its much less expensive counterpart. Particularly for a local travel agent, it can be extremely effective either to cover all households within a given distance of the premises, or to select those areas which it is believed will be most productive. Unlike direct mail, it is not possible to personalise the message, but it can be a very effective way of seeking out the 90 per cent who probably do not use the services of the business. This has been widely used as a method of distributing discount vouchers which can be redeemed only through a given outlet. One particularly successful agency chain produced its own annual newspaper, supported by advertising from principals, and then distributed this on a door-to-door basis throughout the catchment area of all its branches.

Posters

One aspect of advertising widely used in the travel business is that of posters. There are some remarkable successes such as the English Riviera posters of the 1980s, which relied heavily on their artistic quality and were widely displayed in the London Underground stations; but generally posters are used more as point of sale (POS) advertising within travel agencies. Good quality full colour printing on large sheets is expensive, and yet the majority are rarely displayed. Posters are probably at their most cost-effective when used as a medium to distribute display matter for a tactical theme to be used by agents and then discarded.

One of the greatest problems of posters as a medium for selling to the customer is that it is extremely difficult to measure success. It probably needs a very large-scale campaign to have real impact. A major, successful and unusual use of posters is described in the case study covering the launch of First Choice Holidays (see pp. 235–41).

Planning advertising

Few businesses are in a start-up situation and most will have previous practice and expenditure with which to compare when creating an advertising plan for the next season, year, or other period. Once a current level of expenditure has been established, each element needs to be examined to ensure that it is justified, using the best information available. Whatever expenditure is then confirmed should be considered an inherent cost in selling that product, for too often advertising is seen merely as something to be taken out of available profit margins. In reality, advertising is as much a component of selling a holiday as is the brochure or airline ticket.

Against this background a view will undoubtedly be taken as to the adequacy of the overall spend, whether new products or services justify additional funds, and whether new policies need to be implemented. In respect of the forecast period, a timetable will need to be considered, as will the target audience and thus the media to be incorporated. Some flexibility needs to be retained for unforeseen situations and tactical requirements, but an overall plan will be much more likely to achieve the objectives chosen than will *ad-hoc* decisions taken throughout the year.

The following example gives an indication of how this might work in practice for a local travel agent:

Overall spend established at 0.75% of a £2.2 million turnover = £16 500

The three main objectives are:

- maximising business from existing customers
  - method: direct mail
  - budget: £5000
- improving firm's reputation and profile
  - method: by weekly advertisement in local paid newspaper
  - budget: 52 × £100 = £5200
- reaching all residents of the area
  - method: by monthly tactical advertisements in the local freesheet
  - budget: 12 × £400 = £4800

This leaves a figure of £1560 for contingencies to which may be added any funds promised by principals for joint promotions.

Once the budget is established, then it is sensible to establish a plan which anticipates which products are to be featured at what times of the year and by which medium.

Questions, tasks and issues for discussion

1 Discuss and compare present travel advertising for coach and rail services. What are the objectives of each? How far are the advertisements competing for the same markets?

2 Prepare short notes on the four Go-Right Travel ads which appear in this chapter. Suggest how you might change these to improve their appeal to customers.

3 Collect six examples of travel advertisements appearing in the national weekend papers, and

   (a) identify the objective of the message
   (b) suggest the market(s) at which the ads are aimed
   (c) evaluate the extent to which the ads achieve their objectives.

   Analyse their strengths and weaknesses in the light of comments made in this chapter.

4 Which travel advertisements do members of your group remember seeing within the last six months on television? What was it about them that made these ads memorable?

Exercise

Assume you are the advertising manager for a specialist tour operator which, *inter alia*, offers a series of short break and main fishing holiday packages in Britain. The holidays attract some 4000 anglers a year, at an average cost of £135 for the short break holidays (which account for 70 per cent of all the packages) and £210 for the longer packages.

In the past, the company has used a rule of thumb which allowed 3 per cent of the annual turnover to be spent on press advertisements.

Draw up a draft campaign for press advertising, indicating the media which you will use, and the form the advertisements will take.

NB: it will help to have access to a recent copy of BRAD (*British Rate and Data*) for up-to-date advertising costs in the different media.

10 The travel brochure

After studying this chapter, you should be able to:

- understand the importance of the travel brochure as a marketing tool
- recognise the regulatory and other constraints affecting brochure production
- identify design and print needs from the perspective of the consumer, the distributor and the printer
- understand the implications of brochure distribution

The role of the travel brochure

The travel brochure is probably the most important single item in the planning of tourism marketing. Whatever the product being promoted, it is likely that a brochure of some sort will be used. A hotel will need a prospectus; a resort area, a guide or directory; an airline, a timetable booklet; and the holiday company will undoubtedly use a brochure to offer its holidays.

The various travel brochures occupy subtly different roles and the importance placed upon them in each instance reflects the priority they occupy in the plans of the concern they promote. Because the role of the holiday company's brochure is the most significant, this chapter will devote itself mainly to that aspect.

It could be said that issuing a brochure distinguishes the tour operator from the travel agent. When ABTA defined the difference between members, they determined that tour operators were 'those who advertise and offer holidays for sale'. Legal requirements make it essential for anyone in a substantial way of business to describe what is offered in some detail. The practical realities of this call for a brochure to be produced.

Accuracy and statutory requirements

Because it sets out the principal's promise there is an absolute need to ensure that the description of the product in the brochure is completely accurate. The Trade Descriptions Act (1968), the Unfair Contract Terms Act (1977), the Consumer Protection Act (1987), the Package Travel, Package Holidays and Package Tours Regulations (1992), the EU Directive on Package Travel and other consumer legislation – particularly European Union Directives – have all changed the nature of the offence of giving inaccurate information. Formerly to be considered a minor misdemeanour, that is a civil matter which could give rise to claims for compensation, it is now classified as a criminal act which may result in prosecution and punishment. No one would justify knowingly issuing incorrect information, but slovenly compilation itself has become a serious offence. Even the justification that one did not have knowledge of a change of circumstances in unacceptable now as a defence. The travel agent and tour operator must demonstrate that they have exercised 'due diligence': in other words, that they have taken all reasonable steps to prevent inaccuracies or other breaches of legislation. In practice, operational procedures must be in place, documented and regularly reviewed in order to convince the courts that due diligence is indeed being exercised.

The laws place enormous burdens upon a travel company, resort or promoter of any tourist facility. No longer can they rely upon the previous year's definition or tried and tested photographs in their library without checking that each and every fact is still correct. To take a simple example, the tree that stands in front of a hotel may well have grown until it obscures the promised sea view from some of the bedrooms. An operator could not plead ignorance of this and expect to be excused from responsibility.

The scale of the task for the tour operator is put in perspective by the statistic that each brochure page may contain on average one hundred to two hundred facts that must be checked. The major three tour operators between them must therefore verify well over a million individual facts for each summer season. It must also be remembered that much information is supplied from overseas, with the resultant logistics and language problems, and that many details change abruptly over time.

Even after the brochure is printed, the tour operator must continue to monitor that the facts remain true. While the tour operators may use their Viewdata reservations systems to relay corrected information to retailers, it is not necessarily considered sufficient. Once an error is detected, both operator and agent may have a duty to correct the error by such means as printed erratum slips, brochure stickers, 'shelf talkers' on brochure racks, or even reprinting the entire brochure. In practice this is rarely the case, and multi-editions of brochures allow regular updating of errors and changes.

One effect of these laws is to make the travel literature less interesting and flamboyant, and more coldly factual – and sadly, less helpful, as operators seek to avoid illustrative prose to describe a facility that may conceivably not be available or where different interpretation is possible. Better to say nothing than be pilloried is the dictum. To illustrate how such legislation can work against the interest of the consumer, facilities at a hotel which could be of help for disabled travellers may be ignored rather than risk the possibility that they were inadequate; for instance, 'wheelchair accessible' could be true for the majority of wheelchairs, but can the operator be certain it is true of all makes?

Similarly, travel agents are now necessarily wary of keeping and/or handing out resort or country pamphlets, in case they have become obsolete due to a change in circumstances, rendering the agent liable to prosecution for giving wrong information. The acid test must be – is the literature correct, honest and wholly truthful? While the aim of this legislation was clearly to protect the client, it had implications probably not envisaged when the regulations were drawn up.

Further regulatory requirements

ABTA has played a crucial role in regulating the sale of travel products in the UK. Tour operators and travel agents who are members of ABTA have agreed to abide by that organisation's guidelines and Codes of Conduct, which offer clear directives, including those relating to information which must be contained in brochures.

The Package Travel, Package Holidays and Package Tours Regulations (1992) mean that the Trading Standards Departments within local authorities now act to enforce these regulations, and consumers may raise complaints through their local Trading Standards Officers.

As well as the duty to provide accurate information, the legislation places a number of other practical demands upon the travel industry, including:

1 Authoritative, reliable and current health formalities and passport and visa requirements must be supplied to the consumer.
2 Information on the travel aspects of the package must be verified and provided in good time to the consumer.
3 Appropriate insurance policies must be brought to the attention of the consumer.
4 A clear statement must be available of the arrangements in the event of insolvency of travel agent or tour operator, the security of prepayments and arrangements for repatriation – and these arrangements must be satisfactory.

The implications of the EU legislation are far reaching, as they mean that the tour operator is legally responsible not only for monitoring the accuracy of facts but also for ensuring that 'descriptive matter' should not be misleading. In addition, though the operator has no direct control over suppliers such as hoteliers or car hire companies, the operator is legally responsible should a problem occur with these services if they are part of the package.

Breaches of the legislation are now a criminal, rather than a civil, offence. Companies can be heavily fined and individuals can be prosecuted in serious cases. Dissatisfied clients can also claim substantial damages. All of this makes brochure accuracy a high priority, as the results of mistakes are costly in PR as well as financial terms.

The ABTA Code of Conduct released in May 1993 was drawn up to ensure that there are no differences between this and the prevailing UK and EU legislation. Though the obligation to belong to ABTA in order to trade (the so-called 'stabiliser' rule) no longer exists, in practice adhering to the Code ensures correct interpretation of complex legislation. ABTA's position within the industry complements the additional regulatory powers of the Trading Standards Departments.

Style and layout

Every company strives for its brochure to be distinctive and attractive. This publication is the only tangible evidence that the consumer has of the company's promises, unique benefits, financial and management strengths, and style. Yet research shows that the brochure may initially have only a few seconds to influence consumers as they collect a number of brochures at the travel agent for detailed perusal at home. Almost subliminally, a number of factors are weighed up to gauge a 'good' brochure, including:

- the front cover
- cover quality and 'glossiness'
- the extent of use, and appeal, of colours

- the number and quality of photographs
- thickness of brochures
- destinations featured on the front cover
- clarity of the index
- relevance of holiday type.

One might say that travel is a fashion industry in some senses, since as fashions change it is necessary to change not only the product but also the description of it. Conversely, the statutory and other requirements make it difficult to do so.

Logical progression has created a standard approach to writing travel brochures, so that most now follow a three-section pattern:

- introductory pages
- contents pages
- 'extro' or exit pages

The introduction establishes the company's style, makes statements about policies and commercial practices, promotes unique selling points and 'bargain' offers and preferably (though not always) contains an index.

The contents pages are almost always arranged in sections defined by destination country. Most companies lead with their strongest destination, but it is not unknown for the first to be a resort that they wish to emphasise for other reasons (such as launching a new destination).

For touring holidays, Cosmos Tourama Holidays established a winning formula of high quality colour reproduction; descriptive titles for each tour; simple masthead route maps; a day-by-day itinerary; plus three photographs, featuring a place, a tourist attraction and people on holiday. Imitation is said to be the sincerest form of flattery, and this format has become widely emulated throughout the industry.

Similarly for air holidays, winning ways have been developed and much copied. The large number of holidays sold as well as the wide variety of competition has led to many different styles. Among the most successful has been Thomson's Summer Sun layout with larger photographs of hotels (the main distinctive feature of otherwise similar summer holidays) combined with rather fewer words but with price grids featuring a huge choice of flights, departure points, durations and dates. Simply to accommodate these grids on the page is an act of skill. Attempting to make the result understandable and still visually attractive requires abilities approaching genius. However, it has to be said that the task is being made easier in the 1990s by the widespread introduction of desktop publishing software for personal computers, which is capable of handling the entire layout and editing of the package holiday brochure.

The final section of the brochure (jargon phrase 'extro' being the opposite of 'intro') contains details of booking conditions, extraneous information, insurance schemes and all the other 'small print' details required by law and by regulatory bodies such as ABTA. The booking form is frequently to be found on the back cover or on one of the last pages in the brochure, but should not be printed on the back of any booking conditions, since such contractual information should be retained by the customer. The larger tour operators no longer carry booking forms in their brochures, but instead provide retail agents with separate booking form pads.

Brochure covers

The design of the brochure cover is an undoubtedly vital aspect in persuading the customer to consider any product. Tour operators therefore put considerable effort into the design of the front cover. They may, for instance, commission a dedicated photographic shoot just to obtain one special shot. Alternative designs may be researched with panels of consumers before the final cover layout is decided. The choice of design is a difficult one for there are many possibilities, such as:

- a spectacularly attractive photograph of a typical destination
- an attractive holiday situation, such as a family group enjoying themselves in the water
- a markedly different cover from one's competitors
- a pictorial amalgam of the contents

- a statement of what is contained or of sales features.

Each policy has its supporters. Long-haul holidays brochures tend to feature a photograph of some idyllic faraway destination. Most Mediterranean holiday brochures favour a happy or glamorous beach scene. Many comprehensive larger brochures hedge their bets with an amalgam of pictures.

Two examples of different approaches were the Wings brochure which ignored colour photography and for many years stood out on the racks as a blue and white striped brochure, with nothing other than the company logo to relieve its simplicity. In contrast, the original Intasun brochure covers were illustrated each year with a line drawing of an attractive girl in a bathing costume; the use of a drawing in place of the more common photographs made the brochure instantly recognisable. Both companies eventually abandoned this format, and today no major company appears willing to take risks in its brochure design; like the interior of brochures, the formats have for the most part become stale and unimaginative.

Bold statements about special offers and product features have dominated many designs. Cosmos, for example, dropped the pictorial representation altogether and devoted their cover to the offers, displayed in heavy, easily readable type.

Whatever design style is chosen it is wise to ensure that it is relevant to the contents, not merely attractive in itself. Many companies have made the cover so appealing that customers have taken a copy even when they have had no intention of buying anything remotely like the contents.

One aspect of design that should never be forgotten is that brochure space in travel agencies is always limited. The result is that many are overlapped on the racks. Those that are identified or titled in a place that is easily covered will lose their impact.

Design and print

A few brochures are still designed by amateurs, and they stand out like sore thumbs alongside professional offerings. If these companies are successful, it is despite their brochures, not because of them.

Designing a brochure is a highly skilled art needing an exact specification of the intentions, features and statutory provisions necessary. From these, the designer can make a *rough* for approval by the client. A professional design house will have modern technology available, including the ability to simulate photographs by computer.

The number of pages is important in itself. Multiples of four are inevitable, for a folded sheet printed on both sides produces four 'pages'. According to the print run envisaged it may be possible to make substantial economies by utilising the maximum amount of space on each sheet or roll of paper. Rarely will cut sheets be used that equate to the eventual page size. It is more probable that large sheets that incorporate 4, 8, 16 or more pages will be printed at one time, but with really large runs the relationship between several huge rolls of paper fed simultaneously will need to be reflected in the pagination and the layout chosen.

The page size will relate not only to design considerations, but also to the methods of printing chosen. Normally standard ISO (International Standards Organisation) paper sizes will result in the greatest economies in cutting paper. The system was introduced into Britain in the early 1970s and replaced earlier 'Imperial' sizes. Inevitably, some printers still have older equipment, but ISO is now the dominant system.

The system has been developed to be practical and economical. The concept is based upon a square metre of paper arranged in such a way that paper is cut so that the relationship between the two sides is constant when folded (try it out). Thus each 'A' size is exactly half of its next larger counterpart, from 'A0' which uses a square metre of paper down to A6, which is around the size of a postcard (see Fig. 10.1).

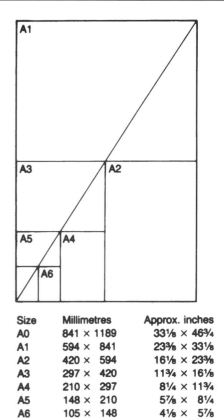

Size	Millimetres	Approx. inches
A0	841 × 1189	33⅛ × 46¾
A1	594 × 841	23⅜ × 33⅛
A2	420 × 594	16⅛ × 23⅜
A3	297 × 420	11¾ × 16⅛
A4	210 × 297	8¼ × 11¾
A5	148 × 210	5⅞ × 8¼
A6	105 × 148	4⅛ × 5⅞

Fig. 10.1 'A' series paper sizes

The fact that the shape is common to whatever 'A' size is chosen makes it much easier for design purposes, as reductions and increases in size can be scaled easily. For large-scale posters and wall charts there is also a 'B' series of larger sizes.

Related to the standard paper sizes are standard envelope sizes. Generally the prefix 'C' is added to the paper size, e.g. C4 for paper size A4, or C5 if you fold the sheet of paper in half before insertion (see Fig. 10.2).

Virtually all brochures are now produced in A4 size (210 × 297 mm), and as a result, display areas are normally designed to fit this requirement too. Woe betide the holiday company that decides to produce a 'king size' brochure that will neither fit the brochure racks nor go into the envelopes that the agent stocks. Even a few millimetres can make all the difference.

An interestingly different brochure was

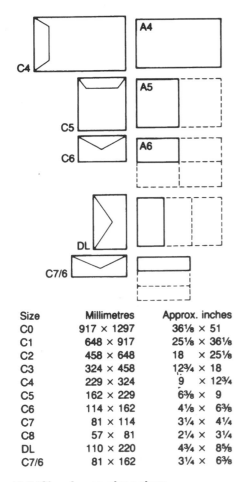

Size	Millimetres	Approx. inches
C0	917 × 1297	36⅛ × 51
C1	648 × 917	25⅛ × 36⅛
C2	458 × 648	18 × 25⅛
C3	324 × 458	12¾ × 18
C4	229 × 324	9 × 12¾
C5	162 × 229	6⅜ × 9
C6	114 × 162	4⅛ × 6⅜
C7	81 × 114	3¼ × 4¼
C8	57 × 81	2¼ × 3¼
DL	110 × 220	4¾ × 8⅝
C7/6	81 × 162	3¼ × 6⅜

Fig. 10.2 'C' series envelope sizes

produced by Tjaereborg when they first started selling their holidays in the UK. As they did not sell through agents they did not need to follow the established pattern. For printing reasons they chose the normal size, but printed the brochure in 'landscape' format (long side at the top) rather than 'portrait'. Later they changed over to the conventional style and lost a unique and original approach to their brochure production. The reason was that they had reduced the thickness of paper to minimise postal charges (a very important item of cost for a direct sell operator) and the pages flopped badly in the wide format.

The thickness and type of paper are important factors. If there are many pages you will wish to reduce the weight by using thinner paper. Often

this will mean using a heavier paper for the cover to prevent floppiness. If the brochure contains few pages, then extra weight will be less important and the 'feel' may be improved by using heavier than average paper.

Matt finish paper will give a certain style to a well-designed publication, especially if full colour is not to be used. Art finished (shiny) paper is, however, essential if high quality colour reproduction is the aim. Within art paper, the heavier the weight, the better the reproduction is likely to be. High quality but lightweight art paper tends to be expensive.

When ordering your brochure it is, therefore, necessary to talk not only about the quality of the printing process but also about paper. It is a critical matter to see that the chosen printer has not only the capability you need, but also access to adequate stocks of the correct paper at the exact time of your print run.

The printing process to be chosen will largely depend upon the number of copies to be printed and the colour requirement. There are almost as many processes as there are paper types, but most modern ones are based upon photographically reproduced images and a lithographic, webb-offset or gravure machine. It is worthwhile getting to know the advantages and disadvantages of each method, and some time spent at your printers will pay off in preventing misunderstandings caused by using the wrong specification.

When it comes to pictures, there are some base rules, too. Photographs should be high in contrasts. Colour pictures should be taken on transparency film on as large a film format as possible (roll film 120 size preferred – 57 mm square). The camera should have an excellent lens. If really necessary, 35 mm photographs can be used, but they should always be originals and not duplicates to ensure reasonable colour and detail.

Modern computers with desktop publishing and graphics software packages have contributed greatly to making the production process both more flexible and streamlined. Nevertheless, it will be appreciated from the following description that considerable project management is required to ensure that each page and section of the brochure is brought together correctly.

Text and pricing information can be received on computer disk by the chosen design studio, who produce a *page make-up* for each page. The design elements and photographs are included with the text, though the flexibility exists to leave the correct amount of space for information that will arrive later in the process. At this stage the pages can be checked from black and white computer printouts, which are quick and inexpensive to produce.

After possibly a number of iterations, a page will be approved to proceed to the next stage – the production of printer's films by a repro house. Even more sophisticated equipment is used to arrive at *colour separated film*. The colour printing process is achieved by the use of four basic coloured inks, magenta, yellow, cyan (blue) and black, which can be combined in different quantities to produce all other colours. The four films represent where each coloured ink is to be applied by the plates of the printing press. At this stage, the films may be developed photographically to produce a full colour chromalin proof for checking.

The colour separated films are then used to produce the metal printing plates for the printing press itself. The press is 'made ready', and as initial pages are printed the press is adjusted for final correct colour balance. Only once the press is running true and the colours are approved will the printer proceed to print production copies.

Corrections should be made at an early stage. Remember that printers correct only their own mistakes free. The type matter is first set up in page layouts in black and white laser printouts. Corrections should be made at this time, before films are produced at the repro house. There is a British Standard (5261C:1976) regarding proof correction instructions (see Appendix 2). Any corrections to the copy, such as grammatical errors that are spotted after the films have been made, are considered author's corrections and are charged at supplementary cost.

Segmentation of the market

The most important dilemma which faces large holiday companies is whether to address different parts of the market with separate and different brochures and/or brands, or whether to include all in one massive authoritative publication.

If a company is known for its expertise in providing summer beach holidays, will it be regarded as expert or even competent if it decides to branch out into coach tours, or into city holidays or fly cruises?

There is no doubt that some customers like to deal with those that they feel are able to provide a personal, caring and expert service. Others may believe that financial strength simply brings better value and that buying from a larger concern is preferable.

The larger the brochure is, the more pages are irrelevant to the eventual purchase and the greater is the cost of distribution. By contrast, several smaller brochures each covering merely a segment (perhaps defined by destination, but also possibly by holiday type, price or activity) will not reach so large a group of potential purchasers. Similarly if the company's offerings for a segment are not contained in the brochure picked up, it might be assumed that they do not undertake the type of holiday required, and the booking will be placed with a competitor.

In the end, costs dictate policy, and it is easy to see why. For example, one major company produced just over 2 million copies of their Summer Sun brochure, at a cost of 85p a copy, while their much smaller Lakes and Mountains brochure cost only 13p. Naturally, the proportion of costs relating to design can be written off more easily on the longer run, but the special brochure undoubtedly paid off for this easily defined holiday type (see Fig. 10.3).

Different approaches inevitably develop as a response to the problem. Some companies put everything into one brochure. Others, such as Thomson Holidays, prefer to segment by holiday type. To give examples in detail of the range of brochures produced by major operators, Table 10.1 lists the summer and winter brochures produced by First Choice Holidays and the Owners Abroad Group.

There is no right or wrong way. What is important is that the marketing executive considers all the merits and demerits of each possibility and formulates a clearly understood policy.

	Summer Sun (%)	Lakes & Mountains (%)
Design/artwork	12	30
Paper	48	35
Print	40	35
	100	100

Fig. 10.3 Comparative percentages of cost for summer brochures

Table 10.1(a) Brochures produced by First Choice Holidays

Brand	Summer	Winter
First Choice	Summersun	Wintersun
	Tropical	Leisurely Days
	Flights	Ski
	Portugal	Tropical
	Florida	Flights
	Lakes and Mountains	Cyprus
		Florida
Freespirit	Go Sunshine	Wintersun
	Go Greek	
	Go Turkey	
	2wentys	
Sovereign	Summer Sunshine	Winter Sunshine
	Villa Collection	Cities
	Cities	Worldwide
	Worldwide	
	Scanscape	
	Small World	
Eclipse	Summer Sun	Winter Sun
	Flights	Flights
	Travelclub	Travelclub

Table 10.1(b) Brochures produced by the Owners Abroad Group

Summer	Winter
Falcon Flights	Falcon Flights
Falcon Corsica	Falcon Far and Wide
Falcon Family	People Like Us
Falcon Summersun	Ski Falcon
Falcon Greece and Turkey	Martyn Holidays
Falcon Florida/Far and Wide	Sunward Holidays
	Falcon Resorts
Falcon Resorts	Sovereign Wintersun
2wenties Holidays	Sovereign Cities
Enterprise Summersun	Enterprise Wintersun
Enterprise Lakes & Mountains	Enterprise Ski
	Go Morocco
Enterprise Florida	Go Canaries
Enterprise Sol	Go Ski
Sovereign Sunshine	Ski Whizz
Sovereign Cities	
Sovereign Golf	
Go Greek	
Go Turkey	
Go Kenya	
Go Morocco	
Martyn Greece	
Martyn Madeira Year Book	
Martyn Canaries	
Martyn Algarve - Private Villas with Pools	
Martyn Portugal	
Sunward Holidays	
Just Turkey	
Villas Italia	
Falcon Sailing	
Small World	
Flairfares	

Evolution problems

Increasingly, there seems to be a 'sameness' about travel brochures. The brightest creative people pour huge amounts of effort into trying to make a brochure distinctive and especially attractive, yet they know that a new formula will be copied quickly if successful. Statutory requirements have to be satisfied, computer logic has to be obeyed (for the booking form, at least), and cost justifications have to be considered.

Consider the case of a small operator who

Fig. 10.4 First Choice Holidays brochures, Summer 1995
(Courtesy: First Choice Holidays)

creates an attractive Villa and Apartment brochure. The company will be proud of the finest properties and will be tempted to give them the most space and best photographic coverage. Initially, this may pay off, and bookings will 'overflow' to the less exceptional properties when the first choice has been sold. Year by year, as the programme becomes more successful, the range of properties will expand. Similarly, and because of the increased number of customers, the number of brochures printed will also grow. Even with economies of scale, the brochure cost per booking will inevitably rise. More impor-

tantly, the cost per page in the brochure will need to be related to the goods on sale there. However nice an individual villa may be, there will normally be only one. How much better, it might be thought, for an apartment to be featured, particularly if it is one of many similar apartments, which are less expensive and easier to sell.

One major company with a programme of villas and apartments followed this road until they produced a brochure with a picture of a villa on the front cover, yet featured only apartments inside! Their product lacked distinction and profits slid into oblivion.

Similar problems regularly occur when small allocations of rooms at popular hotels can no longer justify the cost of the brochure space, and they have to be replaced by less interesting, but more substantial, allocations in larger establishments. Owners of the hotels prefer not to be beholden to any one travel company, and soon a variety of competitors are offering much the same holiday. Customers quickly spot price differences, and the company taking the least profit sells out first.

There is also an implication that the company offers better value throughout its brochure. Customers unable to obtain their first choice may prefer to change, in the belief that, if more is to be paid, the 'cheaper company' will offer them greater satisfaction for the small extra charge being demanded, whereas the 'more expensive company' is simply overcharging. In practice, a sophisticated 'switch selling' technique may be taking place with the cheaper company having only a few rooms at the comparative hotel, but many more at hotels that are not being shared.

Whatever pricing policy is followed, the highly competitive nature of the market means that prices are forced down to very low levels of profit. Thus tour operators are faced with a dilemma: either they take on huge commitments to fill hotels that they reserve for themselves and keep as exclusive offers (where they can control margins more easily), or they take small batches of rooms at a selection of hotels shared with others and face keen price competition.

As hotels have grown larger (over 1000 beds is not uncommon) the chance of exclusivity has receded. Unique advantages are more difficult to justify and price has become an ever more important factor in consumer choice. This places even greater emphasis upon the need for the brochure to create an individuality and character for the company and its products – no simple task.

Successful brochures

It is interesting to take a trip down memory lane and to examine the most successful brochures of each era. There are lessons to be learned from these earlier examples for today's brochure writers. Perhaps the most important lesson is that the best brochures were those able to anticipate developments in consumer demand, and to respond to those developments.

Horizon Holidays brochures of the late 1950s stressed middle-class respectability at a time when the inclusive holiday was rather an unknown quantity, with an introduction by the well-respected Lord Douglas of Kirtleside, retired chairman of the former British European Airways (BEA).

Cosmos coach tours in the early 1960s anticipated the pent-up demand of 'average' Britons to be able to enjoy the sights of Europe at prices they could afford, in an age when foreign travel had been restricted to the rich or those serving in the armed forces. The brochures featured exceptionally high quality colour photographs of tourist attractions at a time when printing was generally of a poor standard.

Universal Sky Tours in the latter half of the 1960s made holidays by air financially accessible for many for the first time. They then improved the quality with such original features as reserved seats on their Britannia aircraft. Their brochure covers were emblazoned with low prices and new features.

In the mid-1960s, Sir Henry Lunn's Everyman Holidays introduced segmentation by promising noticeably cheaper family holidays in parallel with their mainstream product. They stated categorically that the hotels were simpler and that the flights were at less convenient times, that is during the midweek period at night. For those that could accept these constraints, lower prices were available. Another area of potential sales was opened up.

Price has not been the only marketing tool. Kuoni established dominance in the long-haul market as it progressively expanded. Swiss Travel Service has consistently offered a caring personal product to a high price country. Through specialisation and excellence, both have recorded excellent results. Their brochures have been designed to appeal to a more sophisticated clientele, and prices are given much less emphasis.

Originally owned by British Airways, the Sovereign brand was sold to Redwing and then to Owners Abroad. By the early 1990s the brand had somewhat lost its way. Now part of First Choice Holidays, Sovereign has reached a highly respected position in the market. The MORI Travel Agents' Survey investigates travel agents' perceptions of different brands: the 1991–3 surveys showed Sovereign strengthening and becoming ranked no. 2 for both 'trouble free holidays' and 'the quality of their holidays'. The

brochure range has undoubtedly contributed to the success of Sovereign.

The design of the Sovereign brochures was updated to a deliberately classic and up-market feel. The strong use of blue and red is slightly reminiscent of British Airways – a positive association to have in a British travel product's pedigree. The crown logo, the italic typeface and the strapline 'For the Discerning Traveller' all position the brand firmly as a quality product. Most importantly, as can be seen from Fig. 10.5,

Fig. 10.5 The classic range of Sovereign brochures, epitomising the up-market product
(Courtesy: First Choice Holidays)

all the brochures build into a coherent set.

Within the brochure the accommodation is usually 4 star and above, and is also graded by Sovereign's own crown rating. The discerning traveller can choose between categories such as 'Sovereign Hideaways' (which are particularly out of the way and tranquil) and 'Limited Edition' (which represent properties with special character). Taxi transfer from the airport and inclusive car hire reinforce a quality product.

For all the success stories, there have been failures, too. Most were those who believed that yesterday's successful formula was adequate for tomorrow's market, failing to recognise the fast-changing nature of tourism demand. Even one year can produce a huge shift of consumer purchasing compared with the preceding year. Brochures that do not reflect changing demands soon become tired and ineffective. When you realise that the brochure for next season normally goes to press before the current similar season has truly got under way, you can understand the need for a crystal ball in the office of the marketing manager and the brochure planner.

Getting the brochure to the prospective customer

Customers who seek information on an intended holiday have a variety of ways in which to obtain holiday brochures. If they know the company with which they are likely to travel, they can contact them direct. If reacting to a television advertisement, a telephone number for a central response will have been supplied. Most likely, however, customers will visit a travel agent.

In most travel agencies, the brochure racks will be easily accessible and piled high with the offerings of competing companies. In some, the display may reflect company policy regarding commission agreements, customer satisfaction or simply the manager's personal preference. It is probable that the prime positions, that is at eye level and close to the door, will also reflect the policy adopted.

Ideally, the sales staff will wish to discuss requirements and direct the customer to the most

appropriate choice. In reality, however, this rarely happens, and the customer is likely to be significantly influenced by the attractiveness of the brochure cover itself, or by recognition of the name of the tour operator.

Selection can be extremely subjective. The cover picture may well set the scene for consideration of a brochure. Often, it has little relevance to the contents. Sometimes a specialist company will make their brochure cover so attractive that they run out of brochures early. They may take very few bookings because the contents are not what the customer actually sought, or were relatively expensive, when other more reasonable choices were still available.

Timing of distribution is also important. Inevitably, the first brochures tend to be published by the market leaders who feel strong enough to set the price levels for the coming season. They launch with a blaze of publicity and create a consumer demand for brochures, even if only for curiosity's sake. Smaller companies may be tempted to ride along on the crest of that wave. All too frequently they find that their brochure is picked up as a comparison though it is not relevant to the customer's actual needs. One company promoting its summer sun holidays found that the result of coming out early was that their entire year's print order was distributed and 'lost' by the October before the relevant summer, necessitating a reprint and doubling their print costs.

It is equally disastrous to advertise heavily and not have adequate stocks available. Consumers are notoriously fickle and, having got them to the travel agent to obtain the brochure, you may be assured that they will not leave empty-handed when so much choice is available.

The booking process

When someone decides to take a holiday, the normal first reaction is to seek additional information on the probable choice.

The first decisions will probably be:

- whether or not to go abroad

- whether or not to travel independently
- whether or not to travel by air.

In the case of independent overseas travel, the information required may be for car ferry, Eurotunnel or airline information. The literature for these companies might be considered merely as a means of disseminating factual information, and the brochure requirement thought to be for concise details of timetables and fares only. In fact, this is not so.

Car ferry companies are in fierce competition for customers. Their brochures clearly show this: they set out not only the facts but also the competitive advantages of each shipping line. They give details of a wide range of incentives to travel at unpopular times designed to reduce the peaking of demand and to mop up under-used capacity in the off-season.

Similarly, the airlines no longer enjoy monopolies on most routes. On short-haul European routes, they will be faced with strong competition from Eurotunnel, particularly for the business market. The element of competition makes it increasingly important that they also promote their competitive plus points, and they are more than likely to use full colour A4 brochures to attract their market.

If the brochure is important to carriers, it is essential to tour operators. One has only to look on the shelves of a travel agency to appreciate how vast is the selection of holidays, all competing for the consumer's attention.

Research into the booking process identifies that once a decision to take a package tour has been made, the first call is normally on the travel agent, to collect brochures. Disappointingly, the majority of consumers see little difference between different travel agents, just as they do with tour operators.

Brochure collection is influenced by the factors discussed earlier in this chapter, previous experience, recommendation by friends and by the travel agent. Most frequently it is the impact of the front cover and a very cursory examination to 'get a feel' for the brochure and the types of holidays covered.

The brochures are most often collected by women, who are the chief organisers of holidays. Women also do most of the comprehensive homework when brochures are examined and compared in detail. It is clarity and ease of research that makes a winning brochure in the eyes of most consumers, who can regard the process of drawing up a short list as a time-consuming and onerous task.

The role of the brochure is now reduced as the consumer normally returns to the travel agent to make the booking. The ideal travel agent is seen as a source of extra information above and beyond the brochure (possibly first-hand knowledge), and in particular the agent is expected to be able to advise on the suitability of resorts for the kind of holiday required, such as a family with young children. The travel agent is also there to verify the price, flight details and availability, which are often complex for the consumers to work out for themselves.

Brochures in a video age?

The first task of a travel brochure is to describe a facility being offered. How much better can that be done with movement and greater use of pictures? The video now presents both new challenges and opportunities to travel companies.

Travel companies have commissioned a variety of video programmes that give in-depth information about particular holiday areas or types. Some travel agencies have established libraries of such cassettes that can either be used in the shop or taken home on loan so that other members of the household or travel companions can see them.

Videos may be updated and reissued at any time in the season. The video cassette, however, would be an expensive medium for the tour operator. In particular, it does not achieve the same economies of scale as the printing process for very large volumes. Also, there is now a vast investment in existing photography of resorts and hotels: footage that would have to be shot afresh for a video.

Whether potential customers are really interested in going to an agent to see 'more television' is a question that remains unanswered up to this point. There is a widely held view that people use travel agents mainly to obtain opinions and helpful advice to verify their prior decision. If this is the main role (apart from being a convenient outlet for bookings), it is doubtful whether customers will be interested in video, however skilfully presented. Another major flaw in video from the consumer point of view is the fact that it is not interactive. Bearing in mind the booking process described previously in this chapter, it is clear that the consumer 'skips' through brochures seeking specific resorts and information. It is cumbersome to skip backwards and forwards on video cassettes.

CD-ROM

Perhaps an even more interesting development is the CD-ROM, which can hold photographic images of every hotel in every ABTA tour operators' programmes for the complete season. The difficulties inherent in videotape are automatically overcome by a CD-ROM drive attached to a personal computer. The tour operator's investment in existing photography is preserved, as these can be scanned into a computer to be copied on to a CD-ROM disk. Also, the travel agent or consumer accessing information on CD-ROM through the computer is able to find the information instantly, interactively and flexibly.

Other facilities

With a growing tendency towards independence and later bookings, one can see a diminishing role for brochures that attempt to predict customer desires so long in advance. The combination of a database that contains all the flights currently available, and all the accommodation available, will present the agent with the capability of mixing and matching the facilities required by a customer. Having achieved the best possible combination, the agent can then present the result on a screen for the customer to view, alongside pictures of the hotel. The customer could then be provided with a printout of the information, together with any amendments that have occurred and a photographic print of the hotel.

These facilities are no longer science fiction; they are available now, and may spell the end of the traditional travel brochure as we know it. It is but a short step beyond this scenario to recognise that this information could easily be called up on the customer's home television screen, and through interactive booking (already available on satellite television programmes) the customer can book directly with the principal, cutting out the agent entirely. Such a development poses a very real threat to the continued existence of travel retailing.

Questions, tasks and issues for discussion

1 Are brochures issued by the mass market tour operators designed to maximise clarity of understanding about the products and their prices? Examine three major brochures and identify factors which support your view.

2 'A genuinely consumer-orientated brochure would tell the truth about destinations, warts and all'.

    Discuss this point of view in small groups, looking at both sides of the question.

3 Working in groups, prepare a rough draft of artwork for the design of the cover of a package holiday brochure for a company whose aims are:

    (a) to communicate the brand name effectively, and
    (b) to stand out against other brochures in an agency rack.

4   Are the legal or quasi-legal regulations governing the content of brochures
    adequate for consumer protection, or should they be tightened up still further?
    Take the role of an OFT officer whose task is to consider this question, and
    prepare a short report identifying any area where you think controls are currently
    inadequate.

Exercise

Select two current package holiday brochures which are directed at separate
markets, and evaluate their success in terms of the issues discussed in this
chapter.

At what market are they aimed? How successfully do they fulfil their objectives?
What theme and image do they convey, and how do they communicate this?
Consider issues of style, layout, clarity of booking conditions, quality of paper, etc.

11 Sales promotion for travel and tourism

After studying this chapter, you should be able to:

- distinguish between different sales promotion activities
- understand their use in achieving differing objectives
- be aware of the stages in campaign planning for promotions
- understand how to evaluate the effectiveness of campaigns
- appreciate the role of exhibitions, workshops and presentations in the travel industry

The nature of sales promotion

As we explained in Chapter 9, advertising is technically referred to as 'above the line' promotion, and all other forms of promotion are 'below the line'. However, the division between the two is not always clear-cut. Window display, for example, is one of the *merchandising techniques* designed to promote products at the point of sale. Although it could be argued that travel agencies' windows are used to advertise products such as current bargain offers for flights and holidays, window display is still generally treated as a form of below the line promotion.

Most members of the travel industry are familiar with advertising and its uses, but are less confident in the use of sales promotion techniques. This is unfortunate, since there are so many forms of sales promotion which can be undertaken, limited only by the imagination of the marketing staff. However, they must be used with caution, since not all sales promotion is suitable for all forms of product.

Sales promotion activities are *attention getters*, since their objective is to achieve immediate sales impact. However, if this is achieved through money-off or bargain offers, this can have the effect of demeaning the inherent value of the product, suggesting that the seller is anxious to unload the products. Ronnie Corbett's joke that he remembered an event 'because it was the week Allied Carpets were not having a sale' carries an important message for the marketeer: that too much emphasis on 'deals' will degrade the product in the consumers' eyes and at the same time undermine profit levels.

When planning promotional strategies, it is best to think of sales promotion as complementary to advertising. In very few instances is it appropriate to use one or the other communications techniques alone in the marketing plan, even though they may serve different objectives. Each has its place in the overall plan. Often, advertising is seen as the main tool to achieve long-term objectives, such as building the corporate image of the organisation and its products, while sales promotion is used to achieve short-term objectives such as clearing current stock. In fact, making such a clear differentiation is too simple. A travel agent's window display can be used to build a long-term image of the company as much as to sell current products. What is important is that the sales promotion and advertising objectives do not conflict, but rather reinforce one another. If, for instance, the advertising objectives aim to create an image of quality and service for the company, this can be undermined by sales promotion objectives focusing on price bargains.

As sales promotion is designed to appeal particularly to those customers who are price sensitive, such techniques tend to attract buyers who have little brand loyalty. It follows, therefore, that in those areas of travel where brand loyalty is a feature, such as certain cruise markets and holiday centre operators, sales promotion will be a useful tool if it is aimed at present clientele to attract more business from the existing market instead of trying to encourage brand switching from other companies. In other industries such as Fast Moving Consumer Goods (FMCGs) there are powerful sales promotion techniques to encourage brand switching such as free samples to attract trial. With travel there is less opportunity for such techniques (although efforts to sell timeshare apartments in Spain have been accompanied by free trips by air to see the accommodation). We must remember, though, that with less expensive products, in travel as in other businesses, sales promotion using bargain offers can gain many uncommitted consumers. Entrance tickets to theme parks, museums and similar tourist attractions, all make extensive use of vouchers to increase their 'gate'.

While part of today's emphasis on sales promotion in the marketing plan arises from over-use of advertising as a communications tool in the past, another factor is the increased competition in the travel industry, which has caused marketing managers to consider more carefully the use of all methods of communication available to them. Co-operative merchandising in particular, between agents and principals, has been extensively used to increase sales and to generate more agency commission. It also has the attraction of being easily understood and measured in its effectiveness, since it aims for an immediate boost to turnover, while not all advertising is so easily assessed.

The techniques of sales promotion

Before we examine how the techniques are employed, it will be helpful to identify the various tools in the sales promotion 'armoury'. These can be categorised as techniques aimed at the company's staff, such as sales representatives or counter sales staff, those directed at dealers or retailers, and those directed at consumers. The list that follows is not intended to be exhaustive (there are many hundreds of techniques which can be used), but it will cover those more commonly used and which are appropriate for application in the travel and tourism industry.

Promotions directed at a company's staff:
- incentives (financial, travel, etc.)
- bonuses
- contests and competitions.

Promotions directed at dealers or retailers:
- 'give-aways' (pens, ashtrays, calendars, diaries, etc., usually bearing the principal's name)
- contests
- trade exhibitions
- product/brochure launches (presentations, buffets, etc.)
- direct mail (letters, circulars, etc.)
- joint promotion schemes (financial, organisational help).

Promotions directed at consumers (either through retailers or direct):
- point of sale (POS) material (window display, wall display, posters, counter cards, brochure racks, etc.)
- sales literature
- direct mail
- free samples
- 'give-aways' (e.g. flight bags) and 'self-liquidating offers' (products promoting the company's name, and sold at cost price by the company)
- competitions
- low interest financing
- money-off vouchers
- purchase privilege plans (e.g. 'twofers', whereby two are charged the price of one for entrance)
- joint promotions with non-travel companies (e.g. cheap weekends in a major city through the collection of washing powder vouchers).

It will be appreciated from a glance at this list that the scope for new ideas in sales promotion is almost unlimited. Travel companies offer a huge range of give-aways to their clients, including flight bags, carrier bags, wallets for tickets and foreign exchange, and passport covers. Hotels offer a steadily increasing range of useful facilities to their guests, including shoeshine cloths, 'first aid' sewing kits, shower caps and shampoo. Additionally, important clients might receive fruit or flowers in their room.

While most of these promotional tools are designed to do no more than create goodwill among clients and provide a sense of *added value* to the product, they will often also have an underlying purpose; that of ensuring the company or its products are remembered.

Therefore the most successful give-away to be presented to the travel agent is one which will be considered attractive or useful enough to be put on display in the office (see Figs 11.1a and 11.1b). Ashtrays, paperweights and calendars serve this purpose very well. Lists of useful telephone numbers which agents might want to keep in sight next to their desks will ensure that the principal's name is kept prominently displayed throughout the year, and aid recall. Such sales promotion aids serve similar purposes to advertising: they can be used to remind, to inform and to persuade customers to buy and retailers to sell.

Where the product is sold through retailers, the marketing manager can adopt one of two courses of action. One method is to aim the promotion at

Fig. 11.1(a) Effective 'reminder' promotion: Jersey Tourism's crocus promotion

(Courtesy: Jersey Tourism)

Fig. 11.1(b) The crocuses bloom on the agent's desk, a constant reminder of the product they promote

(Courtesy: Jersey Tourism)

the consumer directly, in order to build brand awareness and create a demand that will pull people into the shops to buy the product. This technique is known as *pull strategy*, with the customer pulled into the shop by the effects of the promotion. In effect, the client is pre-sold. Retailers will be persuaded to stock the product through the level of demand they experience. In the second method, sales promotion is geared to merchandising activities, which are designed to persuade retailers to stock the product and help them to sell it. This is termed *push strategy*, with promotion aimed to attract customer sales at the point of sale.

A new tour operator seeking to develop a market will be unlikely to be able to afford the national advertising which a pull strategy would call for, but could successfully develop a push strategy by selecting key retailers and helping them, through 50/50 joint promotional expenditure, to sell to their customers.

Co-operative promotions with non-travel companies are proving a popular way of reaching the travelling public. Travel can be offered as an incentive to purchase other goods or services, or consumer durables can be offered to those booking holidays. Specially priced package tours have been offered as an incentive to purchase FMCGs, while British Rail teamed up with Boots the Chemist to provide free rail travel against purchases in the store. Hoteliers have promoted short-break holidays in this way, while other examples of successful joint promotions include cross-Channel ferry companies and manufacturers of alcoholic drinks. Vouchers, redeemable for travel arrangements, have been successfully used as staff incentives in many large companies, particularly as rewards for the achievement of sales targets. Travel has been found to be a greater incentive than straight financial compensation, in motivating staff.

Most retail promotion activities have tended to focus on price appeal. Thomas Cook, for instance, offered three forms of sales promotion based on price, and one more novel technique:

- *Price Promise*: Cooks agreed to match the price of any holidays they sold which could be purchased more cheaply elsewhere

- *Trading Charter*: a money-back guarantee to Cooks' clients who purchased the products of any tour operator which failed
- *Formal Guarantee*: Cooks would match the customers' need with a particular holiday
- *Business Travel Challenge*: companies could submit to Cooks details of their expenditure on staff business travel booked through other agents over a three-month period and Cooks would then estimate what savings could have been achieved had the bookings been made through them.

Planning the sales promotion

As with any marketing activity, the establishment of a promotional campaign requires careful advance planning. The stages by which such planning is undertaken is found in Fig. 11.2.

We must be clear what our objectives are before we prepare the programme. It is not sufficient to define these in the broadest terms, such as 'increase our winter sports programme sales by 10 per cent'. We need to indicate whether our objective is to attract new buyers or to increase sales to current buyers, since different promotions will be called for in each case.

The target audience will be either our own sales force, our retail agents, or the consumers

Fig. 11.2 Stages in the organisation of a sales promotion campaign

themselves, depending on whether a push or pull strategy is determined upon. It may be appropriate to aim at more than one of these audiences in the promotional plan.

Before considering what methods to use to influence the market, the company should be in possession of as many facts as possible which might affect the decision. The question of the product itself, its nature and quality must be considered. If the image of the product has always been one of quality, what form should the promotion take that will not demean it in the eyes of the target audience? A promotion undertaken jointly with a company that markets a well-established premium product (executive car, up-market alcoholic drink) will enhance the image of the travel company. However, all companies like to believe that theirs is a quality product. It is important that the company first identifies through research what image the firm actually enjoys.

Strategically, it can be useful to take into account the forms of sales promotion which the firm's competitors employ. It may be thought desirable to compete head-on with a competitor by emulating the methods they have used to attract new business, while in other cases it might be better to distance the product from its competitors by deliberately introducing a very different form of promotional strategy.

Strategies will vary according to both the nature of the product and the stage in the product life cycle (PLC). At the launch stage, it will be the intention to build awareness of the new product, and this is best achieved in the case of travel by focusing on advertising and public relations activities, supported by a smaller proportion of the budget spent on sales promotion. This could entail direct mailings to key addresses, or incentives to retailers. A new museum may have different artefacts on display, but to many potential visitors it may be seen as just another museum, and it will be competing for business from local holidaymakers with all other museums and attractions in the area. While local advertising is used to draw attention to the product, co-operative voucher schemes may be introduced to provide discounts for entry to two or more attractions.

As markets for products become saturated in later stages of the PLC, promotional stimuli may have to be increased to draw second or third time visitors, pending product innovation. The use of 'twofer' tickets to increase sales in theatres towards the end of a show's life cycle is an example of a promotion used to boost sales.

As with all forms of communication, decisions on the selection of techniques will be based on which combination of these can be best expected to achieve the desired objectives in the most cost-effective manner. If a money-off deal is being considered for a tourist attraction, marketing staff must decide how many of these discounted tickets are to be offered, and to whom, at what reduction in normal price. Means must be sought of ensuring that those willing to pay full price will not be seduced into paying lower entry prices, and the total cost of the programme and increase in revenue expected must be estimated. The programme cost will be not only the loss in normal entrance price, but also the cost of communicating the offer to the public. Against this, one must weigh the benefits of increased entry numbers, and probable increased spend on facilities at the attraction. The final figure must then be compared with other promotional techniques under consideration, to judge the best package. Figure 11.3 gives examples of sales promotions involving special offers.

In setting up the programme, a decision must be taken on when to start the campaign, how long it is to last, and exactly how it is to be delivered. There must be sufficient *lead time* (time available) to introduce the programme, which in some forms of promotion (such as co-operative ventures involving on-pack coupons in consumer goods) can take months of planning. If the duration of the campaign is too short, there may not be time for it to become effective, while if it is allowed to run for too long, it not only loses its impact, but also may affect the company's image and annual profitability.

The promotion is developed in the context of the overall promotional mix, so that the time scale and activities tie in with any other communications activities. A major promotional campaign may include advertising support, sales

Book a holiday far away...

...and take a break at home.

Up to 50% discount on Hilton and Hilton National weekend breaks when you book with Thomas Cook Holidays.

Book early Go one better!

Here's a real A T Mays offer for you. The Summer'92 Brochures are hot off the press and A T Mays are giving red hot discounts right up to £200 for those who move fast. That means you can book an even better holiday!

BOOK TODAY AT YOUR LOCAL BRANCH

*Per booking form, minimum 2 persons. Discounts apply with selected operators and are subject to purchase of AT MAYS Travelsure at time of booking. Full details on request. Limited period only.

Fig. 11.3 Sales promotions involving special offers
(Courtesy: Thomas Cook/AT Mays the Travel Agent)

calls by sales representatives, and publicity (an innovative campaign could, for example, get coverage in the trade press, or even local press).

If the campaign is to operate on a large scale and involve substantial investment, it is wise to test its effectiveness in advance, wherever that is possible. Market research can be used to question a cross-section of a potential market on the sensitivity towards different prices for a product, or the degree of preference between money-off offers and other forms of promotion. The following could represent the line of questioning to be employed:

1 *How willing would you be to purchase a ticket to this attraction at a price of £3.50?*

very willing ☐
quite willing ☐
uncertain ☐
quite unwilling ☐
very unwilling ☐

2 *If this ticket were to be made available at a discount, how likely would you be to buy it at a price of...*

	£3.00	£2.75	£2.50
very likely	☐	☐	☐
quite likely	☐	☐	☐
uncertain	☐	☐	☐
quite unlikely	☐	☐	☐
very unlikely	☐	☐	☐

3 *If you were planning to visit this attraction, with a regular entrance price of £3.50, would you rather have the offer of*

(a) *a discount of £1.50, or*
(b) *a second ticket free, to use either for yourself for a return visit, or for a friend or relative to accompany you?*

discount ☐
second ticket free ☐
both equally suitable ☐
don't know ☐

An alternative to this form of research is to conduct an experiment with different forms of sales promotions for a limited time, to judge which is most effective. A direct mailing, circulation of brochures to local hotels with money-off vouchers, and an advertisement in a local paper carrying a money-off coupon could each be judged for effectiveness over a given period of time, prior to a full-scale launch. One must take care, however, that other factors do not account for any change experienced in turnover. Where possible, these activities in 'experimental areas' are compared with the results in 'control areas', regions where no campaigns have been mounted, since sales increases may be the result of factors other than the promotion itself. If the increase in turnover is proportionate in all regions, the effect of the campaign itself is likely to have been minimal.

Legal aspects

An essential part in planning any form of promotion that involves a competition or prize draw is to ensure that the promotion is legal. The Lotteries and Amusements Act (1976) lays down the conditions to which these types of sales promotions must adhere. In practical terms, you cannot restrict entry to a lottery or prize draw only to those consumers who order goods. This is, however, possible with a competition.

The Advertising Standards Authority publishes a code of practice to guide marketers in the preparation of a sales promotion and the advertising material that supports it. This covers such aspects as the rules which should always be printed on prize draw and competition entries, and the terms and conditions which should be printed on vouchers. The size and design of money-off or discount vouchers is also covered by the guidelines.

Administration

Meticulous planning will take into account the administration and resource involved in the sales promotion. What is often forgotten is that even relatively simple promotions may generate a significant administration workload. A sales promotion may involve any or all of the following overheads:

- the cost of staff time, e.g. spending several days at an exhibition
- the need to have systems to cope with the logistics of the promotion itself, e.g. checking hundreds of competition entries or issuing vouchers to those qualifying
- the need to provide sufficiently rigorous checks to prevent fraud and financial errors, e.g. invalid use of vouchers
- the need to monitor redemption rates or other measures of take-up.

As with other forms of promotion, there are agencies with specialist knowledge and resources who can be employed to help a company mount a sales promotion.

Evaluating the impact of promotion

There are a number of ways in which the effectiveness of the company's sales promotion efforts can be judged. It is, of course, relatively simple to measure the effectiveness of money-off offers where these are given against vouchers or coupons clipped from advertisements, returned from direct mailshots or redeemed following any other form of distribution. Equally, competitions for consumers or for retailers can be judged from the numbers of entries they attract. Most sales promotions of this kind are designed to generate immediate sales and are judged in those terms. A comparison is then made between the level of sales achieved before the promotion and after it. However, the objective may have been to 'clear current stock' (i.e. to sell off unsold holidays) which may not increase the overall level of sales. Reduced price offers may simply encourage early booking by clients who would have been prepared to pay normal prices later in the year, rather than attracting new customers who would not otherwise have booked a holiday. If the intention was to clear unsold stock in this way, all well and good; but if this unwittingly leads to a slump in later sales and overall reduction in turnover, the campaign can hardly be deemed to have been successful. This is illustrated in Fig. 11.4.

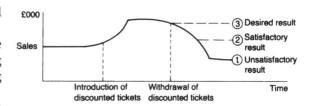

Fig.11.4 Sales resulting from a sales promotion campaign at a tourist attraction

A return to sales at level 2 following the promotion will be satisfactory, since the promotion will have had the effect of increasing sales during the period of the campaign without subsequent losses. But the company may have aimed to attract a larger market through increased awareness, with resulting sales at level 3. If the actual result is a fall to level 1 for the balance of the season, the campaign's objectives will not have been realised.

However, sales promotion should not be judged only in terms of its success at generating sales in the short term, and its success in achieving other objectives should be likewise measured.

Let's take the example of a travel agency window display – an area of unrealised potential for many agents. If it is designed to bring people into the shop to purchase a holiday, a simple count of enquiries and bookings resulting from the products on display is easy to keep. But a window is also designed to attract passers-by to notice and remember the agency and what it sells. It is rarely tested for its effectiveness in achieving this, however. An hour spent observing passers-by and their behaviour in front of the window can be illuminating. How many of those passing glance at the window? How many actually stop to take in the contents? What are they actually looking at in the window: bargain offers or special displays for long-haul travel?

Surveys can be carried out locally, before and after campaigns, to measure increases in awareness of the agency, or changes in the company's perceived image. In the same way, visitors to a tourist attraction can be questioned on leaving, so that patterns of purchase behaviour can be compared between those who took advantage of a promotional offer and those who didn't.

Unfortunately, not all promotions lend themselves to easy means of measurement. Dealer or consumer 'give-aways' are designed to build long-term goodwill and recognition, and their impact is much harder to assess. Finally, it should be borne in mind that the best way to evaluate any tactic is to see how it compares with other sales promotions in its effects. A business must experiment over time with different forms of promotions and learn to judge which seems to work most effectively. Any one technique employed continuously, however, will pall, and a variation in the tactics employed is likely to have greatest impact.

At this point, we shall look at some of the more common methods of sales promotion in use in the travel industry.

Exhibitions

Exhibitions play an important role in the travel industry, providing opportunities for buyers and sellers of travel products to meet and do business. Some, like the World Travel Market (WTM) in London, and the International Tourism Exchange in Berlin, have become of international significance.

Three types of exhibitions can be identified.

- those aimed at the public
- those aimed at the trade
- those which are private, and to which entrance is gained by invitation only.

Events such as the WTM, which is open only to the trade, feature prominently in the travel trade calendar, and their function is as much social as commercial, giving members of the industry an opportunity to see and be seen. Few major companies can afford not to be represented at the show, which covers all sectors of the trade: incoming, domestic and outbound tourism. Retail agents have the chance to enhance their product knowledge, while it provides national and local tourist offices with a rare opportunity to demonstrate publicly their product, the country or region they represent, through the medium of film, wine tasting, national costume, ethnic

dancing and other forms of entertainment. The importance of the show will also ensure that it receives a good press coverage. However, it is undoubtedly the opportunities for personal contact that the trade welcomes most. Often, trade symposia or meetings will be organised to discuss current topics of interest, running concurrently with the exhibition, to take advantage of the presence of so many key figures in the trade.

Against these benefits, however, exhibitions are costly to stage, and to participate in. In addition to rental costs based on the floor area occupied by stands, there are stand design and construction costs, set-up costs for equipment, hospitality and literature costs, and other incidentals to be considered. The competition for status among larger companies means renting larger stands than are strictly needed, and at the most prominent sites, for which premium prices can be commanded by the organisers. Sales staff are tied up while participating in the show, and other marketing staff must be employed in planning and organising the event (a major show can involve year-round planning). In spite of all the planning, attendance figures can disappoint at many unproven travel exhibitions, while even with a good attendance it is not always easy to measure benefits against costs. For this reason, participants may well treat the event as a public relations exercise rather than a sales promotion.

The marketing objective is to make any such ventures as cost-effective as possible. Every attempt should be made to weigh up the cost of reaching and influencing consumers through the medium of the exhibition compared with other means. Participants should obtain in advance an analysis of attendance figures for previous years or audience survey data if published. New exhibitions may be able to provide only calculated guesswork about attendance expectation, which is often wildly optimistic. Some estimate should also be made about the proportion of the audience likely to be interested in visiting a particular stand (something approaching 40 per cent is the Audience Interest Factor for national exhibitions) and an estimate can be made of the cost of reaching that market compared with attempts to communicate with them through other marketing techniques.

An average salesperson can deal with 12–15 enquiries in an hour, and each salesperson will need about 50 sq ft (approx. 5 sq metres) to accommodate visitors. An estimate of the size of the stand can then be made, based on the number of sales staff required to answer enquiries and the space required for display material. This does provide a rule of thumb for the space to be rented, although taking no account of the demands for 'space status' for individual companies. A small cubicle for dealing privately with important visitors to the stand is also recommended.

Some preliminary planning can help to ensure a successful exhibition stand. It is not sufficient merely to staff the stand. Those working on the stand should be well versed in the firm's products, well trained in sales techniques and equally at home dealing with clients and with trade enquiries. Good clients of the company could be sent advance tickets and a map of the exhibition and stand. Adequate supplies of literature should be available, but some control should be exercised over their distribution to ensure brochures are taken by people with a genuine interest in the product rather than children with an avid interest in collecting anything on display! All visitors to the stand should be welcomed, and an attempt made to explore their interests. Potential sales leads should be recorded on stand cards or in a visitors' book for subsequent follow-up. One must never lose sight of the principal purpose of the exhibition, which is to sell travel.

The travel workshop

The travel workshop deserves separate mention here, due to its importance in the travel industry. Strictly speaking it is not so much an exhibition as a forum for trade buyers and sellers of travel products to come together and negotiate business. British travel workshops are often organised under the sponsorship of the National Tourist Boards, with venues in the UK and overseas, in centres wherever there are sufficient numbers of prospective tourists to Britain.

Typical sites for BTA workshops would include New York, Chicago, Los Angeles, Sydney and Frankfurt. Some workshops have particular themes such as coaching holidays, or a regional emphasis, such as tourism in South West England. Suppliers with an interest in incoming tourists, such as hoteliers, coach companies and ground handling agents, arrange to rent desk space in the workshop, which normally runs for between one and three days. Tour operators and others from the tourist generating countries can in this way conveniently meet their suppliers of tourism services under one roof (often without having to travel far from their own home territory) and can negotiate with them for the following season's tour programme requirements – beds, transfer services, excursion programmes, etc. This is one of the most cost-effective means of organising the production of package tours.

Making presentations

A presentation may be defined as an 'act of introducing or bringing to notice'. The presentation is widely used in the travel industry to introduce a company's programme to retail travel agents, although these in turn can run their own presentations for clients, to bring a particular range of holidays to the public's notice. The major tour operators generally organise presentations to agents throughout the country when launching their new programme of holidays for the year.

This will typically take the form of a reception, perhaps a buffet meal, and a formal talk about the new programme or product, given by senior members of the sales force. The approach is typically low key, since it is aimed at young agency counter staff, and the emphasis is on personal contact and a 'fun evening', although it also provides an excellent opportunity for sales staff of the principal to meet agency counter staff at first hand and obtain feedback about the market.

Effective presentations call for good visual promotion: flip charts, overhead projectors or other forms of instructional aids should be used to accompany the formal talk, and it is customary to demonstrate the product with videos, a tape-slide presentation or film. The largest principals mount highly impressive shows, usually in up to half a dozen different centres around the UK, using a tape-slice dissolve unit (or multi-dissolve unit), stereo sound, stroboscopic lights or even laser beams. This will mean a promotional budget running into thousands of pounds.

First Choice brands: sales promotion for brochure launch

The brochure launch for the new First Choice Holiday brands in August 1994 was boosted by large-scale sales promotion activity. This makes an interesting case study, as it ties together many of the aspects of sales promotion already discussed in this chapter.

The sales promotion was seen as complementary to the advertising activity that was also happening at this time (this is discussed in a case study on pp. 235–41). The brand values of 'different' and 'fun' were to be pulled through into the promotion, which was intended to be 80 per cent fun and 20 per cent fact.

The promotion was aimed at consumers to generate a push strategy, as well as travel agents to create a pull strategy. As it was imperative that the retailers accepted the new First Choice brands very quickly, this was to be a very different and memorable kind of brochure launch for travel agents – where the annual round of tour operator brochure launch presentations had perhaps become a little stale.

The consumer aspect of the promotion was created as a co-operative venture with the *Daily Mirror*, as a way of reaching the travelling public and generating awareness: a new brand and name change in themselves were unlikely to be of great interest to the public. In this respect, considerable emphasis was given to keeping the new name 'First Choice' a secret until the launch itself, to maximise its impact.

The consumer promotion was a prize draw. *Daily Mirror* readers collected four tokens from four different days' newspapers and attached these to an entry form. In the UK 550 winners would be selected in the prize draw to receive pairs of tickets to a special 'Walking on Sunshine' game show event staged by First Choice Holidays (although the name was withheld from all pre-launch publicity). The promotion in the *Daily Mirror* is shown in Fig. 11.5.

Just by attending the 'Walking on Sunshine' event, the winners of the prize draw would receive a free Mediterranean holiday for two. The game show was a competition based on the *Don't Forget your Toothbrush* television programme. The events were hosted by a range of celebrities such as Jonathan Ross and Frank Bruno, to add glamour and credibility.

To maximise the value of the investment in venues, sets and personalities, four very different target audiences were addressed on the same day. First, to ensure shareholder interests, the financial analysts were informed of this important corporate development. Second, the press, to ensure maximum PR value. Third, the consumers in the form of the promotion winners. Fourth, travel agents from all the key retailers. The last two constituted three simultaneous events staged in London, Manchester and Glasgow. Altogether, there were 5000 attendees, and the three venues were linked by satellite so that audiences could compete against one another. Three winners received a holiday for two to Florida, and then the venues competed against each other for a holiday to Mexico.

There was a short formal session where the new First Choice brands and the range of brochures were introduced.

The administration and logistics of the promotion were awesome:

- over 1000 people worked on staging the promotion
- 50 000 prize draw entries had to be dealt with
- 550 winners had to be notified, and 4450 other guests selected and invited
- 5000 guests were registered at the three venues by airline staff working at airport-style check-in desks.

Not only was there the need for rigorous security, but the 550 winners of the *Daily Mirror* competition needed to be validated and their details noted for their holiday prize.

The technology involved in the game show itself had to be flawless; the land line routing for the live

£500,000 HOLIDAY BONANZA

Pick up a bonus for fun in the sun

walking on sunshine

Mirror DAILY **Sovereign**

walking on sunshine

ENTRY FORM TO HOLIDAY BONANZA

Send this form together with 4 separately numbered tokens to: Daily Mirror, Walking On Sunshine Bonanza, Hill & Knowlton, 11a West Halkin Street, London SW1X 8JL. All entries must be received by Friday August 5th, 1994. All winners will be notified by Friday August 12th to attend the events in either London, Manchester or Glasgow at midday Tuesday August 16th.

Name:_____
Address:_____
_____
Postcode:_____ Tel. No._____
Signature_____
Name of Guest:_____
Address:_____
_____
Postcode:_____ Tel. No._____
Signature_____
Preferred Game show location (London, Manchester, Glasgow):____

YOU can't beat a bonus, especially if it could be your passport to a sunshine holiday beach

That's why we are reprinting the entry form for our £500,000 'Walking On Sunshine' Holiday Bonanza and a bonus token as well.

Tickets

Use the bonus token, if you need it, to complete the entry form and send the completed form to the address shown.

We have 550 pairs of tickets to give away to popular holiday resorts on the sunny side of Europe.

Each holiday lasts for a glorious week in the summer of 1995.

The charm of Greece, the splendour of Spain or the magic of Portugal are waiting and there is also the chance for you to pick up a holiday in Mexico and the USA. To get

you going, we are giving away 550 pairs of tickets to three celebrity-packed game shows in London, Manchester and Glasgow. During August, the lucky winners of our great prize draw will be invited to a game show of their choice and automatically win a 'Walking On Sunshine' holiday. At each of the

game shows, there will be a great variety of intriguing games to play, including constructing a jigsaw in the fastest possible time, guessing the nationality of different food dishes and lots of holiday questions.

And at all three shows, there will also be a further three Sunshine Holidays for two in Florida to be won.

The shows will be linked by satellite — which means that guests at each show will be able to compete nationwide on a huge TV screen for the biggest prize of all — a holiday for

four in one of the world's top resorts, Puerto Vallarta in Mexico.

The London show will be hosted by Jonathan Ross and the *Big Breakfast's* Gaby Roslin.

In Glasgow, the hosts will be GMTV's Lorraine Kelly and John Leslie of *Blue Peter* fame.

In Manchester, Stuart Hall of *It's A Knockout* and tennis star Annabel Croft will be in charge.

Lucky

If you are lucky enough to win the holiday in Mexico, you will spend two weeks at the 4-star Las Palmas Beach Resort, with private beach, swimming pool and a wide variety of water sports.

The nine winners of the Florida holiday will speed off to Orlando where they could visit Disney World, Universal Studios, Sea World — the world's largest marine life theme park — and the Kennedy Space Centre.

This is your chance to walk on the sunny side — don't miss it!

AFFIX **TOKEN 1** HERE   AFFIX **TOKEN 2** HERE

AFFIX **TOKEN 3** HERE   AFFIX **TOKEN 4** HERE

COMPETITION RULES

1. Winners will receive a pair of non-transferable tickets for themselves and a named companion to the celebrity game show they nominate (either Glasgow, London or Manchester). You and your companion at the gameshow will receive a joint one-week holiday at a Mediterranean resort to be taken in 1995 with a named and fully ABTA bonded operator.

2. All entrants and named companions must be able to attend the Glasgow, London or Man-

chester venues on Tuesday, August 16 during office hours. If either are unable to attend the gameshow, the tickets and holiday will be reallocated.

3. Closing date for entries is Friday August 5, 1994.

4. Winners will be notified in writing.

5. To enter you must be eligible for a British or Irish passport and be over 18 years of age.

6. Tickets and holidays are valid

only for those named on the entry form and are not transferable. Game-show tickets must be presented at the event in order to gain entry.

7. No purchase necessary.

8. Entry to the competition will be deemed acceptance of the above terms and conditions.

9. Normal Mirror Group rules apply.

10. There is no cash alternative.

Mirror DAILY

walking on sunshine

BONUS TOKEN

Fig. 11.5 Co-operative sales promotion to stimulate consumer interest in the new brands of First Choice Holidays. Note the use of the existing brand name 'Sovereign' rather than the new and secret First Choice name
(Courtesy: First Choice Holidays/Mirror Group Newspapers)

television link-ups between the three venues was the most complex ever set up by British Telecommunications. There was enough cable to go around the M25 orbital motorway twice!

The result was a powerful promotionally based launch for the new brands. Coverage of the event was achieved in every national newspaper with an 'advertising value' equivalent of several hundred thousand pounds timed to coincide with substantial above the line investment. And the travel agents were motivated to sell the new brands when they went on sale 36 hours later.

Planning and organising presentations

If a presentation is being made to potential consumers, the aim will be both to generate direct bookings and to build goodwill among the clientele, or potential clientele, of the company. It is therefore well worth taking a little effort with the planning and organisation of the event, to maximise the prospects of its success.

First, the venue and date for presentation must be carefully chosen. Even with the best intentions and with good decorative effects, the local hall can be a depressing venue for such an event, and can depress the image of the company. Better a conference room at a good quality hotel or at a purpose-built conference centre, which will be comfortable, well decorated and geared to meet the company's requirements. The London venue for the First Choice launch, for instance, was the London Television Centre, where the technical facilities were excellent and skilled personnel were available to manage the event effectively. Arrangements for booking these facilities have to be made well in advance to ensure their availability. The company should also make sure there are adequate parking facilities and good public transport to the venue.

An evening meeting will attract more people than a daytime event, especially if the aim is to attract working people to a public presentation. Couples usually consult each other in the arrangement of holiday bookings, so the sale must be made to both partners. Wherever possible, dates should avoid any clashes with local or national events. For example, a presentation designed to attract the public would be unlikely to have succeeded if it had been scheduled to occur at the time the first National Lottery was being broadcast in 1994!

Entry should always be by ticket invitation, to control numbers (this is vital where food and drink have been laid on) and tickets should be

'Dates should avoid any clashes.'

checked at the door. Announcements of the event can be made through a direct mailing to clients, and an invitation in the local paper to others to apply for tickets (with the possible chance of arranging some editorial coverage in the paper alongside your advertisement).

It is advisable to ask people to reply or to book their place so that you can anticipate numbers attending. You should always expect a 'drop-out' rate of people who say they will attend and then do not turn up. The drop-out rate can be reduced by a courtesy phone call a week before the event, confirming that they still intend to come. People will feel more committed if they feel you are expecting them personally.

The formal presentation should be prepared and rehearsed in advance. Not only will you speak more fluently, but also you will be able to time the speech and know if it is the right length. A presentation should follow the general guidelines for other forms of communication:

- gain attention
- generate interest
- build desire
- end with any action you wish the audience to take.

An event and personal presentation gives you the opportunity to live the values you wish to associate with your service: specialist, caring, quality, family oriented, or whatever.

If drinks are to be served, it is sensible to provide not more than one glass before the formal talk: you want your audience to be receptive to the sales talk!

Where a film evening is arranged, it is advisable to run not more than two films, and total running time should not exceed about 20 minutes; the span of attention of many audiences is limited, however good the film. Whoever is responsible for giving the presentation should ensure that they have seen the film in advance, and that the right one has been delivered. All mechanical and electrical equipment should be in good working order, but it still makes good sense to carry spare parts that might be useful – adaptor plugs, new bulbs for overhead projectors (OHPs), etc. – especially if there is any doubt about the reliability of the venue itself to cater for emergencies. Arrangements must be agreed in advance for lighting controls, with someone present to help dim lights for films, OHPs, etc.

Presenter and staff should be at the venue well in advance of the start, to allow ample time to check on, or arrange for, directional signs, and to ensure that the room is decorated with appropriate travel material. A 'publicity pack' of travel material should be placed on each seat in the auditorium. Adequate cloakroom and toilet facilities must be available near to the auditorium, and clearly signposted.

All members of staff present should have name badges, with first name *and* surname (a customer may want to write to you one day.) However, some people may prefer not to display their surname, because of the potential personal security risks. When guests arrive, they should be greeted by a member of staff and given a drink to help 'break the ice'; background music can be useful as an ice-breaker or mood-setter when people arrive and mingle, especially in a large gathering. You will need to ensure sufficient staff to cope with the expected number of attendees. This is not just to smooth administration. You will have worked hard to get people to come, and must now exploit the opportunity to the full. You will therefore want to establish personal contact with as many attendees as possible.

Where the objective is to encourage sales, the company should make it as easy as possible to make a booking. Sales desks can be available and staffed after the presentation to deal with further enquiries. Prepaid reply cards can be inserted in the publicity packs for more information. You may also wish to follow up some or all attendees with a personal phone call or letter afterwards.

Above all, one should exploit whatever opportunities arise for publicity associated with the event. Photographs can be taken during the evening, and sent to the local or trade press with a covering press release, which may gain a few valuable column inches in the local press (especially if local personalities are invited to the event).

The cost of events of this kind can be reduced for smaller companies such as travel agents by linking together with other companies to make a joint presentation. Many tour operators are willing to pay 50 per cent of the costs of mounting an agency presentation to the public, if they are convinced that it will be productive, and they may also contribute staff to talk at the event. However, they may wish to ensure that only their company is represented at the event, so the agent will be wiser to focus on a single principal's products, if seeking support. On the other hand, where a destination is to be promoted, the national tourist board of the country, or a carrier operating to the country, may be willing to support an agent in a joint promotion. Such sharing of costs will ensure that the promotional budget is stretched to gain maximum cost-effectiveness.

Questions, tasks and issues for discussion

1 T-shirts are often used as a medium to promote a message for travel companies. Identify two or three T-shirt campaigns which have caught your imagination, and explain why you think they are good at getting their message across.

   Create and design a T-shirt slogan for a tour operator of your choice, indicating your objectives.

2 The range of accessories available from one supplier which can be personalised to carry the name of the principal includes: address books, attaché cases, bottle openers, business card files, calculators, calendars, clocks, cocktail trays, conference folders, cutlery, desk diaries, flight bags, leatherware (purses,

wallets, etc.), lighters, magnifiers, paperweights, pens, pencils, pen watches, rulers, silver trays, tankards, tape measures, ties and umbrellas.

Discuss the merits of these different 'give-aways', and suggest which you would adopt if you were responsible for promotions in a tour operating company.

3 Study different brochure racks in local travel agencies (there are many different designs in use). Describe how they differ in function and in customer appeal. Which do you think is best, and why?

4 Which is it better to spend a limited promotional budget on: sales promotion activities or advertising? Justify your decision.

Exercise

At the next World Travel Market event, draw up a programme to assess the effectiveness of the stands (each member of the group or class to select one stand to study). Evaluate:

(a) the effectiveness of the stand, its design and display
(b) how good the stand staff are at welcoming visitors to the stand and dealing with their enquiries.

12 Direct marketing: theory and practice

After studying this chapter, you should be able to:

- recognise and distinguish between the various forms of direct marketing
- recognise the benefits which direct marketing offers over other forms of marketing communication
- understand, through the application of basic principles and drawing on examples of successful techniques used in the industry, how each form of direct marketing can be successfully applied
- mount a successful direct mail campaign
- recognise the benefits of the computer database as an aid to direct marketing

What is direct marketing?

All marketing activity by a manufacturer is ultimately directed at the consumer. Most of this activity is designed to create a demand for a product to be supplied through the traditional channels used by the industry concerned. Kelloggs create a demand for their cornflakes through television advertising, but they do not feel it necessary to tell you where you can purchase your next packet.

Direct marketing is a term used in many different ways. It can be defined as the use of non-personal media or telesales to introduce products to consumers and encourage their purchase direct from the company concerned. An alternative, and somewhat wider definition, is 'a communication that creates a direct relationship between a company and its customers and prospects'. Increasingly, direct marketing techniques are being employed within the travel industry in more innovative ways: ways that do not necessarily attempt a direct sale, but attempt instead to establish a relationship with, for instance, loyal customers. The most common techniques in use are:

- mail order
- direct response advertising
- direct mail.

Mail order

Mail order marketing generally makes use of catalogues from which consumers can order products direct, either through the mail or in some cases through direct outlets of the company. An extension of this form of marketing is *party selling*, for example Tupperware kitchen ware, which is sold through a social gathering in the representative's or a friend's home, using catalogues and/or direct demonstration of the product.

The holiday brochure of the direct sell tour operator is, in essence, no different from a mail order catalogue. As such it is likely to be increasingly influenced by the techniques and design style of other such catalogues. Notice the back cover of a direct sell brochure, as illustrated in Fig. 12.1, as distinct from a brochure intended for distribution through the travel agent. The former highlights 'seven easy steps to book'; reservation numbers, 'holiday helplines' and credit card symbols are writ large.

(a)
Fig. 12.1(a) and (b) Two very different brochure styles – the direct sell brochure in Fig. 12.1(b) overleaf works harder
(Courtesy: First Choice Holidays)

Direct response advertising

Direct response advertising involves placing advertisements in the media which encourage consumers to reply direct to the supplier, often using a suitable coupon clipped from a newspaper or magazine advertisement. As these coupons can be coded according to the publication in which the advertisement appears, it is easy for the company to measure the success of each advertisement. A travel advertisement which makes use of this technique, actually providing an attached miniature leaflet (known as a *tip-on coupon*) which can be returned to the company without postage charges ('Freepost') is illustrated in Fig. 12.2.

The technique of direct response advertising can be an effective one, providing the product is well established and its benefits are clearly understood.

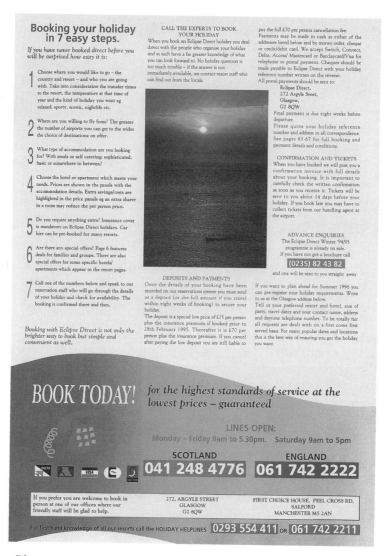

(b)
Fig. 12.1 (continued)

The technique is also used tactically for late sales: this is an important part of the tour operator's activity, as moving unsold stock through last-minute deals is an important contribution to profits. The operators will also encourage brochure requests. Chapter 10 discussed the process of booking a holiday and the key role of the brochure. An operator will know the number of brochures needed to distribute through travel agents, on average, to make a booking. Logically, using direct marketing techniques to get brochures into the hands of a group of prospective customers (who were all interested enough to respond) should generate at least as many bookings.

Direct mail

Direct mail is the technique whereby a company communicates directly with its potential customers by mail, in order to put across a sales message. The technique has the considerable

Fig. 12.2 Brittany Ferries advertisement carrying a direct response voucher
(Courtesy: Brittany Ferries)

advantage that letters can be personalised, and target markets can be clearly identified, so that customers can be expected to be reasonably interested in the product. Wastage is in this way minimised. The process has been greatly aided by the introduction of computer databases which can pinpoint specific target markets and provide comprehensive lists of names and addresses. There are now a number of 'lifestyle' databases which allow for very accurate selection of potential customers. Combinations of age, income, type of occupation, hobbies, residential area, and previous holidays taken are just some of the criteria which can be applied to refine the targeting of the chosen list.

Travel companies are increasingly aware that direct mail can play an important part in their communications mix. Its role can be such aspects as:

- *generating brochure requests* for tour operators, especially where holidays are aimed at very well-defined groups (e.g. golfers), although bookings may still primarily be via the travel agent

- *generating late sales*, especially when aimed at previous customers who booked late the previous year
- *channel support* whereby the travel company communicates sales benefits to the travel agent
- *customer care* where the communication is to strengthen the brand image and customer loyalty for next season, e.g. a client returns from holiday to receive a personal letter from the principal of the travel agency where the holiday was booked.

One of the best known companies in Britain selling through direct mail is the *Reader's Digest Association*, whose offers of products are accompanied by opportunities to enter competitions with substantial money prizes which many customers find hard to resist.

Apart from these well-established techniques, there is a growing number of new forms of direct marketing, such as *telemarketing* (or telesales) to sell products, either using local telephone directories to 'cold call', or telephoning pre-screened lists of prospective customers.

Advances in technology are now providing other means of reaching target markets, such as direct response television selling, which has become available through satellite television in many European countries, personal computer selling and fax sales, where clients are reached through their fascimile machines.

Some see these techniques merely as an unpleasant intrusion into people's personal lives, resenting the increase in unwanted 'junk mail' or the invasion of privacy resulting from the use of personal telephone lines to increase sales. Direct marketers, however, are using these new methods to cut out traditional intermediaries, and in so doing are reducing their selling costs. The result is a wide range of profitable business opportunities for those who dare to be different.

Travel companies are being forced increasingly to make use of them in order to compete for business in the future. Many companies are already doing so. Thomas Cook is just one example of a travel business which has invested heavily in direct selling activities, including a call centre which they estimate will generate up to 20 per cent of their total revenue by 1997. Telesales using cold calling techniques offer great opportunities for the sale of late availability packages, in particular.

About 30 per cent of the travel market in the UK books direct, a 5 per cent increase on 1988. Certainly, there are considerable prospects for expansion in this form of selling, although one must not underestimate the new skills needed by sales staff to succeed in this area. Nor should one over-estimate its impact on the industry; to give one example, while direct mail has indeed grown since the 1980s, as a percentage of all advertising it actually fell slightly in the early 1990s, as new forms of distribution expanded to take a growing share of the retailing business. Nevertheless, the fact that over £42 billion of goods were sold over the telephone in 1992 must encourage many of the larger travel firms, too, to recognise that direct marketing techniques must figure prominently in their planning over the next few years.

The characteristics of direct marketing

It will be seen from examples quoted above that direct marketing of all kinds is becoming increasingly important in the communications mix. Indeed, in the USA it is estimated that more investment is now made in direct marketing than in traditional advertising. The characteristics of the different media should be weighed up when deciding which would be the best technique or techniques for a particular campaign. Direct marketing in particular exhibits the following attributes:

1 *Targeted* the list selection can be very precise, reducing waste and allowing very focused copy and offers that match the prospect's likely requirements accurately.
2 *Personalised* the mailing can be personalised not only by name, but also by accurately reflecting your knowledge of the prospect as an individual, e.g. 'as a valued customer who has booked with us three times before, you are

being extended a special invitation . . .' As most human beings are egocentric to some extent, this is a powerful persuader.

3 *Response orientated* by its very nature, the medium generates high levels of response through coupons, reply cards and telephone. Direct marketing copy can be very 'sales orientated' and directed.

4 *Detailed* the written word and flexibility of format allow a great deal of detail to be imparted – necessary to give customers all the information they need to buy with confidence. The down-side of the detail, and especially with printed items as opposed to advertisements, is that campaigns require careful preparation and cannot be produced overnight.

5 *Short term* the objectives of direct marketing campaigns tend to be more short term and tactical rather than attempting to develop long-term awareness. While a campaign may involve repeat mailing to a prospect a number of times, this is very expensive when compared with, for example, a press advertisement to build awareness that a prospect may see over and over again in the life of the campaign.

6 *Measurable* the medium generates response which can be tracked accurately, whether it is enquiries for more information or actual sales. Therefore the return on the costs of the promotion can be directly measured.

7 *Discreet* television and press advertising will be immediately obvious to a company's competitors. With a little care to exclude competitors from the mailing list, the campaign will take longer to be noticed, or may even escape the competition's notice altogether.

Direct sell holidays

One famous arrival in the ex-UK holiday market was the Danish tour operator Tjaereborg in 1977. This was a new company to the UK, though well established in the sale of holidays in Scandinavia. Although a major operator in these territories, unlike traditional British companies, Tjaereborg sold its holiday products direct to the public, possibly originally because in its home territory travel agents were few and far between. Tjaereborg had built up a considerable expertise in the necessary techniques, and its arrival was greatly feared by the travel trade in the UK. Its advertising promise was that by purchasing direct from Tjaereborg the consumer could 'save' the cost of the travel agent. Old-established tour operators feared being undercut and seemed to believe Tjaereborg's claims, judging by their frightened reactions. Travel agents, too, became agitated, fearing that their livelihoods were under threat.

In the event, while the company prospered in the early years of its UK launch, the market share it enjoyed rapidly stabilised and the major threat to traditional distribution systems which the trade feared did not materialise. Direct sell, at least in the mass market, posed no serious challenge to the retail distribution system.

Of course, it is possible to sell any product by a different method from that adopted by the majority of the suppliers in a given market. The reason for the existence of any distribution channel, however, is because the consumers want it; because they like to purchase their products in a particular way. Clothing is sold in many different ways: though direct catalogue companies exist, selling either to the customer (for example, those of Next) or through an agent (Marshall Ward, for instance), most buyers still prefer to visit shops. So it is with travel.

However, direct sell continues to make inroads into traditional methods of selling. While only 13 per cent of package holidays were booked in this manner in 1983, the proportion had grown to 18 per cent by 1993. This reflects a growing confidence on the part of the consumer, not only in being more familiar with travel, but also by being more comfortable with 'mail order' channels. Nevertheless, this rate of growth is not going to destroy the travel agent route overnight: the future trend is likely to be ever more and different distribution channels co-existing. Consumers will be able to buy a holiday in many different ways, from the local supermarket or via their home computer or television.

The most important factor is that every method of marketing has its own inherent costs. In the case of Tjaereborg, while the company could indeed cut out agents' commission, in doing so it incurred other costs, such as a heavier advertising spend and the need for increased phone lines. In particular, it was less able to sell off at short notice those remaining seats on its flights to customers browsing for last minute opportunities.

When a company is new to a field, or is launching a new product, the cost of selling direct may actually be higher than dependency upon retailers. Unless the company has exceptionally good products, it is likely to need higher than normal profit margins to succeed; however, once a regular clientele has been built up, the position may become easier.

Many businesses in tourism rely almost entirely upon direct sell. These range from small bed and breakfast establishments through visitor attractions and specialist tour operators to large-scale holiday centres like Center Parcs. A glance at the weekend press advertisements for holidays will show that many travel companies rely almost entirely upon direct responses from their customers. The reason for this is simple: if a market is scattered nationally, yet the company is dealing in comparatively small numbers, the cost of using a retailer to distribute one's products is too great. At the same time, fewer agents are willing to stock the products of small specialist operators because individually their sales will be too small to provide rack space and obtain the specialist knowledge required to gain a sale.

Eclipse Direct: successfully exploiting a customer database

A direct sell operator bypasses the travel agent and reaches the market directly. Mail is the major route to distribute brochures and the mailing list chosen for this exercise is crucial. No matter how good the creative design of a mailing, if it is sent to people with no interest in booking that particular type of holiday, then it is doomed to failure.

The mailing pack for the launch of the summer 1995 Eclipse brochure is illustrated in Fig. 12.3. We have already noticed in Fig 12.1 the way that the brochure itself acts as a mail order catalogue. Note these other aspects of the pack:

1 *The letter is personalised to reflect what is already known to be relevant to the recipient.* One section of the database represented previous bookers of Sunfare Holidays, now subsumed into Eclipse. Sunfare had specialised in holidays out of Glasgow Airport, therefore the letter to these customers highlighted no surcharges on Glasgow departures and the existence of a direct sell shop in Argyle Street, Glasgow. Other sections of the database had similar tailoring, for instance the letter to previous Tjaereborg customers highlighted self-catering because Tjaereborg had been particularly strong in villa and apartment holidays.

2 *A separate reply card invites customers to 'recommend a friend'.* This is an established direct marketing technique to gather new names for the database. Experience shows that these names are usually better than cold prospect lists: people are good at providing accurately profiled names for a particular product. Any business that relies on its database for its business, as Eclipse does, will continually seek to draw new names on to the list and to remove older non-productive names. Thus, for instance, one of the objectives of advertising may be to generate response from individuals whose name and address can be added to the mailing list. In this instance brochure requesters from previous years who had not booked were also selected for mailing.

3 *The brochure does not sell hard enough by itself.* A separate flyer was included that aggressively highlights the price advantage of booking with Eclipse. This makes overt but factual comparisons with the immediate competitor to Eclipse, Direct Holidays: 'knocking the competition' is a strategy that has to be treated with great caution. In this instance price is such a strong factor in the direct sell business that it was a successful tactic.

The mailing achieved its overall response targets and a healthy return on the investment. In addition, bookings received were carefully matched back to the original mailing list to establish the conversion

Fig. 12.3 The successful generation of bookings without a travel agent intermediary

(Courtesy: First Choice Holidays)

rates achieved, broken down by the different categories mailed. The results showed that people who had booked for 1994 were eighteen times more likely to convert than people who had not booked since 1990. This should be no great surprise: after four years the previous customers were less likely to book than people who had recently enquired. This emphasises the need to continue contact with customers, to attempt to prolong the life cycle of the relationship. Also, the names and addresses from four years earlier were more likely to be out of date as people move house, marry, die, etc. By tracking conversion rates and cost per conversion, Eclipse are able to calculate the point at which people booked too long in the past to be worth a mailshot.

The results also showed that previous bookers in 1994 were eight times more likely to convert than people who had merely enquired. Again, this should be no surprise – the average figure quoted across all industries is that it is six times easier to sell to an existing customer than to a cold prospect.

First Choice: push strategy to generate travel agency bookings

The launch of the new First Choice brands in 1994 exploited a multi-media approach. As well as extensive advertising, direct marketing was employed to add an extra push into the travel agent. Playing on the strengths of the medium, the campaigns concentrated on specific target groups, known to be the most likely prospects. The television advertising, which was carried out at the same time, was designed to generate awareness and had only an indirect link to sales. The direct mail was intended to put brochures in the hands of prospects and to stimulate bookings at the travel agents.

Measuring actual sales at the travel agent is difficult for the tour operator, as travel agents do not pass on the names and addresses of their clients when they make a booking; indeed, they guard this information jealously out of a fear that the operator will compile a database and begin to sell direct. This fear is probably somewhat unfounded, and tour operators come in contact with their clients whether travel agents like it or not (for example, through customer satisfaction questionnaires). In this case, First

Choice had the names of 340 000 past customers, and was not tempted to sell direct. The strategy was entirely to generate brochure requests and push bookings through agents, to the benefit of all parties.

In the First Choice mailing, a clever ruse was employed to attempt to gain feedback on bookings. The offer of a free beach towel plus the opportunity to win back the cost of the holiday was included in the mailing. Two reply cards were included, one of which requested a brochure, the second of which was to be retained until a booking was made. Upon booking, the travel agent had to stamp the reply card and add in the booking reference number. This could then be returned to claim the towel and competition entry. As not all people booking would necessarily remember to claim, and/or have a co-operative travel agent, the number of towels claimed would represent less than the total likely bookings, but it would at least provide some effective measure of success.

The mailing pack to clients exposed the full range of First Choice Holidays in an interesting 'postcard' approach. Different postcards extolling the virtues and fun of their First Choice holiday destination neatly positioned the different brochures on offer. This is shown in Fig. 12.4.

An overall 5 per cent response for brochures together with revenues in excess of at least £2 million resulted from this part of the launch campaign. The other aspect was a smaller mailing to potential customers, selected from a third party lifestyle database through a process known as *profiling*.

Essentially, the known customers for a particular destination, in our example Portugal, were matched against the third party database. Though First Choice had only the names and addresses of these individuals, as previously observed, lifestyle databases hold information such as age, type of residential area, etc. They are now sufficiently large that they can guarantee that a good proportion of any customer list will also appear on the lifestyle list. This enabled the lifestyle database to fill in the missing details and give First Choice a complete profile of the type of customer booking its holidays in Portugal. The lifestyle database then supplied additional new names from their information of people who matched the profile established – in other words, the most likely prospects.

Fig. 12.4 A successful campaign to generate bookings through travel agents
(Courtesy: First Choice Holidays)

A simpler postcard mailing piece was produced for this part of the campaign as response rates were likely to be lower, and therefore the cost of the mailing had to be less to justify it.

Also the mailing needed only to focus on Portugal. The mailing piece is shown in Fig. 12.5. The same strategy of offering a beach towel and competition entry was employed to track bookings.

As would be expected, the prospect mailing did not generate as good a response as the customer list, but an acceptable 3.5 per cent was achieved.

Noble Caledonia: off the page selling

Noble Caledonia is a good example of a small company which has grown by offering a highly specialised holiday product, so that it has little direct competition. The company is one of a handful of specialist, largely long-haul, operators which are constantly searching for new and unusual destinations, appealing to the frequent traveller who has 'been everywhere' and is seeking something original. The company has prospered by seeking out hard-to-reach destinations but keeping costs under control by chartering foreign-owned (particularly Russian) vessels to provide a cruise programme for comparatively small numbers of like-minded individuals.

Themed cruises are also evident, and the company has found an effective niche in catering to those interested in the more exotic flora and fauna. Ornithologists are attracted by guest lecturer personalities such as Tony Soper, well known for his BBC television programmes on birds. Destinations include the Arctic, Antarctic, and mid-Atlantic Islands. The company reaches its customers through relatively expensive full-page advertisements in the

Fig. 12.5 A successful campaign to achieve bookings through a highly targeted third party list

(Courtesy: First Choice Holidays)

quality weekend press, making particular use of the magazine sections. The customer, once attracted to these relatively high-priced products, can be held on the company's mailing list and will regularly receive news of new products on offer. As a result of this approach, a high level of loyalty and repeat business is achieved.

Direct contact and direct mail

Some 60 million people live in the UK. British people take around 70 million holiday trips of one night or more each year in the UK, and half as many trips abroad. The estimate of those taking package holidays of four nights or more is over 13 million. Trying to reach this huge market is difficult, and can be wasteful unless care is taken to reach those most likely to buy. The key to reducing waste and increasing effective targeting is in the selectivity available in the mailing list chosen. The more information available, the better a list can be refined to mail only the valid prospects. Clearly, the onus is also on the marketer to have a clear view of the nature of potential customers for the product. This can be obtained through a profiling exercise (see pp. 200–1). However, there are many hundreds of third party lists available for use in a mailing exercise, and not all of these are as comprehensive as the lifestyle databases in the information held. Very often an element of 'lateral thinking' can be employed. For example, a list of buyers of thermal underwear probably has the right age and wealth profile for over-55s holidays.

Marketing distinguishes between the 'shotgun' approach, which scatters advertising messages widely in the hope that some of it will reach an interested audience, and the 'rifle' approach, which selects specific target audiences to address. This latter approach will heighten the possibility of success, and contacting potential clients directly through mail or other means is more likely to achieve such success.

Most advertising is designed to get the interest of the consumer. Strengthening the 'brand' and adding value to it also have their place, and these have been described in Chapter 5. Once having established contact, the business should capitalise upon the interest expressed.

Another factor to be considered is the coverage achieved by any medium chosen for one's messages. It might seem simple to consider the case of local advertising by a travel agent, but in reality only about one-third of the homes in a given area normally purchase a local paper; many do so only for specific items such as the classified advertisements and the births and deaths announcements. It may therefore be considered beneficial to create one's own medium for reaching the customer. Saga, the older people's specialist operator, has its own highly regarded magazine dealing with matters that are of interest to that age group; this acts as a regular sales brochure for the company.

At least one travel agency has maintained contact with its local market by the use of a 'freesheet', making use of full colour (few local tabloids yet offer this facility) and accurately targeting the defined catchment area, so that wastage was minimised. Editorial content included travel opportunities and descriptions of travel agency staff and their travel experience, to ensure that potential customers would be aware of the depth and range of personal experience the staff could offer. Advertisements by travel companies were solicited to help offset agency production costs. The success of this direct mail effort was such that eventually a sixteen-page freesheet was being distributed to over 100 000 homes in the catchment area, and it became a recognised vehicle for information on new travel products for the coming season, for details of special trips from the area, and for travel-orientated competitions for readers. The agency group concerned outpaced all local retail competition and achieved blanket coverage in the region – an example of exceptionally effective direct mail activity.

Using databases

There are two possible sources of mailing databases: information held within the company and mailing lists obtained from third parties. A company's own customer list is likely to be the most fruitful in terms of sales; however, any company will lose a number of customers over the course of time. New names should be brought into the process through logging responders to advertising and other promotions, and possibly through the use of third party lists.

Customer lists will perform well only if the data are accurate and well maintained. The administrative burden should not be underestimated. Pitfalls to avoid are such things as duplicates, out-of-date information and names and addresses incorrectly entered. If the information is incomplete, steps should be taken to fill in the gaps. For instance, if the only information held is 'Hilary Morgan', how is a personal letter to be addressed? 'Dear Hilary Morgan', although increasingly finding its way into direct mail communications, is not a correct mode of address, while 'Dear Mr Morgan' takes a risk on both gender and title (the addressee might be a doctor, for example). These facts should be established before sending out material. At all times, as much information as possible should be gathered and stored in the database to help in future mailings.

Any well-run business can now maintain relevant data on their customers inexpensively by the use of computer techniques, as we discussed earlier in this chapter. The equipment needed has plummeted in price during the 1990s, while the capabilities of even the simplest systems now make it possible to compile seemingly individual letters to each customer.

The Data Protection Act (1984) demands that if a database of personal information is held then this must be registered with the Data Protection Authority. Even names and addresses alone constitute personal information. Though you may write to your own customers freely, you may not pass this information on to another company without the permission of the individual. In practice, this is often obtained by 'default', with tick boxes on reply cards that say 'if you do not wish to receive information and offers from other companies at a later date, please tick this box'.

Third party lists are normally available on a 'rental' basis, whereby you rent the information to mail the list once only. You may not be allowed to actually see the list: the owner of the list may designate a mailing house to carry out the mailing, and you deliver the promotional material for them for dispatch. This is because of the value of the information to the list owner, who makes money from the list; if it is sold outright, then the owner loses control over the asset, and would therefore also lose income from it. Some lists are, however, available for sale.

In selecting a third party list, the marketer should exhibit caution, and ask some searching questions of the list owner:

1 Is the list owner registered under the Data Protection Act?
2 Has the list been recently matched against the Mailing Preference File? (This is a list set up under the Data Protection Act where individuals can register that they do not wish to receive direct mail. All lists should in theory be matched against this, and such individuals removed prior to a mailing being dispatched.)
3 What selections can be made on the data to refine the list to more accurately reflect the desired profile?
4 How old are the data?
5 How and why were the data compiled?
6 How are data maintained and kept up to date?

The marketer may wish to mail only a small test quantity of a large list before committing the whole promotion to a particular source.

The more personal any communication becomes, the more effective it is likely to be. At one end of the scale it is easy simply to place an advertisement in a publication produced by others, but at the other end, the single individually compiled sales letter, personally addressed and describing why a specific proposition is appropriate to the addressee, will have a strong sales appeal. Between these two extremes are a myriad of other possibilities, and the initiative of the direct marketer will be tested by the way the customer responds.

Direct marketing for destinations

The proposition need not only be for a product such as a particular holiday, or a service, such as that of a travel agency, but may include the promotion of the destination itself. One particularly effective direct marketing campaign was that carried out by the Tunisian National Tourist Office.

Tunisian National Tourist Office: direct marketing campaign

At the end of the 1980s, the newly appointed director of the Tunisian National Tourist Office in London was faced with disappointing sales for his country in the coming season. His budget was limited, and though a small consumer advertising campaign had been planned around Easter to arouse the public's interest in holidays to Tunisia, he was also aware

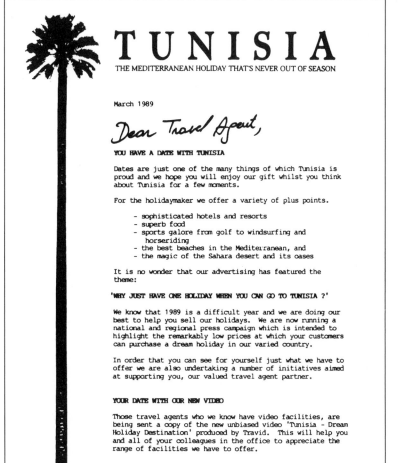

Fig. 12.6 Front page of direct mailshot to travel agents from the Tunisian National Tourist Office

(Courtesy: Tunisian National Tourist Office)

that too few of the 30 000 or so travel agency staff employed by the 7000 UK travel agencies were really conscious of the opportunities that his country's resorts presented. This was hardly surprising, given that the whole of North Africa accounts for only 0.73 per cent of air holidays taken by British tourists in that year. It follows naturally that if less than one in a hundred customers is likely to choose Tunisia, staff of the travel agencies are hardly likely to devote too much time and effort to improving their own knowledge of the travel destination.

The director saw that a major objective must be that of creating awareness of his destination among travel agency staff. At his disposal he had a small but enthusiastic staff in the office to answer enquiries and to give promotional assistance; he had a newly published colour brochure giving information on the main holiday features of the country, and he had a new video cassette which also described the resorts.

With the help of an outside consultant, a scheme was devised to undertake a series of mailings to every travel agency in the UK, in an attempt to capture their attention. In the first instance, humour and local colour were to be established by a pun on the theme. A package was sent out which contained a box of best quality dates from Tunisia, for the travel agency staff to share. The date palm had been used in previous advertising, and it was here used as a visual anchor to promote the theme 'You have a date with Tunisia'.

A letter followed (see Fig. 12.6), produced simply on an office word processor and personally addressed by the director 'Dear Travel Agent', and signed by him (see Fig. 12.6). This set out the five main sales features of Tunisian holidays, then:

- gave details of the video that was available on request
- described a competition for travel agency staff to go on a 'dream trip' to Tunisia themselves
- offered low-price holiday opportunities to travel staff in the early season (to get better product knowledge)
- gave prior notice of study tours for staff in the autumn
- offered promotional help upon request.

Enclosed with the mailing were simple-to-complete postcard entry forms so that each member of the travel agency could enter the 'dream trip' competition after reading the relevant brochures (see Fig. 12.7); a request postcard for a copy of the video; and a list of the names and addresses of all holiday companies publishing brochures to Tunisia, from which the travel agent could sell. The items were enclosed in a specially constructed box carrying an attractive label bearing the date palm symbol and an instruction to 'open immediately', to distinguish it from packets of brochures that might languish in the agency before being opened.

The response of competition entries and video requests confirmed that the contents had been well received and that Tunisia had obtained the high profile attention it sought for the valuable Easter booking period.

The creative quality of this campaign was in marked contrast with competitor countries, and helped Tunisia to return good results in what would otherwise have proved to be difficult season.

Some guidelines for good direct mail letters

The previous section has emphasised the importance of letters being directed personally, by name and by appropriate business title, if relevant. This will ensure that the letter gets to the right person, and makes it more likely to be read. Many people believe that using the name again in the text reinforces the message, but although this can be achieved with most mail-merge software programs, the technique can make the letter appear contrived.

There is inevitably a trade-off between cost and quality, but generally cost savings are counter-productive if the mail is well directed. A fast dot matrix printer will enable many more letters to be produced in a given time than will a daisy wheel or laser printer, but will they make the letters appear more like 'junk mail'? Brown envelopes are cheaper, but they imply penny-pinching economies. Window envelopes may seem less desirable than plain ones, but a personally addressed letter in a window looks better than an envelope with a label, and typing

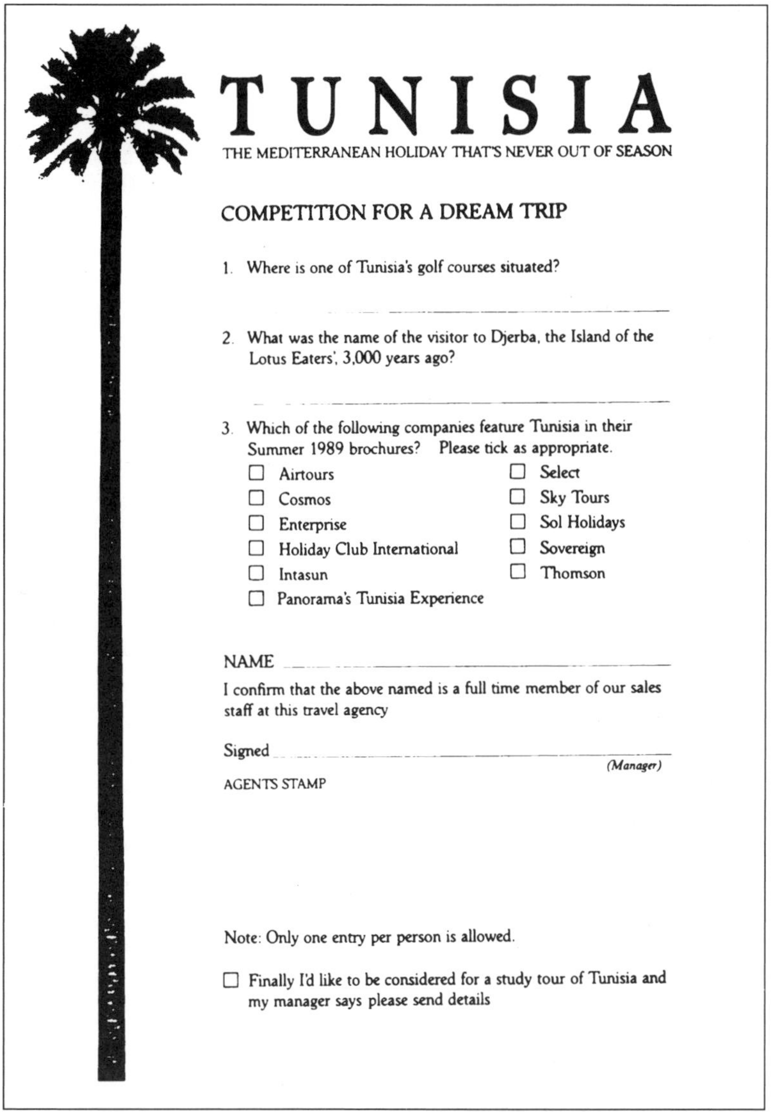

T U N I S I A

THE MEDITERRANEAN HOLIDAY THAT'S NEVER OUT OF SEASON

COMPETITION FOR A DREAM TRIP

1. Where is one of Tunisia's golf courses situated?

   _____

2. What was the name of the visitor to Djerba, the Island of the Lotus Eaters', 3,000 years ago?

3. Which of the following companies feature Tunisia in their Summer 1989 brochures?   Please tick as appropriate.

   ☐ Airtours   ☐ Select
   ☐ Cosmos   ☐ Sky Tours
   ☐ Enterprise   ☐ Sol Holidays
   ☐ Holiday Club International   ☐ Sovereign
   ☐ Intasun   ☐ Thomson
   ☐ Panorama's Tunisia Experience

NAME _____
I confirm that the above named is a full time member of our sales staff at this travel agency

Signed _____
                                        (Manager)
AGENTS STAMP

Note: Only one entry per person is allowed.

☐ Finally I'd like to be considered for a study tour of Tunisia and my manager says please send details

Fig. 12.7 Competition entry for travel agents accompanying the mailshot in Fig. 12.6
(Courtesy: Tunisian National Tourist Office)

individual envelopes requires more sophisticated equipment.

The content of the letter itself is of crucial importance. The aim of the text will be to:

- capture attention with a headline that intrigues
- start by stating how the recipient will benefit
- describe what is offered and demonstrate the product's benefits
- fully detail the offer being made
- explain what the recipient needs to do next, i.e. how to purchase the product.

A direct mail letter is one type of promotion where brevity is not necessarily the best technique. To be effective, the text must capture the reader's attention and interest. The text should be written in good, simple (and correct!) English,

Tŷ Brunel 2 Ffordd Fitzalan
Caerdydd CF2 1UY

Brunel House 2 Fitzalan Road
Cardiff CF2 1UY

(0222) 499909
Telex 497269
Fax 495031

BWRDD CROESO CYMRU
WALES TOURIST BOARD

Miss B G Anderson
8 Tryfan Road
Bristol
BS8 4YA

WHAT DO YOU WANT FROM A
BARGAIN BREAK?

Dear Miss Anderson,

As you've previously expressed an interest in our GREAT LITTLE BREAKS in Wales, I thought you might like a copy of our new brochure.

WALKING?

A typical example of a weekend's walking holiday – two nights at a delightful countryside hotel in the "Heart of Wales." With a variety of guided long and short walks in the locality. Includes room, breakfast and evening meal.

£41 PER PERSON

To receive your free copy, just complete and return the enclosed reply-paid card right away. I'll be happy to send you your brochure by return.

You'll find it's packed full of great ideas for a few days away.

Whatever you want from a bargain break away, you'll find it in Wales.

Perhaps you just want a quiet weekend in the country and a little fresh air. Or, maybe, you'd prefer an active weekend of windsurfing, golfing, fishing or pony trekking.

Our GREAT LITTLE BREAKS will cater for all tastes. Giving you that well-earned rest from your usual routine. Providing a refreshing

Fig. 12.8 A successful direct mail campaign which attracted a 30 per cent response
(Courtesy: Wales Tourist Board)

WINDSURFING?

A two night windsurfing break in a self-catering bungalow for 4 on the Pembrokeshire Coast. Including hire of equipment.

£21·50 PER PERSON

Spring and Autumn are the perfect time for walking or pony trekking. And in Winter you can still enjoy the wild beauty of the Welsh countryside and come back to the welcoming warmth of your hotel lounge for the evening.

So, regardless of the time of year a few days in Wales can always provide a pleasant break.

Send for your GREAT LITTLE BREAKS brochure now.
Just complete and post back the reply-paid card now to claim your free full-colour brochure.

It will have full details of how you can book your GREAT LITTLE BREAK. Do it today and you could be spending a few days in Wales in just a few weeks' time. I hope to hear from you soon.

Yours sincerely,

WYN MEARS
UK Marketing Director

PS. Please do us the favour of answering the few questions you'll find on the brochure request card. This will help us to provide you with an even better service in the future.

WHATEVER YOU WANT, IT'S HERE
322 SPECIAL OFFERS TO HELP YOU GET AWAY

SEND FOR YOUR GREAT LITTLE BREAKS BROCHURE TODAY

Fig. 12.8 (continued)

preferably in relatively short, punchy sentences. Many of the leaders in this field use devices such as indented paragraphs, emboldened or underlined words for emphasis or clarity, and add apparent afterthoughts in postscripts. If inviting a response by mail, then it is essential to encourage action by making it easy to reply. An order form or reply card should serve this purpose. A simple printed, addressed envelope will help to increase replies, but still better is a reply-paid envelope or 'freepost' facility where the cost is met by the promoter (at a small premium on the number of replies received). Most effective of all is actually to put a stamp on the envelope: many people seem to feel guilty about the waste if they don't send it back.

One highly successful promotion undertaken by the Wales Tourist Board, which attracted a 30 per cent response, was a direct mail campaign to promote short breaks in Wales (see Fig. 12.8). The campaign incorporated many of the key points identified here, and was also well illustrated with suitable promotional material.

Questions, tasks and issues for discussion

1 Collect any examples of direct mail letters received by you, your friends or neighbours. Identify the benefits offered by the products being sold, and analyse the strengths and weaknesses of the letters in the light of comments appearing in this chapter.

2 Discuss with your friends how happy or otherwise they are, or would be, to receive telesales messages at home. Does it depend upon the product being offered? How might the sales pitch be modified to make it less offensive to listeners?

3 If you were drawing up a mailing list in order to send out a direct mail letter to people living in your immediate neighbourhood, how would you describe the 'market profile' of the typical resident in the neighbourhood? What kinds of products would be likely to prove attractive to these people?

Exercise

Using the market profile identified above in Question 3, imagine you are a marketing assistant with a package holiday company offering the kind of holiday in which some of your neighbours would be interested. Prepare a direct mail letter to be sent out to these neighbours, and accompany this with a short note identifying:

- the punchy headline and any other attention-getting techniques you have used
- the product benefits you are stressing
- how you are encouraging the recipients to take action
- what material you would plan to include with the mailing.

13 Public relations and its use in the tourism industry

After studying this chapter, you should be able to:

- compare the benefits of a public relations (PR) campaign with other forms of communication
- identify the role of the public relations officer (PRO) and the functions of PR
- understand how PR campaigns are mounted
- evaluate alternative approaches to gaining publicity
- appreciate the importance of measuring the success of all promotional techniques

David Ogilvy, of the advertising agency Ogilvy & Mather and one of Britain's greatest exponents of advertising, once declared to an audience in New York composed of senior travel industry staff that he would choose to spend $250,000 on public relations before he spent a penny on travel advertising. His aim was to highlight the importance of an area of communications that was all too easily overlooked by those in the industry, and to make clear that in his view PR actually produced better value for money than the more traditional avenues for promotion.

One reason why PR has tended to take a lesser role in the communications mix is that it is even more difficult to quantify the benefits of PR expenditure than of other forms of promotion. PR generally takes longer to achieve its results, and it is by definition dependent upon the attitudes and actions of third parties beyond a company's direct control. This adds up to something of a long and difficult task, which sadly defeats the stamina of some organisations. Another reason is that the uses of the technique and what they can achieve are less well understood by the industry. None the less, there are some notable examples of entrepreneurs who have recognised its power and used it: Richard Branson of Virgin Atlantic Airways springs immediately to mind. There are, however, dangers associated with the overuse of the medium, and too high a public profile can attract unwelcome publicity, as Branson would be the first to admit.

PR: its definition, characteristics and role

PR is best defined as a set of communications techniques which are designed to create and maintain favourable relations between an organisation and its publics. The last word is deliberately used in the plural, since an organisation actually has to deal with several different publics, of which its consumers are only one. Companies will want to build good relations with their shareholders, with suppliers, distribution channels, and, where pertinent, with trade unions. External bodies such as trade and professional associations and local chambers of commerce are other organisations that a company might wish to influence, while opinion leaders such as Members of Parliament, travel writers, hotel and restaurant guide publishers are yet more groups with which the organisation must maintain good relations. Finally, companies will wish to be on good terms with their neighbours, and will want to be seen as part of the local community and to support local activities.

Characteristics

The need for PR has arisen with the growth in size of organisations. The resultant lessening of personal contact between a firm and its customers led to criticisms of impersonality, a belief that big corporations had become 'faceless' and 'uncaring'. Some observers such as Robert Townsend[1] believed that the answer was to scrap the PR departments and get back to personal relations again, but it is questionable how far this is practicable once a company has grown to become a major corporation. Until the 1970s, most tour operators handled their reservations systems manually, and specific staff were assigned to handle bookings from agents over the telephone. Retailers were on first-name terms with individual staff members, and knew who to call when they had a problem. This close relationship eased criticisms of the company in other directions. The movement to on-line computer reservations systems, coupled with a reduction in agency calls by sales representatives, depersonalised the company for agents, who found it easier to find fault with the company. Customers, too, grew alienated from the businesses with which they dealt, and organisations were set up to safeguard consumer interests and to lobby for better consumer protection. The Air Transport Users' Committee is one such body in the travel industry which has been established to look after the interests of the travelling public.

Role

Because of the importance of travel and tourism as a service industry, the reputation of a travel company's products hinges on the quality of its staff, and the attitude of that staff to the company's customers. When a company is carrying in excess of a million passengers abroad each year, it has to make greater and greater efforts to retain a friendly and personal image. PR can play a role in supporting and publicising that image, although its creation must still lie with other marketing staff, whose role is to train and to maintain quality control.

As with other communications techniques, public relations plays a part in informing and reminding customers about the company and its products, in order to generate an attitude towards the company favouring the purchase of its products. In generating information, however, the PR message has to be seen as accurate and unbiased, while still reflecting the needs and interests of the company – a considerable challenge for the public relations officer! This objectivity is essential if PR is to do its job effectively. However, it is the media that will determine what appears before the public. Since the aim is to ensure credibility, PR messages, with their perceived objectivity, are more convincing than advertising and in the long run are likely to have a greater impact on sales, if a far more subtle one. This, however, underlines the fact that public relations is essentially a weapon for long-term, rather than immediate, impact on a company's markets. Since consumers are becoming increasingly sophisticated, and hence more immune to the messages carried by advertising, the growing role of PR in an organisation is doubly important.

Lest readers feel that PR concerns only the largest companies, it should be clearly understood that there is a role for it in any organisation, however small. Small companies, too, need the goodwill of the local community and a strong reputation to generate sales, and this can be aided by the application of simple techniques.

In addition to creating favourable publicity for the company, PR is helpful in diminishing the impact of unfavourable publicity. The travel industry has more than its fair share of this, and there are some in the industry who feel that the media are concerned only to report the negative events, focusing on disasters such as overbooking, air traffic controllers' strikes, aircraft near-misses, ferry disasters, coach crashes and the collapse of tour operating companies. Many of these events are beyond the control of individual companies, but the impact of negative publicity will affect them anyway and must be tackled.

There is a misconception in some circles that PR's role is to 'paper over the cracks' which result from poor management or product faults. No amount of publicity will help a company which does not seek to correct underlying problems. PR must be used as an adjunct to good marketing practice, not as a substitute for it.

Five distinct activities are associated with the role of public relations:

1 *Press relations* This requires the company to maintain a close working relationship with press journalists and others associated with the media, with the aim of generating favourable publicity at every available opportunity.
2 *Product publicity* This involves the implementation of tactics designed to bring products to the attention of the public, whether through the use of the media, or in some other manner.
3 *Corporate publicity* This concerns efforts to publicise the firm itself, either internally or externally, in order to create a favourable image.
4 *Lobbying* This involves activities designed to promote a cause. A firm may, for instance, support plans for legislation or regulation, such as airlines' attempts to gain legislation for more night flights out of London airports; or a lobby may be mounted to defeat a proposal for legislation, such as draft European Union plans for certification of travel agents. While lobbying is generally concerned with governmental or local authority issues, it could also be mounted to influence trade regulation, such as a move to defeat ABTA's proposals to increase bonding requirements.
5 *Counselling* The public relations officer (PRO) has the task of counselling management about public issues, identifying developments internally and external to the firm which could influence a company's image. The PRO will then recommend a plan of action to counter any unfavourable developments. Thus the PR department has a monitoring and research function also.

The organisation of public relations

It will be appreciated that while some of the above activities are directly associated with the marketing function, others are only peripheral to it, in the sense that their overall objective will enhance the company's sales opportunities. For this reason, in large organisations some PR activities may be carried out in the marketing department, while others are conducted quite separately, at a senior level. One carrier, for instance, employed a PRO as assistant to the managing director, with all corporate publicity conducted directly under the supervision of the managing director. In such a situation, the PRO becomes a highly influential figure within the organisation, while technically still a member of 'staff' rather than 'line' management.

A difficulty in large companies, where marketing and PR functions are separated, is that the priorities of the two become distinct, although both are concerned with external relations. Where the PR function is not a responsibility of the marketing staff, suspicion of its activities is aroused, since marketing is concerned only with product enhancement. The wider perspectives of the company's interests are of less concern. PR staff, for their part, tend to take the view that marketing staff, with their concern for the customer, may overlook the company's social responsibilities to the community at large, and believe that the PR considerations should play a greater role in product decisions.

By way of example, let us take the case of a major tour operator seeking new destinations for its market. The marketing staff will be principally interested in the attraction of the resort to the company's clients, that the new resort has the right facilities and will be accessible at a price which the company is willing to pay, and that the tourist authorities in the area are supportive. They will be less concerned with issues such as the impact on the local community of the new development, or the political consequences of an intention to file for an increase in flights from regional airports, which might need careful handling. Marketing staff might feel that the use of so-called 'personality girls' to merchandise the launch of a new programme will gain them plenty of press coverage, but PR might urge caution in the portrayal of women in this role, predicting a backlash against such a sexist approach.

In the USA, PR staff are playing a much greater role in marketing decisions, in areas of product policy, pricing, packaging and promotions, as US corporations become more sensitive to their social responsibilities. PR is now exerting considerable influence on British marketing, as companies seek to understand and respond to the changing attitudes and needs of the buying public.

The public relations officer

In the very smallest companies PR may be directly carried out by the managing director or principal. Medium-sized and larger companies are more likely to use the services of an outside PR consultancy. The largest companies will have a senior PRO, and may use one or more PR agencies with specialist talents to support some or all of the following:

- special events and launches
- day-to-day tactical product PR (if this is not carried out by the marketing staff)
- corporate image PR.

PROs usually have a media/communications, rather than marketing, background. In fact, they tend to be former journalists, with good press contacts and an intimate knowledge of media operations. This means they will also have good communications skills. It is their contacts which are valued most highly, though, since they will help to gain increased media coverage for the company.

Where PR activities are intermittent and *ad hoc*, it will be much cheaper for a company to employ a firm of public relations consultants to handle campaigns. External PR companies provide an excellent service, having broad-ranging experience of many businesses and good contacts to exploit. Their sole drawback is their distance from the day-to-day activities of the company, so they must rely on being well briefed by a member of the company in order to do an effective job.

Mounting a PR campaign

Favourable publicity for a company doesn't just happen; it has to be planned and programmed. Those responsible for PR must create news, as well as exploiting opportunities that arise to make news. A publicity campaign should form part of the overall marketing plans for the year, as part of the communications mix.

As a starting-point to the campaign, the PR staff must know who the organisation's publics are, and what their present attitudes towards the organisation and its products are, so that there is knowledge of what needs to be done. While market research should already have a picture of the firm's consumers or potential consumers, additional research will probably be needed to establish the attitudes of other publics, such as staff and shareholders. This will provide an overall picture of the strengths and weaknesses of the company in its public affairs, which will allow a set of objectives to be drawn up for the PR campaign. As with all plans, objectives should be stated in a form which is measurable, for example to raise awareness of the company's social commitment among the local community from a present 20 per cent to 40 per cent within one year.

The next step is to determine the strategies and tactics which are best suited to achieve these aims, and to decide what budget will be required to undertake the campaign. In the case of PR, the implementation of a campaign may last much longer than the usual one-year marketing plan before targets are achieved. Changing attitudes and opinions through PR is a slow process, and a corporate campaign could last as long as five years. Finally, the success or otherwise of the campaign must be monitored. In a campaign lasting several years, this monitoring should take place during the campaign as well as after it, to evaluate its growing effectiveness; some fine-tuning to the campaign, such as tactical adjustments, may be needed in the intervening period.

Gaining publicity

Let us assume that the objective is to generate publicity to develop a favourable attitude towards a local travel agency. How is this best achieved? The first task of an agent is to ensure that the local catchment area is aware of the agency's existence, and of the products it provides. PR can support the advertising and sales promotion activities of the company by, for example, publicising the opening of the offices. New shops and offices open all the time, so in itself, this is hardly newsworthy for the local press. It will be the task of the PRO to make the event newsworthy, in order to attract visitors and gain media coverage. Offering free drinks will bring people through the door, but using a well-known personality (perhaps local, and with some connection to the world of travel and tourism, such as a travel writer) is more likely to gain coverage. It must always be borne in mind that what is newsworthy for the company is not necessarily of interest to the press, and an agency opening will have to contend with many other local events for coverage. Something really attention-getting is needed; perhaps a window display with live models paid to sit in deck chairs for the first few days? This will draw the public's attention, and that of the media too. The important thing about publicity, though, is that it feeds on new ideas all the time, and the agent must continually be thinking up new gimmicks to gain attention.

After the opening, the agent must find ways of keeping the name in front of the public. Some agents have been able to establish themselves with the local press or radio station as the 'gurus' of travel, who are called upon to be interviewed whenever something newsworthy occurs in the industry. This is particularly valuable for long-term image building (it helps if the proprietor's name is the same as the company's, since the company name will probably not receive a mention!). Participation at local fairs, providing raffle prizes at fund-raising events or charities, sponsoring an entrant for a local hot-air balloon race, all offer chances for building community links and generating local goodwill.

A firm can build on the particular strengths of its own staff to gain additional press coverage. One agent employed a counter clerk with excellent skiing skills. This not only enabled the agent to build up a specialist expertise in winter sports holidays, but also gained some useful column inches in the local press. Another well-established agency proprietor is known in the trade and the local community for his enthusiasm for golf, losing no opportunity to publicise his links with golfing personalities, and participating in golf tournaments at home and abroad which get good press coverage. Key names in the retail world, in their role as spokespersons for ABTA, have become well-known faces to hundreds of thousands of television viewers through their appearances on interview programmes or travel programmes. There is a 'caveat' on guesting on television, however. Television is still largely a medium for entertainment, and the role calls for a special kind of talent in presenting oneself effectively on camera.

Press relations

Developing and maintaining links with the press and other media is a critical task of the PRO, who will also need to be on first-name terms with prominent travel writers if representing a major principal. It is to the PRO as spokesperson for the organisation that the media will turn to get information about the company, and the PRO's skills involve the ability to be both tactful and frank when dealing with them.

If the organisation plans to announce some prominent event, such as a takeover, or the establishment of a new trading division, this may be sufficiently newsworthy to merit calling a press conference. This will entail invitations to travel journalists and other representatives from the trade, national and local media to attend a meeting at which senior executives will announce details of the new plans. A press reception will include provision of food and drink (some form of hospitality is normal for all press conferences). The conference itself is usually presaged with a press release, or news release, which is the principal method of communicating to the media information about the company which is thought newsworthy. The press release is a brief summary of the news which the company wishes to publicise, and generally occupies one side, or at most two, of A4 stationery. News releases are always well presented on special letterhead paper which gives the name and address of the company, a contact name (usually that of the PRO) and both home and work phone numbers, as a PRO must be contactable 24 hours a day if journalists want further information. Companies devise their own titles for letterheads, usually a phrase such as 'NEWS FROM . . .' To carry on a policy of integrated communications, the letterhead may carry strong product branding, as well as the company details. The press release in Fig. 13.1 is an example from First Choice Holidays.

Since the press release is the company's main form of communication with the media, it is important that it exemplifies the quality and efficiency of the organisation. It must be well printed (today a word processor and laser printer is almost invariably used) on quality paper incorporating the organisation's logo in the heading. The text needs as much care as any advertising copy, since the material may well be used verbatim by a newspaper's busy editing staff, and if succinct and well written, the copy has a much greater chance of being used. Copy should be double spaced, with wide margins. As with direct mail letters, the opening sentence needs to be an attention getter, conveying the main theme of the message. Information must be accurate and newsworthy, not a company 'plug' which editors will immediately see for what it is and discard. If it is essential to continue on to a second side, the word 'MORE . . .' should appear at the foot of the page. The text should be carefully proof read for grammatical or spelling errors before posting.

Once a press release has been issued, the company must be geared up to respond very quickly and efficiently to any press enquiries.

Journalists usually work to very short deadlines, and rapidly lose interest if they do not get instant answers. As well as easy access to the PRO, the press office may pass a journalist on to other senior staff. These must be specially briefed to talk to the press in order to answer specific questions or provide an interview. Journalists may also need to support their story with photographs of staff, etc., so a small photographic library should be kept for publicity purposes. Good quality black and white prints (not negatives) should be filed. Information about the photos should not be written on the back, but a title and brief description of what the photo portrays should be typed on a separate sheet of paper, fastened with adhesive tape to the bottom of the photo, and folded behind it.

Feature articles

Sometimes an opportunity arises to prepare a 'feature article' on travel and tourism. An example is the Guest Writer's column in *Travel Trade Gazette*, and often local newspapers invite contributions on a travel theme. Feature articles are easiest to arrange with local papers in conjunction with a commitment to advertise in the same edition. Some 'advertising features' such as this almost cross the borders between publicity and promotion, becoming a thinly veiled plug for the company's products. None the less, the material must be newsworthy – a topical issue of interest to readers, for instance – if it is to be used.

When advertising is tied in with potential coverage in this way, care should be taken not to upset the sensibilities of the editorial staff of the publication concerned. They often at least try to take a stance of 'editorial independence'. It may not always be possible overtly to 'buy' coverage by placing advertising.

Press facility visits

One other function falls within the domain of the public relations department. This is the press facility visit. This is organised in a similar fashion to the agents' educational, which will be discussed a little later in the chapter. Its purpose is

Sȯvereign

Astral Towers
Betts Way, Crawley
West Sussex RH10 2GX

Press Office
Tel (0293) 588405
Fax (0293) 588244

SOVEREIGN

Sovereign, one of the largest established premium holiday brands in the UK, has expanded its range of quality holidays and introduced a dedicated villa brochure for Summer 1995. Six new brochures, incorporating the best of the existing Sovereign portfolio, offer a wide choice of holidays, ranging from a weekend city break in Europe to a luxury 4 "Crown" hotel.

Sovereign Summer Sunshine 95 is on sale from 18 August followed by the Sovereign Villa Collection week commencing 22 August. In September, Sovereign World Wide goes on sale, followed in October by Sovereign Small World, Sovereign Scanscape and Sovereign Cities.

Sovereign's new villa brochure now incorporates the best of former market leader Martyn's Villa Collection and Sovereign Italia, plus a selection of villas in new destinations. This means Sovereign now offers an unrivalled collection of 195 villas, all with pools, in 16 different destinations. Prices start from £216 for a 7 night villa holiday in Menorca. There are two regional flight supplements for those who book on or before 30 September 1994.

The Sovereign Summer Sunshine brochure, which now includes the best of Sovereign Just Turkey and Sovereign Corsica, has expanded to offer a range of new destinations including: Puerto Vallarta, Mexico; Costa Dorada and Costa Brava, Spain; Tuscany and Lido di Jesolo, Italy; Corsica and Morocco. Lead price for Sovereign Sunshine is £246. More twin-centre holidays are also available, increasing customers' flexibility of choice.

The Sovereign Summer Sunshine accommodation range has never been broader, ranging from smaller 'Hideaway' hotels to some of the best and most famous hotels in the world.

Aiming to build on already high levels of service, Sovereign Summer Sunshine is offering free entry to the Air 2000 VIP lounge for those travelling with the airline who book before 30 September 1994. Other service features include: private taxi transfers, Sovereign welcome gifts and scheduled flight upgrades where possible.

News Release

First Choice
Sovereign is a member of First Choice Holidays PLC

Fig. 13.1 Launch press release for one of the First Choice Holidays brands for Summer 1995. Such press releases, together with other PR activity, generated extensive coverage in national, regional and trade press
(Courtesy: First Choice Holidays)

to invite the media representatives – travel writers, journalists or correspondents from television and radio – to visit a particular attraction or destination, or to use the services of a particular travel company, in the hope that the trip will receive a favourable commentary in the media.

This can be a two-edged sword, since it invites opportunity for critical comment, too. An example of a press trip backfiring in spectacular fashion was the inaugural trip on the Eurostar train service through the Channel Tunnel. In the autumn of 1994 Eurostar invited a trainload of journalists to travel from London through to Paris on a special trip in advance of normal passenger services. The train broke down at Waterloo Station without travelling an inch and no back-up train was available. The group finally arrived in Paris too late for lunch. The resulting press comment was extremely negative and damaging for a service that hoped to lure business travellers away from the airlines – a target market where punctuality is paramount.

The strategy is widely used, however, by national or regional tourist offices, air and sea carriers, and tour operators, since a favourable press will have a huge impact on bookings. Principals may also invite correspondents from programmes such as *Holiday* or *The Travel Show* to film their product; this again, if favourable, will generate substantial business for the region or company concerned. Occasional opportunities arise for plays or films to be made on location in areas or sites that will attract tourism, and films such as the James Bond series, and television programmes such as *The Lotus Eaters*, *Who Pays the Ferryman?* and *The Aphrodite Inheritance* have all generated interest in visits to the Mediterranean regions in which they were filmed in the 1970s and early 1980s, while the film version of *Hamlet* starring Mel Gibson and set in Dunottar Castle, Scotland, and *The Darling Buds of May*, filmed in Pluckley, Kent, both helped to generate domestic tourism to those regions in the 1990s. Books, too, can perform this feat; one example is that of Peter Mayle's extraordinarily successful *A Year in Provence*.

Sponsorship

Sponsorship is a further means of achieving publicity for the name of a company. An organisation might sponsor the publication of a book or film about the history of the company or the industry, which could not be a commercial success without subsidy. Many long-established companies in the travel industry, such as shipping companies, have used this means of sponsorship. Other companies might choose to sponsor an academic text on travel and tourism, as did Barclays Merchant Services in the case of Alan Beaver's textbook *Mind your Own Travel Business* (1993). Here, the aim was to generate interest in the company's credit card facilities, which are extensively used in travel now. Alternatively, a documentary film might be produced on some subject concerning tourism.

More altruistic forms of sponsorship include financial support for the arts – theatre, fine art, concerts, festivals – and sporting events. The attraction of this form of publicity is that it generates goodwill, while costs can be set against taxes, and suitable activities for sponsorship can be found to fit any organisation's purse. Travel companies have sponsored educational study trips for Youth Training Scheme (YTS) students, or even sponsored staff for educational courses, as a gesture to generate goodwill among employees.

Local goodwill

Apart from sponsoring events in the local community, there are many other ways in which a company can get local goodwill. A retail agent in particular is highly dependent upon good relations with locals, since the catchment area exclusively provides the clients, so it is important to keep the name in front of the public. Events such as anniversaries of the company's founding can be used as a theme for generating news, organising contests and competitions, or mounting exhibitions. One agent saw an opportunity to build goodwill with the local school by offering to provide out-of-date brochures for geography assignments. This simultaneously solved the problem of getting rid of unwanted brochures and preventing the racks being depleted of current brochures.

Contact with shareholders of large companies is usually maintained through the annual report, except where crises emerge such as takeover bids, at which time a hastily mounted corporate advertising campaign aimed at shareholders may have to be mounted to counter the bid. Such campaigns are organised in consultation with management and the advertising agency.

Annual reports have become much more than simply a means of reporting performance to shareholders or would-be shareholders. Reports are now glossy and attractive, designed to create a sense of pride; travel companies, such as Singapore Airlines, have received international acclaim for the quality of their annual reports, which have a readership extending well beyond the shareholders themselves.

Sometimes the 'public' to be influenced are the law-makers. If legislation is planned which is thought to be contrary to interests of the company, a campaign may be launched to persuade Members of Parliament (MPs) to abandon the plans for legislation, or to sway public opinion against it. Such a campaign could be mounted by an individual company, but it is more likely to be taken up by the trade body. The usual vehicle for 'lobbying' is the direct mail letter, or an advertisement may encourage the travelling public to write to their MPs to protest.

Internal goodwill

Internally, too, there are publics to be wooed. Here, the aim may be to improve staff morale, or staff management relations, and in doing so reduce staff turnover or increase productivity.

In a large company, this will mean establishing a campaign just as is done with external publics. A common means of communication in the large travel firm is the house journal, an internal magazine of news and views about the company and its staff. While some of these journals are excellent, many are put together with insufficient time and effort to achieve the aims of good public relations, becoming little more than an in-house joke.

Corporate identity

The public relations department is usually involved in the introduction or modification of the company's corporate livery. The development of a 'house style' is an important element in an organisation's communications strategy, designed to support a particular image of the organisation. The logotype or logo is a symbol, name or combination of these forming a design which will instantly communicate the company and its image to the public. In the travel industry, this 'instant communication' takes on added significance, since the logo will appear on vehicles such as coaches, aircraft, ships and trains, as well as on stationery and shopfronts. It must therefore be instantly recognisable on the sides of fast-moving vehicles as well as under adverse conditions such as poor weather or failing light. Above all, once adopted, the logo should be standardised and appear identically on every form of communication used by the company. If the company wishes to project a modern, dynamic image, the design should be modern, too. Care must be taken, though, not to produce a design which will date quickly. Design fads, for all their contemporary appeal, soon date and will need frequent updating, an expensive undertaking and one where the benefits of a recognisable logo may be lost. Note the huge sums expended by British Telecom (BT) to change their livery and log in the early 1990s – and the adverse response to it expressed by BT consumers.

Thomas Cook was obliged to reappraise its livery in the 1970s as it had neither a recognisable logo nor a standardised company name. The company appeared under various guises around the world, including Thomas Cook and Son, Thos Cook and Wagons Lits / Cook. The decision was taken to standardise the name and incorporate this into a new logo. For the travel division, a bright pillar-box red was chosen for maximum impact, while a more sedate silver grey was selected for the financial services. The result of the redesign was a new, exciting and immediately recognisable insignia on vehicles, stationery and travel shops.

Reputation

Public relations techniques are also used to help develop and maintain the organisation's reputation with suppliers, distributors and colleagues in the industry. Membership of a professional body is one means by which individuals can exert influence through the building up of a circle of contacts. Travel companies are generally pleased to support staff who volunteer to serve on ABTA committees, and may pay subscriptions for staff who qualify for membership in the Institute of Travel and Tourism, or the Tourism Society, the Hotel Catering and Institutional Management Association (HCIMA) or the Chartered Institute of Transport (CIT). Even membership in Skål, the association of travel executives, which is ostensibly designed as a social club, provides a forum for contacts and the strengthening of influence among colleagues in the trade on a local basis, and for this reason some companies are willing to underwrite members' subscriptions.

The travel agents' educational visit

A travel agent who personally knows a destination is more likely to sell it with enthusiasm. There is no stronger force in a selling conversation with a customer than personal experience.

Although agents cannot hope to have knowledge of every area of the world, most can reasonably be expected to have personal knowledge of the nearer and more frequently demanded destinations. The accumulation of such knowledge is aided by the *familiarisation visits* arranged by national tourist offices for travel personnel. Malta is one example of a destination committed to providing agents with personal experience of a destination.

Malta: familiarisation visits for travel agency staff

Following independence in 1964, Malta had a long period of estrangement from Britain, with whom close ties had previously existed. Tourism from the UK had halved during a period of growth for Mediterranean holidays. The only way to rebuild numbers was to be seen to be offering low prices that were directly competitive with nearer destinations. Whereas many Spanish destinations are only two hours' flying time from British airports, Malta is three. This obviously affected costs, and to remain competitive meant effectively discounting the local

costs substantially, by offering a lower 'tour operators' exchange rate. In the longer term, however, it was clear that Malta would have to justify higher prices by offering something different. Higher prices also meant that higher quality would be demanded, and government policies moved towards encouragement of the best in hotels and other facilities.

One problem to be overcome was that Malta's perceived quality in the eyes of past visitors was not always good. It was therefore decided to embark upon a policy of facilitating as many travel agents' visits as possible in order that they could see the improvements for themselves. Careful planning was needed to determine the best time for such visits, when there would be unsold seats on aircraft undertaking regular services, yet when the weather would be kindly, too. All major tour operators with programmes to the island were invited to participate in hosting the visitors and showing off their wares, but within strictly controlled criteria. Visitors were to be generously hosted, given little free time (these were working trips, not substitute holidays) and shown a range of the facilities that Malta offered to emphasise how different it was from other rivals for clients' attention. As well as seeing hotels, visits were included to historic sites and churches, as well as to the ubiquitous high tech disco.

This pattern was repeated many times, with well over a thousand travel agency staff benefiting. All had to make applications to go, to ensure that they actually wanted to visit Malta rather than being pressed by their managers to do so. All paid to go, to ensure commitment, even though the sum was nominal and employers were asked to fund the cost. Returning agents expressed their delight about what they had experienced, and promised to recommend Malta in the future. The formula proved successful in the most important way possible, a visible growth in the size and quality of Malta's tourism against falling levels elsewhere.

Small group visits

Though this pattern of major visits (involving more than 200 agents at a time) has been used by other destinations, more common are small group visits organised by individual tour operators responding to identified gaps in their future sales charts. Sadly, these are often less objective, sometimes being mere excuses for sales executives to entertain favoured agents. Even this, though, will have a beneficial rub-off in cementing relations between supplier and seller concerns.

Progressive agency managements try to plan the attendance of staff on visits that will result in a commercial benefit in the future, but it is also recognised that the provision of fully paid educational opportunities is one of the perks of a fairly low-paid job and, as such, a means of promoting staff loyalty. However, efforts by tax inspectors to make this a taxable perk poses a considerable threat to the educational purposes, as agents rightly argue that gaining product knowledge through training in this way is a vital element in their distribution role.

Preparation for an educational visit

It is important that preparation, organisation of the event itself, and any follow-up, should be faultless, and this does not happen by chance. The organiser needs to establish exactly who is eligible, considering the following points:

- which agencies are eligible for an invitation
- at what level and status of staff the programme is to be aimed, usually those actively working as sales people
- whether those who have been before to the destination will be eligible
- what age range is preferred
- whether more than one person can come from the same agency
- how long those invited should have worked for the agency
- whether, if named invitations are to be issued, substitutes will be accepted.

In addition, it will be sensible to arrange to have adequate information on files such as:

- home emergency contacts
- whether a smoker or non-smoker (for rooming purposes)
- whether the agency requires specific information or specially arranged visits to a particular

property or facility, such as a golf course for golf promoters
- details of the agency's local paper for any publicity shots taken during the trip and copy about the visit.

Before setting out it can be useful to obtain the participants' views on what they think they will see, in order to be able later to compare these with a similar questionnaire completed after their return. It is fairly certain that whatever the views expressed may be, they will represent a microcosm of the opinions of potential clients and may give suitable information for use in later promotional campaigns.

It is also worthwhile attempting to get the agreement of one of the trade press to cover the visit, to maximise the publicity benefits within the trade.

It is to be hoped that the participants' employers will also require a report on the visit, in the employee's own words, that can be circulated to other members of staff, thereby establishing the existence of relative expertise within the agency, as well as giving sales pointers. It is sensible also to furnish the participant with a certificate to display within the agency, to publicise that he or she has 'successfully undertaken a study tour' of the destination concerned.

'Before setting out, it can be useful to obtain the participants' views on what they think they will see . . .'

Handling unfavourable publicity

Having discussed ways in which favourable publicity can be generated, some reference must also be made to dealing with the inevitable unfavourable publicity that will arise from time to time. Negative publicity can develop at both the macro and micro levels. At a *macro level*, the impact of strikes or 'go slows' by air traffic controllers or customs officers can create enormous disruptions to travellers, which the media are not slow to exploit. At a *micro level* the company can be affected by such diverse problems as fires in hotels with locked emergency exits, dangerous hotel lifts, and faulty gas heaters causing asphyxiation in self-catering facilities, to say nothing of major disasters such as aircraft crashes or the extensively reported crisis of the sinking of the Baltic ferry *Estonia* with a loss of over 900 lives in 1994. Quite apart from disasters of this magnitude, many minor problems arise with which PR must deal. Rumours of redundancy or takeovers can affect staff morale, resulting in the loss of key members of the company through resignation at a crucial time, while a CAA refusal to grant an Air Travel Organizer's Licence (ATOL), or a request from ABTA for a company's bond to be increased, may sow seeds of doubt in the minds of the travelling public or within the trade, which can undermine the company's reputation and lead to its collapse.

It may be thought that PROs have a thankless task in having to help 'pick up the pieces' after such events; but their close relationship with the media makes their role invaluable when crises such as these occur. In a situation where a major crisis has occurred, successful PR will depend upon three things:

1 The PRO must be well briefed and in full possession of the facts. A good working relationship with a frank and trusting management is essential if this is to be achieved.
2 PROs must be in turn as frank as is possible with the media. An obvious attempt to cover up will be seized upon by journalists, which will threaten the whole future relationship between the two parties.

3 PROs must act fast, taking the initiative in calling the press and other media to a press conference to announce details of the event, rather than waiting to respond to media pressure. Fast action helps to dispel rumours which may paint a worse picture of the crisis than reality.

An important PR victory was the regeneration of British Airways as an efficient and profitable airline, in the lead up to its privatisation in 1987. The company was overstaffed and inefficient compared with its leading competitors, and suffered a poor public image. The necessary rundown of staff as a prelude to improving productivity worsened already weak morale within the company. A public relations campaign was launched both through a corporate advertising campaign aimed at the public to communicate the new image and the changed nature of the company, while a major internal campaign was launched to retrain staff to improve levels of service and restore their pride in the company. A major element in this campaign involved a one-day presentation 'A Day in the Life of British Airways' with staff from all over the world flown in to participate. The programme provided an opportunity for staff from all levels within the company to meet and learn more about each other's role. The exercise was a highly expensive, but extremely effective, example of good internal PR. Against this, however, must be weighed the damaging conflict with Virgin Airways, in which BA was found to be 'poaching' passengers from the rival airline. The less than frank statements from BA management at the time, and the extensive coverage in the media of the battle between the two rivals, should be an object lesson in how not to handle negative publicity.

Spanish hotel fire: handling by public relations

In February 1992 a fire took place at 4.30 am at a large hotel in Super Molina, Spain. Guests tried to raise the alarm by breaking the glass in a fire alarm, but it failed to go off. Some fire exits were reported as blocked, and guests were forced on to the balconies of their rooms in order to be rescued by ladder. One guest was taken to hospital suffering from smoke inhalation.

The resort office immediately informed the tour operator's head office, who in turn alerted the press officer. This prompt line of communication meant that by the time press calls began at 9 am, a statement had already been prepared. This was a holding statement expressing concern and promising a full investigation.

This investigation revealed a delicate situation in PR terms. The hotel held a proper local fire certificate. In addition, the tour operator concerned had a responsible attitude towards hotel safety, and had its own programme of inspecting hotels. The safety levels demanded by the operator often exceeded local regulations. This particular hotel had been inspected only four weeks earlier, and improvements had been demanded. These were scheduled to be carried out by the hotel, but the fire had taken place prior to their completion.

In PR terms, the situation could go either way. On the one hand, the operator took an extremely responsible attitude in inspecting its hotels and demanding improvements. On the other hand, it could be argued negatively that the operator was aware of the defects following its inspection.

The next move in PR terms was to immediately stop selling holidays to the hotel in question, and to offer attractive alternatives to customers who had already booked. This prompt action further defused the situation. However, as guests returned to the UK to tell their story, local papers began to carry 'death trap' stories. This alerted the *That's Life* TV programme, who contacted the operator asking for a written statement.

It was important to be honest, but also to get across the positive aspects of the case. The hotel was covered by a local fire certificate, and the operator was, in addition, putting a lot of extra effort and money into trying to ensure the highest possible standards for its guests. The prompt and fair action that the operator had already taken in respect of the guests affected or booked to go to the hotel was re-emphasised.

The statement also highlighted that, in conjunction with the Federation of Tour Operators, the operator was putting enormous pressure on the authorities to implement an EU Directive on hotel safety. In the absence of such a Directive, all operators could rely only upon local fire certificates (which might not be up to British standards) and their own efforts (which lacked any real means of enforcement).

Having acted so promptly and honestly, the tour operator had somewhat reduced the negative aspects of the story. By focusing on the lack of an EU Directive (which is a handicap for all tour operators), wider and more important issues were raised. In the event, rather than attempting to expose an 'uncaring and irresponsible' tour operator, the *That's Life* programme featured the need for the extra protection an EU Directive would bring.

Evaluating campaign results

At the beginning of this chapter it was pointed out that evaluating PR campaigns is often more difficult than evaluating the success of other forms of communication, since PR has long-term objectives and these are often qualitative in nature. However, many PR exercises are measurable, providing targets are established initially determining what the campaign is to achieve. One means of measuring PR success is through the measurement of media exposure. An analysis of press cuttings, for instance, will enable the company to measure the number of column inches of publicity received during the period of the PR campaign. Press clipping services are provided by PR agencies, if the company hasn't the resources to undertake this itself. Depending upon the media carrying the coverage, an estimate can be made of the audience reached through these reports, and some comparison made of the comparative costs if this coverage had had to be purchased commercially for advertising. While such tools of measurement are helpful, they provide no measure of the impact of the exposure, or whether goodwill, or recall of the company, would have been more effectively achieved through paid advertisements. Nevertheless, coverage in PR campaigns can be gained at very small cost to the company, and offers a valuable contribution to the overall communications process.

It will also be helpful to attempt some measure of the company's leading competitors, since this will give an indication of the relative success of the two organisations' PR departments.

A more accurate means of measuring PR effectiveness, if more expensive, is through the implementation of a programme of research to check changes in awareness, understanding or attitude. This will require surveys to be carried out before, after and sometimes during campaigns, which can be conducted among a sample of national consumers, among members of the local community, or among the firm's distributors. However, national surveys, involving sampling opinion of 1500–2000 randomly selected respondents, are beyond the resources of all but the largest travel companies, or the public sector.

Within the company, figures on staff turnover can offer pointers on levels of job satisfaction, but must be supported by staff interviews to ascertain reasons for departure.

Finally, the impact of any campaign can be measured in terms of increased sales and profits. It may be difficult to be certain that increases are the result of any PR activities, or what proportion of the increases can be ascribed to PR compared with other communications campaigns of the company. Allowances must be made for external influences on market growth, and increases must be compared with comparative figures achieved by the company's competitors. At best, measurement will be inaccurate, but it will give some indication of the effectiveness of the PR department's activities, and help to justify the budget allocated to this function.

Questions, tasks and issues for discussion

1   This task will involve a role play between two people, one of whom will take the role of spokesperson for a coach company which has just suffered the loss of a vehicle en route from the south of France, killing three and injuring eleven passengers. The second person will take the role of a television reporter interviewing the spokesperson about the crash (if this can be conducted on closed circuit TV for later playback, so much the better). The media have heard rumours that the coach driver fell asleep at the wheel, after having had to curtail his rest hours in France, due to late arrival at the site on the outbound journey.

2   Write a press release designed to publicise the forthcoming launch of a new series of package tours to the Maldives, Mauritius and Madagascar which combine beach and activity (snorkeling, etc.) holidays.

3   Identify key issues which go to make a successful educational visit for travel agents. Now carry out a small-scale survey among agency counter staff who have been on an educational visit, in order to judge how well organised their visits were. Write a brief summary of your conclusions and recommendations.

Exercise

Taking any notable crisis which has affected one travel business during the past two years, plan a PR campaign to handle it.

14 Marketing control

After studying this chapter, you should be able to:

- recognise the importance of control mechanisms in the marketing plan
- distinguish between different techniques of control
- implement simple control procedures in marketing

Control in the marketing process

The marketing function in a business is part of the *business system*. That is to say that certain *inputs* into the business, such as labour, money and enterprise together create a *process* which is designed to produce an end-product for consumers. This end-product is the organisation's *output*. A system can be defined as an input, a process and an output, and the objective of good management is to ensure that the input and process is subject to constant monitoring to ensure that the output is the right product, at the right price, in the right place at the right time; a classical definition of good marketing practice. The key word here is *monitoring*; the process which is designed to provide feedback on the effectiveness and efficiency of the system, to control it, and where necessary to change it. This is illustrated in Fig. 14.1.

In this chapter we shall look at the role of the monitoring procedures which are designed to control the marketing system. All along we have stressed that planning is an essential part of the marketing process, but the plan will be only as good as the control to which it is subject. Plans are not carved on tablets of stone; they have to be adjusted constantly in the light of changing circumstances, as the company reacts to market forces.

Marketing is carried out in an organisation in three stages:

1 *Pre-action* At this stage, activities associated with planning for action have to be undertaken. This includes the development of an information system, and a programme of planned market research. Marketing objectives are established, and strategies devised to achieve objectives. Forecasts are drawn up based on the strategies to be implemented.

2 *Action* At this stage, the marketing plan is implemented. This brings into play the co-ordinating role of the marketing manager, who must ensure that the channels of communication are integrated within the department, so that promotional activities serve a common aim. The co-ordinator must also make certain that where other departments are contributing to the marketing plan, these commitments are met, and in time. Day-to-day activities undertaken as part of the plan will be regularly reviewed and adjusted as necessary.

3 *Post-action* At this final stage, the marketing manager has the responsibility of reviewing the plan in its entirety, both to see whether targets are being achieved and to see if ways can be found to further improve the performance

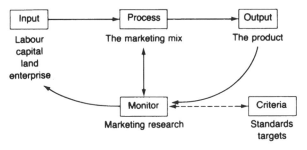

Fig.14.1 The monitoring and control system

of the department. It is this element of the control function which we shall be examining in this chapter.

Although control is a key management function, it should not become a responsibility which exercises too much of a marketing manager's time. The objective of good management is to build a marketing control system which is self-correcting as far as possible. This is achieved by good information systems, the use of management by objectives and the delegation of authority to take corrective action in day-to-day operational activities. Staff within the department need to be aware of what is expected of them as individuals, how they are performing, and to whom they are accountable. It is by no means unusual in a large travel company (as in any other large company) to find staff unclear about their accountability, or staff who are accountable to more than one member of management, each setting different priorities and having different expectations of their staff.

It is equally important that staff not only know their responsibilities but also are given power to regulate their activities, even at the most junior level. A member of a travel agent's counter staff given responsibility for racking brochures must know, for example, what the agency's policy is for racking brochures, procedures for ordering and reordering brochures, what action to take when brochures are refused by a principal or out of stock at the principal's. The clerk must be given full responsibility for maintenance of adequate stock, and control over the stockroom so that brochures are placed in an orderly system so they can be found quickly when needed. With such a system, the manager should seldom have to intervene, and occasional spot checks or an end-of-season survey to ensure that old stock is being cleared is all that is needed to maintain effective control.

Five different forms of control can be identified in a control system:

- performance control
- quality control
- financial control
- efficiency control
- strategic control.

Each of these will be examined in the light of travel and tourism practice.

Performance control

This is designed to make sure the organisation meets its set targets. The normal targets identified in the marketing plan will include issues such as:

- turnover
- profitability
- market share
- return on investment
- quality
- consumer attitudes.

The extent to which these targets are being met can be monitored on a daily or weekly basis, and control is therefore dependent upon a regular flow of information which will indicate performance variance coming to those responsible for corrective action. These members of staff must ascertain why the deviance is occurring and whether action can be taken to bring it back into line with forecasts.

Actual identification of variance is a largely mechanical process, but correcting it calls for management skills, both in interpreting data and in the suitable deployment of resources. Here the manager must distinguish between controllable factors, and those outside the control of the business which will require readjustment of the forecast or the marketing plan. Let us say that the sale of tours to Britain from the United States has declined, and is failing to reach the targets set. This may be accounted for entirely by changing economic or political circumstances, such as the drop in US visitors to Europe resulting from a combination of the Gulf War, threats of Arab terrorist activity and a recession at home, or fluctuating exchange rates between the two countries.

Nevertheless, it is important that the decline in the company's bookings is compared with those of other businesses handling US traffic to Britain, since it may be that internal factors account for part of the deviance. Assuming the organisation's performance is broadly in line with that of the total market, the marketing plan will require adjustment, so that targets are less dependent on US traffic in the coming year. The marketing manager will also want to look at the original objectives, and determine whether they were realistic. A close look will be taken of the controllable elements in the marketing plan; is the structure of the department designed to get the results sought in the marketing plan, for example? What factors in the marketing mix require to be changed to achieve the targets set?

Remedial action to bring performance back on target needs to be taken quickly, but not so quickly as to reflect a panic response to a temporary aberration, which may be self-correcting. At the time of the 1987 British general election, for example, overseas tour bookings in Britain fell sharply, leading to a rapid slashing of prices on forthcoming tours. While response is needed to clear current stock, in the long term price reductions may not be needed, and in fact the market picked up after the election. Price reductions through the season led to a serious fall in seasonal margins.

In looking at profitability control, the organisation will be concerned not only with overall profitability but also with the profitability of each 'profit centre', or product range. A tour operator will be observing its profitability on each programme operated, just as a travel agent should examine its profitability for each type of travel service it sells. In fact, the tour operator will be looking at profitability not only at the programme level, but also by brand, season, resort and hotel. This allows for continual adjustment throughout the season to attempt to maintain profit levels. Resort and hotel performance will also influence the following season in terms of the rates the operator is willing to pay hoteliers and the overall balance of destinations.

As we have seen, the tour operator's business is extremely competitive and all operators are very conscious of their overall market share as well as individual sales levels. It is relatively easy for an operator to assess its own sales. Those of the competition pose a rather more difficult problem. Yet even if sales are up, an operator will wish to know that this increase is not in fact less than it ought to be, relative to the whole market and the competition.

Recognition of the need for timely (often weekly) performance information within the travel industry has led several research companies to provide a statistics service to travel organisations. Basically, third party research companies pull together information that individual companies would find difficult or costly to prepare. This consolidated information is then sold to a number of companies who use it for performance monitoring. An example of this is the Holiday Booking Audit from STATS MR, which provides detailed weekly statistics on sales made through ABTA travel agents, including sales by destination, party size, holiday type, operator and booking month.

Interestingly, even though the tour operators are fiercely competitive, the hunger for performance measures means that the industry is rich in syndicated research. This is research where operators join together to share the costs of a particular research programme. They may also provide information knowing that the only way they will know what their competitors are doing is by revealing their own position.

One of the most significant factors affecting profitability of a tour operator is *load factor*, or the extent to which individual flights are filled. In Chapter 6 we discussed fixed and marginal costs; an aeroplane represents a very high fixed cost, and with the low individual margins of the travel business, if less than around 90 per cent full, it is unlikely to be generating any profit contribution at all. Thus, for instance, an operator may 'consolidate' two undersold flights into one in order to reduce costs. This of course is unpopular with consumers who have their travel arrangements altered, perhaps at short notice; there may be a hidden cost to the savings overtly made in terms of compensation and lost future business. However, the operator may simply have no option if it is to remain in business making a profit.

Tour operators will track the performance of individual retailers closely in order to identify the most productive outlets. One of the most significant trends in the retail channel has been the growth of the multiple chains, so that some 70 per cent of a mainstream tour operator's bookings now come from outlets of the top six multiples. Again, performance needs to be assessed in a wider context: though a large multiple may sell more holidays, it may also have used its size to negotiate higher commission rates, to the detriment of the operator's overall profit margins.

Quality control

Measuring quality and ensuring that quality is maintained is a relatively simple matter in the production of durable goods; these can be inspected, rejected if below standard, and some tolerance agreed for the proportion falling below standard. Maintaining quality control over a product such as tourism is far less straightforward. Uncontrollable factors such as weather exert a considerable influence over the perceived quality of a tourism service.

Tour operators pay close attention to the requirement that their products live up to their description in their brochure, because this is required under law. Increasingly, they are establishing acceptable tolerances for levels of complaints, as this is a measure of quality control. This can be easily measured, since complaints can be measured through letters of complaint received by the company, or complaints made to the resort representatives, which can be easily recorded. The correct operation of a monitoring system means that complaints are fed back in the form of corrective actions that prevent complaints in the future. Thus, as well as counting overall numbers of complaints, even just one complaint could mean, for instance, a change implemented in copy for the next edition of the brochure. The use of questionnaires is less effective in monitoring complaints, as most questionnaires used require only that clients list their levels of satisfaction or dissatisfaction with the product; there is insufficient information to take action to correct a situation if a high level of complaints is registered. One needs to know *exactly*

what is wrong with the service, and what *action* is needed to correct the situation. Suggestion boxes can provide a good picture of consumer dissatisfaction, as can debriefing of staff such as resort representatives at the end of a season.

All the major tour operators have for many years monitored performance through customer satisfaction questionnaires. Some companies such as Thomson and First Choice have also empowered their resort representatives to pay compensation to clients on the spot in order to satisfy complaints at the earliest opportunity. Research has shown that prompt and appropriate action of this kind not only saves future costly customer service, but also makes the client more likely to repeat book.

It is all too easy to believe that if levels of complaint are low, all is well with the company. In fact, there may be a high level of 'disguised dissatisfaction' with the company. Many British holidaymakers make vociferous complaints to resort representatives on the first day of their holidays. A good rep is able to placate clients who might otherwise return home with a simmering dissatisfaction, leading them to book with another company in the following year. Consequently the level of repeat bookings must be taken into account in measuring quality control.

For this reason again the major operators subscribe to syndicated 'attitude' surveys which sample both consumers and the retail trade to ascertain their true opinions of the different operators. An example of this is the annual MORI survey of travel agents' perceptions of tour operator performance.

Financial control

It is not only the financial controller who will be concerned that departments keep within their budgets. While the budget itself is designed to exercise an automatic control over the operations of the business, the marketing department must constantly check that sales, promotion and other expenses remain within the agreed limits. However, too tight control can lead to missed marketing opportunities. The marketing plan must not become a strait-jacket.

The use of ratios to determine marketing mix expenditure is a common means of judging performance, but can be misleading if it is based on what 'the average company in the industry' is achieving. While it is common to determine that a fixed proportion of turnover be allocated to promotion, the earlier discussion on communications budgets will have made it clear that spend will need to vary according to the established objectives of the marketing plan. In a time of falling sales, too often the control mechanisms go into operation to cut promotional spend where it might be more appropriate to increase it to generate more sales.

Changing circumstances can also result in a particular product carrying too high a proportion of the company's overheads. Let us say that fuel prices have been increased. This could lead to a disproportionately large fall in long-haul tour bookings, which will require some readjustment to the allocation of overheads to those programmes.

Efficiency control

If performance control has indicated a weakness in some aspect of the organisation's marketing, analysis will be needed to determine whether the marketing activities or the structure of the department needs to be changed in some way to make the marketing more efficient. Even if marketing targets are being met, sheer pressures of competition between principals or between retailers requires that ways be constantly sought to reduce costs without impairing efficiency. This means constant re-evaluation of the marketing mix. All means of measuring success must be taken into account, not merely levels of turnover.

Reviewing the organisational structure of the department might mean considering whether sales should be separated from marketing and given its own head; or whether the department has grown to a point where it is worth introducing a marketing controller to co-ordinate activities in the department. Should the market-

ing functions become increasingly centralised, as has happened in some large hotel chains, or should they be more decentralised, as other chains have done? Does the administrative structure facilitate the marketing function, or does it hinder it? Above all, is the quality of the staff up to the standard required?

This last question is a crucial one for the travel and tourism industry. In most sectors of the industry, the belief remains that profit levels do not allow better salaries to be paid, and therefore better staff cannot be recruited. However, performance standards do vary between companies, and different management styles are a major contribution to these variations. Are staff being properly trained in marketing techniques? Are they being promoted beyond their capabilities? Are they adequately motivated? What does the manager know about levels of satisfaction among the staff? How is the staff managed – by sanctions, rewards, or, simplest of all but surprisingly rare, by thanking them for a job well done? Frequent examples can be shown of small companies in travel (employing between 20 and 50 members of staff) where the manager seldom meets or greets the staff, but nevertheless expects them to give of their best for the company. Measures of staff turnover and levels of staff satisfaction are important methods of judging the efficiency of the organisation with respect to staff. It is not sufficient simply to count the proportion of staff leaving the company; managers must know for what *reasons* the staff are leaving.

Even with a good workforce and organisation, the communications mix must be monitored constantly to compare the relative performance of different promotional tactics and seek ways of making these more cost-effective. Some of these ongoing monitoring processes were described in Chapter 10, dealing with promotional techniques. Such procedures are an integral part of the control system.

The production of the holiday brochure has been made far more efficient through the use of computer technology. Computers now help work out the hundreds of thousands of individual prices, and carry out the complex matching of hotel beds and flights. The use of modern desk top publishing has also greatly facilitated the compilation and printing of the brochures themselves. Since the travel brochure is such a critical element in the promotional mix, a company should regularly monitor its brochures by soliciting consumer and retailer views about its brochures compared with those of the competition. Tests of awareness and recall must be carried out, and sales representatives calling on travel agents will be required to report which brochures are racked and where.

The sales manager will monitor the ratio of sales to cost of sales, both for the sales force and for the company's retail agents. The efficiency of the reservation process has also come under scrutiny and is supported by technology. Viewdata reservation systems mean that a much smaller proportion of bookings need involve any human agent at all within the tour operating company. This has resulted in large cost savings for the larger operators. Those reservations staff who remain are supported with sophisticated telephone and computer systems.

Identification of more productive distribution outlets will determine future levels of support and should permit analysis of the relative performance of national multiples versus independent agents and small chains. Results of joint promotional schemes will be assessed, as will the effect of different incentives provided to retailers.

Carriers are seeking to employ new technology in their drive for cost efficiency. The introduction of ticket printing machines at some airports internationally is one means by which they are responding both to the needs and needs to improve cost control.

Strategic control

From time to time it becomes necessary to look at the total process by which strategic marketing is undertaken in the company, in order to judge whether the organisation is taking advantage of the marketing opportunities open to it. This will require senior staff from outside the department to consider the extent of market orientation of the department and of the company as a whole, how

well organised it is to spot opportunities when they occur and exploit them, and how well the organisation plans its strategies. No travel business today can afford to rest on its laurels; markets change rapidly, and complacency over present occupancy levels, load factors or bookings can quickly change to concern as new challenges emerge to face the company. The rebirth of First Choice Holidays from the former Owners Abroad is an example of an organisation reappraising its place in the market and making substantial changes accordingly, as will be seen from the numerous examples we have drawn on in this text.

Management will want to review the effectiveness of its internal, as well as its external, communications. Do the staff share common objectives, and are they working towards a common aim? How well do other departments co-operate with the marketing staff to meet their needs? These are important questions which relate to the operating efficiency of the company as a whole. Where there are divisions of the company on separate sites, or staff are employed far from head office, communications can easily suffer. One of the most common management problems in tour operating is the failure to communicate, and above all the failure to establish common aims between the head office staff and staff in the field such as area managers and resort representatives. Head office staff making field visits may not even take the time to meet their field representatives; yet it is the resort representative who is closest to the company's clients, knows their problems and can best offer suggestions for the improvement of services.

If a serious weakness is found in some aspect of the organisation's marketing, a full marketing audit may be commissioned. This generally means bringing in outside consultants to undertake a systematic investigation into every aspect of the company's marketing operation.

Where responsibility is delegated, as is the case in large organisations, control is easier to exercise in one sense because a system of checks and balances is introduced by assigning individual responsibility and accountability. A very small company, where management is vested in a single individual who takes on total responsibility for marketing, as well as general management of the company's day-to-day affairs, will be less likely, and less willing, to build in a system of control. It is this aspect of marketing management which poses the greatest threat to the many small units which still make up the bulk of companies operating in the travel and tourism industry, and which are today struggling to survive in the face of the more professional marketing management of the large corporations.

Questions, tasks and issues for discussion

1 What levels of control do travel agents actually exercise at the pre-action, action and post-action stages of marketing?

2 Should control over racking policy, window display and other merchandising activities of a 'major multiple' travel agency chain be exercised by head office, or by the individual branches?

   What arguments would you offer in favour of each of these approaches?

3 The aim of controlling sales reps is to achieve a balance between giving them total autonomy to do their jobs properly, and ensuring that their performance is monitored adequately. How will a good sales manager tackle this problem?

Exercise

As part of the year's current marketing plan for a tour operator, develop a programme of quality control, giving details of how this will be measured, and what standards will be imposed.

Part 2   Case studies

Case study 1
Successfully relaunching a major tour operator: transforming Owners Abroad into First Choice Holidays

(Prepared by Chris Robinson, Group Marketing Manager, First Choice Holidays, with the help of Ogilvy & Mather, advertising agents)

Background

The 1993 season was an unhappy time for Owners Abroad. Market share and share price alike were adversely affected by an attempted hostile takeover bid by arch-rival Airtours, and though this was ultimately unsuccessful, the bitter six-month battle left Owners Abroad seriously weakened. The old board of directors made way for a new team who went on to carry out one of the most far-reaching business and marketing reviews ever undertaken by the travel industry in Britain.

This review resulted in the establishment of a radical and ambitious objective: to transform the entire company within a period of eight months. Market share was to be regained and increased, profits were to be restored and the company re-engineered from top to bottom in terms of management structure and product line. In addition, the market perception of Owners Abroad and its brands was to be rebuilt around a fresh, new and positive image.

Role of advertising

The old Owners Abroad had a marketing communications legacy that was recognised as an insuperable barrier to business progress:

1 The name Owners Abroad was little known and, where it *was* known, the associations were either of timeshare or, thanks to the takeover battle, of a company about to go under. Both of these misconceptions needed to be addressed.

2 The fourteen separate brands in the company portfolio presented a confused and disparate image to the consumer. No individual brand had the strength to compete against the 'monolithic' brands of Thomson Holidays and Airtours.

Nevertheless, it takes courage to wipe the slate clean on a company and products that represent over 86 per cent of their sales, 12 per cent of the total market and over 2 million individual holidays.

The primary objective of the advertising campaign was to effect the change of the company from Owners Abroad to First Choice Holidays and its three new brands without loss of market share or volume. Naturally, this was not the task of advertising alone: the brochures and their launch, public relations, direct mail and the sales force calling on travel agents all contributed to this primary objective.

Each brand was approached differently, according to its specific target market and contribution to overall sales. Thus the smallest budget (12 per cent of total spend) and colour advertisements in the prestige press were considered sufficient for the already established Sovereign brand name. The largest share of the budget (52 per cent of total spend) and extensive television coverage were deemed appropriate for the mass volume brand First Choice. This, of course, was also raising awareness of the new company, First Choice Holidays. The advertising campaign for First Choice is considered in detail in this case study.

Campaign objectives

The advertising campaign was specifically aimed at achieving the following objectives:

- to achieve a high level of awareness of First Choice Holidays in the crucial booking periods, that is, August/September, which were the two months post-launch, and January/February, when there is a traditional post-Christmas peak in holiday bookings
- to increase market share by a minimum of 1 per cent over the previous season as Owners Abroad
- to reach the target of adults who habitually take a two-week summer package to Mediterranean destinations; one-third of these travel as families with children; women are particularly important as 'brochure collectors' and influencers of potential destination and operator
- a secondary target was the travel agent, both independent and multiple
- to get people excited about the idea of a holiday with First Choice, while subtly reassuring them that this was a large, firmly established and substantial company
- to differentiate First Choice from Thomson and Airtours
- to get people to pick up the Summer 1995 brochures at travel agents
- to get travel agents to recommend First Choice
- to integrate the campaign with the other communications activity through use of the new designs, colours and logos developed for the brand
- to be consistent and true to the brand values established for First Choice: 'a fresh new approach to holidays'; brighter, more lively, trying harder, yet safe and experienced; full of sun, fun and colour.

Advertising strategy

These were to be advertisements like no other holiday advertisements. A lively, humorous and highly creative approach, together with an innovative use of media, were chosen as best fitting the new brand image.

The campaign basically was a series of parodies of recognisable and clichéd advertisements for other products, taking the ridiculous claims made in ads and comparing them to two weeks in Spain.

The first advertisement featured a no-hoper who is suffering from a headache at work. A scientific looking woman walks into his office and says, 'If you are suffering from tense nervous headaches you could try a leading brand of painkillers, or you could choose a holiday from First Choice'. She then hits him on the head with a First Choice brochure and the man is transported to sunny Spain, where his dull life takes on a new look. The advertisement bursts into music and colour, while our hero gets a girlfriend, a suntan and a jaunt on a jet-ski.

The second advertisement featured a weary housewife cleaning a typical black-and-white kitchen floor. She is given the choice between a new floor cleaner or a holiday as a guaranteed way of keeping floors clean for two weeks. Cut to a series of funny shots of the family on holiday, ending with a Spanish woman cleaning her floor, to which the housewife quips, 'I know how she feels'.

The final advertisement promised a slightly overweight couple 'a new you in just two weeks'.

The campaign started with 10-second 'teaser' TV advertisements, supported by a saturation poster campaign. These ran for the two weeks prior to the launch. They did not reveal the name First Choice, but tongue-in-cheek proclaimed a new miracle product that could cure tense, nervous headaches, etc.

The posters were revealed overnight to coincide with extensive launch and PR events on 16 August 1993. At the same time the full 30-second advertisements started to appear on television in a campaign that ran for six weeks.

Pre-campaign research methodology

A campaign costing in total something in the order of £5 million should not be left to chance. A vital part of the process was extensive research to aid the development of the campaign.

The research during the creative development phase was carried out with a number of discussion groups of six C1C2 adults in the London area, the Midlands and the North. It had the following key aims:

- to verify the brand awareness created by the advertisements
- to establish the likely 'life' of the campaign, and in particular its ability to last into February of the following year
- to verify that correct image and positioning is created by the advertisements
- to optimise the response stimulus
- to gauge the effectiveness of the teasers
- to provide guidance for final execution of the advertisement and on the choice of music.

The research not only provided reassurance about the overall approach, but also provided positive direction for the final advertisements.

- research highlighted that the 'Walking on Sunshine' music selected for the advertisement was by far the best choice and a very positive asset
- research threw up the vital information that in the trial versions the First Choice branding and logo sequence was not long enough to achieve the high levels of brand awareness required, enabling these to be considerably strengthened in the final versions
- research sent one advertisement back to the cutting room as the research showed that the 'mickey take' of the fat people advertisement had gone just a bit too far
- research warned the media planners that the teasers had maximum impact on the main television campaign if different teasers for the different advertisements were seen in conjunction, which caused them to book poster sites

in close proximity and always two 10-second teaser advertisement slots within each commercial break.

Media strategy

Television

Television was immediately determined as an important medium to achieve the advertising objectives, thanks to its mass coverage, rapid penetration and ability to imbue a product with status just by its being seen on that medium.

The television space buying strategy demanded the greatest possible coverage of TVRs (television viewing ratings) for the available budget. It also took into account the following:

- the target market: ABC1C2 adults aged 25–54, ideally those who have taken a holiday abroad in the previous twelve months, with secondary emphasis on housebound women with children and on couples
- the need to reach high levels of coverage quickly so frequency should be maximised against high cover base
- extra emphasis on daytime slots to weight towards women at home
- extra emphasis on those programmes researched as having greatest appeal to adults who have taken holidays in the previous twelve months
- extra weight around the launch date and switch from teasers to full 30-second advertisements; attempts were made to buy simultaneous slots on all channels including satellite
- extra weight on key regions, e.g. London, and lowest coverage in least productive sales areas, e.g. northern Scotland.

The full media schedule appears in the following table.

MEDIA SUMMARY PLAN 1994

TARGET AUDIENCE = ADULTS

20th June 1994

	SEC	JAN 3	10	17	24	31	FEB 7	14	21	28	MAR 7	14	21	28	APR 4	11	18	25	MAY 2	9	16	23	30	JUN 6	13	20	27	SPEND Jan/Jun	TVR Jan/Jun
ITV																												0	0
CHANNEL 4																												0	0
GMTV																												0	0
SATELLITE																												0	0
TOT NWRK TVR		0	0	0	0	0	0	0	0	0	0	0	0	0	0	0	0	0	0	0	0	0	0	0	0	0	0	**0**	**0**

	SEC	JUL 4	11	18	25	AUG 1	8	15	22	29	SEP 5	12	19	26	OCT 3	10	17	24	31	NOV 7	14	21	28	DEC 5	12	19	26	SP PCT	SPEND Jul/Dec	TVR Jul/Dec
ITV	10/30"						200	200	150	150	100	100	100	100														65%	2 232 000	1100
CHANNEL 4	10/30"						50	50	50	50	50	50	50	50														26%	876 000	400
GMTV	10/30"						40	40																				3%	96 000	80
SAT NWRK	10/30"						20	20	20	20	10	10	10	10														6%	216 000	120
SAT ACT							100	100	100	100	50	50	50	50															0	600
TOT NWRK TVR		0	0	0	0		310	310	220	220	160	160	160	160	0	0	0	0	0	0	0	0	0	0	0	0	0		**3 420 000**	**1700**

Start date = 6th Aug

TOTALS	SPEND 1994	TVR 1994
ITV	2 232 000	1100
CH4	876 000	400
GMTV	96 000	80
SAT	216 000	120
	0	600
TV TOTAL	3 420 000	1700

TOTAL SPEND 3 420 000

NOTES

1ST TWO WEEKS ARE 10" ONLY, 3 ADS, 2 PER BREAK

SUBSEQUENT 6 WEEKS ARE 30" ONLY, 3 ADS, 1 PER BREAK

CHANNEL 4, GMTV & SATELLITE ARE BOUGHT NATIONALLY GIVING REGIONAL BIAS

ITV TO BE BOUGHT IN ORDER TO ACHIEVE AS CLOSE AS POSSIBLE EQUAL TVRS BY AREA AND IS SUBJECT TO NEGOTIATION

SPEND FIGURES ARE DISGUISED TO PROTECT CONFIDENTIALITY

Media schedule for the launch of First Choice Holidays

(Courtesy: First Choice Holidays)

Posters

A saturation poster campaign was chosen to support both the teasers and the 'revealed' main television advertisement. Not only was this approach very different from the competition, but also it positioned the company as fun and colourful through an innovative use of media.

The poster site buying strategy took account of four main factors.

First, it was necessary to identify quality sites that could be booked for a consecutive four-week period, with the opportunity to 'reveal' the name First Choice after two weeks. This practical implication of the creative approach was very important. Poster sites are usually booked in two-week periods, and sites in demand might not be free for four consecutive weeks. Also, for example, though they would have been ideal sites, Cross Track sites on London Underground could not be used. London Transport Advertising could not provide the service of changing the poster overnight at the end of the second week, which was so essential for the impact of the launch.

Second, following on from initial research, the sites needed to be clustered to ensure that different teasers were seen together in close proximity.

Third, the weight and coverage of the different television areas were also reflected in the poster sites chosen.

Finally, a number of poster sites are classified as 'specials' or 'spectaculars', due to the particularly high numbers of people able to view them. Locations such as the Cromwell Road in West London and Waterloo Station main concourse fall into these categories and play an important part in raising the profile of an outdoor campaign. Sites such as those at major airports and on the main road routes into London were chosen to strengthen the media schedule.

Integration with other marketing activity

The project to effect the relaunch and rebranding exercise within Owners Abroad was a large and complex undertaking. Twelve working parties were set up to consider different aspects of the

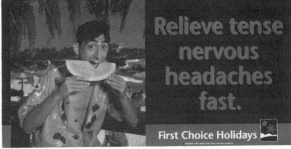

Teaser posters heralding the First Choice advertisements
(Courtesy: Ogilvy & Mather Advertising / First Choice Holidays)

Win your First Choice Holiday FREE

Winning a First Choice Summer Sun Holiday couldn't be easier. Just follow the step by step guide below.

Step 1
Study the four First Choice Summer Sun holidays overleaf and choose the one you would most like to win.

Step 2
Pick up a First Choice Summer Sun '95 brochure from any ABTA Travel Agent.

Step 3
Complete the application form below, filling in the destination of your choice and the page number from the First Choice Summer Sun '95 brochure that your destination is featured on.

Step 4
Post your entry to the following address:
First Choice Free Holiday Offer,
FREEPOST, PO Box 100,
Swadlincote, Derbyshire
DE12 6BR.
(No stamp required)

£10 off your First Choice holiday
All entrants will receive a £10 First Choice holiday voucher to spend on any First Choice Summer Sun holiday. So, even if you don't win a free holiday, you can still enjoy £10 off any holiday in the First Choice Summer Sun '95 brochure. Just pay your deposit now and use the voucher when the balance is due.

APPLICATION FORM

Please complete in block capitals:

Mr/Mrs/Miss/Ms (Please delete as applicable)

Name

Address

Post Code

Tel. Number

My chosen destination is

This holiday appears on page No(s).
of the First Choice Summer Sun '95 brochure.

Send this completed application form by 30th September 1994 to:

First Choice Free Holiday Offer,
FREEPOST, PO Box 100, Swadlincote,
Derbyshire DE12 6BR.

(No stamp required)

RULES

1. Open to all UK residents aged 18 or over except employees (or members of their families) of First Choice Holidays PLC, Promotional Campaigns Ltd or anyone connected with the administration of the draw.
2. There will be a total of ten prizes of First Choice Summer Sun holidays as featured in this leaflet. These will be awarded to the first ten correct entrants drawn after the closing date.
3. The draw will be conducted by an independent person. No correspondence will be entered into.
4. If you win, you will be awarded the holiday you have chosen from the 4 overleaf, to be booked from the First Choice Summer Sun '95 brochure subject to availability and normal booking conditions. If you have already booked a holiday with First Choice, we'll pay for that holiday or give you the option to change to your winning holiday instead. No cash alternative will be available. All holidays must be taken by 31st October 1995. Prize holidays may not exceed £1,000 in value. Each holiday prize is for 24 people; dependent upon cost conditions above.
5. All entrants will receive a voucher worth £10 which is valid against any holiday booked from the First Choice Summer Sun '95 brochure. This voucher cannot be used in conjunction with any other First Choice offer. Please allow 28 days for delivery of your voucher.
6. Only one entry per household.
7. The winners will be notified by 17th October 1994. Results can be obtained by sending a SAE marked "winners" to the above address after 23rd October 1994.
8. Winners may be required to take part in the publicity connected in connection with the free prize draw.
9. Entry is to be that entrant's demand to be signed to acceptance of these rules and the instructions above.

Promoters address: First Choice Holidays PLC, Groundstar House, London Road, Crawley, West Sussex RH10 7TB.
No applications to this address.

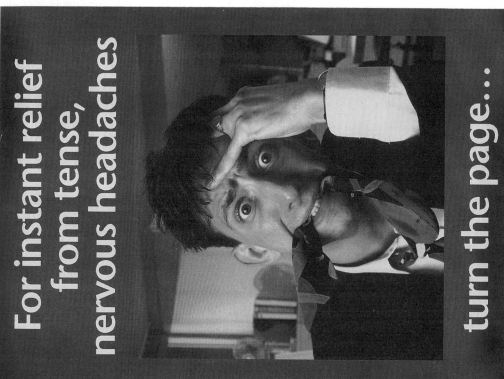

For instant relief from tense, nervous headaches

turn the page….

Mailshot carrying First Choice advertising theme
(Courtesy: Ogilvy & Mather Advertising /First Choice Holidays)

task, such as advertising or PR, with the relevant senior management forming part of all working parties. In addition, the many external agencies working on advertising, design, launch events and the like were also required to form part of the working parties. This ensured that the exercise was an integrated whole. It also had the positive effect on the different marketing communications that they built upon each other and reinforced consistent brand values.

Just one small example of many is the way that the music chosen for the television advertisement was cross-fertilised. The 'Walking on Sunshine' music was the theme tune of the launch events; a major sales promotion in conjunction with the *Daily Mirror* was called 'Walking on Sunshine' (see pp. 187–8); the phone systems at all offices were set up so that callers to First Choice who are 'on hold' also hear this tune; while from the date of launch, holidaymakers boarded the company's airline, Air 2000, to the same music.

The mailshot illustrated shows how the advertising theme was translated into the medium of direct marketing.

Evaluation of the campaign

The sales performance of First Choice Holidays was carefully evaluated in the weeks following launch. Six weeks after launch, sales were up 42 per cent on the same period for the previous year, in a flat market.

Post-launch research was also conducted which had demonstrated the effect of the promotion on the awareness and image of First Choice.

Conclusion

The high risk strategy paid off, and a new company has essentially risen in place of the old Owners Abroad. After the pain of transformation, First Choice Holidays has become well placed to strengthen still further its position as a major tour operator. Its image is fresh, strong and much clearer to consumers. Its three strong brands were set to enjoy a good summer season by the start of 1995. The next step would be to ensure that the delivery of the product matched the initial high expectations created by the initial launch promotion.

This advertising campaign clearly played a crucial part in the success of the company. Without a creative, memorable and effective campaign the new company could not have been so successful in its launch. Sales momentum was maintained and improved in the face of radical changes – a vital factor for business survival. The campaign itself had provided an excellent platform from which to build future marketing communications.

Case study 2
Promoting an established tourist attraction: the island of Mainau

(Prepared with the help of Herr Winfried Nesensohn of Blumeninsel Mainau GmbH, Mainau)

Background

The island of Mainau is situated in Überlinger Lake, the north-western part of Lake Constance (German: Bodensee), near the border of north-eastern Switzerland, western Austria and south-western Germany. The island has an over-all size of 45 hectares; it boasts an eventful and colourful history and offers an attractive destina-tion for an outing.

During the time of the Roman Empire, the island was the fleet base of the Roman comman-der Tiberius. In the fifth and sixth centuries, the island became an Alemannic ducal estate. From AD 724 it passed into the hands of the Reichenau Monastery. In 1272 it was given to the Teutonic Knights, a religious brotherhood of knights, who retained it until 1805. Between 1739 and 1746 the castle and the baroque St Mary's Church were constructed under the supervision of the Teutonic Knights' master builder Johann Caspar Bagnato. In 1806 the island became part of the Grand Duchy of Baden, later changing hands a number of times before eventually returning to Baden's ownership in 1853. That year also saw the construction of the present-day botanical park which was to provide the foundation of the island's success as a major international tourist destination. In 1932, through hereditary succes-sion in the Duchy of Baden, ownership passed to the Swedish Count Bernadotte, who successfully developed those parts of the park formerly used as agricultural land into a botanical garden. In 1974, the island of Mainau became a charitable institution, ensuring that it would remain as an excursion destination with unique cultural and historical interest.

Market for the island

Mainau, which has been open year round since 1986, remains a predominantly summer holiday destination. The 'Mainau Flower Year' is the more popular season, from the middle of March to mid-October; the autumn/winter season lasts from October to March. In the high season, between 1.7 million and 2 million visitors arrive, of which:

> 60% are holidaymakers visiting the neighbouring holiday regions in Germany, Austria and Switzerland
> 32% are nationals of these three countries
> 8% are travellers passing through.

About a quarter of all visitors are non-German nationals, led by 10 per cent Swiss, 5 per cent Austrian, 4 per cent French and 3 per cent Swedish. The catchment area for day excursions extends to around 200 km.

Visitors arrive by various means: 38 per cent arrive by private car or motorcycle; 35 per cent come on ships of the Lake Constance fleet, 25 per cent arrive on tour buses and 2 per cent are pedestrians or cyclists. Nearly half the visitors, (46 per cent) come as couples, while 25 per cent arrive in family groups and 25 per cent arrive in organised groups. Only 4 per cent are on their own.

During the winter period, some 100,000 visi-tors are still attracted to the island, although the catchment area is limited to a radius of only about 50 km. Visitors at this time of the year are largely German nationals.

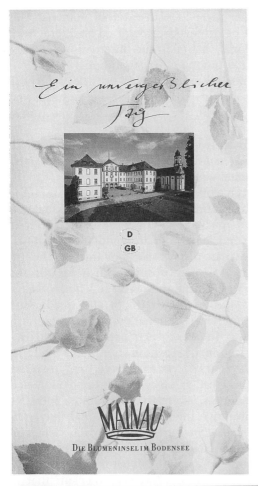

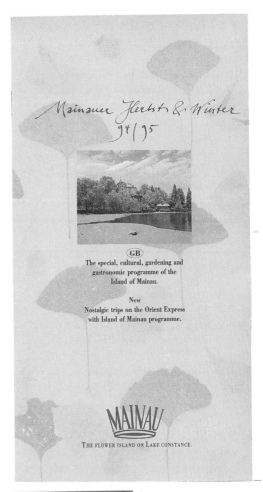

Promotional material for the island of Mainau
(Courtesy: Blumeninsel Mainau GmbH, Mainau)

The island of Mainau
(Courtesy: Blumeninsel Mainau GmbH, Mainau)

Economics of Mainau as a tourist attraction

The island is reached by lake steamer or a narrow bridge, across which pedestrians may walk (vehicles are prohibited on the island itself). Tourism to the island is promoted and operated through a private limited company, Blumeninsel Mainau GmbH, which employs about 450 staff in summer and 220 in winter. Annual turnover for the enterprise amounts to around DM40 million, broken down as follows:

    admission charges   44%
    catering 41%
    shop   10%
    car parking charges 5%

Break-even is usually achieved with around 1.7 million visitors per year.

Since 1991, when the company recorded 2 million visitors in the high season, there has been an annual drop in visitors of around 8 per cent, reflecting a similar downturn in visitors to the region generally in the early 1990s. Turnover could be raised through increases in admission and other charges, but there is concern that the profit zone of 1.7 million visitors during the high season would no longer be reached. Mainau has not proved to be a sufficiently popular winter destination for local visitors, and the company hopes to address this problem in the future.

The marketing plan and objectives

The company aims to achieve ten objectives:

1 To achieve *quality* is the primary aim, in both corporate and marketing terms. The maintenance and improvement of the product is fundamental to the company, and attention to the quality of existing and future facilities, while giving due consideration to ecological issues, is a major marketing objective.

2 To retain the already high level of *awareness* (approximately 90 per cent) of the destination in the German market, while achieving higher awareness in external markets. This will be achieved through co-operation with regional, national and international tourist boards, among other institutions.

3 To increase *visitor numbers* outside of the peak season, but particularly in the autumn and winter, with the co-operation of the tourist boards.

4 To foster existing *target groups*, while expanding demand, particularly among local and regional visitors.

5 To develop *new responsibilities* within the organisation, including hotel booking services, package holiday booking services, souvenir mail order and renting of premises.

6 To increase *turnover per guest* through the creation of a more positive consumer climate, and by extending the average length of stay.

7 To improve the *image* of the destination through clearer, more comprehensible information in areas such as ecology, quality, motivation and identification.

8 To develop *Practised Hospitality*: this term refers to the creation of customer orientation and friendliness, as a matter of corporate policy.

9 To improve internal and external *interactive communication* through the introduction of an information system for quality assurance and the implementation of visitor requirements.

10 To implement *regular checks* to ensure that all marketing aims are being satisfactorily achieved.

Strategy

The drop in visitor numbers since 1991 can be ascribed to a number of factors, including poor weather, the international recession, competition from garden shows and leisure parks, and a general failure to achieve awareness consistently for the Lake Constance region as a holiday destination. However, it is also recognised that no updating of attractions has occurred on the island since 1989. Repetition of identical subject matter in promotional material leads to fatigue and a drop-off in interest, as other attractions come on-stream.

This problem is being tackled by the construction of a butterfly house with an exotic collection of plants: a new palm house with a princely orangery; the organisation of additional flower shows, especially during the low season; and the expansion of the exotic plant collection outdoors. Existing flower shows, such as tulip, rhododendron and rose blossom displays and the dahlia show, will be improved. Steps will be taken to ensure that new facilities and attractions such as catering, cultural events and the sale of souvenirs, will be attractive, up-to-date and in keeping with the overall corporate image of the 'flower island'.

Events will play a key role in the future. A wide variety of services will be brought together to form individual packages. Where previously emphasis has been placed on restaurant reservations, rental of premises and the implementation of small to medium-sized events, new, more ambitious packages will now be developed, in co-operation with partners such as the Lake Constance Shipping Company, hotels, operators of old-time train trips and tour operators. The distribution channels and reservation systems of these operators will be used extensively to reach the market. This strategy takes on particular significance in efforts to reach the market for autumn and winter visits (when outdoor flower displays are not possible). During this season, cultural and restaurant facilities will be promoted.

The island offers seminar courses for the educational market, including school classes, training for teachers and management courses on the nature trail. The ecology and nature education department is also drawing up plans for reasonably priced all-in packages, organised with relevant partners, offering environmentally friendly trips to the island using public transport. The island's expertise in green matters is illustrated by its 'Green Telephone' service, offering advice on plants.

Pricing strategy on the island takes into account the varying levels of demand according to season and market. In the Mainau Flower Year in 1994, admission to the park and gardens cost DM14, with a scale of reduced charges for concessions. Additional special exhibition fees of DM1 are charged during the Flower Year. In the autumn and winter low season, admission falls to DM5, but this is waived where restaurant bookings are made, and exhibitions are free. Prices are broadly comparable with similar attractions in the area, and are considered moderate. Catering is offered in two forms: good, cheap lunches served quickly for day visitors are available at budget prices, while dinner is provided at a much higher price and standard, reflecting the demand for evening meals on the island.

Promotion

A variety of means is used to reach the destination's markets. Direct advertising to the public is used only within a radius of 200 km of Mainau, to generate day trips among both locals and holidaymakers in the region. Newspaper advertisements, posters, radio spot advertising, and direct mail and public relations campaigns are all used to stimulate demand within this market. The major national and international consumer markets located 200 km or more from the destination are canvassed through PR methods and joint advertising campaigns in partnership with the tourist boards and other interested parties. Reference to Mainau is included in generic advertising for the Lake Constance region, and the island co-operates in joint appearances at fairs and exhibitions which admit the general public.

The trade is also reached through a number of distinct tactics. Direct mail campaigns are undertaken to hotels and guesthouses within the 200 km radius; employees of tourist offices in the region are invited to presentations on the island, and all employees receive a free yearly season ticket for their family. Direct mail campaigns are targeted at tour operators, both in Germany and abroad. The island, working with its Lake Constance partners, is represented at all key trade fairs throughout Europe.

Canvassing of principals is undertaken by a field sales force employed by the island. Six sales representatives are employed, to cover respectively the local region, Britain, France and Spain, Italy and Switzerland, Eastern Europe, and Scandinavia. These representatives, supported by a wide range of merchandising material including posters, brochures and multilingual videos, aim in particular to increase awareness of the destination in their regions through PR measures, and to encourage tour operators to arrange a Lake Constance trip which will include a visit to Mainau. Finally, Mainau is in the process of establishing an incoming travel agency to handle the inbound market generated by these efforts.

Case study 3
Direct marketing in the retail sector: the case of Bakers Dolphin

(Prepared with the help of Gail Izzard, Senior Marketing Manager, Bakers Dolphin Travel)

Background

Bakers Dolphin was formed in Britain in 1984 through the merger of two West Country travel businesses, Baker's Travel and Dolphin Travel. Baker's Travel was an old-established coaching and travel company tracing its origins back to pony-and-chair rides on the beach at Weston-super-Mare in 1889. Dolphin Travel had been founded in the early 1970s, a single retail shop in a Bristol suburb which had survived through the 1970s virtually unchanged.

The merger had resulted from the desire of Baker's Travel to expand further in Bristol, as previously their strength lay in the West Country's market towns. Dolphin Travel at the same time wished to expand outside of Bristol. Both companies recognised the benefits of uniting instead of competing. A second factor was the wish of Dolphin's founder to retire, leaving the company relatively under-capitalised – a problem not shared by the much longer-established Baker's Travel. The merger of the two transformed the company into by far the largest and strongest chain in the area.

Following the acquisition of Dolphin by Baker's in 1984, the company immediately engaged in a programme of expansion and heavy advertising, gaining a strong profile in the area and increasing turnover thirteen-fold in the space of a year. It became the first agency chain in the area to offer inducements to gain market share, by providing free transfers to the local airport, and by the early 1980s it had become the leading independent chain in the region, particularly for the sale of package holidays.

By 1994, with its head office split between Bristol and Weston-super-Mare, and with 43 branches, the group had grown to employ over 400 staff, and was operating 80 of its own coaches. In addition to running a regular scheduled service between Bristol and London in competition with National Express and other local coach operators, it has further developed this sector by establishing a new nationwide coaching operation under the brand name Travel Savers. It has established a new division specialising in arranging holidays to Australia and New Zealand, and a separate division (Wildwings) devoted to providing travel services for birdwatchers; it has also set up a flight consolidator division, Bravo Delta.

The problem

Retail travel had become increasingly competitive throughout the 1980s and early 1990s, as competition from the multiples, heavy discounting and low price package tours cut into profits. The company had already mounted a highly successful campaign to retain their market dominance in the area (see Case Study 3 in the second edition of this textbook) but now accepted that long-term planning and development, involving substantial investment in resources, was necessary for their future success. An evaluation of trends in retailing convinced the company that more emphasis on direct marketing was the key to future sales and profitability. This required that the company review its own current direct marketing activities and determine ways in which these might be strengthened.

The success enjoyed by the company over the previous decade had arisen primarily as a result of aggressive marketing campaigns which encouraged customers to switch from other agencies. The company was concerned that the existing direct mail activity was not sufficient to retain these new customers. It accepted that a proportion of new customers would always book with the agent offering the biggest discount, irrespective of factors such as service and expertise. Nevertheless, it believed that well-targeted direct marketing activity could be effective in retaining much of this new market.

Crucial into this development would be an expansion into telemarketing, both incoming and outgoing. This would give the company a national market without the expense of national advertising. At the same time, it would ensure better targeted, more effective, marketing.

The trend to telesales, in which customers looked to purchase goods and services over the phone, had already been apparent to the marketing team of the company. It offered customers the benefits of simplicity, convenience and low cost.

Implementation of direct marketing activities

Earlier direct marketing had been undertaken, but this was comparatively unsophisticated; shops and staff would largely react to travel enquiries rather than proactively develop new business.

Most Bakers Dolphin shops held on file enquiries from five different market segments: those interested in skiing holidays, those expressing an interest in coach holidays, those seeking to book holidays to Australia, those enquiring about a cruise, and group enquiries. Mailings were made to these customers, but in a somewhat ad-hoc manner, with individual staff using their own personal style in preparing letters. No supervision was carried out of the accuracy of spelling or grammar in out-going letters, nor were they addressed personally. Lack of investment in software meant that the direct mail lists had to be prepared manually – a lengthy

process – nor were mailing lists brought up to date regularly. Furthermore, a marketing weakness was recognised as it became clear that few clients wished to purchase the same or similar products again. Meanwhile, the company was either failing to communicate with the bulk of its regular clients, or where it did communicate, the mailings were not proving effective.

Now the company set out to get new business through its direct marketing activities. Mass leaflet drops, involving up to 750,000 leaflets and segmented by market, were undertaken to reach the company's principal booking markets. Typical of these was the campaign to reach early bookers following the August launch of tour operators' new products. Such campaigns have achieved notable success in boosting awareness of destinations and their appeal to specific markets.

The company had run a telesales department for a number of years, linked to the sale of holiday products sold to credit card holders and villa/apartment owners. Sales to the latter were based on low fares or discounts on flights and car hire. Servicing holiday club members was a further function of this department, and the sales it achieved helped the company to reach the target figures set by tour operators to justify higher incentive commissions. At the same time, this proved to be an effective way of disposing of late availability offers.

A first stage in developing an improved direct marketing section was to invest in the technology necessary to handle much more information. The purchase of a Concord computer system helped to overcome this problem. This was primarily a booking system, therefore the information it carried was up to date, and any changes of address, etc., would be registered automatically. The company was now in a position to access much fuller information about their customers, including the number booked, the type of holiday they took, and the time of year they had travelled.

The second stage involved the development of a new marketing database which recorded all information on bookings made through the company. Key data such as postcodes, ages and

Promotional material for Bakers Dolphin

(Courtesy: Bakers Dolphin)

full details of previous bookings were now available, including information on whether the clients had purchased car hire at the destination or overnight hotel accommodation en route to the destination. The database can be searched to see whether a customer has already booked through Bakers Dolphin for the current year, before any direct mail activity is undertaken.

As an example of how direct mailing is now undertaken, customers who have booked a ski holiday with the company at any point in the previous three years now receive a sales letter when the new skiing holidays brochures become available. This is followed up by a wintersports newsletter at a later date, and finally a third mailing provides the customer with late availability information.

The Travel Savers campaign

In late 1993, the company launched a new direct marketing initiative designed to boost sales to organisers of group travel. Seven telesales staff were each assigned a region of the country, and, working with a private list built up within the firm of some 30,000 organisers, set out to contact these potential customers to offer charter coach trips within the UK and in mainland Europe. Revenue from these sales is boosted by selling optional insurance and excursions tied to the coach charter. In the first year of operation, this initiative is expected to achieve a turnover of over half a million pounds.

Telesales success

Investment of some £50,000 in state-of-the-art telephones have given the company a highly effective telesales operation in its handling of incoming calls. Information which can be logged includes calls answered, calls waiting and how long customers have been waiting, as well as those calls abandoned by callers.

Telesales are coupled with direct mail addressed to 'closed-user' groups and the general public, allowing the company to introduce its specialist lines. Opening times which are convenient for its customers (there is a substantial increase in demand between 7 pm and 8 pm) lead not only to increased sales, but also more flexible staffing hours to meet peak demand. The result is a turnover approaching £4 million in 1994.

Case study 4
The specialist product: letting self-catering cottages through Lakelovers of Cumbria

(Prepared with the help of Carol Latham-Warde, Proprietor of Lakelovers Holiday Homes)

Background

A notable success story in new tourism product development during the 1980s was the growth of self-catering holidays, based on rented cottages, villas or apartments, both in the UK and abroad. Lakelovers is an example of a small, independently owned company which recognised this trend, took the initiative to develop the concept and, after an initial slow growth, has now developed a well-established niche product in the Lake District in north-west England

Lakelovers was founded by Carol Latham-Warde in 1980. As with many small companies, its origins lie with one entrepreneur without expertise in the field but with an eye to changing demand. The business started when Carol rented out her own property through an agent. She herself knew very little about either self-catering or the tourism industry, but she had a legal background and substantial business experience to draw on. With security provided by her husband's job, she could afford to gamble in looking for business opportunities in her area, and soon recognised that many local people seeking to rent out their property to the summer tourist market needed a good agent who would both manage and let out their properties.

In her first year, 1980, Carol let out a flat in her own home, getting the feel of the self-catering business. In the second year, she extended this to the management of five properties in the area, and created the present company name and logo. A leaflet was produced on the home typewriter, with line drawings by a friend, a graphic designer, who helped in the translation of the concept into name and logo. Two cleaners were employed, sufficient for five properties on change-over day (formerly she had cleaned the properties herself). Working in co-operation with her accountant, she was able to route calls to his office, where his staff provided an effective answering service. When the office was closed, or incoming calls could not be answered, Carol installed an answerphone, and made it a point to provide a long, personal message for callers.

By the third year, 1982, the scope for further development had become apparent. At this point, she conveniently met up with an old friend who was in marketing, who offered her helpful marketing advice. In his words, 'pretend you are a customer – try selling to yourself as that customer'. Her previous legal experience, dealing with clients with problems and under stress, made this easy. She now felt sufficiently confident to invest in an advertising campaign, and placed advertisements in the *Daily Mail* and *Daily Telegraph*, along with the *Yorkshire Post*, which brought in business. She joined the Cumbria and Lakeland Self-caterers' Association, and a year later registered with the local tourist board and Tourist Information Centre (TIC).

In 1983, Carol faced the personal trauma of a marriage break-up, and the operation of her business became no longer a sideline but a necessary means of earning her living. Money was invested in the business to employ further staff, including a manager and, eventually, a full-time secretary. An office site was purchased in

Bowness – an old confectionery manufacturing site known as the Toffee Loft – at a cost of £15 000, and additional funds were borrowed to convert it into suitable business premises. By the mid-1980s, Lakelovers had become a small but well-established company acting as agents for a substantial number of properties in the region.

Operating a self-catering holiday letting agency

The company operates not by contract with property owners, but with a simple (and legally binding) 'Letter of Intent'. The company's earnings are made in the form of commissions on lettings; rates of commission vary between 23 per cent and 25 per cent. (The higher rates apply to properties located further away from the company's offices, which increases maintenance and cleaning costs. Distances above nine miles are negotiated individually.)

Lakelovers now deals with some 150 properties in the region, and undertakes between 3500 and 4000 lettings a year. Virtually all sales are made directly with the public. This enables the company to retain some control over the suitability of the customers booked – an important point for those letting their properties through the agency. A clause in the booking conditions allows the company to refuse bookings to those they feel are 'unsuitable'. The company feels that it 'has an ear' for its customers, and certainly, based on 60–70 per cent of its sales being either repeat business or based on personal recommendation, it appears to achieve an excellent match between the clients and the properties rented. A small number of bookings are obtained through agents, especially in Northern Ireland and Scotland.

The quality of the company's brochures has been steadily improved each year, and some 21 000 copies are now printed annually. Of these, 500 are distributed to Tourist Information Centres and other pick-up points in the district.

Some late bookings are obtained through the TICs, who are paid 10 per cent commission, and the few travel agents undertaking bookings are also renumerated with a flat 10 per cent commis-

sion (half of which Lakelovers pays, the other half being paid by the owner of the property). Not all owners are willing to pay this additional 5 per cent to obtain business, however.

The company is often approached by overseas agents who have seen it mentioned in the BTA Marketing Guides. It presently has three agents (based in the USA, the Netherlands and Germany) who select a small number of the properties to include in their own brochures; rental prices are marked up by 10 per cent to cover the added costs of sales through these outlets. Overseas visitors currently comprise only a small number of total bookings (some 2 to 3 per cent) and many of these bookings are made via fax from the USA or Australia, through BTA offices abroad. The continuing relationship with the German agent is in doubt at the time of writing, given the strict German interpretation of the EU Directive on package holidays, which includes severe constraints on direct selling methods and may therefore inhibit the use of European agents.

The company now employs three full-time booking clerks, with two telephone lines and an answerphone line to handle enquiries for brochures. The acquisition of a computerised quick address system speeded up the handling of enquiries. Enquiries and requests for bookings can be taken round-the-clock and throughout the year, apart from two weeks in November when staff visit the properties they are selling. This training through personal experience of the properties is seen as vital to maintain the enthusiasm and loyalty of staff in promoting sales through the company.

The company's advertising message features the theme of 'selected properties, personally managed'. The company will help owners furnish their properties, and provide the basic amenities needed. The cost for this service is held down through Lakelovers having negotiated trade prices for furnishings, making it an attractive proposition for owners. About a quarter of the properties are furnished in this way, and this ensures consistency and standardisation of quality. It also results in easier replacement of items broken or missing.

Advertising and promotion

The company invests some 7–8 per cent of its previous year's turnover in above the line and below the line expenditure, including 3 per cent on advertising spend. The pattern of response to advertising appears difficult to judge, and the company's press advertisements are placed as much to satisfy property owners as to generate new business: many owners complained that they saw more rival advertisements than those for their own properties. Consequently, the company has invested in drip-feeding small ads throughout the year which results in a relatively small number of bookings but acts to reassure the property owners themselves.

The company has tried both direct mail and coupon-response campaigns but found neither very cost-effective. Coupon-response advertising generated a substantial volume of enquiries but few conversions into bookings; as these advertisements required more space in the press, the increased cost was not justified.

As yet, the company has not engaged in formal public relations activities, but will respond to individual travel writers' enquiries by providing free accommodation in properties out of season.

Recent developments

New patterns in bookings have emerged in the early 1990s. The season for bookings has lengthened, with a substantial boost in lettings at Christmas, New Year and the February school half-term holiday. The usual pattern of week-long bookings is giving way to shorter lets, for which a supplementary booking fee is charged, although lettings for less than a week are accepted only at present out of season or as late availability offers during the summer season.

With the growth of properties handled, the company has introduced computers for storage of its bookings, but still does not use computers to check availability. As Carol herself puts it, 'the computer simply doesn't allow one so quickly or effectively to glance at a sheet and find alternative accommodation which will suit the needs of the client'. However, once a booking is confirmed, full details are entered into the computer.

Lakelovers recognises that, as well as having its advantages, there are also disadvantages in being small – not least, in the shortage of finance for investment and, in a competitive environment which inhibits expansion of staff, the added pressures this creates on the existing small team. The marketing focus has to be on the theme of 'small but beautiful', with a strong emphasis on high and consistent quality and personal service. So far, as witness the high level of repeat bookings and recommendations, this has created an environment in which the company can prosper. Customers are provided with 'questionnaires' left in their properties, inviting suggestions for improvement. These are, in fact, requests for comments and suggestions which are cunningly combined with a meter reading sheet, ensuring that virtually all will be returned to the office anyway. Few other forms of research could be expected to achieve such a high rate of return, and the fact that these responses also indicate exceptionally high levels of customer satisfaction is confirmation that the programme is a good illustration of a market-orientated company.

Case study 5
A new approach to retailing travel: Marco Polo Travel Advisory Service

(Prepared with the help of Polly Davies, Proprietor of Marco Polo Travel Advisory Service)

Background

Polly Davies formed Marco Polo as a sole trader in 1989. She had had substantial experience of travel and work abroad, and was at that time employed by Trailfinders, arranging bookings for long-haul flights and overland tours for independent travellers. She recognised that there was an inevitable conflict in the way in which travel sales were transacted through retail agencies, with customers seeking information and advice from their agent, while agents themselves were necessarily more concerned with selling flights and overland tours and speeding up transactions, in order to improve their turnover and remain profitable in the very competitive environment in which retail travel was now operating.

To substantiate her belief in this market gap, Polly undertook a small research exercise, taking advantage of another marketing strength she possessed – a circle of well-connected young, mainly single, and relatively well-off professional friends in London and Bristol. These she saw as the prime market for a new kind of travel retailer, who could provide knowledgeable advice and information for a fee. The idea shares some similarities with the US concept of Certified Travel Counsellors, who, having demonstrated their expertise through formal vocational examinations, can charge for consultations with their clients planning tailor-made travel arrangements. This form of specialist agency has operated for a number of years in North America, but has not taken off in the UK up till now.

Polly distributed 150 questionnaires among friends and their contacts, and a good response (about 60 per cent) was obtained. The information provided convinced her that current levels of service in travel agents were proving inadequate to meet the growing needs of 'independent' travellers, and that – at least on paper – most people would be willing to pay a fee of up to £25 for a consultation with a knowledgeable expert, in addition to their travel costs.

The launch and growth of Marco Polo

Polly initially worked for a while as an accountancy clerk in order to save sufficient money to launch her new project. Then, supported by the evidence of her research, she applied for and received an award under the national Enterprise Allowance Scheme which was in operation at that time. The £40 a week government grant allocated for the first year of her business was supplemented by her own investment of £2000 to launch the company (mainly to cover the cost of acquiring a computer). Initially, she planned to operate from her own home.

Her initial investment in marketing was tiny. With the limited amount of capital available, Polly recognised that it would be impractical to launch a national advertising campaign. Instead, she produced a simple six-page two-fold leaflet setting out the philosophy behind the project – an organisation of integrity, knowledge based on many years' experience of travel and work in the industry, and Fellowship of the Royal Geographical Society. This leaflet, with a covering letter, was distributed to her earlier questionnaire respondents, inviting names and addresses of other contacts who might be interested in such a service. A reply paid coupon was included in the leaflet.

The establishment of a clientele was painfully slow; in the first year, around 50 clients were dealt with. Contact was made through the telephone, and those clients seeking a personal meeting were given appointments either in her home, or with consultants that she had recruited, who could offer specialist expertise, such as knowledge of mountaineering or cycling opportunities. Her own network of friends was to prove invaluable in developing this network of consultants, who are now distributed throughout the country. The real challenge of the job at this point was to persuade prospective clients, who expected to be able to walk into a traditional

MARCO POLO TRAVEL ADVISORY SERVICE

NEWSLETTER AUTUMN 1994

AITO 100 CLUB

The Association of Independent Tour Operators (AITO) was founded in 1976 by a group of small, specialist tour operators who saw the need for coming together as a group to promote their products. The organisation has grown in numbers and stature over the years and now provides a bonding facility for members. Many of the tour operators represented by Marco Polo are AITO members and it is an organisation for which we have a great deal of respect - in fact we have been trying to persuade them to take travel agent members for some time!

Recently AITO has recognised the advantages of working in association with chosen specialist agencies and have launched The AITO 100 Club. Marco Polo is pleased to announce that we have accepted the invitation to join this select band of 100 Travel Agents and look forward to working with both old AITO friends as well as new ones in the future.

This means that Marco Polo will be able to offer a broader choice of interesting specialist holidays, particularly villa holidays in Europe as well as more unusual activity holidays worldwide, such as swimming with dolphins, whale watching, truffle hunting, wine drinking and language learning. We will keep you posted of these developments in future newsletters.

We continue to represent all our old tour operators so still offer a wide variety of tried and tested tours, treks, safaris, overland expeditions, walking holidays and tropical beaches.

CHINA AND HONG KONG

A few words from Polly who has just returned from a trip to China and Hong Kong: "China is a vast country offering enormous variety - deserts, mountains, lush forests as well as the well-known sights of the Great Wall, Grand Canal, Forbidden City and Summer Palace and the dramatic landscape of Guilin. Independent traveller China tend to stress the difficulties expe with getting around and communicati booked independent travel arrangem advance. After a long flight it is co know that you do not have to con and hotel bookings. Because of decided not to spend my time instead based myself on a sm a strong connection with th religious life of ancient Ch The kindness and charm overwhelming - I even me across a busy roa

A week in Hong K Frantic commerci gastronomic exp space on pave and magnific bronze stat experienc thinking go now immi

AIR PASSENGER DUTY

Last year's budget paved the way for the introduction of Air Passenger Duty which will become payable on 01 November 1994. Details of payment and collection have not yet been finalised but be prepared to pay an additional £5 on European flights and £10 on Intercontinental flights for all departures on or after that date.

THE BRISTOL TRAVELLERS' CLUB

Future meetings of the club, which is run by Marco Polo, include talks on Argentina, the remote Kamchatka Peninsula in Russia, Rumania, Travels in Thailand with Children, India, Java and the Baltic Republics. As active members of Tourism Concern we always aim to promote awareness of responsible tourism and many of the talks inspire discussion on this subject which is an integral part of the Marco Polo philosophy.

For dates and further information please call us on 0272 294123.

WOMEN & TRAVEL SEMINARS
Getting Going and Staying Safe

The one-day Women and Travel Seminars, now in their 4th year, continue to attract great media interest. Some of you may have seen Polly Davies' appearance on Granada TV's Travellers' Checks in May, heard her on BBC Radio or read about the Seminars in The Guardian, Telegraph or Independent. As well as media interest the seminars continue to attract participants from all over the country and postcards to the Marco Polo office from all over the world from women inspired to set off on their own adventure.

If you have friends thinking of setting off please mention the seminars as it may give them extra encouragement as well as practical advice on staying safe. The next one takes place in Bristol on October 1994. Ring us for a Programme on 0272 294123.

MARCO POLO TRAVEL ADVISORY SERVICE

Are you an imaginative and independent traveller looking for an extra dimension to your holiday?

Do you need a travel agent who can answer all your questions and fulfil all your travel requirements?

For the complete travel service come to the experts. We can help you decide.

**WHERE TO GO
HOW TO GO
WHAT TO DO**

MARCO POLO
TRAVEL ADVISORY SERVICE

The travel experts who offer you more!

24A PARK STREET, BRISTOL BS1 5JA
TEL: 0272 294123 FAX: 0272 292972

ABTA

Promotional material for Marco Polo Travel Advisory Service

(Courtesy: Marco Polo Travel Advisory Service)

travel shop, to accept this highly untraditional method of consulting their travel agent – via a home telephone and a system of appointments.

Polly expected to do little more than survive in the first 18 months. However, she married in 1990, moving to Bristol. With her husband a practising solicitor, she no longer needed to be totally self-sufficient, and invested her slender profits in building up the business. The success of her venture enabled her to open an office in Bristol in 1992.

Fees are based on a set charge (at the time of writing, £30 per hour), and that this was seen as good value by clients is evident from the growth of business during the 1990s. In 1994 the company dealt with nearly 1100 clients, of whom 95 per cent are either repeat clients or arrive through word of mouth recommendation.

Limited budget marketing

A small company such as this can never expect to generate sufficient funds to undertake a national marketing campaign on a major scale to reach the niche market clients who might be interested in its services. Consequently, Polly has wisely chosen to maintain an emphasis on direct marketing activities, backed up by substantial free publicity achieved through media coverage.

The leaflet remains the key promotional tool, and this is now supported with a regular newsletter providing information about destinations and new services. The newsletter is useful in drawing attention to the services provided by the company for women travelling alone, a newly recognised niche market. Women and travel seminars are organised four times a year in Bristol; these are designed to build confidence through sensible and practical advice, and they have proved very popular. These seminars also form a useful vehicle for press releases, and are well publicised as a result. Apart from the local press, *The Times, Daily Telegraph, Guardian, Independent, Sunday Times, Observer* and the *European* have all run features on the company, and Polly has appeared on Granada TV, as well as the BBC's *Breakaway* and other radio programmes devoted to travel issues. A weekend *Telegraph* article which appeared one week before a seminar not only filled the seminar but also drew an additional 80 enquiries about the service. Seminars in turn produce a good mailing list for potential future business.

Apart from these techniques, a small amount of advertising is undertaken – in the Yellow Pages, and the local magazine *Venue* – but the other key promotion is participation in the Independent Travel Show. This was originally a public exhibition for alternative travellers based once a year in Bristol, but is now staged twice a year – once in London, and once in Bristol. She also speaks at these exhibitions on the potential and pitfalls of being a woman traveller; this has proved to be a major draw for exhibition visitors, attracting audiences of 250 or more.

The company is now a member of ABTA and the '100 Club' of the Association of Independent Tour Operators (AITO), membership of which is made up of smaller independent specialist agencies. In addition to consultancy fees, revenue is achieved through commission on air tickets and tours. The company does not package its own tours, but works with small specialist operators to develop tailor-made arrangements for its clients. Success has meant that many small operators are now keen to work with them. While remaining small, the company has expanded to take on one full-time and two part-time consultants at the Bristol office, and is now proving self-sufficient.

Case study 6
Image and reality: promoting RCI through public relations

(A case study prepared in collaboration with Jane Evans, Head of Corporate Affairs, RCI Europe Ltd)

Background

It is hard to imagine a tourism activity with greater contradictions than timeshare: an almost universal bad press, with a correspondingly poor public image, yet one which delivers high levels of consumer satisfaction, and has become one of the fastest growing sectors of the industry.

Timeshare has been described as one of tourism's best kept secrets. The activities of exchange company RCI are an even better kept secret – or at least, they were, until 1991 when RCI set out to change things.

RCI is an unusual business. The company offers a service to timeshare owners (RCI 'members') allowing them to swap the holiday weeks they own for alternative weeks in different resort properties around the world. To become a member of RCI, consumers must buy one or more weeks of timeshare in a resort affiliated to the RCI network. Once enrolled as RCI members, they can choose each year either to return to their own resort at the specified time, or to request an alternative from among the 2700 properties affiliated to RCI.

This idea of timeshare exchange is such an attractive one that it is regularly cited as the most important reason why people buy timeshare.

The success of the concept can be demonstrated by the fact that by 1994, more than 1.7 million families had become members of RCI; in 1993 the company had been responsible for arranging the holidays of some 4 million people around the world.

RCI's customers also offer confirmation of success. Regular customer satisfaction surveys have consistently revealed around 85 per cent of members are satisfied or very satisfied with the service they receive. Moreover, satisfaction with the timeshare purchase and its use is graphically demonstrated by the fact that one-third of the new enrolments into RCI's system in the UK are from existing timeshare owners who have bought more weeks.

However, the fact is that the company is working within a very negative business climate because it is part of the timeshare industry. That negative image has principally been generated because of the hard-sell methods of a small number of rogues in the timeshare business who use high-pressure methods to lure unsuspecting consumers into sales presentations. Often, the consumer does not actually buy or experience the timeshare product itself – but is left with a bad impression of the business.

For many years, other players in the timeshare business have looked to RCI to work on the negative image of the industry as a whole. Although RCI is not a 'timeshare company' in that it does not build, sell or run timeshare resorts, the company has commercial relationships with developers, marketers and financiers of timeshare resorts (through its affiliated properties). Given that the company also has a relationship with timeshare owners (the RCI members), RCI occupies a pivotal position within the industry. It is also one of the biggest single entities in timeshare, with its 56 offices and 3 500 employees worldwide.

For a long time, however, RCI in the UK did not desire any promotion outside of its immediate business circle. There was no point in advertising, the argument went, because RCI did not sell its product direct to the consumer. The company's reputation with both developers and members was high. There was no need to go outside this circle and risk being tarred with the same brush as timeshare in general. The expenditure needed and the risk to be taken were just too great.

In time, however, this view changed. The pressure from other players became irresistible. Legislation was threatened, and if the industry was not very careful, legislators would make decisions based on the poor image and not on the reality of a successful and popular concept of timeshare plus exchange.

It was time to tell the world how timeshare worked and where exchange fitted into the picture.

A profile-raising exercise

The proposed profile-raising exercise was no easy proposition. First, the brief. Not the usual marketing support brief (because, remember, RCI has no product to sell direct to the consumer). More a corporate affairs exercise, to influence the whole climate of opinion about timeshare and RCI – with the marketing aspect as an important spin-off, since a better climate of opinion ought to lead to more sales of timeshare.

RCI therefore decided that public relations, rather than advertising or promotions, was the route to take. A public relations manager was appointed, based at RCI's European and UK headquarters in Kettering, Northamptonshire. She was selected on the basis of her background in politics and the public sector, having worked with exactly the people RCI decided it wanted to influence. She was also well used to handling a difficult brief – and she happened to be a time-share owner and RCI member!

Public relations is, by its nature, a long-term exercise. Few PR campaigns can have the instant effect that high profile advertising or marketing does. Campaign evaluation is made in terms of years, not months. Phrases such as 'drip-drip' and 'building bricks' come to mind.

It is also very important, when judging the likely success of a PR campaign, to take account of the background against which it is carried out.

PR's role is to create the climate against which sales can be made, good legislation drafted, investors encouraged to enter the business – or whatever the final objective is. Good PR sets the scene, generates understanding about an organisation, business or industry. PR is the art of getting other people to say good things about your organisation instead of saying them yourself. PR happens anyway: if the communications of an organisation are not managed to the benefit of that organisation, they do not simply go away. Communications still happen. Perceptions are still formed. And they might just be the wrong ones.

That was the problem which RCI faced: the immense amount of negative press coverage about timeshare had already created a background which would interfere with the positive messages which the company wanted to promote. Moreover, the negative coverage of timeshare was not invented by the press. Most of the reports were actually true, based on incidents which really did take place.

A journalist who takes a regular interest in timeshare matters, Jeremy Gates of the *Daily Express*, once commented that the trouble with writing a positive article about timeshare was that he was promptly inundated with letters from unhappy consumers relating their negative experiences. Needless to say, when he wrote a negative article, he was not inundated with happy timeshare owners writing to tell him how contented they were!

It was not possible, therefore, for RCI to deny the negatives – the public would see through that. Nor could they try to defend indefensible actions on the part of some rogues. But this goes further. Nor could the company try to stand up and say, 'timeshare is good really, despite the cowboys' (a statement which the company earnestly believes): it would simply not be believed. The campaign would have to be much more subtle in its approach.

First, there had to be an acknowledgement that the negatives did exist. The company would do itself no good by denying it. Next, there had to be a clear definition of what the positive message should be – and what it realistically could be. And of course there had to be an identification of the target audiences to be reached.

One thing RCI could not do – despite pressure to the contrary from various sectors of the industry – was to act as a spokesperson for the whole industry. This was the role, not of any one company occupying a particular niche, but of the embryonic and developing trade association, the Timeshare Council. Indeed, it could be said that part of RCI's PR exercise, and a part that had been going on for some years, was its active support for that association.

Strategy

The following objective was set:

> to address and influence positively all audiences, trades and professions which impact on RCI's business and on which RCI impacts. Further, to show by implication that there is a good and responsible core to the timeshare industry, which will help to alleviate the industry's consistently bad image in the UK.

The statement of objectives affirmed strongly that it was 'NOT single-handedly to represent the industry publicly, nor to defend the indefensible'.

The objective was to position RCI as

- a major player in the leisure, travel and tourism industry
- a quality organisation
- a 'blue chip' company, part of the business 'establishment'.

The strategy was therefore articulated as follows:

> To raise the profile of RCI (in the UK) through the press and through direct contact with target audiences and individuals, demonstrating by showing what we do that RCI is a large, successful, important, ethical, well-established company.

Tactics

The tactics used during the first part of the PR campaign (the first two years) were principally those of a corporate or business to business campaign, promoting RCI as a company and aimed at opinion formers more than consumers.

A list of target audiences was drawn up. This included:

- *the press*: local, national (travel and business correspondents), regional, sectoral
- *politicians*: MPs, MEPs, civil servants, councillors and their advisers
- *the professions*: solicitors, banks, finance houses
- *public bodies and enforcers*: Office of Fair Trading, trading standards officers, Consumers' Association, Advertising Standards Authority, Citizens' Advice Bureaux and others whose job it is to receive complaints
- *travel and tourism*: hotels, tourist boards, ABTA
- *business groups*: Chambers of Commerce, Confederation of British Industry (CBI), Institute of Directors
- *the education world*, with emphasis on academics engaged in travel and tourism work.

Tactically, RCI decided to raise its profile slowly and gradually, rather than in one great burst which was likely to be more expensive but which was also much more likely to backfire. Consequently, a relatively modest budget of around £100 000 was set for PR projects.

One of the priorities was to talk to the opinion formers direct, by inviting them to visit RCI's European and UK headquarters in Kettering, Northamptonshire. This exercise was to pay dividends far in excess of the considerable time and energy expended; any image of a back-street cowboy operation was dispelled by impressions gained of the new £10 million building, while personal contact with some of the 500 staff who worked there convinced the visitors of the quality of the personnel and their dedication to customer service. The level of investment in the industry was apparent when visitors were shown the highly sophisticated, state-of-the-art international computer systems which controlled RCI's global exchange business. Opinion formers such as the Director-General of Fair Trading, the local MP, the editor of *Travel Weekly* and the managing director of Anglia Television were in this

(a)

(b)

(c)

(d)

Components of RCI's public relations campaign: (a) opinion formers invited to RCI's European and UK headquarters; (b) RCI's seminar for travel and tourism course tutors; (c) and (d) raising RCI's profile through national advertising and promotional campaigns.
(Courtesy: RCI Europe Ltd)

way given reason to believe that the timeshare business could be serious, ethical and highly successful.

The computer systems spearheaded another line of attack. This was the tactic of securing press coverage about various aspects of RCI's corporate life, quite divorced from the nature of its business. A major feature placed in *Which*

Computer magazine demonstrated the kind of hardware and software used by RCI to meet its needs, exemplifying a company ahead of its field in the use of technology, and which also happened to be involved in timeshare.

Further publicity was secured through an article in the *Financial Times*, covering the company's employment policies relating to pregnancy and maternity leave, an issue which the company had had to tackle with some urgency, given that the majority of its workforce was female and aged in their mid-twenties. Again, the responsible way in which the company had approached this issue demonstrated a commitment to ethical business practice. Coverage was gained in a prestigious newspaper without laying too much emphasis on the timeshare angle.

This was followed by a write-up in *The Linguist* (a specialist magazine for translaters) illustrating the company's international activities by featuring the work of its multilingual publications team.

These 'oblique' approaches to press coverage went some way to countering the reluctance on the part of some journalists to cover timeshare as a story. However, the task of persuading newspapers and magazines to carry timeshare pieces was, and is, an ongoing part of RCI's PR activity. The editor of the BBC *Holidays* magazine was persuaded that timeshare exchange was a form of holidaytaking worth the attention of a member of her staff, and a positive article resulted; an article about timeshare was initiated in *Business Life*, the British Airways in-flight business magazine; the *Sunday Express* has carried an article about RCI's activities and the timeshare business. All positive, and all the result of a huge amount of proactive PR work.

Intelligence as to who is planning to write articles about timeshare is part of the PR campaign. Because of its key role in the industry, RCI is a fund of facts and figures about timeshare generally and is able to provide a constant stream of information to illustrate timeshare's success. This stream is not only directed at journalists. RCI also gives a great deal of help to the writers of reports and surveys on timeshare specifically, and on tourism generally. Mintel's report on timeshare published in 1993 contained much background information from RCI. The Economist Intelligence Unit has twice published a review of the European timeshare industry written by RCI's managing director, and a similar report has been published by *Tourism Management*. A digest of information about the timeshare industry worldwide and in Europe

was put together by RCI and circulated, this time through the trade association, to politicians all over Europe.

Seminars have been used to raise the profile of the company and its business and to reach some of the target audiences direct. A seminar for people involved in the hospitality industry was staged at the World Travel Market in London. This achieved two objectives, as well as addressing key people: RCI was able to establish a presence at WTM, thus positioning itself as part of the travel industry.

Another exercise based around a seminar was the drive to reach academics. RCI's long-term thinking requires that future travel and tourism professionals understand the timeshare business and are aware of how it works. RCI therefore selected the principals of university tourism courses and invited them to take part in a seminar, held at a timeshare resort, to brief them on the growth, marketing and operation of the business. The seminar was accompanied by a set of course notes giving background information on the industry and designed to be used when planning courses. The idea was that aspects of the information could be incorporated into different course units to ensure that timeshare was seen as an intrinsic part of the travel industry. The seminar also included a visit to RCI's offices.

Addressing conference audiences is another important part of RCI's PR campaign. An international tourism conference, a management seminar or an address to business studies students again all establish RCI as a company that matters.

Creating a presence at the professional conferences of key target audiences has been an important and useful exercise. For example, the professional institute of trading standards officers holds an annual conference with an associated exhibition. RCI has taken a stand there for two consecutive years, appearing in conjunction with the Timeshare Council. The number of conference delegates visiting the stand to speak to RCI did not drop from one year to the next. However, the number of awkward questions and complaints almost disappeared between one year and the next. In 1994, RCI coupled the conference stand with an organised visit for a small group of delegates to the nearest timeshare resort. The guests were shown around the resort, not by sales people but by timeshare owners, who were able to explain in their own words why they found the product so good. And, of course, the guests saw with their own eyes the high quality of the timeshare accommodation.

Evaluation

Two years into the PR campaign, RCI was confident that the image of its business was improving. Some external factors helped: a reduction almost to zero in the use of direct mail by timeshare companies virtually cut out the negative newspaper stories about timeshare sales presentations; legislation coupled with the recession caused some of the more aggressive timeshare sales companies to pull out of the UK market, which may not have been good for the business, but helped the image problem; and the sheer number of people who had now come to own timeshare – over 250 000 in the UK alone – meant that most people knew someone with direct experience of happy timeshare holidays.

The extensive press monitoring exercise carried out by RCI revealed that negative stories about timeshare had been significantly reduced. There were almost no articles appearing which described disappointed families attending unpleasant and high-pressure sales presentations. The small number of critical stories that continued to appear were concerned with specific timeshare companies causing easily identifiable problems.

The academic world heard the message, resulting in an increase in the number of invitations received by RCI to attend universities and colleges to make presentations to students about the timeshare business. Politicians, too, had become more willing to listen to the case the industry was attempting to make: during discussions on the draft EU Directive on timeshare, for example, a proposed penal cooling off period of 28 days was reduced to a much more acceptable 10 days.

The press, too, had started to take notice. Some of the more adamant representatives of the travel press had come to acknowledge that timeshare was a growing force which they should be covering from time to time. The result was that articles began to appear in the *Travel Trade Gazette* as well as in national papers such as the *Sunday Express*.

The next stage

At the time of writing, the campaign is ongoing. Success up to this point, coupled with an improving business climate, suggest that the future direction of the campaign can be bolder. A more proactive press campaign has been launched, and a number of editors of the national press have been persuaded to run articles on timeshare exchange, as well as on RCI itself. Advertising is being used to supplement the PR activities, with a generic-style campaign in conjunction with a number of magazines, mainly the Sunday colour supplements. These are run in collaboration with several of RCI's affiliated resorts, and are designed to encourage readers to send for more information about buying timeshare, and about the specific properties. Competition-style promotions are being mounted in national newspapers, with timeshare holidays as prizes.

However, much remains to be done to improve the image of timeshare. RCI's budget for this is relatively small, given the magnitude of the task, but achievements to date have been notable, and have reinforced the view that a sustained PR campaign is an essential tool in building the future of the timeshare business.

Case study 7
Destination marketing and the USP: the City of Nottingham

(Prepared with the help of Phil Nodding, Tourism Manager, City of Nottingham Leisure and Community Services)

Making the most of Robin Hood!

Destination marketing is nothing new, but the promotion of cities as tourist and conference locations has become a competitive and technical business since the 1980s. Nottingham's Unique Selling Proposition (USP) was its world-wide reputation for being the home of Robin Hood, but in the mid-1980s Nottingham, situated in the centre of England, could offer no 4 star hotels, no conference facilities and no commercial tourist attractions.

In less than ten years the city saw a dramatic increase in both tourism infrastructure and visitor numbers. Ten new hotels with over 2000 bed spaces, two major conference venues, three major tourist attractions drawing in an extra 250 000 paying visitors each year, and an annual programme of over 200 events have changed the face of Nottingham tourism.

In 1991, Nottingham won the British Tourist Authority's UK Tourism Marketing Award for its work around the *Robin Hood – Prince of Thieves* film. In 1992, the city was awarded the East Midlands Tourist Board's Resort of the Year Award. In 1993, Nottingham won the English Tourist Board's England for Excellence 'Holiday Destination of the Year' Award for its work in tourism promotion.

Success on such a scale is due to a complex combination of initiatives and hard work by a number of individuals, but the Robin Hood Film Campaign gives an interesting insight into the methods employed to exploit a particular product USP and media opportunity. The marketing campaign carried out to achieve this was extensive and complex, and comprises a number of elements which are examined in this case study.

Movie magic

In 1991 Kevin Costner's *Robin Hood – Prince of Thieves* became an unexpected world box office success. Before the film had even finished production, however, Nottingham City's Tourism and Marketing team had started planning joint promotions with the film's distributors and national cinema chains to fully exploit the visitor potential that renewed Robin Hood publicity offered the city.

Although Nottingham boasted a famous castle, a new Robin Hood visitor centre (opened 1989) attracting 200 000 visitors per year, and two Robin Hood festivals (one in Sherwood Forest in August and one at Nottingham Castle in October), it needed a boost to put all these ventures on a sound commercial footing. The film would undoubtedly have had some small effect on visitor figures to the area without the joint promotion, but a concerted effort to exploit every business angle was what turned hype into measurable economic impact.

The opportunity: the *Prince of Thieves* film première

Background

As far back as August 1990 the City Tourism Office became aware that two Robin Hood films were in pre-production. In September 1990, it was confirmed that Kevin Costner was to star in Morgan Creek's production *Robin Hood – Prince of Thieves*, and that Patrick Bergin was to head the cast in Twentieth Century Fox's version, called simply *Robin Hood*.

Nottingham City Council decided to contact the film companies to offer 'historical advice', details on possible locations, and joint publicity opportunities. The prestige of a European première of a Robin Hood film in Nottingham itself, and in the presence of the real-life Sheriff of Nottingham, was also suggested.

Strategy

The objective was to link in with the massive world-wide publicity machine behind each film and to gain prominent exposure of the Robin Hood product in Nottingham.

National Amusements UK Ltd, developers of the Showcase Cinemas chain in the UK, had built their first and most successful multi-screen cinema in Nottingham and had always experienced a good working relationship with the local authority Tourism Office. With their US connections it made them the obvious choice as partners in the bid for the première. Their Vice-President of Publicity used his influence in the USA to suggest various Nottingham-linked promotional opportunities, and to identify the most successful film. He established that Kevin Costner's version of the Robin Hood story was to be the more popular because of the cast, script and its massive publicity budget.

In January 1991 Nottingham Tourism Office decided to put the majority support into association with the *Prince of Thieves* version. Meetings were soon held in London between National Amusements, Morgan Creek, Warner Bros (the film distributors), and the City.

Pre-première publicity

The promotional company chosen by Warner Bros to publicise *Prince of Thieves* was keen on a première in Nottingham, with a party afterwards at Nottingham Castle. The initial bid to the US directors of Morgan Creek to host the première was made by the Sheriff, and helped to tip the balance.

Prior to the film's release a whole package of competitions, photo-opportunities, news stories, and a comprehensive advertising schedule were produced. Media invitations for the première were sent out with an arrow and a signed scroll from the Sheriff of Nottingham.

The première press launch

On 19 July 1991 there was a champagne breakfast for national journalists at the 800-year-old 'Trip to Jerusalem', purported to be the oldest inn in England, hewn into Nottingham Castle rock. A local medieval re-enactment group, 'Black Knights', were assigned the task of providing atmosphere for the day. Following a breakfast, the 'Black Knights' raided the Inn and rounded up the journalists, taking them into the Castle via Mortimer's Hole, a vast tunnel leading from the foot of the Castle Rock. The journalists were ushered into the Sheriff's room in Nottingham Castle for an audience with the Sheriff of Nottingham. Later, over lunch, they were able to interview actors from the film.

The première

The evening saw the charity première of the film at the Showcase Cinema. Many stars were present including Alan Rickman, who played the evil Sheriff, and who was introduced to the real Sheriff of Nottingham, creating another photo-opportunity. The 1200 guests were greeted by a medieval guard of honour outside the cinema.

The post-première party

Celebrities, civic dignitaries and film executives attended a special private party in the Long Gallery at Nottingham Castle. The VIP guests arrived at the Castle to be greeted by minstrels and fire eaters as they arrived through an avenue of flaming torches.

Evaluation

The première achieved wide publicity in both local and national media. The benefits are unquantifiable, but helped to provide a link to the general Robin Hood awareness campaign surrounding the film. The successful organisation of the event helped to develop the idea of Nottingham as a new media centre with the ability to attract film premières and other key media events. The potential of Nottingham Castle as a major function venue was also proven.

Awareness campaign

In conjunction with the film première of *Robin Hood – Prince of Thieves*, a full-scale public awareness campaign was launched, comprising the following aspects:

- regional press weekend
- national and international press coverage
- Robin Hood film campaign
- product building and trade liaison
- Robin Hood Rate 1991
- co-operative campaign with British Midland Airways
- BTA familiarisation visit
- consumer promotion.

Each part of the promotional campaign will now be described.

Regional press weekend

Objectives

This was a familiarisation 'Robin Hood Weekend', aimed at regional journalists. The objective was to target regional newspapers to run articles about products in Nottingham, particularly the discount 'Robin Hood Rate' and the selection of special themed weekends including 'In Search of Robin Hood' in July and October. The opportunity was also taken to highlight the area's many other attractions.

Strategy

The target market was the British domestic market, particularly families. The overall budget was £2100 to cover coach transport, guiding services, photography and entertainment. It was funded jointly by the City and County Tourism Offices. The private sector was closely involved and provided most services free of charge. Accommodation and the farewell lunch reception were hosted by two city centre hotels. 'The Tales of Robin Hood' gave free admission and a new ground handler hosted and ran a medieval banquet in conjunction with a local hotel. Rangers at Sherwood Forest Visitor Centre provided an informative tour of the forest.

Evaluation

The weekend was very positively received by the guests, many of whom claimed to be pleasantly surprised at the diversity of facilities and products on offer in Nottingham.

Articles appeared in the following papers:

Scarborough Evening News
Plymouth Evening Herald
Café Society
South Wales Argos
Blackpool Evening Gazette (special Robin Hood feature)
Bournemouth Evening Echo
Esher and Elmbridge and *Leatherhead and Mole Valley Couriers*
Ealing and Southall Informer
Middlesborough Evening Gazette (special pull-out feature)

The BBC World Service broadcast a half-hour programme on Nottingham and the Robin Hood legend. The newspaper articles alone equate to over £12 000, based on standard advertising rates.

National and international press coverage

Objective

To gain maximum free exposure in the media on the Nottingham holiday product in the wake of two Robin Hood films.

Strategy

To respond positively to any requests for interviews, press visits, photographs or articles on Robin Hood or Nottingham, and to actively seek the attention of local, regional, national and international press.

Evaluation

Both tourism offices experienced an increased number of calls relating to Robin Hood and the area in relation to the new films. A number of journalists and film crew, and radio broadcasters visited the area to do stories based on the real Nottingham behind the Robin Hood legend. Assistance was rendered to radio and film crews from the UK, USA (CBS), and the Middle East. As well as visits from domestic journalists, others visited from Japan, the Netherlands, North America, Europe, and from Reuters News Agency.

Over 1000 column inches of copy were written on Nottingham as a tourism destination, including articles appearing in *In Britain* magazine, *Journo do Brasil* and the *New York Times Première*.

Robin Hood film campaign

Objectives

Following the resurgence of interest in Robin Hood after the general release of the two major films in the summer of 1991, a further marketing initiative was undertaken by the City of Nottingham. The objective was to link the interest in the films with leisure and holiday visits to the city and county, thus reinforcing the public's association of Robin Hood with Nottingham. The target markets were cinema-goers and those living in the West Midlands who were aware of the films but had not actually seen them.

Cinema-goers

Showcase Cinema agreed to a series of exhibitions and associated literature was produced and displayed in their cinemas nationwide. The message 'You've seen the film, now live the legend in Robin Hood's Nottinghamshire' reached a predominantly young, cinema-going audience.

West Midlands residents

Survey work carried out in 1990 at Sherwood Forest Visitor Centre showed that despite its vast population, the West Midlands was a poor visitor-generating region for Nottingham. The area was therefore chosen for an outdoor poster campaign to help redress this situation and to maximise the effects of the new M42 Birmingham to Nottingham motorway link road. The new connection added potentially some 3 million extra visitors within an hour's drive of the county.

Exhibitions and leaflets

Emblazoned with the slogan 'You've seen the film, now live the legend', eight full-colour panelled exhibitions were produced featuring shots of Kevin Costner, Patrick Bergin, Sherwood Forest Visitor Centre, Nottingham Castle, The Tales of Robin Hood and the Robin Hood Festival. These were displayed at Showcase Cinemas in Nottingham, Birmingham, Leeds, Manchester, Liverpool and Peterborough from mid-July to the beginning of October. They were accompanied by a leaflet in the same style, with stills of past and present Robin Hood films and copy which focused interest on Nottingham attractions linked with Robin Hood. Each of the 25 000 leaflets distributed included a Freepost coupon response for further information, along with a 'where did you pick this up?' question.

Outdoor posters

Adopting the corporate campaign and design style, a four-sheet poster campaign was undertaken at main railway stations throughout the West Midlands between mid-July and mid-September. The campaign took the form of two companion posters positioned alongside each other depicting a selection of Robin Hood film reel cases and attractions in Nottingham depicting Robin Hood.

Product building and trade liaison

Objectives

Essential to the success of many of the initiatives relating to the release of *Prince of Thieves* was the relationship and co-operation between the public and private sector. The objective was to provide an attractive themed product to sell to the consumer and travel trade.

Local trade liaison

Initial discussions were held between tourism officers, hotel managers of the city's main hotels, and other private sector companies including the attraction 'The Tales of Robin Hood' and Heritage Classics, a specialist ground handling agent. There were three main ideas idea behind this liaison:

1   To ensure that all sectors were aware of plans and promotions relating to the release of the Robin Hood films.
2   To elicit support from the private sector for the initiatives that were being planned. These included complimentary weekend breaks and free or discounted entry to 'The Tales of Robin Hood', with a complimentary banquet to use as competition prizes for journalists on familiarisation visits.
3   To identify the need for a county-wide discounted product that would encourage visitors to the area and so compete effectively with discount offers available in other areas.

The award-winning Robin Hood film campaign for Nottingham and Phil Nodding, Tourism Manager for Nottingham City Council, receiving the UK Tourism Marketing Award

(Courtesy: City of Nottingham Leisure and Community Services and Martin I. Ellis Associates)

The resulting 'Robin Hood Rate' scheme was an excellent example of local trade liaison and product building.

The promotion also led to the establishment of the Greater Nottingham Hoteliers' Association, membership of which was composed of hotel general managers. This association serves to maintain and build upon the initial relationships made, to continue the established initiatives and to develop new ones.

Robin Hood Rate 1991

Objectives

To produce, in conjunction with the private sector, a discounted package available throughout the area and an incentive to encourage weekend and longer stay visitors to come to Nottingham.

Strategy

A special accommodation rate of £25 per person per night was introduced for bed and breakfast, available on weekend nights at a choice of fourteen top hotels. Children under 14 sharing their parents' room were charged £5 for bed and breakfast. This was available on Friday and Saturday evenings throughout the year and every day in August. The rate was at all times subject to availability, and acceptance of bookings was at the discretion of the individual hotel. The scheme included a free information pack and discount vouchers for 'The Tales of Robin Hood'.

PHASE I

A sales brochure was prepared by Nottinghamshire County Council in close liaison with hotel managers.

Budget: Phase I

The cost of the brochure was met jointly by both City and County Tourism Offices.

Design:	£700
Print (30 000):	£2500
Advertising:	£10 000
Distribution:	£3000
Total:	£16 200

Launch and promotion

The launch of the Robin Hood Rate scheme was set up to coincide with the general release of *Prince of Thieves* following its July 1991 première in Nottingham. The major thrust of the promotion was a national advertising campaign in the major consumer press including *Radio Times* and the weekend press.

The brochure was also distributed via

- every tourist information centre in England
- British Tourist Authority offices, via BTA London
- British Travel Centre, London
- National Tourist Information Centre, Victoria Station, London
- London and South East network outlets of Brochure Display
- publicity campaign: a press release was sent to all travel editors on national and regional papers, television and radio
- The county's special break mailing list of 2500 individuals.

Evaluation: Phase I

Bed nights from mid-July until 30 September 1991 were approximately:

751 adults @ £25	£18 775
192 children @ £5	£960
Total	£19 735

PHASE II

Following the success of the initial campaign, it was felt necessary to maintain the momentum by further advertising in the off-peak autumn season. The aim was to increase public awareness of key events including the Robin Hood Pageant and Nottingham Goose Fair, both in October, and to use the Robin Hood Rate to attend these events or for Christmas shopping and sightseeing visits.

Budget: Phase II

The budget for the Phase II advertising campaign amounted to £10 000, and was met in full by the Tourism Development Action Programme. It was agreed to concentrate efforts into those publications producing the greatest responses from Phase I advertising, that is, the *Radio Times*, *Daily Mail*, and *Mail on Sunday*. The column space for each advertisement was smaller, so that repeat advertisements could be placed throughout the autumn.

Evaluation: Phase II

Bed nights from 1 October to 31 December 1991 were approximately:

565 adults @ £25	£14 125
32 children @ £5	£160
Total	£14 285

The figures for Phases I and II identify only bookings made in advance, not those booked and taken on the same day. Based on these figures, over 1500 extra bed nights were achieved between July and December, with an accommodation spend of over £34 000. On a conservative multiplier of 1:1 an equal amount was spent in the area on souvenirs, admissions, drinks and meals. The success of the Robin Hood Rate led to the launch of an ongoing promotion which saw the concept develop still further:

1 A banding structure was introduced to discriminate between the slightly differing facilities on offer by the hotels.
2 Emphasis was placed upon the rate per couple as opposed to a single rate, to further encourage tourist rather than business trade, with a slight discount for two persons:

  Band I £39 per couple (£20 single rate)
  Band II £44.50 per couple (£22.50 single rate)
  Band III £49 per couple (£25 single rate)

3 The monitoring process was further

improved, each hotel formally notifying the Tourism Section of monthly bookings taken. A further six hotels later joined the scheme.

The Robin Hood Rate became an established marketing tool for the destination, and generated over 10 000 bookings between 1991 and 1994.

Co-operative campaign with British Midland Airways

British Midland Airways (BMA) is the prime local carrier flying from East Midlands International Airport. Existing contacts were approached with a scheme to develop traffic on the Amsterdam, Paris and Belfast routes, linked to the increased interest in Robin Hood.

Amsterdam

A joint leaflet was designed to promote Nottingham and the BMA East Midlands to Amsterdam route. This featured a scheduled flight timetable and five major Nottingham hotels that could be booked direct in the Netherlands. Of the initial print run of 10 000, BMA requested a further run of 10 000 to distribute to the trade and leisure markets. The overall costs to the City and County Tourism Office was £450, while BMA contributed £470.

This venture proved highly successful. BMA reported that they achieved an increase in traffic on the route of 30 per cent for leisure travellers, against 12 per cent for business travellers.

In May 1991, eight Dutch journalists and two BMA representatives were invited on a two-day tour of Nottingham. The resulting press articles were very favourable, with prominent features in major Dutch papers highlighting Sherwood Forest, the Robin Hood Festival and the Robin Hood legend.

The May visit led to a journalist from the Dutch magazine *Elegance* (broadly comparable with *Vogue* magazine) making contact with Incento Travel, a company who organised reader holidays for the magazine. The County Tourism Office arranged a complete itinerary including car hire, welcome gift of lace, and vouchers for entry into selected attractions. Incento completed the package which was published as a three-page special feature in September 1991. However, while the press coverage was excellent, the take-up was in this instance disappointing.

Both the Tourism Office and BMA worked closely with the promotional publicity company in the Netherlands which had responsibility for publicising the *Prince of Thieves* film. BMA secured a competition with prize weekends in the cinema magazine *Skoop*, and were further able to promote Sherwood Forest and its Robin Hood connections in a national leisure magazine. The results of the competition featured in a number of Dutch newspapers, with the prize winners enjoying a weekend in Nottingham in October 1991.

Paris

Two joint leaflets were designed to promote Nottingham and the East Midlands–Paris route. One leaflet was aimed at the trade, while a second tapped the leisure markets; 10 000 of each were printed, featuring a double-page spread on Nottingham itself, a scheduled flight timetable, and five major Nottingham hotels that could be booked directly in France. The overall cost for these leaflets was £1200, with costs split between the city, county and BMA.

Three weekend familiarisation visits for the trade were organised in April 1991 to raise awareness of Nottingham as a short-break destination. Two were aimed at leisure travel agents, and the third was directed at business travel agents. All achieved prominent press coverage in France.

A later familiarisation trip was organised for the head of LCA Publicity, following a contact from BMA Paris. This top advertising agency had a client, Geo Foods (the second largest delicatessen chain in France) who undertook annual promotions to boost sales. Geo expressed interest in promoting Robin Hood as a theme targeting children.

A promotion was undertaken, which consisted of Robin Hood wrappers around the Geo Food product 'sautines' sold through supermarkets. In-store displays featured a Nottingham fold-out poster. A competition in connection with vouchers found on the food wrapper offered a prize of five weekends for two in Nottingham during Easter 1992. The added publicity from the prize winners' list added to the very cost-effective promotion.

Belfast

Five journalists and a BMA representative from Northern Ireland were hosted in September 1991 by the Tourism Office on a day's itinerary around Nottingham, resulting in features on the region in the Irish regional and national press.

BTA familiarisation visit

A familiarisation trip was organised for staff from the BTA, with the aim of building on the increased Robin Hood awareness, and to develop personal contacts for future promotions which would allow BTA staff to act as 'ambassadors' for Nottingham.

In May 1991, Nottingham officials made a formal invitation to key BTA staff to visit the city and view its tourism products at first hand. The following September, fourteen staff from BTA paid a two-day visit, led by the assistant director of marketing. Visits were paid to tourism attractions in the city and county, and an evening Tourism Forum was held at a local hotel. Over fifty representatives from the local tourism industry attended the Forum to learn at first hand how to use the BTA in promoting overseas. The budget of around £1000 was shared equally by the City and County Tourism Offices for this venture.

The visit was featured in the local press and on both local radio stations, and was also included in BTA's in-house staff newsletter. All who attended agreed that the visit had enhanced their knowledge and image of the area. Further contacts with the staff have been maintained.

Consumer promotion

Finally, an advertising campaign was carried out to increase the demand for visits to Nottingham. The primary motive was to increase weekend and off-peak bed occupancy, with a subsidiary aim of increasing visitors to events and attractions in the City.

The target markets were principally day visitors, short-break family groups, overseas visitors and the travel trade. The budget for this venture was once again met jointly by the City and County Tourism Offices, with 40 per cent spent on domestic consumers, 30 per cent on overseas markets and 30 per cent on promotions to the trade.

Publications with proven records for their effectiveness and response rates were used to reach consumers, while the trade were targeted mainly via group and coach journals. The domestic market advertising included free tourism newspapers distributed via TICs, and regional tourist board publications. Overseas, BTA guides were used for the first time, in Europe, Japan and the Republic of Ireland, using the special 'Live the Legend' themed advertisements. *In Britain* magazine also carried advertisements.

The overseas advertising proved to be highly successful, with encouraging responses to the *In Britain* and BTA advertisements, particularly within Germany.

Appraisal of the promotional campaign

The campaign was designed to take advantage of a unique opportunity. The enormous success of the film *Robin Hood – Prince of Thieves* generated a world-wide awareness and interest in the Robin Hood legend. Tourism officials were able to build a campaign on the back of this popularity, and lost no opportunity to maximise the potential of the event.

A wide range of promotions were organised, targeting both consumers and trade. An attractive 'Robin Hood Package' was designed; its aim was to stimulate awareness of the area and a desire to visit Nottingham in particular. The success of the package, coupled with the 'Robin Hood Rate' and increased attendance at events, attractions and the growth of incoming enquiries revealed that the message was successfully communicated, and the campaign provided a solid base to build on in future years, highlighting other products in addition to the Robin Hood theme itself.

Visitor figures for the period August 1991 to September 1992 for hotels, visitor attractions and tourism-related retailing were up 22, 24 and 17 per cent respectively. The campaign provided the boost in image, visitors and confidence that Nottingham needed, and business to the city has remained strong throughout the recession of the early 1990s. The Robin Hood events and attractions have continued to prosper, and now provide the framework for a thriving tourist industry in the city.

Case study 8
A quality partnership programme: the Sun Project of Thomson Holidays

(Prepared with the help of Marco Antonio Robledo and Francisco Julio Batle, Escola Oficial de Turisme, University of the Balearics)

The tour operator's quality dilemma

The quality of holiday provision has been acknowledged by tour operators to be of considerably more importance in the late 1980s and early 1990s than in the past. By the end of the 1980s, tour operators were seen to take a more conscientious attitude, reflecting greater concern with quality than quantity (price, or number of visitors). Behind this concern lay the belief that, given improved quality of accommodation and surroundings, tourists would be willing to pay more for their holidays and spend more in the resorts, especially in the hotels, thus increasing the industry's overall profitability. A quality strategy means achieving the level of excellence that is demanded by the target market. However, the problem that the tour operator faces in attempting to achieve high satisfaction levels among its customers is that so many of the components of its packaged product are outside its immediate control. The 'service journey' theory states that tourists have a global perception of their holiday, and therefore it is very difficult for them to assess individually its separate elements, such as the hotel. Perception of this element will be influenced to some extent by other parameters such as the destination itself, or the flight. No matter how hard the hotel tries to satisfy its customers, if the other components making up the holiday are not of a similar standard, the overall satisfaction of the tourist will be affected. The old adage remains true: the chain of quality is as strong as its weakest link.

For tour operators, this concept is of para-mount importance, since what they are attempting is to create a holiday experience that is hard to match for all-round value. This entails ensuring there is a balance in all parts of the experience. The problem is how to guarantee good standards of provision from all the different organisations that the tourist experiences while on holiday.

One means of achieving this is through vertical integration, that is, ownership of all the companies that the tour operator handles, in order to control directly all the links in the chain. Thomson Holidays has its own airline, Britannia, and has owned hotels in the past. However, accommodation ownership is accompanied by reduced flexibility in the form of pressure to use the accommodation, even if alternative provision is of better quality and/or cheaper. Therefore tour operators have generally pursued strategies for monitoring the quality of accommodation and catering provision which are more cost-effective than that of ownership.

Another interesting although unusual option is to establish co-operative links with the tourist suppliers. The idea underlying such initiatives is that for tour operators to engage in repeat business (by means of regular annual contracts) with a core of hotels of consistent quality is a workable and highly commendable option from the strategic point of view, for three reasons:

1 It is a way of avoiding the multiple problems associated with ownership (vertical integration) while at the same time securing high standards of service quality, since by focusing on a few hotels, the tour operator can set a desired standard.

2 It also allows them to reduce their dependency on smaller, older hotels which do not meet rising quality requirements.

3 It is a way of putting an end to the confrontational relationship that operators and hoteliers have maintained for a very long time, and that has been a source of great dissatisfaction to the hoteliers themselves.

Tour operators' and hoteliers' partnership programmes: the 'Sun Project'

The Total Quality Management (TQM) philosophy has been an important step in recognising the need to improve the relationship between customer and supplier. Such a relationship has special importance in the tourism industry. A partnership strategy is radically different from the traditional confrontation strategy that often characterises the relationship between operators and hoteliers as they struggle to negotiate the best price.

In the new competitive environment, it becomes appropriate to leave behind earlier confrontational attitudes and initiate a period of closer collaboration, trust and teamwork in setting higher quality standards (and at the same time setting higher prices), and marketing the product in a different way. The new strategy is based upon closer teamwork between operators and hoteliers, a longer term relationship and absolute reciprocal trust. The result of this collaboration should be increased customer satisfaction, which is essential for both parties.

The Sun Project is an ambitious scheme in this idiom, launched by Thomson Holidays in 1990. Thomson is the leading UK operator, and one of the biggest operators globally, with offices in 53 destinations all over the world.

This important new strategy, entitled 'Thomson Sun', is concerned with quality specification and quality assurance. The project applies to some carefully selected hotels in the Mediterranean area that had in the past had a satisfactory performance with Thomson, as far as the operator was concerned, and met certain pre-established criteria, including:

- excellent management
- total (or at least, British) exclusivity
- good overall CSQ (Customer Service Questionnaire) performance
- good location and environment
- adequate size and existing standards.

Thomson Holidays' objectives (as they relate to Sun Hotels) are as follows:

- to raise occupancy levels in the best hotels
- to build loyalty, repeat purchasing frequency, and word of mouth recommendation
- to improve value for money, i.e. improve existing features
- to add value, i.e. incorporate new features
- to give a more detailed brochure description of the hotel and its facilities
- to make a Thomson Sun holiday different
- to be foremost in the field of improving quality.

To some extent, Thomson views the Sun Hotels as flagships in their search for quality. The dominant UK tour operator has taken the lead in creating a better quality product. Initially, they identified ten 3-star hotels in the Balearic Islands and invested £10 million in them to bring them up to a standard and style of service which their research had shown British clients demanded in the 1990s. At the time of writing, there are seventeen Sun Hotels and apartments (five in Majorca, five in Ibiza, two in Minorca, one in Tenerife, one in Costa Brava, one in Rhodes, and two in Corfu). The company's goal is to have thirty Sun Hotels by the year 2000.

Before getting started, Thomson carried out market research among 80 000 British tourists, the results of which would be incorporated into the Thomson Sun product. This research had led to four key conclusions:

- quality is the key issue for the 1990s
- minimum levels of quality (i.e. standards) must be specified, consistent and guaranteed
- new and enhanced features must be introduced to give better value for money

- four key areas would have to be addressed: food, facilities, entertainment and service.

Accordingly, each hotel is now given a 300-point specification handbook covering the following areas:

- *Furniture, fixtures, fittings and facilities* The objective is to offer specially upgraded facilities, acceptable to the UK customers, with attention paid to small details.
- *Food and food service* According to the research undertaken, 72 per cent of the respondents prefer British food; as a result, extensive training courses have been introduced for chefs to know the UK techniques of preparation and cooking, meals are available at times desired by the customers, and rotating, balanced and varied menus are introduced (since the average stay is between two and three weeks, menus vary every fifteen days).
- *Service* In order to ensure a consistent service quality, staff training courses are put together and run by Thomson, training manuals are provided, and repair and maintenance standards are agreed.
- *Entertainment* The results of the research revealed that entertainment was the most important element for the British tourist, therefore a full and varied entertainment programme has to be offered, tailored to British tastes.

All the specifications aim at ensuring that all the Sun Hotels offer the same consistently high standards, plus the added benefits of some extra touches, for example, co-ordinated furnishings in all rooms, and many other convenient requirements (the specifications even establish the exact wattage for the bulb in each bedside reading lamp). These specifications are based totally on the outcome of the research mentioned earlier, and on results obtained through the company's own CSQs which 70 per cent of their clients complete while on their flight home with Britannia. Results are tabulated monthly, and corrective actions implemented immediately: this is the most important tool in quality control.

The hotels are branded in Thomson's brochure as 'Sun Hotels', offering 'a touch more comfort, a touch more care, a touch more style and a lot more value'. Clearly, customers perceive they are getting good value for the extra money paid. They always find these 'special extras' that make the difference:

- well-maintained accommodation and high standards of cleanliness
- rooms that are tastefully decorated and thoughtfully designed
- a 'Welcome' information pack, including a map and hotel guide
- free pool towels for personal use during the stay, and free sunbeds by the pool
- menus offering British-style meals, plus local specialities and vegetarian dishes
- the choice of a full British or Continental breakfast
- friendly and helpful staff
- a team of Thomson representatives, plus a 24-hour emergency contact service
- full daytime and evening entertainment programmes which feature professional British cabaret acts, dancing, theme nights, sunstretch, water polo, French boules and cookery demonstrations, all organised by Thomson Sun entertainments representatives.

This should not be described by the overworked phrase 'going up-market'. Thomson's Charles Newbold described the Sun Hotels scheme as a middle-of-the-road product aimed at the average holidaymaker: 'We don't want to create an upmarket product. I'm sure that the market will develop new sectors, but . . . the traditional holiday will continue to be the largest single sector'. The idea is to upgrade gradually ('with leaden steps') the existing hotels and products, aiming at exactly the same clients who have filled the hotels in the past.

The Thomson Sun Project has a strong marketing and promotion support that includes the following:

- greater exposure of hotels (two whole, highlighted pages) in the Summer Sun brochure
- special Sun Hotels brochure for travel agents

- a new image, name, logo and look
- a special introductory spread at the front of the Summer Sun brochure
- a full press and media launch
- comprehensive travel agent and leisure trade training and promotions, including a special video
- priority in Thomson reservations systems
- priority for tactical sales and marketing action.

Prices for Sun Hotels are about £15–35 higher per week than comparable hotels in the same brochure, in the belief that people will pay more for quality. The sales they have achieved are a good indication of whether holidaymakers are really prepared to pay extra for quality.

The project is regarded as extremely successful so far, both by Thomson and by the hoteliers themselves. For the latter, the satisfaction is understandable, since the Sun Project is making a heavy contribution to upgrading and repositioning their hotels in terms of price and image. Added to that, there are several other advantages as far as the hotelier is concerned:

- higher utilisation of contracted beds (via enhanced marketing)
- the reassurance of being one of Thomson's premier Sun Hotels
- access to research data and Thomson consultants (e.g. for training, catering, costing, design, entertainments)
- increased in-hotel revenue (from bar sales, snacks and restaurants) due to enhanced in-hotel activities and higher spending customers
- optional benefits from central purchasing (of materials and services)
- improved Thomson representative service and rep ratio
- better satisfied customers and more repeat business.

Benefits for Mediterranean resorts

Apart from the advantages for hoteliers and for Thomson, this strategy can also be regarded as extremely positive and beneficial for the Mediterranean destinations where the Sun Hotels are located. There is a clear need to reverse the negative 'lager lout' image that many Mediterranean destinations such as certain resorts in Majorca have acquired, and this could help to be achieved by the adoption of the Sun Project on a massive scale. For many people, Majorca, where the Sun Project was initiated, is a classic illustration of the theory of the product life cycle: after years of growth Majorca has reached its maturity as a tourist product and is about to go into decline. The new tourist demand trends show that the package holiday as we know it is going out of fashion, making it necessary to change the marketing mix and the positioning of the product. This strategy makes sense, in that what satisfied C1C2 families in the early 1980s is no longer good enough. Followers of Maslow would explain this by saying that the lower needs – for relaxation, the security of packaged arrangements, the social pleasure of holidays with people from similar backgrounds – are all now taken for granted. Today, people also want holidays with an element of status, of self-development (learning new activities, discovering new places) and of aesthetic pleasure. That is what the Sun Project attempts to provide. Its contribution to the necessary change of image of the Mediterranean remains to be assessed, but in the long term the proliferation of similar schemes will be evident.

Other tour operators such as First Choice Holidays have also launched comparable projects in collaboration with hoteliers, in the inevitable and imperative search for quality and sustainability.

Appendix 1 Sources of tourism research data

The following is a short list of principal sources of data which are relevant to travel and tourism research:

A *International Tourism Statistics*

CAB International
- World Travel and Tourism Review

Economist Intelligence Unit (EIU)
- International Tourism Quarterly (ITQ)
- Special reports on tourism
- Travel and Tourism in the Single European Market (Ed. Storey, A) 1990
- Travel and Tourism Analyst

European Union (EU)
- Basic Statistics of the Community
- General statistics Bulletin

International Air Transport Association (IATA)
- World Air Traffic Statistics

International Civil Aviation Organisation (ICAO)
- Civil Aviation Statistics of the World
- Digest of Statistics

Organisation for Economic Co-operation and Development (OECD)
- International Tourism and Tourism Policy in OECD Member Countries

United Nations
- Statistical Yearbook
- Monthly Bulletin of Statistics

World Tourism Organisation (WTO)
- Current Travel and Tourism Indicators
- Economic Review of World Tourism
- Tourism Departures and Main Destinations
- Yearbook of Tourism Statistics

B *National Statistics*

British Tourist Authority (BTA)
- Annual Report
- British National Travel Survey
- Digest of Tourist Statistics
- Market guides to overseas countries
- UK Tourism Survey

Civil Aviation Authority
- Statistics

Economist Intelligence Unit
- Travel and Tourism Analyst

Employment, Department of
- International Passenger Survey (IPS)
  The main results are summarised in the Business Monitor MQ6
- Overseas Travel and Tourism (Quarterly)

English Tourist Board (ETB)
- Annual Report
- English Heritage Monitor (annual)
- The English Hotel Occupancy Survey (annual)
- Insights: The Tourism Marketing Intelligence Service
- Overseas Visitor Survey 1990
- Regional Fact Sheets (for the Regional Tourist Boards)
- Sightseeing in 19— (annual)
- Visits to Tourist Attractions (annual)

Harvest Information Services
- Airlines 1990
- Hotels 1990
- Travel Agents 1990

Jordan & Sons
- Britain's Tour and Travel Industry 1990
- The British Hotel Industry 1988

Keynote Reports
- Airlines 1993
- Bus and Coach Operators 1989
- Business Travel 1991
- Cross Channel Ferries 1992
- Hotels 1992
- Tourism in the UK 1988
- Tourist Attractions 1992
- Travel Agents and Overseas Tour Operators 1991
- UK Airports 1988
- UK Tourism and Travel 1992 (Market Review)

Market Assessment Reports
- Development of the UK Tourism Market to 1993 1990
- Travel 1992

Marketline
- Cross Channel and North Sea Ferries 1993

Mintel
- Market Intelligence Reports
MORI
- Travel Agents' Survey (annual)
Scottish Tourist Board
- Annual Report
STATS MR
- Holiday Booking Audit (monthly)
The Tourism Society
- The Tourism Industry 1990/91
Transport, Department of
- National Travel Survey (NTS)
- Transport Statistics in Great Britain
Wales Tourist Board
- Annual Report

In addition to the above statistics which focus on travel and tourism, there are a number of other statistical publications which may include travel and tourism statistics, or are pertinent to tourism. These include:

Bank of England Quarterly Bulletin
BMRB TGI (Target Group Index)
Central Statistical Office (CSO)
- Annual Abstract of Statistics
- National Income and Expenditure ('Blue Book')
- Regional Trends
- Social Trends
- Economic Trends
- Monthly Digest of Statistics
Employment, Department of
- Family Expenditure Survey
- General Household Survey
Information Division, The Treasury
- Economic Progress Report
National Institute Economic Review
Trade and Industry (DTI), Department of
- British Business Weekly

Appendix 2

Proof-reading marks

There are standard correction marks, as follows:

Text	Marginal mark	Meaning
One thing is quite certain and that is that few brochures are any longer designed by amateurs.	c/	Insert 'c'
There are some and they STAnd out like sore thumbs among the professional offerings. If the companies concerned are are successful it is despite their brochures, not because of them.	≢	Change to lower case
	ℓ)	Delete word
	bold	Bold
Designing a brochure is a highly skilled art needing an exact specification of the intentions, features and statuHtory provisions necessary. From these the designer can make a 'rough' for approval by his client. a professional design house will have amazing moderntechnology available even including the ability to simulate photographs by computer	⊗/	Damaged characters on print supplied
	ℓ]	Delete and close up
	≡/	Change to capital
	⋎	Insert space
	⊙/	Insert full stop
The number pages of is important in itself. According to the print run envisaged it may be possible to make substantial economies by utilising the maximum amount of space on each sheet or roll of paper.	⊔⌐/	Transpose words
	⌐/	Start new paragraph
	⌐/	Take over to next line
	⌐	Run on
Rarely will cut sheets be used that equate to the eventual page size. It is possible that large sheets that incorporate 4, 8, 16, or more pages will be printed at one time, but with large runs the relationship between huge rolls of paper fed simutaneously will need to be reflected in the pagination.	ital	Change to italic
	rom	Change to roman
	⋔	Reduce space between words
	←⊏	Cancel indent
The page size will relate not	✓	Leave unchanged

References

Chapter 1
1. Levitt, T, *Marketing Myopia*, Harvard Business Review July/August 1960, pp 45–56

Chapter 2
1. Kotler, P, *Marketing Management, Analysis, Planning, Implementation and Control*, Hemel Hempstead, Prentice Hall, 8th Ed. 1994, p 98

Chapter 3
1. Economist Intelligence Unit, *Choosing Holiday Destinations: the Impact of Exchange Rates and Inflation*, London, EIU 1987

Chapter 4
1. Maslow, A, *Motivation and Personality*, London, Harper and Row, 1984
2. Howard, J A & J N Seth, *The Theory of Buyer Behaviour*, New York, John Wiley, 1969
3. Plog, S, *Why Destination Areas Rise and Fall in Popularity*, paper presented to the Southern California Chapter of the Travel Research Association, 10 Oct 1972
4. Pearce, P, *The Social Psychology of Tourist Behaviour*, Oxford, Pergamon, 1982

Chapter 6
1. *Marketing*, 'Discretion Plays a Bigger Part', 13 August 1987
2. Rogers, A, *Pricing in the Hotel Industry*, Oxford Polytechnic, 1974

Chapter 7
1. Colley, I R, *Defining Advertising Goals for Measured Advertising Results*, New York, Association of National Advertisers, 1961

Chapter 13
1. Townsend, R, *Up the Organisation: How to Stop the Corporation Stifling People and Strangling Profits*, London, Coronet, 1971

Bibliography

Ashworth, G J & Goodall, B, *Marketing Tourism Places*, London, Routledge, 1990

Ashworth, G & Tunbridge, J, *The Tourist-Historic City*, London, Belhaven Press, 1990

Ashworth, G & Voogd, H, *Selling the City*, London, Belhaven Press, 1991

Bishop, J, *Travel Marketing*, New Romney, Bailey Bros and Swinfen, 1981

Brann, C, *Cost Effective Direct Marketing by Mail, Telephone and Direct Response Advertising*, Cirencester, Collectors Books, 1984

British Tourist Authority, *Cross Channel Marketing Strategy*, London, BTA, 1993

British Tourist Authority, *First Impressions: Reception of Overseas Visitors' Enquiry*, London, BTA, 1986

British Tourist Authority, *Gaining Your Share of an £8 Billion Market* (including market guides to 27 countries), London, BTA, 1990

British Tourist Authority, *The Independent Hotel: a Guide to Overseas Marketing*, London, BTA, 1977

Buttle, F, *Hotel and Food Service Marketing*, London, Holt Rinehart, 1986

Campbell-Smith, G, *Marketing of the Meal Experience: a Fundamental Approach*, Guildford, University of Surrey, 1967

Coltman, M, *Tourism Marketing*, New York, Van Nostrand Reinhold, 1989

Cooper, C & Latham, J, *The Market for Educational Visits to Tourism Attractions*, Poole, Dorset Institute of HE, 1985

Cross, D, *Please Follow Me: The Practical Tourist Guide's Handbook*, Salisbury, Wessexplore/ETB 4th edn, 1991

Davidoff, D M, *Contact: Customer Service in the Hospitality and Tourism Industry*, London, Prentice Hall, 1994

Doswell, R & Gamble, P R, *Marketing and Planning Hotels and Tourism Projects*, London, Barrie & Jenkins, 1979

English Tourist Board, *The Arts and Tourism Marketing Handbook*, London, ETB, 1993

English Tourist Board, *The Future for England's Smaller Seaside Resorts*, London, ETB, 1991

English Tourist Board, *Putting on the Style*, London, ETB, 1981

English Tourist Board, *Report of the Working Party to Review Tourist Information Centre Services and Support Policies*, London, ETB, 1981

English Tourist Board, *The VFR Market: Marketing Opportunities and Guidance*, London, ETB, 1988

Foster, D, *Sales and Marketing for the Travel Professional*, London, McGraw-Hill, 1991

French, Y, *The Handbook of Public Relations for Museums, Galleries, Historic Houses, the Visual Arts and Heritage Attractions*, Milton Keynes, Museum Development Co, 1991

Gartrell, R, *Destination Marketing for Convention and Visitors' Bureaus*, Dubuque, Iowa, Kendall Hunt, 1989

Gayle, D & Goodrich, J (Eds) *Tourism Marketing and Management in the Caribbean*, London, Routledge, 1993

Getz, D, *Festivals, Special Events and Tourism*, New York, Van Nostrand Reinhold, 1990

Gold, J R & Ward, S V, *Place Promotion: the Use of Publicity and Public Relations to Sell Places*, London, Belhaven Press, 1993

Goldblatt, J J, *Special Events, the Art and Science of Celebration*, New York, van Nostrand Reinhold, 1990

Goodall, B & Ashworth, G, *Marketing in the Tourism Industry: the Promotion of Destination Regions*, Beckenham, Croom Helm, 1988

Greene, M, *Marketing Hotels into the 90s*, London, Heinemann, 2nd edn, 1987

Hart, C W L and Troy, D A, *Strategic Hotel/Motel Marketing*, East Lansing, MI, Educational Institute, American Hotel and Motel Association, 1995

Hawkins, D E, Shafer, E L & Rovelstad, J M (Eds) *Tourism Marketing and Management Issues*, Washington, DC, George Washington University, 1980

Heath E & Wall G, *Marketing Tourism Destinations: a Strategic Planning Approach*, New York, John Wiley, 1992

Henley Centre, *Inbound Tourism: a Packaged Future?*, 1992

Hotel and Catering Industry Training Board, Marketing for Independent Hoteliers, Wembley, Middx, HCITB, nd

Hotel and Catering Industry Training Board, *Marketing for Publicans*, Wembley, Middx, HCITB, 1982

King, B & Hyde, G, *Tourism Marketing in Australia*, Melbourne, Hospitality Press, 1989

Kotas, R (Ed) *Market Orientation in the Hotel and Catering Industry*, Guildford, Surrey University Press, 1975

Kotler, P, *Marketing Management: Analysis, Planning and Control*, Hemel Hempstead, Prentice Hall International, 8th edn, 1994

Lanquar, R & Hollier, R, *Le Marketing Touristique*, Paris, Presses Univ de France, 1981

Laws, E, *Tourism Marketing: Service and Quality Management Perspectives*, Cheltenham, Stanley Thornes, 1991

Lewis, R and Chambers, R, *Marketing Leadership in Hospitality*, New York, van Nostrand Reinhold, 1989

Lickorish, L, Bodlender, J, Jefferson, A & Jenkins, C L, *Developing Tourism Destinations: Policies and Perspectives*, London, Longman, 1991

Lickorish, L J & Jefferson, A, *Marketing Tourism*, London, Longman, 2nd edn, 1991

Lumsdon, L, *Marketing for Tourism: Case Study Assignments*, Macmillan, 1992

MacSweeney, E F, *Public Relations and Publicity for Hotels and Restaurants*, London, Barrie & Jenkins, 1970

Mayo, E J & Jarvis, L P, *The Psychology of Leisure Travel: Effective Marketing and Selling of Travel Services*, Boston, CBI, 1981

Middleton, V, *Marketing in Travel and Tourism*, Oxford, Heinemann, 2nd edn, 1994

Moutinho, L, *Consumer Behaviour in Tourism, Management Bibliographies and Reviews*, Vol 12 No 3, MCB University Press, 1986

Pearce, D G & Butler, R W (Eds) *Tourism Research: Critiques and Challenges*, London, Routledge, 1993

Poynter, J M, *Tourism Design, Marketing and Management*, Englewood Cliffs NJ, Regents/Prentice Hall, 1993

Reilly, R, *Travel and Tourism Marketing Techniques*, Albany, NY, Delmar, 1980

Richards, B, *How to Market Tourist Attractions, Festivals and Special Events*, London, Longman, 1992

Ritchie, J & Goeldner, C (Eds) *Travel, Tourism and Hospitality Research: a Handbook for Managers*, New York, John Wiley, 1987

Schmoll, G A, *Tourism Promotion*, London, Tourism International Press, 1977

Seaton, A V and Bennett M, *Marketing Tourism Products*, London, Chapman and Hall, 1966

Shaw, S, *Airline Marketing and Management*, London, Pitman, 3rd edn, 1990

Shepherd, J W, *Marketing Practice in the Hotel and Catering Industry*, London, Batsford, 1982

Sumner, J R, *Improve your Marketing Techniques: a Guide for Hotel Managers and Caterers*, London, Northwood, 1982

Taneja, N K, *Airline Planning: Corporate, Financial and Marketing*, USA, Lexington Books, 1982

Teare, R, Calver, S & Costa, J, *Hospitality and Tourism Marketing Management*, London, Cassell, 1994

Teare, R, Calver, S, Mazanec, J & Crawford-Welch, S, *Marketing in Hospitality and Tourism*, London, Cassell, 1994

Tourism and *Recreation Research Unit, Recreation Site Survey Manual: Methods and Techniques for Conducting Visitor Surveys*, London, E & F N Spon, 1983

Veal, A J, *Research Methods for Leisure and Tourism*, London, Longman, 1992

Vladimir, A, *The Complete Travel Marketing Handbook*, Lincolnwood, Illinois, NTC Business Books, 1988

Wahab, S, Crampon, L, & Rothfield, L, *Tourism Marketing*, London, Tourism International Press, 1976

Witt, S & Moutinho, L, *Tourism Marketing and Management Handbook*, Hemel Hempstead, Prentice Hall, 2nd edn, 1994

Wood, M (Ed) *Tourism Marketing for the Small Business*, London, English Tourist Board, 1980

Index